Social Work

THIRD
EDITION

Social Work
Issues and
Opportunities

IN A CHALLENGING PROFESSION

DIANA M.
DiNitto
UNIVERSITY OF TEXAS
AT AUSTIN

C. AARON
McNeece
FLORIDA STATE UNIVERSITY

LYCEUM
BOOKS, INC.

5758 South Blackstone Avenue
Chicago, Illinois 60637

Published by
LYCEUM BOOKS, INC.
5758 S. Blackstone Ave.
Chicago, IL 60637
773+643-1903 (Fax)
773+643-1902 (Phone)
lyceum@lyceumbooks.com
http://www.lyceumbooks.com

11 10 09 08   1 2 3 4 5

Library of Congress Cataloging-in-Publication Data

DiNitto, Diana M.
  Social work : issues and opportunities in a challenging profession /
Diana M. DiNitto, C. Aaron McNeece.—3rd ed.
      p. cm.
  Includes bibliographical references and index.
  ISBN 978-0-925065-86-5 (alk. paper)
  1. Social service—United States. I. McNeece, Carl Aaron. II. Title.
HV10.5D56 2007
  361.3′2—dc22

                                                                    200702177

Quotation by H. M. Bartlett in chapter 1 used by permission: Copyright 1970,
National Association of Social Workers, Inc., The Common Base of Social Work
Practice.
Figure 1.1 used by permission: Copyright 2006, National Association of Social
Workers, Inc., Assuring the Sufficiency of a Frontline Workforce: A National Study
of Licensed Social Workers.
Figure 6.1 used by permission: Copyright 2007, Human Rights Campaign.
Boxes 7.1 and 7.3 used by permission: Mental Health America, www.mental-
healthamerica.net.
Box 8.2 used by permission: Drug Policy Alliance.

Dan, so many years have passed, but I miss you every day and wish you were here with us.

    —Diana M. DiNitto

For my grandchildren—Dylan, Britney, Kelsey, Cy, Emily, and Jared

    —C. Aaron McNeece

ABOUT THE EDITORS

Diana M. DiNitto is Cullen Trust Centennial Professor in Alcohol Studies and Education and a University Distinguished Teaching Professor at the University of Texas at Austin School of Social Work. Her professional interests include social welfare policy, chemical dependency, and violence against women. She earned her MSW and PhD from Florida State University. Professor DiNitto has been co-director of the NIDA-funded Social Work Research Development Program at the University of Texas at Austin. She has received the Texas Exes Excellence Teaching Award twice and has also been a recipient of the Lora Lee Pederson Teaching Award, as well as the Lifetime Achievement Award from the Social Welfare Policy and Practice Group. Professor DiNitto has served on the board of the Council on Social Work Education and on the editorial boards of the nineteenth and twentieth editions of *The Encyclopedia of Social Work*.

C. Aaron McNeece is Walter W. Hudson Professor and dean of the College of Social Work at Florida State University, where he teaches courses on social welfare policy and administration, substance abuse and treatment, and criminal justice system issues. A former probation officer, he has worked as a consultant to the Federal Bureau of Prisons on substance abuse issues and to the Irish National Council on Alcoholism and since 1989 has conducted evaluations of approximately 130 criminal justice systems programs. Professor McNeece has also served as the director of the Institute for Health and Human Services Research at Florida State University. He earned an MA in political science from Texas Tech University, an MSW and PhD from the University of Michigan, and is the author of over 100 articles and books.

■ Contents

FIGURES, TABLES, AND BOXES

■ Preface

Social Work: Issues and Opportunities in a Challenging Profession offers college students a realistic introduction to the social work profession within the context of a rapidly changing domestic and global world. It describes many of the challenges and controversies that social workers in the twenty-first century encounter. Many accounts of the profession written for beginning students present a picture of social workers helping clients who want their services, and clients always doing better as a result. Social workers have a positive impact on the lives of many of the people they serve, but readers also need to know that many clients have little interest in seeing social workers and do not seek help voluntarily, and that social workers face many obstacles in serving clients, not all of which are easily resolved. This text balances the many exciting and rewarding aspects of social work practice with the difficulties, struggles, and problems that social workers face as they do their jobs, uphold the profession's values and ethics, and remain true to themselves.

Since the world and the profession of social work have changed significantly in recent years, the content of this edition of *Social Work: Issues and Opportunities in a Challenging Profession* is new in almost every respect. We invited social work colleagues with intimate knowledge of the subject matter to contribute to the text. The contributors are a diverse group of faculty from social work education programs around the country. Some have many years of faculty experience and are deans or program directors. Others are newer to social work education but are experienced practitioners and have a good deal of experience teaching introductory social work courses. A number of contributors to the last edition have authored the chapters in this edition, while several others worked with us for the first time. One thing about the authors is consistent—their enthusiasm for the subject matter shines through in their writing.

We loosely organized the book in four parts; this framework reflects the way we have taught introductory social work courses for many years. The first three chapters provide an introduction to the profession's history and value base as well as some of the early pioneers and prototypes of social work; address social work theory; and introduce students to the concepts of micro-, mezzo-, and macropractice. These chapters also introduce some provocative issues related to the profession for students to think about as they take their first social work course, including lack of diversity among practitioners, the privatization of services, and the increasing emphasis the profession is placing on research and evidence-based practice.

We next offer information on culturally competent practice with diverse groups within the context of the increasing ethnic and racial diversity of the United States, as well as gender issues and practice with male and female clients, and broach the topic of sexual orientation and social work with clients who are gay, lesbian, bisexual, and/or transgender. These chapters challenge readers to examine their own values in regard to a variety of topics.

The next section discusses a number of social work practice areas, as well the role of the social worker in relation to other professionals with whom social workers may work in these contexts, such as psychologists, psychiatrists, and nurses. These chapters also offer a look at the types of issues that clients in these areas may face and some of the interventions that are commonly used to address them. Students are introduced to such relevant issues as organ donation, health insurance parity and managed care, legislation affecting people with disabilities and social work practice with them, the child welfare system, and the shortage of social workers to meet the growing need for gerontological services among aging baby boomers in the coming years.

The last chapters deal with some of the environments in which social workers practice. The overlap between some of the topics covered in these chapters—for example, poverty and rural America and poverty and the justice system—provides interesting opportunities for student discussion. These chapters tackle the topic of advocacy as well as the ethical dilemmas social workers may encounter in working in these contexts. They also provide information on the major public assistance programs with which social workers must be familiar in order to help clients, as well as some of the unique challenges these social workers often face.

We conclude with a look at the profession's future, particularly the expanded role technology will play in service delivery and the rapid development and dissemination of knowledge, as well as trends in the field, and the impact these factors will have on social work education and practice.

The text is illustrated throughout by engaging and realistic case studies, many of which provide examples of situations that students are likely to face as social workers. In addition, an instructor's manual with class exercises, activities, and assignments to keep classes lively as well as test questions for each chapter is available online.

We are grateful to all the contributors to this book, and to Mary Tijerina, Kelly Ward, Nancy Stewart, Sara Sanders Claudia Triche, Sepora Fisher, Linda Wells-Glover, Glenn Rohrer, Karen Harper-Dorton, Bob Vernon, Ann Lampkin, Romel Mackelprang, Karen Bullock, Susan Cole, John McNutt, Tara Larrison, Cal Streeter, Catherine Crisp, and Dina Wilke for taking time to review portions of the manuscript. We also wish to express our gratitude to Christie Fisher, Christina Miller, Nina Nelson, Monica Pignotti, and Cathy Nipper. Finally, we want to thank David Follmer of Lyceum Books, Sonia E. Fulop, and Joann Hoy, who gave so much attention to the big picture of this book as well as the details and were ever patient with the process.

1 Social Work: A Challenging Profession

Daniel Harkness and Will Rainford

This chapter introduces the profession of social work—past, present, and future. Social workers share a deep concern for the welfare of individuals and groups. Guided by a common core of professional values and ethics, social workers have many ways of helping others develop, function, and achieve their greatest potential.

SOCIAL WORKERS IN ACTION

Child Abuse Case Coordinator

Marlene is a case coordinator for child protective services. She uses the knowledge and experience she gained in her bachelor of social work (BSW) program to conduct intake assessments and see cases through the process of investigation, prosecution, treatment, and resolution. One of her main tasks is to advocate for children at risk, ensuring that each receives consideration and care from all the professionals involved. The agency receives a large number of referrals, many of which come to Marlene. Because Marlene may coordinate one hundred or more cases at any time, her job can be daunting, but her colleagues and supervisors are supportive and helpful, and Marlene knows her work is important. She earns $32,000 a year and a full package of employee benefits.

Gerontology Case Manager

After earning his BSW, Joseph became a case manager at a senior center in downtown Detroit that is supported by grants from the city, state, and federal government, as well as private donations. Joseph begins each workday with a morning staff meeting with a nutritionist, nurse practitioner, occupational therapist, and mental health worker. Joseph is responsible for knowing each person who uses the center's services. He completes an intake assessment for each new client, in which he asks about family structure and functioning, health, mental health, economic needs, and any other concerns the client may have. Joseph provides this information to other staff by writing a psychosocial assessment. He records ongoing case

1

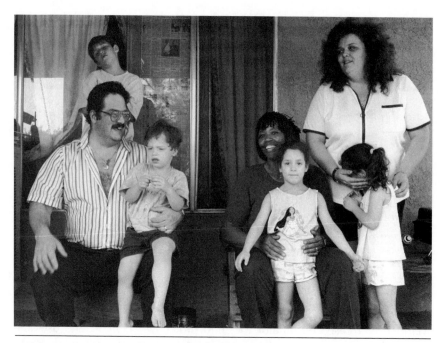

When these four children had to be removed from their home by child protective services, a social work-er helped their parents learn better parenting skills so that the family could be reunited.
© Richard Bermack

notes to keep staff apprised of each client's current situation. Joseph further supports clients by locating and brokering resources in the community; that is, he connects clients to other social service providers who can help meet their needs. In order to ensure continuity of care across service systems, he also visits clients who enter hospitals or nursing homes. Joseph takes great satisfaction in seeing that his clients get the services they need. He earns $27,000 a year and benefits. Joseph has enrolled in a master of social work (MSW) program because he would like to become director of a senior center.

Mental Health Case Worker

Melissa works for a state department of mental health. She is responsible for providing case management services for forty-five clients in the rural community where she lives. Melissa ensures that clients have access to mental health care in area clinics. She helps clients apply for government benefits, including Social Security, Medicaid, and food stamps. She also assists her clients by connecting them to employment support, education, and housing services. She sees clients in her office, in their homes, and at community agencies as needed. The majority of Melissa's clients are low-income individuals. A frequent challenge she deals with is seeing that clients have transportation to get to appointments. With a BSW, Melissa is a qualified case manager. She relies on mental health professionals who hold graduate degrees in social work or counseling to provide psychotherapy for her clients. Melissa earns $30,000 a year. Her agency has an educational incentive program that pays tuition and book costs for a master of social work. Melissa hopes to earn an MSW and is looking forward to continuing her education. She will be able to work part-time for the department while attending school. In exchange, Melissa will be required to work for the department for three years after obtaining her MSW.

Agency Administrator

Rosio, who has an MSW, is executive director of a private adoption agency. She is responsible for domestic and international adoptions from source countries such as Azerbaijan, China, and Guatemala. Rosio supervises a number of social workers and other professional staff, providing them with in-service training and evaluative feedback to ensure adopting families receive the best services possible. She also develops training curriculum for adopting parents, which she provides in community workshops. In addition to staying abreast of domestic and international adoption laws, Rosio writes grant proposals for funding, evaluates agency outcomes, and provides critical information to her board of directors for ongoing planning. Always on the lookout for talented staff, she provides internships for social work students. Rosio finds great satisfaction in helping the agency run effectively, allowing hundreds of parents to adopt children in need of "forever" families. Having worked her way to the top of her field, Rosio earns $65,000 a year, plus benefits. She enjoys a well-appointed, comfortable office with enough support staff to help her achieve the agency's mission.

Policy Advocate

Scott, who also has an MSW, provides policy advocacy and analysis for the American Civil Liberties Union. In support of the ACLU's mission to protect and expand constitutional rights, he conducts research and writes grant proposals to fund new programs. Scott recently completed an analysis of school district policies related to nondiscrimination and prevention of harassment. In particular, he has been investigating which regional school districts identify gay and lesbian youths as a protected group. He also crafted an anti-bullying bill, which was introduced to the state legislature in March 2005. In another effort to protect constitutional rights in his state, Scott worked hard to defeat a state-level anti-gay constitutional marriage amendment in the summer of 2004. In that campaign, he coordinated the distribution of educational materials to raise public awareness about discrimination against gays and lesbians, gave interviews to the media, and spoke at many community events. Scott also works with educators in local schools to help them become more supportive of their lesbian, gay, bisexual, and transgender students. He is able to do so because his agency is supported by large contributions made primarily by private donors. Scott's salary of $40,000 a year with full benefits is paid for from a mix of agency funds and external grants he has written to strengthen his office's budget. Because of the fiscal strength of his organization, Scott has an office downtown with the latest computer equipment.

WHO IS A SOCIAL WORKER?

According to the U.S. Bureau of Labor Statistics (2001), over 826,000 U.S. citizens call their occupation social work, which is more people than the population of Alaska, Delaware, North or South Dakota, or Wyoming. To describe the common base of a large profession, the National Association of Social Workers (2007) defines social work as the professional activity of helping individuals, groups, and communities enhance or restore their capacity for social functioning and creating societal conditions favorable to this goal. Traditionally, social work has involved helping people obtain services; providing counseling and psychotherapy to individuals, families, and groups; helping communities or groups provide or improve health and social services; and participating in legislative processes that affect human welfare. In what is called *generalist practice*, social workers demonstrate effective helping and problem-solving skills and engage in solution-building processes with individuals, families, and groups. This requires knowledge about how to engage clients, assess their needs, develop a plan to help, implement the plan, and evaluate the outcomes.

THE ORIGINS OF SOCIAL WORK

Many social workers choose this helping profession out of an altruistic desire to help others. Since the dawn of civilization, altruism has been found in almost every organized society. Altruism has been called a survival impulse (Kristeller & Johnson, 2005; Kropotkin, 1925) because mutual aid helps people survive in hard times. The altruistic impulse that drives social workers to help others may be a natural human response to those in need (Sanchez & Cuesta, 2005).

Some social workers would describe their motivation to help people as a spiritual response based on their religion or faith. Like altruism, the tradition of religious stewardship or community care is found in most civilizations, both ancient and contemporary (Trattner, 1999). Religious beliefs have long promoted efforts to help individuals in need. Individual charitable obligation is a central tenet of most organized religions, in which the more materialistically endowed members of the group are expected to help those less fortunate. Sometimes this obligation has extended to governments as well. In ancient Egypt, for example, the government stored grain to be distributed in times of famine. Out of religious duty, strangers also received assistance.

Charity toward those in need is a central tenet of the world's largest religions. In ancient Judaic law, the Torah directed the owners of agricultural enterprise to glean their fields, setting aside a portion of crops for the poor. Early Christians often carried their obligatory compassion for the unfortunate to extremes. The sanctification of the poor and castigation of those ensnared in worshipping materialistic consumption arose from church teachings at that time. The thirteenth-century monk St. Francis of Assisi typifies the response of the early church to the impoverished. St. Francis came from a wealthy family, chose to live a life of poverty and service to the poor, and was subsequently beatified. Like St. Francis, people in the very early church sometimes sold their worldly possessions to provide for the poor. Indeed, as early as the second century CE, charity had become highly organized (Trattner, 1999). An important principle of Islam is that wealth emanates from God and should be passed on. Charity toward the poor is one of the Five Pillars of Islam.

Whether altruism is an innate human response, a religious tradition, or a civic responsibility in a democratic society, its public expressions wax and wane. From its origins in eighteenth-century English poor laws, organized public charity has undergone major transformations in American society. Behind recent welfare reform, for example, is the fear that people will become dependent on government assistance unless they are forced to work. In return for cash benefits, the poor may have to go to various extremes, including relocating, if necessary, to obtain employment (Rainford, 2004). For an overview of the U.S. social welfare system and its history, read Axinn and Stern (2005) or Popple and Leighninger (2005), or visit the Social Work History Station (n.d.) online.

SOCIAL WORK PIONEERS

Many notable individuals have devoted their lives to helping others. The social work profession traces its central tenets of helping vulnerable and oppressed groups in society to the efforts of many historic figures. A few of those individuals who have given social work its present shape and meaning are noted here.

John Augustus

Augustus, a shoemaker who lived in Boston in the early 1800s, was concerned with the plight of juveniles placed under the jurisdiction of the magistrate for minor offenses; while their crimes were often minor, incarceration was not. Augustus argued to the court that these young people were capable of reform, but not while housed with heinous and hardened criminals. He pledged to the court that he would be personally responsible for the behavior of any juveniles released to his custody and care. The court accepted his offer. Over the course of the next eighteen years, Augustus took into care almost two thousand juveniles, providing them opportunities to reenter society as productive, responsible adults. His efforts evolved into the current system of probationary rehabilitation (Allen, Eskridge, Latessa, & Vito, 1985).

Dorothea L. Dix

Before the onset of the Civil War, Dix lobbied the government for humane treatment for people with mental health problems. In the mid-1800s, she pushed the U.S. Congress to allocate five million acres of public land for the support of institutions for the insane. Responding to Dix's pleas, Congress authorized the allocation of twice the amount of land requested. Unfortunately, President Pierce vetoed the legislation, but the debate Dix generated resulted in an era of mental health institutional reform at both the state and local levels (Axinn & Stern, 2005).

Jane Addams

In the late 1800s, Chicago, like other midwestern and northeastern urban areas, experienced a large influx of immigrants from Europe. Immigrants generally lived in densely populated impoverished neighborhoods where disease, malnutrition, illiteracy, substandard housing, and unemployment flourished, threatening the health and welfare of residents. In response, Addams, who had toured England's community settlement houses, opened Hull House, which offered social services and community development programs to neighborhood residents. While the family unit was the target of intervention, the desired outcome was improved well-being for the entire neighborhood. Change resulted from casework, environmental reform (much more than merely cleaning the air, water, and living space, environmental reform addresses all elements in a person's world, including crime, inadequate shelter, poor housing, and lack of employment opportunities), and societal change through legislative and judicial actions. In her description of Hull House, Addams (1897) wrote, "To adjust an individual to civilization as he finds it round him, to get him to the pitch which shall induce him to push up that civilization a little higher . . . is perhaps the chief function of a settlement" (p. 339).

A. Clayton Powell

In the early twentieth century, the Reverend A. Clayton Powell was the spiritual leader of the largest African American church in New York. Recognizing the growing needs of residents in Harlem, he moved his church there in 1920. Powell responded to individual needs and community problems by establishing the first community center from which educational and social service programs were launched. Facing racial oppression and violence head-on, Powell became a social activist, organizing rallies and lectures, and participating in community groups designed to elevate the status of African Americans. He co-founded the National Urban League and was an active member of the National Association for the Advancement of Colored People (Powell, 1923). When Powell died in 1953, he left a living legacy—the church he founded is still the largest, most active faith organization in Harlem today.

Maggie Walker

Walker was an African American woman far ahead of her time. She was born in 1867 in the segregated South. Her central concern was to teach African American families to save and invest their money to better their futures. In opening the St. Luke Penny Savings Bank, a bank owned and run by and for African Americans, in 1903, Walker became the first female bank founder and owner in the United States. By 1920, the bank had helped six hundred families purchase homes. Walker was also a community organizer and joined the Richmond Council of Colored Women and the National Urban League. She co-founded the Richmond, Virginia, branch of the National Association for the Advancement of Colored People. Walker's dream of a bank owned by African Americans for the benefit of elevating the welfare of families and the community lives on—the bank she started still operates today as Consolidated Bank and Trust Company. It is the oldest minority-owned bank in America.

Ida B. Wells

Emancipation made it possible for this nineteenth-century African American woman who was born a slave to attend Rust College and Fisk University, after which she became a teacher and supported her orphaned siblings. Ordered to relinquish her seat to a white man on the Chesapeake & Ohio Railroad, Wells refused and resisted, biting the hand of a conductor who sought to drag her out of her seat. Forcefully removed from the train, the twenty-five-year-old teacher entered public life by suing the railroad. Wells left teaching to launch a crusade through her work as an author, intellectual, journalist, and speaker with national and international audiences. The lynching of three of her friends, whose fledgling grocery store threatened white businesses, triggered the publication of *Southern Horrors*, Wells's exposé of the murder of African Americans in the American South. A founding member of the National Association for the Advancement of Colored People, Wells also founded the Negro Fellowship League for men, the first suffrage club for African American women, and the nation's first kindergarten for African American children. Settling in Chicago, Wells helped elect the city's first African American alderman and became one of the first African American women to run for election to the state legislature.

Mary Richmond

Richmond devoted her life to helping people in poverty. As a member of the Baltimore Charity Society Organization, founded in 1897, Richmond became a specialist in visiting impoverished families in their homes in order to learn about them, analyze their environments, and then help them improve their lives (Richmond & Hall, 1974). She found that the systematic collection of information on families enabled her to prescribe remedies for their economic plight (Hiersteiner & Peterson, 1999). Richmond (1917) authored the authoritative text on casework and "friendly visiting," entitled *Social Diagnosis*. The text became a pillar of clinical social work. Richmond worked to formalize social work education, contributing much to the early years of the professionalization of social work. Incredibly, Richmond's formal education ended with high school. She, like many of the early heroes of social work, was self-taught and field-trained to help others, rather than benefiting from the rigorous curriculum required of social work students today. Richmond was a true pioneer of social work as a profession.

SOCIAL WORK'S PAST: LIBERAL OR CONSERVATIVE?

The profession of social work is often depicted as liberal in today's political climate. Compared to professions such as accounting, banking, and finance, social work is a liberal profession. The term "liberal" has various meanings. Used here, it is meant as social liberalism, which advocates freedom from government intrusion on personal liberties, coupled with individual rights and governmental regulation of economic markets so that all individuals are afforded equal access to economic opportunities in society. In the past, social work was depicted as being more conservative in its approach to helping people. The term "conservative" also has various meanings. Here it is meant as both fiscal and social conservatism, wherein the economic market is free from government intrusion, government programs are reduced or eliminated, and individual freedoms are subject to governmental scrutiny only where "moral" issues such as reproductive rights and sexual diversity are concerned. The social welfare historian Walter Trattner (1999) charts the evolution of American social welfare in a grand narrative in which major trends and developments are punctuated by events like depression and famine, insurrection and war. In its early days, the United States was comprised of mostly farmers and frontiersmen who were faced with abundant land but a scarce labor force. In such an economic environment, organized welfare was not possible. Prior to the twentieth century, most welfare programs were funded by private sources and administered by private agencies. Helping the poor began to change when the brutal American Civil War left many men dead and their families without a breadwinner, or wounded and disabled with dependent wives and children to support. The federal government levied the nation's first income tax to finance the war. However, it wasn't until the Sixteenth Amendment to the Constitution in 1913 that Congress authorized an ongoing income tax that allowed the United States to develop a financial structure for a national response to the country's problems.

One instance of a national response was the effort to relieve suffering caused by wholesale poverty during the Great Depression of the twentieth century, during which one-third of the nation's private welfare programs disappeared. The New Deal (engineered by Harry Hopkins, a social worker in the Franklin D. Roosevelt administration) created an array of federal programs to assist the nation's destitute, hungry, and jobless, who numbered in the millions. Thus, social workers and the nation adopted a liberal approach using public, rather than private, support to affect individual welfare. In recent years, it seems that much of the nation may have forgotten the lessons of social welfare history. The aftermath of Hurricane Katrina in 2005 is a reminder of the vulnerability of a sizeable portion of the population of the United States to the problems of poverty and the need for governmental assistance.

SOCIAL WORK'S PRESENT: LIBERAL OR CONSERVATIVE?

Compared to the reform-minded social workers of the late nineteenth and early twentieth centuries, some academics believe contemporary social workers "lack the necessary zeal or strength to influence social policy change" (Sanders, 1973, p. 176; also see O'Connell, 1993). If social work began as a noble movement to eradicate poverty and societal inequality, it soon became grounded in the practical realities of working with the poor and other vulnerable persons. Although social workers still champion social advocacy and reform, most professional social workers now earn a living by helping individual clients, one at a time. With the popularization of psychological thinking during the first half of the twentieth century (influenced largely by Sigmund Freud), social work embraced counseling and psychotherapy as primary professional tools. During the turbulent civil rights movement of the 1950s and 1960s, social work experienced a resurgence of activism and advocacy, swinging the profession back toward its progressive roots and espousing a new commitment to social justice (Specht, 1972). "Social justice" is a term widely used in the profession of social work. It refers to the idea that all people, regardless of race, gender, age, sexual orientation, religion, socioeconomic status, or disability, should have the same basic rights, opportunities, benefits, and obligations in society. However, as social work's role grew in a health-care and mental health-care system financed by third-party insurance, many social workers left public service to pursue clinical practice in private agencies (Frumkin & O'Connor, 1985). The perceived abandonment of the poor and vulnerable by the sizeable majority in social work led Specht and Courtney (1994) to label such social workers "unfaithful angels." In retrospect it appears some of the "unfaithful" were demonized for taking part-time second jobs to augment their salaries (Gibelman & Schervish, 1997) or seeking other employment as government social service programs were cut (Krugman, 2003).

Although the debate over social work's commitment to public service and social activism continues, social workers share common values, education, and purpose. Social workers are a diverse group of people who do many things. The profession consists of at least two different groups. One group is those who rely on direct face-to-face intervention efforts to help individuals and families, often called *micro-level* interventions. The other group uses advocacy or other approaches, called indirect methods, to achieve community, state, and national change. Community interventions are often referred to as *mezzo-level* work, and state and national interventions as *macro-level* work. Social workers don't own the market when it comes to helping people, of course. Some of the many others involved are the members of volunteer groups such as the Junior League, the Veterans of Foreign Wars, and the Socialist Party of America.

SOCIAL WORK AND ITS SISTER PROFESSIONS

Many other professions also serve people in need. Psychology, sociology, counseling, psychiatry, nursing, and public administration are among social work's sister helping professions.

Psychology

Social workers and psychologists, especially clinical psychologists, often work together as part of a team, and there is a great deal of overlap in what they do. Both are interested in people's behaviors and patterns of interaction. Both deal with human beings' thinking and feeling processes. The psychologist, however, is interested primarily in understanding the human mind and behavior. Many psychologists base this understanding on the behavior of animals. While the clinical psychologist focuses on individual behavior, the social worker focuses on the social functioning of the individual. While the psychologist, especially the clinical psychologist, may work intensively with clients to help them change their individual beliefs or behavior, the social worker is just as often interested in changing the individual's environment. Social workers focus more on the client's social roles and on using community resources to meet a client's needs. In recent years the field of psychology has become increasingly specialized, resulting in the fields of social, industrial, counseling, and community psychology. Some of these newer areas may resemble social work more than experimental or clinical psychology because they deal with environmental conditions that affect clients. Box 1.1 provides an example of how a social worker and a psychologist might handle the same case in different ways.

Box 1.1   Social Work and Psychology

Juan has been in and out of juvenile institutions most of his life. Abandoned by his mother at an early age, and never having known his father, he went first to a faith-based children's home and then to a foster home. After running away from his foster home, he stole a car. The police apprehended him. By the time he was thirteen, he had been committed to a public "training school" for delinquent boys. Upon arriving, he saw a psychologist, who gave him a battery of psychological tests to determine his level of intellectual functioning, his mental status, and the prospects for adjustment to his new environment. Based on these test results, the psychologist recommended that Juan see a clinical psychologist once a week. This psychologist thinks it is important for Juan to change his thought processes so he can adapt to life in the institution and earn his release.

Juan was also assigned to a social worker who will be his case manager while he is in the training school, and who will also be responsible for planning Juan's eventual return to the community. The social worker is interested in how and what Juan thinks, but he is more concerned with the problems in Juan's social relationships that have gotten him into the institution. The social worker realizes that in order for Juan is to readjust to a normal life in the community, he must try to help Juan build relationships that will be supportive and provide incentives for normal, healthy behavior. The social worker spends more time building a network of community support systems for Juan and helping him engage in pro-social activities than counseling Juan about his psychological problems.

If you are interested in a job that is primarily concerned with administering psychological tests and counseling clients, you might prefer a career in clinical or counseling psychology. If you want to improve the environment as well as counsel clients, you might want to choose social work.

Sociology

Sociology is primarily an academic discipline focused on understanding the human condition, while social work is an academic discipline and a helping profession dedicated to improving the human condition. Sociologists study social organizations and institutions. Unlike social workers, who act on the social context in which people live, sociologists are interested in the context itself. Although some radical or reform-minded sociologists hold political beliefs that lead them into social action, and there are subfields called applied and clinical sociology, sociologists are generally more interested in theory than in working with people. While sociological literature has contributed heavily to modern social work practice, it is social workers who have attempted to apply theories of social organization and interaction to improve social functioning.

Counseling

There are many different types of counselors—for example, rehabilitation counselors, vocational counselors, guidance counselors, and marriage counselors. In many respects, counselors and social workers in direct practice provide similar services. However, counselors differ from social workers in an important way. Counselors emphasize the establishment of a relationship with their clients as the primary means of helping clients change (Timms & Timms, 1982). Most social workers also view helping relationships as very important, but they are equally committed to seeking opportunities for change in the client's external environment. As in clinical psychology, the practice of counseling rarely extends beyond the counselor's office. Take, for example, the behavioral problems of a junior high school student. The school counselor would most likely try to engage the student in talk therapy, meeting with the student on a regular basis to establish a bond. The school social worker, on the other hand, is also likely to consider such factors as the student's health and her relationship with her parents, whether the family can afford to feed the student three meals a day, and how the student's ethnic group affects her behavior. Instead of (or in addition to) counseling, the social worker's assessment may suggest the importance of interceding with parents, helping the family obtain food stamps, or developing a program to improve race relations in the school. The social worker is also more likely to go to the client's home to complete an assessment and provide assistance to the family.

Psychiatry

Social workers are also quite likely to work with psychiatrists as part of a multidisciplinary team, but social work and psychiatry are vastly different. Psychiatrists are medical doctors who prescribe treatments (which might include education, diet, exercise, and medication). Psychiatrists use the medical model. They act mostly as experts telling patients how to manage mental disorders or illnesses. Social workers are also experts, but they generally take a collaborative role, working with clients to jointly decide on treatment goals and approaches. Social workers cannot prescribe medications, but they frequently help clients with serious mental disorders. They also work with people whose problems may not meet strict definitions of mental disorders, but who nevertheless need intervention. In the scenario presented in box 1.1, while a psychiatrist might view Juan's delinquency as the sign of a developing personality disorder, the social worker might see it as normal behavior for a young man coping with a difficult life. For the social worker, the challenge then becomes not changing Juan but changing Juan's situation.

Nursing

Nursing may have more in common with social work than any of the professions previously discussed. The American Nurses Association (2007) defines nursing as "the protection, promotion, and optimization of health and abilities, prevention of illness and injury, alleviation of human suffering through the diagnosis and treatment of human response, and advocacy in the care of individuals, families, communities, and population." Like social workers, nurses attend to client-environment interactions, not just to the client's physiological or intrapsychic functioning.

The major difference between nursing and social work, of course, is that nurses employ skills based on medical training, and the nurse's primary focus is on the patient's physiological functioning. Some nurses do specialize in psychiatric nursing or public health nursing. In particular, many nurses working in public health or community clinics and hospitals function quite similarly to social workers in medical settings. This is especially true where nurses function as case managers or discharge planners, roles traditionally held by social workers.

Public Administration

Not all social workers prepare for careers in which they work directly with individual clients. Managers or directors of large public welfare organizations are as likely to have a degree in social work as in public administration. A growing number of social workers—some with specific training in social welfare administration—manage or direct such agencies. You might be surprised at the similarities between social work and public administration. Administrative training for professional social workers has been available on a significant scale only during the past three decades, but some evidence suggests that the management and administration of public agencies by individuals with a degree in public administration, business, or social work has become virtually indistinguishable (Wuenschel, 2005). All are also likely to manage nonprofit and for-profit agencies.

The difference between the social work administrator and the public administrator with no professional social work education has to do with values and orientations. The public administrator learns management methods that can be applied to any public organization—for example, a state highway department, bureau of fisheries, or the Internal Revenue Service. The social work administrator seeks to work in an agency that helps clients with problems of social functioning or advocates for those who are oppressed or disadvantaged. Economy and efficiency are primary values that guide public administrators, while the social work administrator is guided more by the value of optimizing client well-being. Social workers, whether administrators or direct service providers, share the foundation of values described in box 1.2.

Box 1.2   Do You Have Social Work Values?

After seven years of negotiation to establish the National Association of Social Workers, another three years were necessary for the group to agree on the profession's core values. In 1958, those values were published in *Social Work*, the flagship journal of the profession. According to Bartlett (1970), the following values provide the philosophical foundation for social work practice:

- The individual is the primary concern of this society.
- There is interdependence between individuals in this society.
- They have social responsibility for one another.

- There are human needs common to each person, yet each person is essentially unique and different from others.
- An essential attribute of a democratic society is the realization of the full potential of each individual and the assumption of his social responsibility through active participation in society.
- Society has a responsibility to provide ways in which obstacles to this self-realization (i.e., disequilibrium between the individual and his environment) can be overcome or prevented. (p. 221)

PROFESSIONAL SOCIAL WORK: EDUCATION AND TRAINING

Because the social work profession is so diverse, there must be a core base or foundation of knowledge upon which more specialized forms of social work practice can be built. In the United States, the Council on Social Work

Education (CSWE), which accredits baccalaureate and master's social work programs, determines that foundation, including many aspects of the curriculum you are studying.

Curriculum

The CSWE (2003) mandates that social work education be grounded in a liberal arts perspective. If you select social work as a major, you will study the following subjects: (1) social work values and ethics, (2) human diversity, (3) social and economic justice, (4) populations at risk, (5) human behavior and the social environment, (6) social welfare policies and services, (7) social work practice, (8) research, and (9) field education.

Social work values and ethics are central to the profession. Students must study them and decide whether they can make them their own, because without these values, it is difficult to call oneself a social worker. Internalization starts with awareness of one's current value system and how it affects one's interactions with the world (Barkow, 1978). Three core values provide social workers with a framework for ethical practice: (1) the right to self-determination, (2) social justice, and (3) the dignity and worth of the individual. In a democratic society, for example, the right of self-determination means that individuals should have the freedom to chart their own course in the world. The value of social justice means every individual deserves an equal opportunity for full and effective participation in what the world has to offer. Valuing the dignity and worth of each person compels social workers to resist forces such as racism, ageism, sexism, and homophobia that devalue individuals and groups and diminish their spirit. This does not mean social workers are naive do-gooders or Pollyannas. It does mean social workers believe individuals and groups deserve freedom of choice, equal access to opportunity, and freedom from fear. Students enacting democratic values learn to engage their clients in a professional manner that fosters each individual's potential.

Human diversity expresses itself in myriad ways. Social workers help people of every color and "stripe"—individuals, families, and groups from all parts of the world. In addition to human variation in ability, age, color, ethnicity, gender, political affiliation, race, religion, sexual orientation, and socioeconomic status, social workers and their clients may bring different cultural views and behavior to the table. To help a diverse clientele, students must develop awareness of their own diversity relative to others. Through self-awareness of our own ethnic identities, for example, we open ourselves up to other ethnic experiences and perspectives.

Social work is very much concerned with helping disenfranchised groups and individuals, sometimes referred to as *populations at risk*, achieve *social and economic justice*. Social work students learn to identify contemporary and historical forces of discrimination, prejudice, and oppression. All too often history seems to unfold by the rules of a zero-sum game, in which some social groups gain privilege and advantage at the expense of others. Examples are found in groups with limited educational and economic opportunity and access to health care and high rates of poverty, disease, and despair and in the wholesale patterns and consequences of discrimination and prejudice that deny the basic human rights of whole groups of citizens—gays and lesbians, religious minorities, women, people of color, individuals with disabilities, children, and older people—based on their differences from what is perceived to be the norm. Social work is very much concerned with helping disenfranchised groups and individuals achieve social and economic justice.

Social work majors also study *human behavior and the social environment,* content devoted to human development. The work of developmental theoreticians Jean Piaget and Eric Erikson is often stressed, along with general models of biological, psychological, and social development, but more consideration is being given to alternative models, such as those that consider differences in the socialization of boys and girls and of different cultural groups. In addition to individual behavior, human behavior courses also focus on developmental models for families, groups, communities, and organizations, and how these systems promote or hinder human development.

Content on *social welfare policies and services* covers major federal and state policies and programs, including social insurance (e.g., Social Security), public assistance (e.g., food stamps), and social services (e.g., protective services) for a variety of client groups. In addition to identifying social problems, those affected by the problems, and how government responds, social welfare policy content includes approaches to social policy analysis. Such analysis enables the social worker to determine if a policy is appropriate, given its costs, benefits, and effectiveness, and whether a program is achieving its intended goals. This prepares social workers to compare and contrast various social policies in order to select the ones that best promote human development. One problem, of course, is that what seems best to one individual may not seem best to another; hence, students learn skills such as negotiation and coalition building to reach an agreement. Social work students are also taught how to influence social policy through legislative advocacy, which introduces them to social policy practice as a career option.

The foundation of *social work practice* is the integration of values, knowledge, and skills for helping people in systems of all sizes, from individuals, families, and groups to whole communities. Direct practice skills with clients include interviewing, establishing and managing professional relationships, defining issues, assessing client strengths, setting goals, choosing and applying appropriate interventions, and evaluating practice outcomes. Social workers must do all these things with an understanding of human diversity. MSW education builds on the foundation courses in social work practice, providing students with an array of possible specializations or concentrations to pursue, including working with children, youths and families, people with disabilities, or the elderly. Some graduate students elect to focus on practice at the mezzo or macro level in community development, policy, or administration.

Social work once assumed its interventions were effective solely because the intervention seemed to be the right thing to do. More recently, social work has placed increased emphasis on the value of *research* and evaluation in testing the efficacy of its interventions (Gambrill, 2003). Research courses teach students to be critical consumers of helping-science research and to evaluate their own practice on an ongoing basis. Research content includes the design of evaluation projects, from individual case studies to large-scale experiments. Professional social workers use knowledge gained in research coursework to identify and provide effective and efficient interventions, bring about change that clients desire, improve programs and services, develop policy, and evaluate their practice (Council on Social Work Education, 2003). Social work has also come to value many ways of knowing, including quantitative and qualitative research methods.

Field education allows students to develop and practice their skills under the supervision of an experienced professional, usually a social worker who holds a baccalaureate or graduate social work degree. Fieldwork occurs in the many types of agencies and other settings in which social workers practice. Designed to integrate and synthesize social work values, knowledge, and skills, this capstone experience is described by many students as their most rewarding social work course.

Undergraduate, Master's, and Doctoral Social Work Programs

Although the Council on Social Work Education accredits only master's and four-year undergraduate programs, community colleges may also offer a few introductory courses in social work, and a number of universities offer a social work doctoral degree.

Accredited undergraduate programs prepare students for beginning or entry-level generalist social work practice in a variety of settings. Many undergraduate programs call the degree they offer the bachelor of social work, while a few offer the bachelor of science in social work (BSSW). Others offer a bachelor of arts in social work. Since accredited programs meet the same standards, these are considered equivalent degrees. Colleges and universities differ in the number of credits in English, history, and science required in order for students to earn a degree. The Council on Social

Work Education mandates certain subject areas be taught, but program faculty determine the number of required social work courses and their specific content.

In 2003, the 380 undergraduate programs that responded to the Council on Social Work Education's inquiry reported that approximately 25,000 juniors and seniors were enrolled as social work majors (Lennon, 2005). Of the full- and part-time junior and senior social work majors, nearly 82 percent were women. Thirty-five percent of seniors were students of color (22% were African American, and about 8% were Hispanic/Latino). Representation of other minority groups was relatively small, although this varied by program. For example, the University of Hawaiʻi attracts a considerable number of Asian American students because of that state's ethnic heritage, and American Indians have traditionally made up more than one-third of the juniors and seniors enrolled at Northeastern State University in Tahlequah, Oklahoma.

Social workers who obtain an MSW enjoy a vast array of opportunities and career choices. Many states require practitioners to hold the MSW or an equivalent degree in order to engage in private clinical practice. Likewise, a majority of social service agencies require that social workers hired to provide psychotherapy hold an MSW. The MSW is a versatile degree, enabling graduates to work in a variety of settings from hospitals to schools, private practice, and a whole host of other settings. Like schools offering the baccalaureate degree in social work, any graduate program accredited by the Council on Social Work Education will have the same basic requirements, regardless of its title. All accredited master's programs offer a two-year course of study, and many also offer an accelerated course of study called advanced standing for those who have a baccalaureate degree in social work from an accredited program. Possessing an undergraduate social work degree does not guarantee admittance to advanced standing, but it is a requirement for applying.

Many master's programs offer students an opportunity to select a concentration or track of study. Students often have a choice of two tracks. One track is usually called something like direct practice or clinical social work, and the other may be called administration and planning or policy practice. Master's programs may also educate social workers for advanced generalist practice, or they may provide education for practice in specialty areas such as gerontology, child welfare, chemical dependency, or occupational social work.

More than 37,000 students pursued social work master's degrees in 163 graduate programs in 2003. Although enrollment in social work graduate programs declined in the 1980s, from 1993 to 2003, full-time student enrollment increased by more than 40 percent. About 83 percent of master's students are women, and about 31 percent of full-time students are individuals of color. Fifty-five percent of students are enrolled in clinical concentrations. The remaining students are enrolled in administration, community organizing, a combination of direct and indirect practice, or other specializations such as mental health or child welfare, or they have not yet declared a concentration (Lennon, 2005).

Many faculty are concerned that enrollment in indirect practice tracks has declined. They may associate indirect practice with social change and see this as evidence that social work has abandoned the core values of the profession. For others, it means fewer social work students will be prepared to manage social welfare programs. However, the numbers suggest the proportion of students in indirect practice has not changed much and student concentrations reflect the social work marketplace. For most of the past thirty-five years, the number of full-time students enrolled in indirect practice tracks has hovered between 7 and 11 percent.

Moreover, face-to-face client services are the primary function of three-quarters of the members of the National Association of Social Workers who hold master's degrees (Gibelman & Schervisch, 1997). And because direct service experience and time in grade are typically required for promotion, the direct practice curriculum is often the route to administrative and supervisory social work jobs. Even social workers who specialized in administration in their master's programs often do direct practice before moving into management and administrative roles. Less than 2 percent of social workers devote their time primarily to the challenging and exciting world of policy, consultation, research, and planning. Social workers have many important career decisions to make about the methods and field of practice they pursue.

You may never have thought about a doctoral degree, but social work needs more professionals who have the preparation necessary to conduct research and hold faculty positions. Approximately 2,600 students were enrolled in fifty-eight social work doctoral programs in 2003. Enrollment has increased 30 percent in the last ten years. About 70 percent of doctoral degrees are awarded to women, and 27 percent to individuals of color. Most doctoral programs offer a PhD in social work; a few call the degree the doctor of social work (DSW). Doctoral programs generally prepare professionals for careers in teaching and research or high-level administrative or policy analysis positions. A few emphasize clinical practice. Doctoral programs usually require two years of classroom work, followed by qualifying examinations and the completion of a dissertation. Since CSWE does not accredit doctoral programs, their content and design can be quite flexible, and much of the coursework may be structured around students' individual interests. Doctoral programs must, of course, meet the parent university's regulations for conferring graduate degrees.

By now you may be thinking about the social work program in which you would like to enroll. What degree or degrees does it offer, is it housed in a separate school or college or in combination with other degree programs, how many students are enrolled, and what is their ethnic and gender composition? Faculty composition is also important, as are interactions among students and faculty, program deans, directors, and staff. For example, how is academic advising of students done? Is there sufficient opportunity for contact between administrators, faculty, and students? What agencies are used for field placements?

WHO REPRESENTS SOCIAL WORKERS?

Professional social workers in the United States are represented by a variety of organizations. Two of the largest are described in this chapter. Others related to social work education and specific areas of practice are mentioned here or discussed in subsequent chapters. The growing number of social work organizations may be a sign of the profession's vitality or a sign of splintering due to social workers' many interests and activities.

The National Association of Social Workers

The largest membership organization of social workers in the world is the National Association of Social Workers (NASW). It was founded in 1955. The organization's purpose is to enhance the professional growth and development of its members, create and maintain professional standards, and advance sound social policies. NASW's Web site expresses its overriding concern for the eradication of racism, sexism, and poverty. In recent years its agenda has been to advance the profession, to influence public policy, to advocate on behalf of clients and professional social workers, to promote the image of the profession, and to improve compensation for social workers.

NASW (2003) has about 153,000 members, slightly more than half of the nation's 300,000 licensed social workers. Of NASW members, 79 percent are female, 87 percent are white, 5 percent are African American, 3 percent are Hispanic, 2 percent are Asian American, and 1 percent are American Indian. Regular members (as opposed to student members) hold a baccalaureate or graduate degree from a program accredited by the CSWE. Those whose highest educational level is a bachelor's degree make up only about 10 percent of the total membership. In part this is because many individuals with undergraduate degrees who remain in the profession eventually earn a master's degree and are no longer counted as baccalaureate members. However, the number of members whose highest degree is a baccalaureate degree is disproportionately small. Some believe NASW's programming is more responsive to social workers who hold graduate degrees and that membership costs discourage baccalaureate membership.

NASW has specialty practice sections in aging, addictions, child welfare, health, mental health, poverty and social justice, private practice, and school social work and plans to add more sections. All members receive *Social Work*, NASW's flagship journal. Articles address topics such as original research, new practice techniques, and policy issues. Members also receive the organization's newspaper, the *NASW News*, which keeps them abreast of current events such as the latest policy developments in Washington, actions of the NASW board of directors, and upcoming conferences in the United States and abroad. Organizations conducting national job searches may advertise in the *News*. Other NASW journals are *Children and Schools*, *Social Work Research*, *Social Work Abstracts*, and *Health and Social Work*. NASW also publishes *The Encyclopedia of Social Work*, as well as an extensive list of books, reports, manuals, and standards for social work practice.

The Council on Social Work Education

The Council on Social Work Education provides leadership in social work education. CSWE works to ensure that there is a sufficient number of high-quality social work education programs to meet the country's need for social work professionals. The organization is best known for its role in accrediting social work education programs, but holding conferences, publishing, providing consultation, and creating curriculum development projects that improve social work education and practice are also important functions of the organization. Accreditation criteria are available online under the title *Educational Policy and Accreditation Standards*. After a program receives initial accreditation, it is reviewed again in four years, and every eight years thereafter. Failure to meet the standards can result in sanctions against the program, the most severe of which is loss of accreditation. Although more than six hundred graduate and undergraduate programs voluntarily comply with accreditation, there is never a lack of discussion or concern about the process. Some believe the standards are too broad and vague. For example, undergraduate students must have knowledge of the biological, sociological, cultural, psychological, and spiritual development of people across the life span, but the specific nature and amount of content are left to each program to determine. Others argue that some aspects of accreditation (e.g., curriculum requirements, faculty qualifications) are so specific that they stifle educational innovation. One of the most significant recent changes in accreditation standards is a greater emphasis on globalization.

CSWE publishes the *Journal of Social Work Education* as well as statistical reports and directories of social work education programs and books on social work education and practice. CSWE holds an annual conference that is a major vehicle for disseminating information to improve social work education, such as new models for social work practice, curriculum innovations, and information on a host of other topics ranging from student advising to the development of international field placements.

Other Membership Organizations

Social work education is also represented by organizations composed of the deans or directors of bachelor's, master's, and doctoral programs. The profession of social work also has a growing number of specialized membership and credentialing organizations in addition to those discussed in this chapter. They include the American Board of Examiners in Clinical Social Work, the Association of Oncology Social Work, the Clinical Social Work Association, the Institute for the Advancement of Social Work Research, the National Association of Black Social Workers, the National Association of Puerto Rican/Hispanic Social Workers, the National Organization of Forensic Social Work, the North American Association of Christians in Social Work, and the Rural Social Work Caucus. To learn more about these organizations, visit their Web sites.

STATUS OF THE PROFESSION

According to Greenwood (1957), a profession's status is a reflection of its self-regulating powers and privileges, rooted in monopolistic authority derived from unique and valuable knowledge and skills, and sanctioned by its clients and the public. This sounds like a mouthful of jargon, but it is important because social workers have powers and privileges that affect human lives. Recognizing the critical roles social workers fill, all fifty states, the District of Columbia, the U.S. Virgin Islands, and Puerto Rico regulate social work practice, ensuring that license or certification holders meet prescribed qualifications or standards. Other important benchmarks of professional status include income and image.

Licensure

Licensure or certification is intended to protect the public by regulating social work practice, and a certification or license may be required for one to call oneself a social worker (Association of Social Work Boards, 2005). Although each jurisdiction defines by law its requirements for social work licensure, typically there are four categories of practice subject to state regulation: (1) baccalaureate (requiring an undergraduate social work degree), (2) master's (requiring an MSW degree), (3) advanced generalist (requiring an MSW degree and two years of supervised post-master's experience), and

(4) clinical (requiring an MSW and two years of supervised post-master's direct clinical practice experience). Applications for licensure are evaluated on the basis of the applicant's education and experience, and tests of knowledge, judgment, and skill. State board of social work examiners usually require a passing score on a written examination for licensure. The Association of Social Work Boards, a central resource for information on the regulation of social work practice, develops and maintains national examinations used to evaluate applicants for social work licensing and certification. The Association of Social Work Boards also helps individual social workers and social work students with questions they may have about licensing laws, rules, and examinations.

By specifying the knowledge and skills required for a given level of social work practice, and a common code of professional conduct, individual state boards use licensure to protect those using social work services. Of course, the rigor of qualifications and standards differs according to the particular methods used to grant licensure, and, through "grandparenting," social workers are sometimes exempted from examination for licensure or from meeting other new standards. Moreover, according to many state licensing laws, employees of state welfare and social service departments are exempt from the licensure requirement. Unfortunately, some evidence suggests social workers exempted from examination by grandparenting are more likely than their examined counterparts to be named in ethics complaints, and it is much more likely for ethics complaints against them to be substantiated by evidence (Kinderknecht, 1995). Although licensure does not guarantee professional competence, it usually allows complaints against social workers accused of failing to provide services in a professionally competent manner to be filed. It also provides sanctions for those found to have violated professional standards.

About 300,000 social workers are currently licensed by the state boards of social work examiners (National Association of Social Workers, 2006). According to a national survey of a representative sample of 10,000 licensed social workers, 86 percent identified their ethnicity as non-Hispanic white (National Association of Social Workers, 2006). This tells us that the social work profession has not kept pace with population trends. For example, African Americans are 12 percent of the U.S. population and the largest minority group represented in social work, but only 7 percent of licensed social workers are African American. Also telling is that a mere 5 percent of the NASW membership are African American. The gap for Hispanics and Latinos is even larger. Asians/Pacific Islanders and American Indians/Alaskan natives are also underrepresented in the social work profession. There is a concern that professional social workers do not demographically represent the clients they serve as the U.S. population and those needing social work services become increasingly diverse (see figure 1.1).

Figure 1.1   Racial/ethnic distribution of active licensed social workers and the U.S. population, 2004

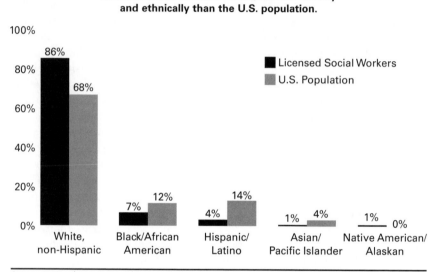

Source: National Association of Social Workers. (2006). *Assuring the sufficiency of a frontline workforce: A national study of licensed social workers.* Washington, DC: Author.

Salary

Based on a broad definition of self-identified social workers (one that includes individuals without a social work education or license), the U.S. Bureau of Labor Statistics (2005) reports the median annual earnings for social workers are $33,150 for child, family, and school social workers; $37,380 for medical and health social workers; and $32,850 for social workers working in the fields of mental health and substance abuse. The lowest 10 percent earn less than $21,270, and the top 10 percent earn more than $54,250. Based on a national survey of people with at least a baccalaureate degree in social work and a social work license, the estimated median annual social work salary is $47,689, while 25 percent earn $60,000 or more (National Association of Social Workers, 2006).

By and large, attorneys, dentists, nurses, and physicians earn more than social workers, but exactly how much individual social workers earn depends upon their academic and practice credentials, what they do, where they work, and where they live. Incomes in New England and the Pacific states have generally been higher than those in the South Central United States, and salaries in the U.S. territories have been the lowest of all. Other variables also affect salaries. For example, small nonprofit agencies such as battered women's shelters and rape crisis centers often operate on limited budgets and depend heavily on donations and volunteer services. The paid staff of these programs may be motivated more by dedication to these fields of service than the goal of a large income. Like other professions comprised primarily of women, social workers operate in a job market where salaries are affected by gender discrimination. It is not uncommon for students interested in a social work major to say that family and friends have tried to dissuade them from selecting a social service career in favor of something more lucrative. Given their generally modest salaries, it is likely social workers choose their profession because their primary motivation is service, and they believe they can effect positive changes in the lives of individuals, groups, and communities.

Image

The image of social workers in movies may not be particularly flattering (Freeman & Valentine, 2004), and it may be even worse on TV (Gibelman & Sweifach, 2004). But Davenport and Davenport (1997) find that in print, social workers' image is positive. Social workers are viewed as experts doing good work. The 1995 *Consumer Reports* study of psychotherapy outcomes, for example, ranked social workers' effectiveness on par with that of clinical psychologists and psychiatrists, and superior to that of marriage and family counselors and primary-care physicians, in treating mental disorders (Seligman, 1995). The public also appears to hold a generally accurate and positive image of social work. Most of the 386 respondents to a nationally representative random-digit telephone survey knew social workers need a bachelor's or master's degree to practice and evaluated their community value as second only to nurses (LeCroy & Stinson, 2004). On the other hand, social workers were viewed as less helpful than psychologists in managing problems, with the exception of domestic violence and homelessness, and respondents tended to associate the social work role with child abuse.

What about social workers' self-image? Professional social workers are no different from the general public in satisfaction with our financial situation, health, general happiness, and job satisfaction (Hodge, 2004). However, we are significantly more likely to describe our lives as exciting, particularly those of us with master's degrees! Social workers with master's degrees are also more likely to describe their family income as higher than that of the general public and as having gotten better over the past few years.

TRENDS IN THE PROFESSION

An increase in the number of jobs and schools of social work and growing privatization are important trends in the profession of social work. As the

United States grows and changes, the social work profession grows and changes with it.

More Jobs

The U.S. Bureau of Labor Statistics (2005) predicts social work employment will increase faster than average for all occupations through 2012, and some states have already reported a critical shortage of social workers. The majority of licensed social workers are employed in mental health and health care (National Association of Social Workers, 2006), and rapid growth and demand for social work services are expected in the fields of addictions, gerontology, and home health care (U.S. Bureau of Labor Statistics, 2005).

Much of the increased public demand for the health and social services that social workers provide is being fueled by demographic changes, and the social work profession, like the U.S. population, is rapidly aging. With nearly 30 percent of the social work labor force over fifty-five years of age and facing retirement (National Association of Social Workers, 2006), many new social workers are going to be needed to fill the void that is looming.

More Schools of Social Work

In response to perceived need, the number and size of social work baccalaureate, master's, and doctoral programs have grown rapidly in the past twenty years, and some states have aggressive plans for further expansion. Karger and Stoesz (2003) suggest that this rapid growth has produced a number of low-quality programs at all degree levels, resulting in a surplus of social workers and educators of dubious competence, and a reduction in social work salaries to levels that cause some of the best and brightest to leave the profession. Such critical appraisal is needed, but there are also many high-quality social work education programs from which to choose. If you are considering a degree program in social work, you can find a list of all accredited undergraduate and master's programs in the United States on the CSWE Web site. Social workers must work together to ensure the high quality of social work education and practice.

More Privatization

In the foreseeable future, new social workers are more likely to enter the profession in private, not public, settings. The privatization of social work practice has been a trend for some time (Gibelman & Schervish, 1997); 67 percent of licensed social workers are now employed in the private sector, and 17 percent of them are self-employed (National Association of Social

Workers, 2006). Apparently, the privatization of social work has done little to erode core social work values. A national survey of licensed social workers found the "unfaithful angels" with private-sector jobs were more likely to enact social work values through volunteer service than their public service counterparts or the public at large (Gibelman & Sweifach, 2004).

SUMMARY

Social work is a helping profession. Although social workers have common values rooted in altruism, the helping methods they use are as diverse as the places they work and the people they serve. This chapter provided a brief historical overview of the social work profession; introduced social work education, licensure, opportunities, and challenges; and took a stab at predicting the future of the profession. Social work is an honorable way to earn a living by helping others, an exciting field of practice for those wishing to tackle big social problems, and a way to make a difference that counts. The following chapters look further at issues and opportunities in this challenging profession.

SUGGESTED READING

Addams, J. (1990). *Twenty years at Hull House: With autobiographical notes.* Urbana: University of Illinois Press. Social work has deep roots in social action and social reform. Written by social work's Nobel laureate, *Twenty Years at Hull House* is a grand narrative of the interplay between the private personal development and public human engagement of a social work hero.

Bartlett, H. (1970). *The common base of social work practice.* New York: NASW. Social work is a pluralistic profession of such diversity that seven years of negotiation were necessary to establish the National Association of Social Workers in 1955 through the merger of seven social work organizations. In this book, Bartlett seeks to explain what social workers have in common.

Gibelman, M. (2004). *What social workers do* (2nd ed.). Washington, DC: NASW Press. This work addresses many questions about the profession: What is a social worker? How do social workers think? Where do social workers work? What do employers look for? What will social workers do in the future?

Hamilton, G. (1951). *Theory and practice of social casework* (2nd ed., rev.). New York: Columbia University Press. If social work has deep roots in social action and social reform, then its roots in social casework and psychotherapy run just as deep. Although the profession of social work can be fractious, Hamilton was a big-picture thinker who provided an integrative view of social casework with individuals, families, and groups.

Richmond, M. (1917). *Social diagnosis*. New York: Russell Sage Foundation. In this classic statement, Richmond established an intellectual foundation for a science of social work practice. Reflecting American pragmatism and a can-do spirit in an era of progressive faith in our ability to improve the human condition, Richmond proffered social diagnosis as a model for building social work knowledge and selecting effective methods of helping.

THE WORLD WIDE WEB OF SOCIAL WORK

Association of Social Work Boards http://www.aswb.org

ASWB is the association of boards that regulate social work practice. It develops and maintains the social work licensing examinations used across the country and is a central resource for information on the legal regulation of social work. ASWB is also available to answer the questions individual social workers and social work students may have about licensing and the social work examinations.

Council on Social Work Education http://www.cswe.org

CSWE is responsible for developing accreditation standards that define competent preparation and ensuring that social work programs meet them. Visit this Web site to deepen your understanding of the goals and curricula of social work education.

**George Warren Brown School of Social Work: Jobs Online
http://gwbweb.wustl.edu/jobs**

This Web site is for social workers and employers alike. It can be used to explore career opportunities and search for or post jobs by location or keyword.

National Association of Social Workers http://www.naswdc.org

NASW is the largest social work membership organization in the world. It publishes model standards and ethical guidelines for social work practice. NASW's Web site is an important source of information on many aspects of professional practice, such as specialty practice areas, positions on issues of concern to the profession, advocacy activities on behalf of professional social workers and their clients, and professional liability insurance.

Social Work History Station http://www.idbsu.edu/socwork/dhuff/XX.htm

This interactive Web site was developed through the Council on Social Work Education Millennium Project. It offers a visual history of social work and social welfare as well as biographies and essays of contemporary interest.

Social Work Today http://www.socialworktoday.com/index.php

Social Work Today is a newsmagazine, available online, that provides articles about many aspects of social work practice. It also offers an e-newsletter.

**U.S. Department of Labor: Bureau of Labor Statistics
http://www.bls.gov/oco/ocos060.htm**

This Web site offers statistics on the occupational outlook for social workers, including information on the nature of social work, its working conditions, education and training, employment and earnings, and the job outlook for the future.

2 Theory and Practice of Social Work with Individuals, Families, and Groups

Virginia Rondero Hernandez and Cynthia Franklin

This chapter introduces some of the most widely used social work practice theories, models, and approaches for helping others. Social workers use theory as a guide in assessing the needs of clients, developing interventions, and evaluating the effectiveness of interventions. This chapter will help you understand the role of theory in social work practice, especially in working with individuals, families, and groups. As chapter 1 noted, social workers call this type of work *direct practice* or *micropractice*.

THEORY AND EVIDENCE-BASED PRACTICE

Social work practice theory comprises concepts, facts, hypotheses, and principles (Turner, 1995). *Concepts* are idea statements that are used to describe a human behavior or social circumstance, *facts* are pieces of information that can be verified in a scientific way, *hypotheses* are statements intended to predict an outcome, and *principles* are statements upon which we depend to explain an observed behavior. When all four are present, we have a theory. *Practice models*, on the other hand, do not meet all four criteria of theory, but they are useful because they tend to be less abstract and more concrete than theories. Practice models help social workers organize concepts and theories for working with clients (Berger, Federico, & McBreen, 1991).

Vicki is a thirty-eight-year-old widow who has come to your agency asking for help. Her husband committed suicide six months ago. Vicki talks about her husband's unexpected and tragic death and the financial problems it has created for the family. She is especially distressed about why her husband committed suicide and is worried she will lose her house. She understands that your agency might be able to help her. As a social worker for a family services agency, your job is to work with Vicki to identify her needs and refer her to the appropriate community resources. Where do you begin?

Cases like Vicki's are common in social work practice. When they occur, social workers use theory to guide the way they approach the situation.

Theory is used in social work "to seek and understand the complex reality of the person-in-situation" (Turner, 1995, p. 2258). The discipline of social work often uses the word *theory* in a general sense to describe a number of practice theories, practice models, and practice approaches. These theories, models, and approaches are conceptual frameworks that guide practice and equip social workers with knowledge for helping people in many different situations.

A unique aspect of social work is that it embraces theories from different disciplines, including psychology, sociology, political science, and education. The use of theories from other disciplines to build social work practice theory enriches the social work profession and has resulted in a transdisciplinary approach to practice that allows social workers to apply a broad perspective for helping people. This broad perspective is important because it helps social workers envision how to work with an individual client within the context of his or her social environment and the other systems that surround him or her. Theory also helps social workers conduct informed or evidence-based practice, which in turn helps to support and refine the theories they use.

Evidence-based practice focuses on the need for a scientific base in the theories and methods used in social work practice. Paula Allen-Mears (2006) notes: "The theoretical must be tested and proven, in order to generate best practices, which ultimately support a sound knowledge base, and to ensure the very same effectiveness and efficiency in service delivery" (p. 1189). She describes two different understandings of what constitutes evidence-based practice. The first comes from the medical field, where practitioners are concerned with using the best available evidence to make decisions about patients' health care. These best practices are typically combined with clinical experience and knowledge of patients' beliefs and experiences. The second understanding comes from the mental health field, which has strongly influenced social work practice. In mental health, evidence-based practice is considered "any practice that has been established as effective through scientific research according to some set of explicit criteria" (Mullen, cited in Allen-Meares, 2006, p. 1189). Criteria may include a particular way to do treatment, evaluation, research trials, or other scientifically tested or measured outcomes. Once those criteria are selected, theories or practices that meet them are considered part of the evidence base, or best practices. These practices are used to assist clients.

Social workers across the nation attempt to improve social work practice and systems of care (e.g., health and mental health care) by using evidence-based practices. The evidence-based practice movement calls on social workers to view all theories through the lens of best practices so that clients receive the best care possible.

THEORY FOR GENERALIST SOCIAL WORK PRACTICE

All social workers are expected to be familiar with social work practice theory and practice models. Levels of knowledge about social work practice theory for BSWs and for MSWs differ. Social workers with a BSW are expected to understand and apply core theories such as systems theory, the ecological perspective, and the strengths perspective to conduct *generalist social work practice*. Generalist social work practice involves demonstrating effective helping and problem-solving skills and engaging in solution-building processes with individuals, families, and groups; it also involves knowing how to engage a client, assess a client's needs, develop a plan to help, implement the plan, and evaluate how well the plan assists the client. Knowing what practice theory or practice model to use gives a social worker with a BSW some direction in how to begin helping clients.

The ability to integrate knowledge across disciplines and to critically assess and use knowledge increases with advanced social work education. Social workers with an MSW are expected to perform more complex tasks that require higher levels of knowledge and skills than those practiced by social workers with a BSW; this is *advanced generalist social work practice*. Examples of advanced practice are conducting mental health or substance abuse counseling, working on a public school campus as a school social worker, and providing marriage and family therapy. In Vicki's situation, a social worker with a BSW would probably concentrate on offering Vicki resources and referrals, while a social worker with an MSW would more than likely concentrate on applying counseling theories that can help sustain Vicki and her children as they work through the grief and loss they are experiencing. Distinctions between BSW- and MSW-level social work are highly dependent on the agency in which one works, but all social workers, regardless of their level of education, are required to learn about and use theories supported by empirical evidence to understand individuals, families, groups, organizations, and communities (Council on Social Work Education, 2002).

MAJOR SOCIAL WORK PRACTICE THEORIES AND PERSPECTIVES

Social workers use a variety of different theories and models. Social workers must understand the differences between these theories and models in order to decide what approach to use with an individual, family, or group. The theories and models featured in this chapter are systems theory, the ecological perspective, problem-solving theory, task-centered theory, cognitive-behavioral theory, and the strengths perspective (see table 2.1). Although social workers use numerous other theories and models as well, these particular ones are taught in all accredited social work education programs in order to prepare students for the dynamic and challenging profession of social work.

Table 2.1   Major theories and models used by social workers

Theory/model	Emphasis of application
Systems theory	Assessing systems in interaction
Ecological perspective	Assessing transactions of person in environment
Problem-solving theory	Facilitating problem resolution
Task-centered theory	Supporting goal accomplishment
Cognitive-behavioral theory	Modifying thoughts and behaviors
Strengths perspective	Identifying internal/external resources

Systems Theory

Systems theory (sometimes referred to as general systems theory) is an overarching framework borrowed from the physical sciences to help explain the dynamic and recurring process of human interactions (Beckett & Johnson, 1995). It is a core theory that social workers use to organize their thoughts or theorize about the interactions and effects of interactions that occur among individuals, families, and groups. For example, systems theory can help a social worker envision and understand the effects of suicide on various systems, but it does not prescribe exactly what a social worker should do to respond. This is a function of other social work practice theories discussed later in this chapter. Nevertheless, systems theory has had a huge impact on how social workers practice and intervene with clients. Some of the key concepts of systems theory are environment, systems and subsystems, boundaries, and inputs/outputs.

Environment describes the environ or setting in which a system functions. In social work, the word *environment* has also come to mean *social environment*, or the outer, surrounding environment in which all human systems reside. These human systems include individuals, couples, families, and groups; they can also include larger systems, such as neighborhoods, communities, or the broader society. Systems theory proposes that regardless of its size, any system is embedded in a larger overarching social environment. Defining the environment can be tricky because it can often be defined in several ways (see box 2.1).

Another key concept of systems theory is *systems* and *subsystems*. Systems are composed of component parts, or subsystems, that interact to serve a particular function within the structure of a larger system. A family system comprises individuals, each with distinct individual systems of personality, biological traits, and social habits. Likewise, a family system may be part of a larger system such as extended family, neighborhood, or religion. All these systems are parts of a community, which is a part of a city or

---

Box 2.1   Defining Client Systems

Fifteen-year-old Gus keeps coming home late at night, even during the school week. His parents start talking to him about his failure to come home on time in front of his grandparents, who are visiting the family. Soon, all three of them—mother, father, and son—are yelling back and forth at each other about Gus's behavior. The fight then switches to the two parents, who start blaming each other for Gus's behavior. As the two continue yelling and Gus exits the room, the grandmother leans over to the grandfather and whispers, "If those two just got along better, Gus wouldn't have this problem." The grandfather whispers back, "What do you mean? They're all to blame!" Based on her observation, the grandmother believes that the problematic behavior occurs within the environment, or setting, of the couple or parental system. The grandfather, on the other hand, believes the problematic behavior occurs within the environment of the family system. Although their assessments differ, they have each described the way various systems interrelate in the family environment.

---

town, and so forth. For example, a nuclear family (mother, father, and child) exists in its own right, but it is also a subsystem within a larger system of extended family (i.e., grandmother, grandfather, aunts, uncles, and cousins).

Boundaries delineate systems and subsystems. Social workers use the term *boundary* to define the limits of a social system. Simply stated, anything outside the boundary of a system belongs to the environment; anything inside the boundary of the system belongs to the system. Boundaries serve two important functions: they help to give the system an identity (Zastrow & Kirst-Ashman, 2004) and, when properly managed, they prevent a system from being intruded upon and allow the system to preserve its integrity and autonomy. The concept of boundaries takes on special importance for families because the quality of family system boundaries affects family functioning. Enmeshed, overlapping, or diffuse boundaries between subsystems and between individuals may prevent a family member from developing his or her own identity or independence. Rigid boundaries, on the other hand, prevent communication between subsystems and the exchange of information or communication, which also threatens each member's integrity. Incest is an example of both enmeshed and rigid boundaries: a father who is seeking adult sexual gratification from his daughter invades her boundaries—her body and sense of self. Another dynamic of incest is the rigid boundaries that exist between the father and the mother, who may avoid acknowledging the relationship between the father and daughter because the father has established rigid rules for the family in order to protect himself and cover up his actions.

Anything (e.g., information, communication, transactions) that enters a system from the outside environment is an *input* to that system; anything leaving it is an *output*. Both inputs and outputs filter through system boundaries. Inputs may transform or convert to either energize or maintain a system. Let's say that several mothers of children with developmental disabilities have organized themselves into a group system (i.e., support group). Let's also say that a mother who has just moved to the area learns about the support group through her child's special education teacher. She attends a meeting and shares that she belonged to a group in her home state where the mothers took turns watching each other's children so each mother could have some respite—time to relax or run errands. The ideas and experiences that the mother shares with the others are inputs of energy into the support group. The group listens to the new mother and shares that they use the services of a respite agency in the community and give her its phone number. Outputs of this system are the support and resources offered to the new mother. According to systems theory, inputs and outputs function in relationship to each other to energize or maintain a system; however, a system can be destabilized if too many inputs overwhelm it or too many outputs drain the system of energy or resources.

Systems theory is a template for theorizing about the interactions of individuals, families, and groups against the background of the larger social environment. It helps to explain how dysfunction in individual, family, and group systems occurs and to identify behavioral patterns that create and maintain dysfunctional behavior. Over the past decade, family system research has produced considerable empirical evidence that systems theory concepts can be used to help manage problematic behaviors. For example, brief strategic/structural family interventions have shown positive results in helping Hispanic youths with substance abuse problems. These positive results are achieved through the building of therapeutic alliances between the youths' family members and practitioners, the identification of family interactional patterns, and the creation of opportunities for family members to interact in new ways that discourage substance abuse and promote self-control (Jantzen, Harris, Jordan, & Franklin, 2006).

The Ecological Perspective

Social workers use the ecological perspective to help explain how individual, family, and group systems interact with each other and with the larger social systems that surround them. This perspective is very helpful for theorizing about the reciprocal interactions that occur between these systems and the resulting effects. The significance of the ecological perspective is that it promotes a broader vision for understanding and explaining the person-in-environment perspective. Key concepts related to the ecological perspective are social environment, transactions, reciprocal exchange, adaptation, stress, coping, and relatedness.

The ecological perspective extends the systems concept of environment to the *social environment*. The social environment includes "conditions, circumstances, and human interactions that encompass human beings" (Zastrow & Kirst-Ashman, 2004, p. 7). More simply put, the social environment includes all social settings that make up an individual's world and influence his or her behavior (Germain, 1991). Take, for example, the case of a third-grade student who is caught stealing money from his teacher's purse. When caught, he admits that he took the money and says he did it to give the money to his mom, who lost her job the day before. He says he wanted to make her feel better. Knowledge of an individual's social environment lends insight into the circumstances that motivate his or her actions.

The ecological perspective helps us understand the nature and outcomes of exchanges or *transactions* between a person and the surrounding social environment. Transactions reflect active involvement between people and their environments; they are energetic and dynamic and can be positive or negative (Zastrow & Kirst-Ashman, 2004). A person is influenced and shaped by transactions with the environment, and the social environment is influenced and shaped by a person through various transactions. This concept is illustrated in box 2.2.

Box 2.2   Understanding Transactions and Adaptations

Kia, age nineteen, emigrated from Thailand to the United States with her parents twelve years ago. She was seven years old when her family arrived. Neither she nor anyone in her immediate family spoke English. Upon their arrival in the United States, Kia's parents enrolled her in elementary school. This environment was completely new to her, but the classroom aide and some children in her class spoke both Hmong and English. Her teacher would talk to her in English, and the aide and other children would translate. Interactions with her teacher, the aide, and other children helped Kia adapt to the school setting.

Kia did well academically and graduated from high school with honors. She plans to study medicine. Her cousin Mouen is also nineteen years old. He arrived with his family at the same time that Kia's family did, but he struggled with school, lost interest in learning, dropped out of the ninth grade, and got involved with a neighborhood gang. His involvement in a shooting resulted in a ten-year prison sentence. Kia and Mouen come from the same Hmong clan. They had similar experiences and were exposed to the same family values; however, their adaptations to the social environment resulted in very different outcomes.

According to the ecological perspective, transactions between systems are rooted in a process known as *reciprocal exchange* (Germain, 1991). Exchanges between a person and a social environment are mutual and run on a circular feedback loop that over time shapes the behaviors and responses of the person and his or her social environment (Barker, 1995; Berger et al., 1991). In the vignette in box 2.2, Kia learned to adapt to the school setting through reciprocal exchanges with school personnel and peers. Reciprocal exchanges can often be observed in relationships between people. For example, Joe is often late and does not follow through on obligations very well, and Suzi makes excuses for him and takes care of everything to make him look good. Even though at first it may seem that Suzi is in a position in which she is giving and not getting, a closer examination would indicate that a mutual exchange is taking place. Both Suzi and Joe are getting something out of this relationship pattern. Since Joe lets Suzi be in charge all the time, she gets to organize everything, which is something she enjoys. In addition, she gets lots of praise for being so responsible.

The ecological perspective theorizes that humans either adapt or fail to adapt to their surrounding social environment through a series of transactions and reciprocal exchanges. Systems must adapt in times of environmental stress. For example, John was recently in a diving accident in which he acquired a spinal cord injury. As a result, he had to learn to use a wheelchair and adapt to his injury over time. John was very depressed initially, but through contact with others in similar circumstances, he has become

The relationship that this social worker has developed with her fourteen-year-old client, who was removed from her drug-addicted mother when she was eighteen months old, has helped the teenager to adapt as she has been moved from one foster home to another.
© Richard Bermack

skillful at negotiating his environment (home and community). John has also used his political acumen and Internet skills to become active in the disability rights movement. These reciprocal exchanges have helped John grow and move forward in his life. This is a good example of *adaptation*.

Stress is a common human experience that occurs when a person feels overwhelmed by multiple demands or stressors found in the environment. Stress can be positive (e.g., applying for a job you really want) or it can be negative (e.g., the destruction of your house by a hurricane). Positive stress challenges us to grow and bolsters our self-esteem, whereas negative stress can debilitate us or even jeopardize our lives (Lazarus & Launier, 1978). The ability to cope with life's problems is a measure of one's capacity to manage stress. *Coping* is a mechanism of "behavioral and personality patterns used to adjust or adapt to environmental pressures without altering goals or purposes" (Barker, 1995, p. 81). In other words, coping is not letting a negative situation or circumstance get the best of us. If we are able to cope with stress, we reduce the effects of a perceived threat or stressor. On the other hand, if we are overwhelmed by the stress and unable to cope with the perceived threat, we may succumb to pressures or stressors around us and fall into a state of dysfunction. Dysfunction is synonymous with problematic behaviors. John faced many negative stressors in learning to use a wheelchair, but he was able to cope with them and function well.

Relatedness refers to the social attachments that surround a person. Attachment is mediated by the quality of relationships. In families, relatedness is enhanced or diminished by the mutually perceived roles of each member and mutually understood rules (Helton & Jackson, 1997). Like adaptation, relatedness can be a healthy or unhealthy process and is regulated by how well the person fits into the environment.

The ecological perspective helps social workers focus on the total picture of the individual, family, and larger systems, but it does not prescribe the specific steps a social worker must take to intervene. In spite of this limitation, the ecological perspective has been helpful in developing evidence-based therapeutic interventions that effect change. For example, multisystemic therapy is an intervention that incorporates concepts of the ecological perspective. This therapeutic intervention, which has been well researched and is considered by many to be evidence based, targets a young person's day-to-day transactions so that the reciprocal exchanges that take place between the youth and other systems (e.g., family members, foster parents, teachers) in the social environment become more positive and pro-social. Multisystemic therapy can help young people strengthen their coping abilities in the face of stressful situations, thereby increasing their confidence and sense of competency and belonging (Henggeler, Schoenwald, Borduin, Rowland, & Cunningham, 1998).

Problem-Solving Theory

Helen Harris Perlman (1986) developed problem-solving theory in response to the medical model, which was the theoretical framework most social workers used to develop interventions during the early twentieth century. Perlman questioned the medical model's appropriateness for resolving personal and social problems. She suggested that the medical model is expert based and rests on the practitioner's authority. Perlman proposed an alternative perspective that encouraged social workers to engage clients in a problem-solving process characterized by compassion, collaboration, and practical support (Turner & Jaco, 1996). Problem-solving theory emphasizes the importance of the setting in which problem resolution begins, predictable responses from clients who engage in the problem-solving process, how to define a problem, and a process in which the client and social worker work together to resolve a problematic behavior or situation. Key concepts related to problem-solving theory are a focus on the here and now, place, use of relationship, time, and partialization.

Perlman viewed the desire to confront a problem in the *here and now* as an opportunity for change. Being in the here and now with a client allows the social worker to capitalize on the client's motivation to engage in the problem-solving process. For example, a client may reach the point where she believes her boyfriend will never stop using drugs and lying to her about it. Her frustration motivates her to end the relationship. Acknowledging and discussing the client's conclusion may provide her with support to take steps toward liberating herself from this relationship. Rather than discussing how the client's relationship with her boyfriend continues a destructive path that emanates from her relationship with her father, the social worker makes an effort to stay in the here and now. This demonstrates that she thinks the client's concern is important and worthy of support and may be enough to encourage the client to take needed action at this moment in time. If discussing the relationship with her father is necessary for the client's future well-being, that may occur at a later point. Box 2.3 provides another example of use of the here and now.

Box 2.3   Supporting Client Motivation

Ana has just learned that her son, Javier, has been suspended from his high school for violating the campus dress code. He came to school wearing the colors of a local gang. Up to this point, Ana had suspected that Javier might be infatuated with gangs. Now she is convinced! Ana is both angry and frightened. At the assistant principal's recommendation, she meets with the school social worker. She is anxious to learn how to keep her son out of gangs. Perlman (1986) states that "potential powers for change and movement are mobilized best when the 'iron is hot'" (p. 249). The sense of urgency that Ana feels right here, right now, provides fertile ground for change.

When people go to a place like a social service agency, they may have expectations about what can be done to help them. They may also feel intimidated. *Place* is the arena for help, but if people feel intimidated asking for help or have unrealistic expectations about the help they can get, this can spell disaster for the helping relationship. Perlman states that "the client's perceptions and expectations of the agency need to fit within the service mandate of the agency" in order for the client to get the help he or she needs (Turner & Jaco, 1996, p. 513). In the case presented in box 2.3, Ana may feel intimidated about going to the school for help, but she does it anyway because she believes the people there can help her son. Whether her expectations are fulfilled depends on how she is greeted and assisted at the school.

Use of *relationship* refers to the task of building a compassionate and supportive relationship with a client. Perlman (1986) characterizes relationship as "empathic," "caring," "supportive," and "enhancing" (p. 250). It is more likely that change will occur and the client will resolve the problem if the relationship is characterized by these qualities. For example, in the case of Ana and Javier, if the school social worker offers a positive and encouraging response, Ana will probably walk away with a sense of accomplishment and hope. This outcome is likely to intensify Ana's motivation to do whatever it takes to get Javier away from the gang. However, if the

A woman and her new baby visit with the social worker who helped her when she was in foster care and stricken with cancer. She is now an adult and is doing well, and the two have stayed in touch.
© Richard Bermack

school social worker seems bored with Ana's concern or focuses on the amount of gang activity in the area, rather than what can be done for Javier, Ana will probably leave feeling frustrated and even more confused about what to do. Not all clients seek help voluntarily, as Ana did. In fact, social workers often work with involuntary clients, such as batterers, parolees, and others who are ordered by the courts to get services. In all cases, social workers strive for positive connections that reflect goodwill and compassion for clients (Perlman, 1986, p. 250).

Time is an element of the social environment. It takes time to grow and develop, to learn to manage the multiple demands of living, and to solve problems. Time is a key concept of problem-solving theory. Perlman's (1986) consideration of time is a major contribution to the social work profession. She proposed that the helping process consists of a beginning, middle, and end. The beginning or *contact phase* focuses on (1) establishing the helping relationship, (2) identifying the client's problem, (3) identifying the desired goal, (4) developing a preliminary contract for working on the problem, and (5) exploring the client's level of motivation, capacities, and opportunities. The middle phase is the *contract phase*. The focus during this period of the helping relationship is on (1) assessing and evaluating the identified problem, (2) formulating a plan of action for resolving the problem, and (3) predicting if the problem can be resolved. The end phase is the *action phase*, in which (1) the agreed-upon plan is carried out and goals are met (or not), (2) the termination of the helping relationship begins, and (3) the social worker and client take stock of what was accomplished and evaluate the outcomes (Turner & Jaco, 1996).

Partialization is the "cutting down of a complex problem to such size and specificity as to make it manageable for discussion and work-over by the client at a given time" (Perlman, 1986, p. 251). It is the process of breaking down a goal into specific sequential steps. Breaking down goals into attainable subgoals reduces the sense of intimidation the client may feel and his or her resistance to change and allows for little successes that bring a client that much closer to the goal.

Problem-solving theory operationalizes (puts into action) key concepts of systems theory and the ecological perspective and has been adapted over time for use with individuals, couples, families, and groups (Hepworth, Rooney, & Larsen, 2002). Although little empirical research has been conducted on Perlman's problem-solving model, social workers believe that teaching problem-solving skills is an effective method for helping people. Research does suggest that skills-training approaches that teach the step-by-step processes of problem solving are effective in helping adolescents who experience substance abuse, conduct problems, depression, and teen pregnancy (Harris & Franklin, 2004).

Task-Centered Theory

Task-centered theory is a practice approach developed within the discipline of social work in the 1960s that incorporates features of problem-solving theory. The task-centered approach is characterized by three phases of helping: case planning, implementation, and termination. Task-centered theory functions as both a practice model and a theoretical approach. Its emphasis on the planning and completion of tasks helps to move clients toward problem resolution within a relatively short period of time. It also is one of the few social work practice theories that is securely anchored in empirical research; it has been described as a "technology for alleviating specific target problems that clients recognize, understand, acknowledge, and want to attend to" (Epstein, 1995, p. 313). Key concepts related to task-centered theory are the practitioner-client relationship, contextual change, brevity, and basic procedures.

According to task-centered theory, a solid *practitioner-client relationship* is necessary for conducting an adequate assessment of the client's problems and developing realistic strategies for alleviating them. The effectiveness of the practitioner-client relationship depends on the level of motivation and the energy the client invests in completing the tasks required to reach goals and realize change. Reid (1996) acknowledges this when he observes that "the primary agent of change is not the social worker but the client. The worker's role is to help the client bring about changes the client wishes and is willing to work for" (p. 620).

The task-centered model strives for *contextual change* for the client. Task-centered theory proposes that specific tasks can be introduced into the social context (or immediate surroundings) of a client to reduce a problematic behavior. If these tasks are successfully executed within one's social context, they can help to promote and sustain change. However, the social context does have the potential to exert influences that extend beyond the client's control, effectively diluting the successful completion of tasks. For example, a practitioner might advise a client struggling with an anger problem to count to ten whenever he feels like responding angrily to another person, but the client may live in a household where family members share angry exchanges with each other on a regular basis. In this instance, completing the task of counting to ten might be difficult for the client to accomplish due to the influences of the social context. Contextual change is more likely to occur when the client is successful in getting support from his or her social context (e.g., supportive family members, friends, colleagues).

The task-centered approach was intended for use in time-limited treatment. Reid (1996) demonstrated that time-limited treatment achieves results similar to those achieved in long-term treatment. Other studies also provide evidence that imposing limits on treatment does not reduce the effectiveness of the task-centered model (Epstein, 1995). The *brevity* of the task-centered approach is relevant in the current era of cost containment since third-party payers (e.g., insurance companies and government agencies) are demanding that social workers and other service providers demonstrate effective treatment outcomes over relatively short periods of time (Epstein, 1995).

The task-centered model comprises a series of *basic procedures* or steps that are taken in sequential order, generally over a treatment period of six to twelve weeks. These procedures represent the case planning, implementation, and termination phases of treatment. But before case planning can begin, start-up activities must occur. The conditions under which clients come to the agency will affect their attitudes about the need to change and their willingness to work on the problem and must be considered. Clients who come voluntarily generally have a basic desire to alleviate a problematic behavior or situation. They are ready to work and understand the importance of change. Involuntary clients generally enter treatment because they have to (e.g., through a court order, or a family member has pressured them to come). Start-up activities with an involuntary client may include finding out what the referring agency (e.g., the court, child protective services) requires or what goals the family member has in mind and how they differ from the client's perspective.

The first step in a task-centered approach is case planning. As part of this step, the social worker and client work together to identify and prioritize the problems that require intervention. The social worker assesses if the way a client identifies problems and prioritizes them is realistic. If not, the social worker is obligated to counsel the client about this. In the case of an involuntary client, the social worker must also work with the client to reconcile personal priorities with those of the referral agency.

The second step is contracting. The social worker and clients work together to develop a contract for intervention that entails a number of goals and tasks. They prioritize which problems they will work on together, and in what order. Specific goals are identified, and both the client and social worker identify and are assigned tasks to help the client reach the treatment goal. The social worker offers support and consultation throughout the process. A schedule of interventions with specific deadlines is developed, as are periodic reviews of the client's progress. The contract can be revised over time to include new problems or modify the length of treatment.

The third step is problem solving, which involves implementing the contract. Each target problem is assessed in depth to determine its particulars (e.g., frequency, circumstances under which it occurs, significance, and consequences). The social context in which the problem occurs (e.g., home, school, or workplace, socioeconomic status, family structure, peer group structure, cultural/ethnic background) is also defined. Cognitive and emotional factors are also assessed (e.g., typical conduct of the client when the problem occurs, whether the client has received treatment for the problem in the past). The sources and range of supports for goal attainment are also identified (e.g., family, physician, religious organizations, mutual-help groups like Alcoholics Anonymous). Decisions are also made about rehearsing how to complete a task, identifying and reducing barriers to task completion, and monitoring the client's progress.

Termination marks the final step of the task-centered model. If the client completes the negotiated tasks and meets the treatment goals, treatment ends. If the tasks are not completed or the goals are not met, the social worker and client might negotiate to extend the treatment or try a different approach; or in the case of an involuntary client, the social worker may recommend that treatment continue. After treatment formally ends, the social worker and client continue to monitor progress. Box 2.4 provides a simplified version of how the task-centered model might be used.

Box 2.4   Using a Task-Centered Approach with an Involuntary Client

Vince is an involuntary client ordered by the court to go to the local family services agency for treatment. He lost his temper at work, punched his co-worker in the face, and broke his jaw. Vince was found guilty of misdemeanor assault. The judge ordered him to pay his co-worker's medical bills, complete one hundred hours of community service, and get anger management counseling. The problem and priority are predefined by the court. The social worker determines that Vince is a good candidate for counseling; he shows remorse, accepts the consequences of what he did, and says he wants to change. The social worker and Vince agree that the treatment goals are to strengthen Vince's abilities to handle anger and increase his tolerance for disagreement. Vince enrolls in the agency's eight-week anger management course and agrees to meet with the social worker for fifty-five minutes once a week during the same eight-week time period. Vince takes the class and sees the social worker as planned. He completes various tasks developed to improve his communication skills and strengthen his patience (e.g., practicing listening techniques with his wife, refraining from making comments or rebuttals to statements with which he disagrees, purposely standing in long lines in stores to develop patience). Throughout the process, the social worker supports Vince's efforts, offers suggestions and guidance, and keeps progress notes. Vince is making progress. By the sixth week, he is ready to move into the termination phase. During the last two sessions, Vince and the social worker review what he has learned. Vince has reached the goals he set out to meet and feels affirmed by the treatment process. The social worker signs off on a report to the court testifying that Vince has met the conditions of the court order. The helping relationship ends.

Interventions using task-centered models with individuals, families, and groups have been tested extensively over the past forty years. The model also has been used with a variety of client systems, including school-age children, couples, families seeking to regain custody of their children from the foster care system, elderly individuals, adolescents, and sex offenders (Reid, 1996). An example of a task-centered intervention is Taking Charge, a school-based curriculum designed to help pregnant and parenting adolescents stay in school. One or two adult leaders lead the intervention over a period of eight to twelve weeks. During this time, participants learn and practice various strategies for coping with the social and emotional challenges of teen pregnancy and adolescent parenthood. This task-centered intervention has been tested over time, and evidence shows it is helpful for adolescent mothers (Harris & Franklin, 2004).

Cognitive-Behavioral Theory

Cognitive-behavioral theory combines information from the fields of psychology, philosophy, and behavioral medicine to describe the reciprocal effects of thought processes, emotions, and behaviors. Cognitive-behavioral theory shares some of the qualities of problem-solving theory and task-centered theory and has produced a model for treatment. Its emphasis, however, is on information processing. The cognitive-behavioral model is considered especially effective for treating dysfunctional thinking that contributes to low self-esteem and lack of assertiveness, as well as mental health problems. Social workers who use cognitive-behavioral theory methods need to be well educated in the component parts of cognition. Key concepts of cognitive-behavioral theory are cognitive structure, cognitive propositions, cognitive operations, cognitive products, and cognitive-behavioral sequencing.

Cognitive structure is the first of the four components of human cognition. Cognitive structure relates to "the way in which information is organized and internally represented" (Ingram, quoted in Granvold, 1994, p. 6). This includes how the mind stores information and how that information is used to respond to internal and external influences on the human experience. For example, a soldier assigned to combat duty already has information stored in her cognitive structure about what war might be like. Cognitive structure helps the soldier prepare for what to anticipate.

Cognitive propositions, the second component of cognition, relate to the specific content stored in a person's cognitive structure. Cognitive propositions "may be knowledge received from external sources or internally generated" (Ingram, quoted in Granvold, 1994, p. 7). In the case of the soldier, her knowledge about combat may have been acquired from the surrounding social environment (e.g., the classroom, training, briefings). The soldier may also have constructed the information herself (e.g., personal opinions, observations, or experiences).

The third component of cognition, *cognitive operations*, involves how the mind attends to internal and external stimuli and how those stimuli are perceived, encoded, stored, and retrieved. Cognitive operations or processes can be defined as "the processes by which the system (mind) operates to input, transform, and output information" (Kendall & Ingram, quoted in Granvold, 1994, p. 7). The soldier preparing for combat duty will be relying heavily on cognitive operations to survive the experience of war.

The final component of cognition is *cognitive products*, which are the results of the previous components of cognition. Some cognitive products that result from information processing are "thoughts, self-verbalizations, and explicitly held outcomes such as beliefs, opinions, attitudes, values, judgments, and conclusions" (Ingram, quoted in Granvold, 1994, p. 7). For example, if the soldier experiences active duty in a war zone, she may experience post-traumatic stress disorder, a cognitive product that is the result of trauma.

Cognitive-behavioral sequencing refers to the series of cognitive processes that result in an observable behavior. This concept rests on the principle of reciprocal determinism, which proposes that human behavior is the "product of an array of interacting variables and processes" (Granvold, 1994, p. 4). These processes may include biophysical factors such as genetic predisposition, temperament, or medical condition; psychological factors such as cognition, emotion, or motivation; and social and environmental factors. Reciprocal determinism suggests that a practitioner using cognitive-behavioral theory and interventions must address these variables and processes when assessing human behavior and developing interventions. Box 2.5 provides an example of how cognitive-behavioral theory might be used.

Box 2.5   Using Cognitive-Behavioral Group Therapy to Increase Coping Skills

Larry has returned from his twelve-month combat tour of duty in Baghdad. During his tour, he was part of a ground forces platoon that conducted house-to-house searches. Larry was trained to expect the unexpected and to practice hypervigilance at all times during search operations. Larry saw three fellow platoon members die and witnessed a number of civilian causalities. His tour of duty is now over, but he carries intense grief and guilt about not having done enough to save his friends from death and protect innocent bystanders. During a visit to the veterans' hospital, he sees a flyer for a support group for soldiers who have been to Iraq. He goes to the behavioral health clinic, where the social worker concludes he is an appropriate candidate for this group. Ever since he got back two months ago, he has been having a tough time suppressing thoughts about his friends' deaths. He is also having difficulties sleeping and has been having nightmares about combat. Sometimes he wakes up with his heart racing. The group meets once a week for eight weeks and is conducted by a licensed clinical social worker who uses cognitive-behavioral theory and techniques. By the time Larry finishes the group, he should understand the effects of post-traumatic stress disorder, and his ability to cope with the trauma of combat should be stronger.

Over the past twenty years, researchers have produced an abundance of evidence supporting the use of cognitive-behavioral practices with individuals, couples, families, and psychoeducational groups (Granvold, 1995). Much of this evidence has come from clinical work with veterans of war. Cognitive-behavioral interventions are considered effective and can produce positive results in relatively short periods of time with diverse client populations (Fanger, 1995). One such intervention is Beck's cognitive-behavioral therapy for depression, which has been tested in numerous clinical trials funded by the National Institute of Mental Health (Beck, 1982; Craighead, Hart, Craighead & Ilardi, 2002). This approach helps clients change depressive thinking about themselves, their future, and others.

The Strengths Perspective

The strengths perspective is a theoretical approach that encourages social workers to look at the strengths and resources that are present in a client's life as means for solving problems. Schriver (2004) calls the strengths perspective an "alternative" theoretical approach because it "shifts away from traditional approaches to practice" (p. 129). Traditional approaches, which include some of the theories and models we have discussed in this chapter, focus more on an individual's problems than an individual's strengths. Although many traditional approaches incorporate similar concepts, the strengths perspective is unique because of its strong emphasis on identifying and building up the strengths of an individual's system. The key concepts of the strengths perspective are empowerment, membership, resilience, healing and wholeness, dialogue and collaboration, and suspension of belief.

Schriver (2004) defines *empowerment* as "the process through which people gain the power and resources necessary to shape their worlds and reach their full human potential" (p. 27). Empowerment approaches require social workers and clients to "co-investigate" the realities of their situations (Lee, 1996). Knowledge of clients' social, economic, political, and cultural realities and the consequences of these realities provides insight into their lives and how they have been diminished or disempowered by long-standing oppression, discrimination, mistreatment, or neglect.

We've all heard phrases like "Well, that's because she's a member of 'the club.'" It really doesn't matter what the club is; the important message is that the person in question belongs to something. According to the strengths perspective, *membership* implies a sense of belonging to something, someone, or someplace. Like the ecological perspective concept of relatedness, membership underscores the importance of being attached to a social network that supports and protects a person. When people lack membership, they risk feeling isolated, neglected, and unimportant; when they experience membership, they usually achieve a sense of connectedness. Saleebey (1997) views membership as a precursor to empowerment.

A simplified definition of *resilience* is the ability to bounce back from an adverse situation. In a longitudinal study that followed individuals who grew up in adverse social environments from birth to young adulthood, Werner (1989) used the term *resilience* to describe those who exhibited competence, determination, and self-efficacy (a can-do attitude) and maintained a sense of faith, hope, and confidence in the future. They also had access to a caring person, someone who made them feel like they belonged. This research affirms the strengths perspective and the innate capacity of human beings to bear the demands and challenges of life and thrive, no matter how adverse the situation might be.

One of the most remarkable features of human nature is the tendency to recover or heal from trauma, abuse, or injury. How else can we explain the experiences of Holocaust survivors; South African civil rights leader Nelson Mandela, who was imprisoned for three decades but went on to lead his country; or the late Christopher Reeve, the actor who was paralyzed in a riding accident yet advanced the cause of those with spinal cord injuries and continued to make films? Saleebey (1997) states that "healing and self-generation are intrinsic life support systems, always working and, for most of the time, on call" to help us surpass the worst of circumstances (p. 10). This innate drive toward *healing and wholeness* is similar to the concept of wellness, which recognizes the interrelatedness of the mind, body, and spirit and the drive to achieve a good fit with one's social environment (Germain, 1991).

Dialogue and collaboration are how a social worker engages a client using the strengths perspective. Dialogue refers to the ways social workers verbally connect with clients. You already know that communication is a vehicle for interacting with another person. But dialogue, as defined by the strengths perspective, "requires the social worker to listen, really listen, to what the other person has to say and to value the client's voice as essential to understanding and action" (Schriver, 2004, p. 132). Meaningful dialogue sets the stage for the process of collaboration. Collaboration, a central concept of other social work practice theories, takes on a different meaning in the strengths perspective. Collaboration results in "mutually crafted projects" (Saleebey, 1997, p. 10). According to the strengths perspective, collaboration suggests that clients are experts about their own experiences, that their points of view are valid and meaningful, and that the social worker represents only one half of a collaborative exchange.

The last key concept of the strengths perspective is *suspension of belief*, which refers to the social worker's purposeful efforts to divest himself or herself of preconceived notions about the client and the helping process. Saleebey (1997) acknowledges that social workers are not immune to pessimism and cynicism but argues this is not an excuse for discounting clients' points of view, diminishing their qualities, labeling them, passively encouraging stereotypes, or using one-upmanship over clients. The strengths perspective discourages the perpetuation of "isms" (e.g., racism, sexism, ageism, ableism) and encourages social workers to withhold judgment and maintain a positive perspective about clients, no matter what.

The strengths perspective promotes hope, optimism, and opportunities for clients to realize their full potential (see box 2.6). This perspective also elaborates on the positive aspects of a client's characteristics and proposes a *revisioning* of the client–social worker relationship that focuses on clients' inherent strengths. Strengths-based practice is somewhat antithetical to empirical research because it views empirical research methods as generally restrictive and as disregarding the richness and depth of human behavior and the context in which human behavior occurs. One strengths-based approach that has opened itself to empirical research is solution-focused, brief therapy (Gingerich & Eisengart, 2000). This model offers several easily applied techniques for helping both adults and children. It is used in diverse practice settings throughout the world (Franklin & Moore, 1999) and is being studied using experimental and quasi-experimental designs.

Box 2.6　Building an Adolescent's Strengths in the Transition to Independent Living

Sixteen-year-old Shauntay has been in foster care since age five. Her mother suffers from mental illness and cannot provide for herself or Shauntay. There are no other relatives who can care for Shauntay, so she has remained in foster care. Shauntay has lived in five foster homes and has not stayed in one place for much longer than two years. Her current placement is the best so far, and she hopes to stay there until she graduates from high school. Shauntay has managed to keep her grades up and has gotten close to a few of her teachers. They say they believe in her. Shauntay has a social worker and wants to talk to the social worker about how she is going to support herself when she leaves foster care. She'd like to go college to be a nurse, but she isn't sure how she will pay for it. If the social worker embraces a strengths perspec-

tive, he will understand that it is important to get Shauntay enrolled in the county's independent living skills program as soon as she is eligible. These programs teach adolescents in foster care skill sets for self-sufficiency (e.g., money management, communication skills, job-seeking skills, hygiene and wellness care, housekeeping skills). Independent living skills programs can forge youths' connections to peer and community networks that support competency, self-efficacy, and aspiration. These networks can help youths make successful transitions to community living, college or vocational training, and employment. Obviously, Shauntay has a number of strengths. What she needs is encouragement, direction, support, and resources so she can build on her strengths to reach the goals she has set for herself.

This research has shown positive results with children and in school social work practice settings (Franklin, Kim, & Tripodi, 2006).

SUMMARY

Social workers are ethically bound "to ensure the competence of their work and to protect clients from harm," especially as it relates to clients' "race, ethnicity, national origin, color, sex, sexual orientation, age, marital status, political belief, religion, and mental or physical disability" (National Association of Social Workers, 1999). Therefore, it is imperative that social workers seek the very best knowledge available to ensure they practice in a competent way with a typically diverse array of clients. To do this, social workers seek to educate themselves about the current best practices in the field. Best practices are informed by "practice experience, a commitment to placing the concerns of the client first, and a determination to utilize the current best evidence to guide decision making" (Gibbs, 2003, p. xx). This definition suggests that social workers not only need to know about the latest social work practice methods; they also need to be informed about the theories and models that drive practice in order to become more effective practitioners.

As you study social work, do volunteer work, and pursue practicum experiences, you will try different practice approaches to determine which ones are most effective for your work, and which ones suit you best. If the examples in this chapter sound like the kind of work you want to do, the following chapters will be of special interest to you. They explore theories and methods that social workers use to help individuals, families, communities, and larger client systems achieve their full potential.

SUGGESTED READING

Germain, C. B., & Bloom, M. (1999). *Human behavior in the social environment: An ecological view* (2nd ed.). New York: Columbia University Press. This is a classic text on the ecological perspective in social work.

Payne, M. (2005). *Modern social work theory* (3rd ed.). Chicago: Lyceum Books. This book discusses theories that social workers commonly use in their practice, including cognitive-behavioral theories, systems and ecological perspectives, and crisis intervention and task-centered models, as well as radical and feminist perspectives.

Rivas, R. F., & Hull, G. H. (2004). *Case studies in generalist practice*. Belmont, CA: Brooks/Cole. These case studies demonstrate how social workers use the problem-solving method to assist individuals, families, groups, communities, and organizations. They also demonstrate the diverse situations in which social workers practice and how they use practice theories to guide them.

Saleebey, D. (1990). *The strengths perspective in social work practice.* Boston: Allyn and Bacon. Saleebey defines the philosophy, principles, and language of the strengths perspective. He discusses the importance of using a practice framework based on the strengths of individual clients as well as families, groups, and communities.

Tolson, E. R., Reid, W. J., & Garvin, C. D. (2003). *Generalist practice: A task-centered approach.* New York: Columbia University Press. This text presents the task-centered methodology, a structured, short-term problem-solving approach, and discusses its use with individuals, families, groups, organizations, and communities. It provides information on systems theory and includes case studies.

THE WORLD WIDE WEB OF SOCIAL WORK

Association for the Advancement of Social Work with Groups
http://www.aaswg.org

AASWG is a nonprofit organization of group workers, group work educators, and others who are interested in group work and support its program of advocacy and action for professional practice, education, research, training, and writing about social work with groups.

BMJ Clinical Evidence http://www.clinicalevidence.org/ceweb/index.jsp

BMJ Clinical Evidence is a peer-reviewed international online journal that publishes systematic reviews to help clinicians select treatments for various disorders.

Campbell Collaboration http://www.campbellcollaboration.org

C2 is an international nonprofit organization that provides systematic reviews of research studies to help people make decisions about the use of social, behavioral, and educational interventions. Systematic reviews are considered by many social work researchers to offer the gold standard for evaluating best practices. The online reviews are available to the public for a fee and offer both consumers and professionals an opportunity to evaluate the best evidence for different interventions and problem areas.

Clinical Social Work Association http://www.associationsites.com/main-pub.cfm?usr=CSWA

CSWA is a national professional membership organization of clinical social workers. It focuses on clinical work, particularly mental health treatment in agencies, clinics, institutions, hospitals, and private practice. CSWA provides clinical training; legislative advocacy on mental health matters, including protection of clients' rights; and professional development and support for clinical social workers.

3 Social Work with Organizations, Communities, and Larger Systems

Stephen P. Wernet

This chapter introduces students to mezzo- and macropractice social work, also called *indirect practice*. Though the term *mezzo* is often used for community practice, for the sake of brevity, the term *macropractice* will be used to describe community, administration, and policy practice. The chapter reviews the history of this cluster of complementary and influential social work methods; discusses the scope of macropractice; and highlights careers in social work administration, community organization, and policy practice.

Macropractice is a hallmark of the social work profession. Community organization, policy planning, administration, and social research have developed in parallel fashion as social work practice methods. There are obvious areas of overlap among these four methods. All are concerned with resolving and preventing social problems at the organizational, community, and societal levels. However, each method uses a somewhat different approach to achieving these goals. In recent years, attempts have been made to combine community organization, administration, and policy practice into an integrated macromethod. Some see this as a logical outgrowth of the generalist social work practice approach discussed in chapters 1 and 2. Others prefer to maintain distinctions among these methods because of the differences in perspective, intent, and focus. For example, social workers who are community organizers see themselves as agents focused on structural change, while those who are administrators focus on implementing and managing social programs.

HISTORY OF SOCIAL WORK MACROPRACTICE

Early Social Work

Social workers have been involved in macropractice from the beginning of the profession in the United States (R. Fisher, 2005). Macropractice has its roots in the social reform and Social Gospel movements of the nineteenth century, which produced both the Charity Organization Society and the settlement house movements and provided macropractice with its dual foci of administration and social reform. On the administrative side, residual solutions (those that happen after a problem has occurred) predominate, and program and logistical planning, interorganizational and service coordination, and administrative practice are emphasized. When macropractice emphasizes social reform, institutional change (usually efforts to prevent a problem before it occurs) predominates. The emphasis is social action, citizen participation, inclusion, and empowerment. For example, the Temporary Assistance for Needy Families program (and its predecessors) helps parents and children only after they fall into poverty, while the Social Security program attempts to prevent people from becoming poor.

The Progressive Era

The Progressive Era was the first watershed event for the profession of social work. After the economic depression of 1873, industrialization, immigration, and the movement of rural populations into urban areas created new social problems. Two responses evolved among socially concerned citizens. One was the Charity Organization Society movement, which focused on solving the problems of fraud, duplication of services, and indiscriminate giving that were sometimes associated with charity. The Charity Organization Society melded the new organizational form of American business with businessmen's reluctance to pay taxes to a corrupt public governmental system. Charity Organization Societies were private organizations that addressed the growing urban social problems and unrest of the Progressive Era. Charity Organization Society workers were concerned with providing charity efficiently and scientifically, but they also believed in developing personal relationships between donors and aid recipients.

The second response was the settlement house movement, which combined the outreach and proselytizing of mainstream Protestant denominations with the impetus of the social reform movements of the era. Settlement houses focused on social action to promote social, political, and economic justice. Child labor laws, workers' compensation laws, and mothers' pensions were all partially the result of the settlement house movement. Settlement house workers sought solidarity with neighborhood residents by living in the settlement houses and helping immigrants from other countries and migrants from rural communities adjust to American society and city life.

The Charity Organization Society movement spawned councils of social agencies, which were organized shortly after the turn of the century. The councils emphasized efficiency, centralization, and specialization in the planning and delivery of services by private community agencies. By the beginning of World War I, the term *community organization* had come into general use. During the war, these community organizations designed services to meet the needs and solve the problems of servicemen and their families. Fund-raising agencies called community chests were developed to centralize planning and achieve more efficiency in the utilization of community resources.

In 1929 the Milford Conference provided a forum for leaders in the social work profession to define the nature of practice. Although the conferees paid lip service to administrative practice by calling for professional training in this area and by recognizing the organizational context as critical to effective service delivery, little was said about specific administrative skills (American Association of Social Workers, 1929). That year the first *Social Work Yearbook* was published; it was glaringly silent on the topic of administration. By 1930, social casework (micropractice) had become the dominant method in social work and was assumed to be the foundation for all forms of professional practice.

During the 1920s and 1930s, the labor movement and a few state and local government experiments kept the social change aspect of macropractice alive. One notable experiment, the Chicago Area Project, began in 1934 as an attempt to organize residents of slum areas in a juvenile delinquency prevention program (Kobrin, 1959). Shortly before World War II, the *Lane Report* to the National Conference of Social Work identified community organization as a method of social work practice.

The Great Depression

Following the Progressive Era, the Great Depression was the second watershed event to influence the development of social work and macropractice. The Great Depression produced massive public problems of poverty and unemployment. The social response was public programs built upon a philosophy of social insurance rather than charity. Social workers and like-minded individuals who advocated an institutional response to these societal problems developed the policies and programs of the New Deal (e.g., the Social Security Act of 1935) and an array of public works (employment) projects like the Civilian Conservation Corps and the Works Progress Administration. Theirs is the legacy of a social safety net for all citizens.

The Great Depression also gave birth to a rank-and-file movement of radical social workers who believed that the federal government's response was inadequate and that the New Deal programs could not significantly affect unemployment rates (J. Fisher, 1980; R. Fisher, 2005). Most radical social workers during this era were strongly influenced by Marxist-Leninist thought. They attributed the Depression to the imminent collapse of the capitalist order and were committed to the complete dissolution of capitalism and its replacement by socialism (J. Fisher, 1980). At the height of the movement in 1935, there were forty-eight local organizations of radical social workers in twenty-three cities (Burghardt & Fabricant, 1987).

World War II

The social change and social action aspect of macropractice continued during World War II. Citizen participation and coordination gained prominence through community councils, neighborhood associations, and block committees established to support the war effort. Another macropractice landmark was the Back of the Yards movement in Chicago, organized by Saul Alinsky. Although he was not a professional social worker, Alinsky did much to change macropractice's direction by championing conflict-oriented techniques. Alinsky's ideology was socialist and class directed, but he generally soft-pedaled ideological principles in favor of organizing and bargaining for power. His ideas helped shape much of macro social work's orientation to the protest movements of the 1960s.

Postwar and Civil Rights

Following World War II, macropractice shifted from social reform to administration. The political environment following World War II, and the subsequent political repression of the McCarthy era, made social change initiatives and radical social work unpopular, suspect, and highly risky. The new emphasis on science and technology that evolved from the country's success in World War II bolstered the shift to administration.

Coterminous with the conservative 1950s was the confrontation of inequities both at home and abroad. National rebellions and challenges to colonial rule were occurring throughout the developing world. Radical social workers shifted their focus from economic oppression to discrimination, racism, and inadequate housing. Their objectives included increasing services and benefits while equalizing power between clients and bureaucracies. The civil rights movement, aided by African American veterans of World War II, ushered in a dramatically altered model of community organization practice similar to Alinsky's strategy of conflict and confrontation. The efforts to desegregate schools and public accommodations; the 1955 Montgomery bus boycott in Alabama; and the growth of organizations such as the Southern Christian Leadership Conference, the Congress of Racial Equality, the Student Nonviolent Coordinating Committee, the Mississippi Freedom Democratic Party, the Black Panther Party, and the National Association for the Advancement of Colored People are all examples of this type of community organization (Garvin & Cox, 1995). Urban renewal caused neighbors to band together to fight displacement from their neighborhoods. Riots in Detroit, Michigan; Newark, New Jersey; Watts, California; and other urban areas created a new climate favoring social reform.

Confrontation of inequalities was furthered by the 1954 amendments to the Housing Act of 1949, which required citizen participation in the planning of community programs. This trend continued through the mandate of "maximum feasible participation" of residents of low-income communities in the Economic Opportunity Act of 1964, a major component of the war on poverty. Mandates in planning aging, education, mental health, and health-care services further encouraged citizen participation.

Beginning in the mid-1960s, job opportunities for social workers in administration and health care increased, fueled by amendments to the Social Security Act. Title XIX (Medicaid) was the single largest stimulus to the growth of the nursing home industry. Together with Title VIII (Medicare), it increased access to outpatient health care for older and impoverished Americans.

The Modern Era

The 1967 Amendments to the Social Security Act separated social services from public assistance, creating a new demand for social work administrators. These amendments also allowed state governments to purchase social services from nonprofit organizations, enabling governments to outsource direct care. Jobs developed at the state, county, and local levels of government in departments and divisions of mental health and child welfare and in the nongovernmental sector as well. Social work administrators were pushed to develop greater technical competencies in program planning, budgeting, contract compliance, evaluation, and grant writing. Small and informal voluntary associations began to evolve into bureaucracies with large operations, professional staff, and sizeable budgets.

In the 1970s, the community organizers who came to head community action programs needed greater administrative expertise to manage the multimillion-dollar budgets that supported service programs in nonprofit and public agencies. The 1972 Social Security Amendments, also known as Title XX, caused an explosion in the use of government funds for the provision of social services. Class action suits to deinstitutionalize individuals with mental retardation and mental illness and to provide community-based alternative treatment helped drive the growth of social work administration. The 1976 election of President Jimmy Carter shifted the approach of social welfare policies, programs, and services away from cash entitlements and benefits toward training and job readiness. Social work administration needed new budgeting and contract compliance skills for use in performance-based contracting for these work programs.

Since the 1980s, social workers have practiced in an increasingly wide array of settings requiring the complete range of administrative skills. Due to the privatization, outsourcing, and load shifting of public services, macropractice occurs in for-profit and nonprofit settings as well as government agencies. Social work administrators must possess a broader range of technical and interpersonal skills to succeed in today's world. Community practitioners engage in economic and social development as well as traditional neighborhood building to create stable, revitalized communities. Radical practitioners, now referred to as progressive or political social workers, have returned to union organizing and direct political action. They are focused on social issues such as hunger, homelessness, gay rights, sexism, ageism, and domestic violence.

EDUCATION FOR MACROPRACTICE

The Great Depression profoundly affected social work education as well as social work practice. Shortly after the Federal Emergency Relief Administration was created in 1934, grants were made available to schools of social work to support short-term courses of study that would prepare personnel to work in public relief agencies. Schools of social work were asked to analyze casework and group work skills and suggest how they might be adapted to administrative tasks in public welfare agencies (Brown, 1940). At this time, the field of public administration began to emerge as a distinct discipline. Theories concerning such matters as span of control, specialization of function, and general management principles evolved during this period (Patti, 1983). This body of literature, adapted for social agency management, inspired practitioners and educators who advocated a specialized social work administration curriculum.

By the early 1950s, administration had gained a foothold in social work education, but social workers still lacked adequate preparation for administrative practice (Hollis & Taylor, 1951). Resistance to specialized administrative training for social workers remained strong. The dominant pattern in graduate programs throughout the 1950s was to offer one introductory administration course in a curriculum otherwise oriented toward preparation for direct practice.

During the 1960s, several events renewed the profession's interest in the range of macropractice methods. First, the National Conference on Social Welfare featured a number of papers on administration, one of which challenged the idea that casework training and experience were the essential prerequisites for social welfare administration (Thompson, 1961). Shortly afterward, Eveline Burns (1961), a leading social work educator, presented a paper to the Council on Social Work Education criticizing the professional schools for neglecting administration and policy content. By 1963 there was sufficient interest in administration to bring about the establishment of the Council on Social Work Administration within the National Association of Social Workers (Trecker, 1977).

By 1962, the Council on Social Work Education recognized community organization as a separate field of specialization for graduate study. Fueled by the grassroots movements in civil rights, poverty, and housing, it became an increasingly popular course of study during the 1960s. The controversial Vietnam War also increased its popularity. Within a decade, however, regard for community organization as a field of practice waned as the war ended, and student protest as well as populist activism diminished. The dismantling of many war on poverty programs also contributed to declining interest in community organization practice. However, civil rights and social service reform legislation grew.

During the mid-1970s, jobs for community organizers disappeared, while employment opportunities for community and economic developers flourished. Many schools formally merged community organization and administration specializations into macropractice tracks, but interest continued to wane.

The 1980s, however, brought renewed interest in macropractice. In 1985, the Network for Social Work Managers (now the National Network for Social Work Managers) was founded. In 1998, the Academy of Certified Social Work Managers was established. It offers the Certified Social Work Manager, a management certification comparable to NASW's direct practice credential, the Academy of Certified Social Workers (ACSW). In 1987, a group of social work faculty committed to both community practice and social work administration founded the Association for Community Organization and Social Administration, which is dedicated to advancing community organization and social work administration education and practice and now has over four hundred members. Today both the Academy of Certified Social Work Managers and the Association for Community Organization and Social Administration are alive and well and continue to advocate macropractice in social work.

MACROPRACTICE CONCEPTS

Four concepts—social justice, civil society, social capital, and community—form the conceptual foundation for social work macropractice.

Social Justice

The social work profession's overriding goal is social justice. Generally speaking, social justice is fairness in dealings with others, but not everyone defines it in the same way (Weil, 2005). One major approach to defining social justice is utilitarianism, which espouses the notion that social justice is the greatest good for the greatest number of people. It is sometimes thought of as advocating equality of outcome—that is, everyone should receive the same benefits, regardless of effort. Another approach to social justice is social contract theory. According to this school of thought, social justice is equality of opportunity, but not necessarily of outcome. Social contract theory posits that members of a society agree to undertake minimal obligations to meet the basic needs of all members of society. We have interpreted these basic needs to include material goods as well as social, civil, political, and cultural rights. Citizens are also expected to be productive, contributing members of society. In other words, outcomes are contingent on individuals' efforts and abilities.

The social contract position on social justice seeks to benefit the disadvantaged and protect the rights of victims of oppression and systemic injustice while arguing for the primacy of the individual and small communities over larger communities and the state. A community organizer who registers new voters and an administrator who develops a new program for aiding underemployed and unemployed workers are applying the principle of social justice.

Civil Society

Civil society refers to interpersonal relationships within a public sphere (Jacobs, 2003). It is guided by the principle of association (Lynn, 2002), in which citizens come together in voluntary, democratic, private groups free of state control to address issues of concern (Smith, 1997). Such associations range from bowling leagues to anti-hunger coalitions to Alcoholics Anonymous to political parties. Structurally, they may be informal or formal (Smith, 1992). Membership size frequently oscillates, and the membership boundaries are permeable. Association members, sometimes called volunteers, share similar values and commitment to a common goal. Associations serve as mechanisms for self-expression, personal growth, and social integration; many also provide training in the skills necessary for political activity and civic engagement. Members frequently accrue personal benefits, often through some form of mutual-help activity. Associations are public spheres in which citizens meet the human need for affiliation and intimacy and deliberate with one another. Associations are deemed essential for the success of a democratic society (Eikenberry & Kluver, 2004).

Social workers support people who coalesce to build a better society, integrate socially, and become engaged in the community (i.e., build a civil society). For example, macropractice social workers who work with neighborhood organizations, youth groups, and boards of directors are helping to build civil society.

Social Capital

A vibrant society is predicated upon a rich, dense social fabric, or social capital. Social capital refers to the features of social organization that facilitate generalized reciprocity—that is, coordination and cooperation for mutual benefit (Putnam, 1995). It is built through repeated interactions among individuals that create communication pathways, predictable positive outcomes, and the potential for trust. Trust develops because individuals assume they can call on one another for assistance and the call will be honored. These relationships are sometimes referred to as goodwill ties (Backman & Smith, 2000).

Social capital resides within social networks. These networks are composed of individuals within a group, referred to as bonding capital (the networking strength between or among people), or individuals across groups, referred to as bridging capital (the networking strength between and among groups of people). A vibrant society also requires many social connections that are less intense, called weak ties (Backman & Smith, 2000). The multitude of horizontal social interactions among individuals and across social groups builds a fabric of social connections and networks and produces social capital.

Social workers promote a society that is rich in social capital. Examples of macropractitioners building social capital are a community organizer working on an interracial dialogue project, a policy planner bringing together diverse groups to comment on proposed legislation, and a social work administrator working on a statewide task force addressing the need for new senior citizens' programs.

Community

A community is composed of webs of relationships that create interdependence (Palloff & Pratt, 1999; Wernet, 2002). Community develops because of mutual or common interests, shared experience, and common norms. It is a voluntary experience one chooses to enter because of affinity. It is created when each member assumes some part of the common work of the community and development of reciprocal responsibility, and each member surrenders some part of his or her individual interests to fellow community members.

Some communities, like neighborhoods, are space or place based (Chaskin, Brown, Venkatesh, & Vidal, 2001). Some believe that a shared physical environment is essential for the development of community. Other communities are based on relationships among people independent of a physical environment; these are called conscious communities (Palloff & Pratt, 1999). Social workers believe in building mutual understanding, shared experience, and reciprocity. That is, social workers believe in and support community. Helping to form a neighborhood watch group is an example of working with a place-based community. Facilitating an Internet-based advocacy group for health-care reform is an example of working with a conscious community.

MACROPRACTICE METHODS

Social workers are change agents committed to advancing fairness; protecting the vulnerable and oppressed; and ensuring equality of opportunity and, in some cases, equality of outcome. Macropractice social workers focus on public issues and target both mezzo social structures (e.g., communities) and macro social structures (e.g., governments, criminal justice, and educational systems) for intervention. Macropractice social workers' goal is to create a civil society. This can only be achieved by building community and developing social capital. To achieve a socially just society, macropractice social workers develop webs of relationships among people and groups. Through these interactions in public spheres, cooperation and mutual assistance evolve, common interests and affinities are identified, and social networks and trust are built.

When these relationships and interdependencies are aggregated and become formalized, people form an array of voluntary associations and functional communities. These mezzo sociological structures become the mechanisms through which citizens exercise their societal responsibilities and contribute to the community. Helping people learn the importance of mutual benefit and interdependence is the key. Through reciprocity, trust grows and community and civil society are built. The macropractice social worker achieves these goals by working in one of three areas of the profession: social work administration, community practice, and policy practice.

Administration

Social work administration shares a common body of knowledge and skills with business management and public administration, and professionals from these three disciplines often compete for the same jobs. But social workers bring something distinct to administrative work. This is the profession's value base. Social work administration is moral work (Hasenfeld, 2000). It begins with an understanding of desirable human behavior—of the good society—and a commitment to social justice (Hasenfeld, 2000; Patti, 2000). Social work administration consists of all the roles and tasks performed by staff in middle and upper levels of an organization to accomplish its goals (Patti, 2000). Social work managers sit at the junction of the organization and its operating environment. They must be multitalented in order to bring out the talents of others. They must translate the environment to the organization, and the organization to its environment. They accomplish their work through other individuals and groups. For example, a chief executive officer helps the agency's board of directors understand the programs offered to clients while also helping agency staff understand the priorities and policies established by the board. Likewise, a social work administrator educates public groups about the mission and purpose of the agency while educating the staff and board about the public's needs and desires for services and programs.

The National Network for Social Work Managers has promulgated forty-six practice standards and ten competencies that every social work manager should possess (Wimpfheimer, 2004). They reflect the principal tasks that social work administrators and managers consider to be most important in their jobs (Hoefer, 2003; Patti, 1983). These standards and competencies reflect an open and complex systems perspective emphasizing the need to balance competing interests—that is, balancing the influence and impact of the operating environment on the social work organization's design, structure, services, and performance (Hasenfeld, 2000; Wernet, 1994). A competent social work manager has skills in both external relations and internal relations (Wimpfheimer, 2004). In *external relations*, social work administrators

- Stay current on social and public policy issues that affect the organization
- Advocate a position on an issue
- Promote and seek visibility for the organization and its services
- Hold the organization's values, assets, and purpose in public trust while advancing the organization's vision and mission and maximizing the return to stakeholders

In *internal relations*, social work administrators

- Balance the demands of managing daily operations with charting a future path
- Design and deliver services that meet community needs, are high quality and efficient, and achieve reasonable outcomes
- Provide financial oversight and assess the financial need of the organization's operations
- Use evaluative information and results in decision making
- Manage personnel
- Help staff enhance their professional skills by matching staff needs to training opportunities

Not every social work manager must be equally skilled in all these competencies. Social work administrators seek staff who have complementary skills and talents. The key to successful social work administration is leadership. The focus and type of leadership depend upon the administrator's level of responsibility. There are two levels of social work administrative leadership: operational and executive. At the operational level, leadership positions are the supervisor or program administrator. These middle managers are responsible for the integrity of an agency's services and projects. A supervisor is concerned with ensuring that policies become program services implemented according to the original plan. The supervisor must possess a range of technical and interpersonal skills, including managing programs, projects, and personnel; interviewing; assessment; and research design. He or she ensures the quality of agency services through oversight and education of social workers, case record sampling, and document analysis.

The other level of social work administrative leadership is executive leadership. At the executive level, leadership positions are the chief executive (or chief operating) officer, president, and vice president. Upper managers and executive staff are responsible for both internal operations and external relationships. In the area of internal operations, the executive leader ensures that the organization has operating policies that guide the agency's work, including policies that guide program services, and that programs and services are implemented according to the agency's operating policies. In the area of external relationships, the executive ensures that the organization is involved with and connected to every major stakeholder who can influence the organization's survival and success. A social work executive must build networks and maintain interpersonal relationships with those stakeholders in addition to other social work and human service professionals and organizations. A social work executive must be able to raise funds, develop policy, lobby, speak publicly, plan programs, and do budgeting (see box 3.1). This is a tall order, and many social workers are motivated by the challenge.

Box 3.1   Building an Effective Social Welfare Agency

There are at least five key elements that have helped us build and maintain an effective organization. The first element is having a clear mission. Every piece of agency work should be centered in the mission. Your mission is your identity. It is who you are and what you are about. Lutheran Family and Children's Services is about kids and families. Our motto is "Caring for kids from two days to ninety years." That's a great sell because we were all kids once; many of us have kids or grandkids; we grow hope by building families.

Second is the CEO's relationship with the operating board. If board members don't understand the vision and the goals of agency leadership, they won't be involved. Another way to say this is that if they don't understand the passion of the CEO for this work, effectiveness will be drastically diminished. Our board is now structured so that we know who our board chairs will be four to five years in advance. This builds trust in the board because other board members have a clear picture of where the organization is going and how the board works.

Third is institutional integrity. An agency must "walk the walk" and uphold its values. Our agency communications must convey our values and mission. Accreditation, licensing, and recognition are all marks of good management. The greatest situation is when things don't go right and your supporters and friends commend you for the way the things were handled. The deadliest situation occurs when an agency won't deal with its problems or simply goes into denial.

Fourth is cultivating friends and constituency. Your heart must be open to the people and institutions you call friends. Depending on its size, an effec-

---

Box 3.1   *Continued*

tive agency may have upwards of thirty to forty different kinds of relationships that need to be constantly balanced. These range from the United Ways of your region to corporations to church bodies to individual congregations to thousands of donors. Each entity wants to be valued and respected. Organizations and individuals want to believe that their relationship with the agency is making a difference in the community or the lives of others. Never pass by an opportunity to say thank you and tell someone how important he or she is to your mission. The more often you interact with those with whom you have a relationship, the stronger are the ties that bind you together. Your communication of results and needs helps individuals and institutions identify with you.

Finally, your staff defines the difference between being an okay agency and an effective agency. We have a tremendous reputation as a child welfare and adoption agency. That is a reflection of the talented and dedicated staff we employ at Lutheran Family. My job is building the team and letting them work. A good leader is always willing to listen to the perspectives of others. Our senior management needs to know that they can disagree with me and help lead in a better direction. There are always several roads to a destina-

tion, and even if you're not on my road, we still might get to the same place.

The fact that someone is good and effective does not mean he or she is right for your organization. Some people are not team players, or they are individuals with their own agendas. Good leadership sets the course of action and gives employees the freedom to do their jobs. Good leadership also values all the employees of an organization and weighs carefully how situations are handled. I have the option of saying, "Because I'm the boss," but that card must be played carefully and honestly, and always with the goal of institutional harmony in mind.

It's all about relationships. It's not just me. It's relationships with boards, ambassadors, donors, clients, and staff. I love people, I like talking to people, and I'm always learning and listening. Throughout the many services we offer at Lutheran Family, we grow hope. Hope is the promise that tomorrow can be different. Hope is the assurance that you are valued. Hope is all about possibilities, healing, and the future. Hope makes organizations effective.

Rev. Alan M. Erdman
President/CEO
Lutheran Family and Children's
Services of Missouri

Social work administrators typically work in public and nonprofit organizations. With the current emphasis on privatizing social welfare services, social work administrators may also be employed by private for-profit organizations. Social work administrators' responsibilities vary across these sectors. In the public sector, the social work administrator answers to elected officials or executives appointed by elected officials. For example, a governor may appoint a social worker to head the state's health and human service agency. Or the head of the state's health and human service agency may appoint a social worker to lead a division of the agency. The role of the social work administrator is to implement public policy and aid the governing board of elected officials in developing policy.

In the nonprofit sector, the social work administrator is responsible to a self-perpetuating board of directors (organization members elect new board members or board members select new members) and implements policies the board establishes. Examples of nonprofit organizations where social workers may be employed in administration (as well as direct service or other staff positions) are Big Brothers and Big Sisters of America (which provides children with mentors), America's Second Harvest (which helps those in need obtain food), and the Arc of the United States (an organization that helps children and adults with intellectual and developmental disabilities).

Social work administrators in the public and nonprofit sectors can have a great deal of influence in service delivery and development. Public administrators carry out legislative mandates with government-allocated funds, while those in the nonprofit sector often have a greater role in policy development. All administrators have fiduciary responsibilities, and most deal with multiple funding sources. In the public sector, administrators of state and local agencies often seek funding from other government entities like the federal government. Nonprofit administrators often seek government funding and also raise money from private donors, frequently through annual drives and capital campaigns. Many also work with their boards to invest assets that will generate income for the organization. All administrators are responsible for ensuring that clients and employees are treated fairly and are not subjected to situations like sexual harassment. They also face the challenge of balancing the interests of multiple constituencies—boards or government bodies with oversight authority, clients, staff, and other stakeholders. In the for-profit sector, social work administrators are judged largely by their ability to generate a profit for the corporation that owns the agency. Clients are generally charged for services at market rates. Administrators are involved in marketing or selling the agency's services to individuals or insurers. Examples of organizations that may operate on a for-profit basis are private residential treatment facilities for youths with mental illnesses or alcohol and drug problems, nursing homes, and child-care centers. Governments are increasingly contracting with for-profit groups to provide social welfare services such as child welfare services, the determination of eligibility for public assistance and administration of benefits, and the operation of correctional facilities. The trend toward privatization has created new challenges for social work administrators who have traditionally focused on client needs and outcomes rather than profit. Private-sector work may require a new mentality about social services and new skills that focus on increasing the bottom line.

Community Practice

Social workers in community practice help individuals form groups to address social problems that negatively affect a community (Weil, 2005;

Wernet, 2004). These social workers build the collective power of the citizenry through participation, thereby strengthening and building a democratic society. They help people help themselves to develop social and political power and build resources. The client system is a community (Valocchi, n.d.); the goal is a socially just democratic society in which the plurality participates on an equal footing.

Community practitioners must understand why and how humans form social organizations as well as the processes of these dyads, groups, organizations, and communities. The practitioner must understand the nature of community power and the logic of social change and innovation and must possess a host of related skills.

Several themes and assumptions permeate community practice. First, economic and social injustice result from the failure of the larger society to assist all individuals in meeting their potential. Second, all citizens have the right to participate directly in decisions that affect them. Third, when provided with information, citizens will participate in the decision-making process. Fourth, failure of citizens to participate in the democratic process is attributable either to their lack of knowledge about the process or injustices that disenfranchise them. Outside intervention is sometimes required to promote citizens' participation in order to achieve a socially just society.

Community practice consists of four related sets of practice skills—planning, development, community organizing, and political social work (Weil, 2005). The first approach is *planning*, sometimes called community building, social planning, program development, and community liaison (R. Fisher, 2005; Valocchi, n.d.; Weil, 2005; Weil & Gamble, 2005). Planning is generally concerned with coordination of services and policies with representatives of organizations. The approach has a strong technical orientation and is based on several assumptions. It is predicated on the existence of strong bonds within the community, and agreement and cooperation about community needs, desires, and interventions. Activities include developing intra- and interorganizational planning and coordinating systems, utilizing administrative and political leadership, developing mechanisms of citizen participation, interacting with administrators and political leaders, handling budgets, and understanding the laws and administrative regulations governing agencies that provide social services. This approach to community practice is used in community needs assessments and the work of organizations such as United Way community planning councils and coalitions. Planning has long been a major practice area for social workers (see box 3.2).

A second approach to community practice is *development*, sometimes called social or economic development. The emphasis is on building sustainable communities (Valocchi, n.d.) through partnerships focused on

Box 3.2 Community Planning and Employment Training

Board chair: "Thanks for meeting with the executive committee tonight to report on your findings. We hope you can help us deal with this problem."

Community social worker: "I'm pleased you invited me to assist in addressing this challenge."

Board chair: "As you know, we are very concerned about falling short of our goal in the job training program. Our objective is to provide training for unemployed and underemployed job seekers and link them with career-path jobs that offer family-supporting wages and benefits. We just are not meeting the self-sufficiency objective in the program. We are very concerned that we are missing something in assessing our program and this will jeopardize our relationship with the foundation that funds this program."

Community social worker: "Can we talk about how you define success in this job training program?"

Board chair: "We define success by the overall percentage of people who graduate from the training program, end up finding jobs with family-supporting wages and benefits, and stay in those jobs for twelve months. Only a small percentage of program participants who complete the training are actually able to find and keep these types of jobs."

Community social worker: "Besides your agency, who else has a vested interest in seeing this program succeed?"

Board chair: "Well, there is the private foundation that funds the program. They are interested in and support innovative community-based initiatives that help young low-income workers find meaningful jobs. They are trying to identify national employment and training models by funding these workforce development initiatives. Our regional planning agency has been collaborating with political and business partners who are interested in this project's success."

Community social worker: "What are they looking for from the project?"

Board chair: "Well, high-quality workers would help signal to employers that there is a good, qualified workforce here, and they should keep their businesses in the region. It would also help attract other new businesses into the region, thereby helping to create more job opportunities for people. Another issue is that if we can demonstrate success, we might be able to attract more funding to showcase the joint regional efforts in matching job seekers with job opportunities. And I guess the success of this program would help low-skilled individuals and families in an age when public assistance is no longer a fallback option."

Community social worker: "You know, your project has very ambitious goals. And it sounds as though you have spent lots of time thinking this through and talking with employers and regional development people. But did you talk to the potential program participants before you designed this program?"

Board chair: "Yes, of course."

Community social worker: "I figured you had, but your project goals might need to reflect barriers the participants are facing."

Board chair: "Oh."

Community social worker: "I had an opportunity to speak with some of the program participants and gradu-

Box 3.2 *Continued*

ates, and even some folks who might be eligible to participate in the program. I'm sure you already know many of the things that I am about to share with you, but let me review them with you. The people you are targeting face a host of employment barriers and challenges. They already have low incomes and live in areas of concentrated poverty and joblessness. So jobs are not readily accessible, and job opportunities are limited. Transportation is a major obstacle for them—just getting to and from a job can be a nightmare. You already know that many lack formal education or have very limited education and skills training, or else why would you be offering this training program? Some of these folks also experience health challenges. When you put all these factors together, it is clear that the people you are trying to assist with the training program have difficulty finding and keeping jobs. So, you may be overly ambitious in your project goal."

Board chair: "Well, we may have missed the implications of the life situation factors challenging our target population for the project."

Community social worker: "Have you thought about redefining success for this program?"

Board chair: "What do you mean?"

Community social worker: "Have you asked your program participants and clientele how they define success in the project?"

Board chair: "Gee, I don't know."

Community social worker: "When I asked them, they suggested a different understanding of success for your program. They saw self-

sufficiency as what I would call a psychological process."

Board chair: "Hmmm."

Community social worker: "Your clients' definition of success requires some steps even before they get job skills. Their comments indicated that they need to develop a sense that they are moving forward from where they have been; they need to overcome their feelings of hopelessness. When they can do this, they develop a sense of inner strength. Then they are able to think about acquiring job skills and jobs. As I was saying earlier, these are people who live in some pretty dire situations. They need to feel and believe they can overcome these circumstances before you put them into job training. They need to feel hope before they can learn concrete skills. If you don't have hope, then nothing else really matters. We call this self-efficacy. You know, another problem might be an adequate supply of family-sustaining jobs. I can't speak to this issue without further study, but if your graduates are having trouble finding and holding jobs that pay a family-sustaining wage, then there might also be a problem with adequate job opportunities. You might need to do some more work with the business community on this. Perhaps we can work on this issue as well."

Board chair: "Well, you certainly have given us a lot to think about and talk about. Thank you for your time and assistance."

Philip Young P. Hong, PhD
Assistant professor
School of Social Work,
Loyola University Chicago

Social workers promote programs like Operation Joseph, a program in rural Zimbabwe that prepares residents for periods of draught and famine by teaching them conservation farming.
© Visual & Written SL/Alamy

developing a community's economic resources and infrastructure. Community development promotes an array of opportunities for citizens to increase their social and economic security, thereby helping them out of poverty (Weil & Gamble, 2005). This approach to community practice requires technical proficiencies as well as a good measure of interpersonal skills. Social and economic development may require skills comparable to those necessary for social planning and skills more typically used in business, such as economic and business planning, finance and financial planning, and project management, as well as knowledge of bonding and taxation. Social workers specializing in social and economic development may work in community development corporations, housing corporations, urban renewal departments, coordinating councils, and regional growth councils. This practice arena is based on the assumption that participants can come to agree on problems and problem solutions. It also assumes a level of sophistication in economic and business planning (see box 3.3).

The third and fourth approaches to community practice are *community organizing* and *political social work*. Both entail social change efforts

Box 3.3   Tallahassee Equality Action Ministry:
Community Organizing for Health Care

Formed in 2002, Tallahassee Equality Action Ministry (TEAM) is a faith-based community organization that has grown to represent twenty congregations (including the Buddhist Faith Fellowship, the Unitarian Universalist Church, the Friends Meeting, and a number of Jewish and Christian congregations) in Tallahassee-Leon County, where Florida's capital is located. TEAM's mission is to identify community-wide social justice issues and undertake direct actions to redress injustices, especially those experienced by the least privileged among us—the poor, low income, disenfranchised, and powerless. Membership is diverse, and all ethnic, racial, and socioeconomic groups from a wide spectrum of faiths are represented.

TEAM uses a direct action bottom-up community organizing and decision-making model, the first step of which is called listening. In this step, congregation members engage in one-on-one and small-group house meetings. During the listening process, which occurs early in the year, broad topical issues facing the community are identified and discussed—for example, transportation and the homeless. These are then brought to an annual assembly of TEAM members by mid- to late spring. The TEAM congregations choose which issues will be the organization's priority for the year. TEAM then forms issue-specific research committees made up of thirty to forty people. During their work, which takes place during the summer months, issue committees speak with experts, service providers, local government, and other local stakeholders. The committee is charged to develop winnable measures that will alleviate problems of injustice. The solutions are then taken to a citywide direct action meeting in mid-fall and are presented to people who have the authority and influence to make the appropriate changes.

Health care for the uninsured has been a recognized community-wide problem for over ten years. In 2001, following several years of discussions and recommendations, the county adopted a municipal services tax to pay for services to meet the growing needs of the uninsured and relieve the increasing pressure on emergency services. However, tax revenues were far less than the estimated amounts needed for service coverage. Meanwhile, unpaid debts incurred at local hospitals continued to mount, bringing about higher rates for the insured. The advisory committee overseeing implementation of the program was unable to come to an agreement on strategies and stopped work in June 2005. That's when TEAM stepped in and got involved.

Health care for the uninsured was adopted as a TEAM priority issue for 2005, and a request to the county to get the plan back on track was presented to elected officials at the 2005 fall action meeting. They agreed. From there, representatives from TEAM congregations attended and spoke at several commission meetings to ensure that health care for the uninsured stayed on the public agenda. It did. By the end of January 2006, the county had hired a national health-care consultant, Mercer Consultant Group, to draft the plan. This was accomplished by April 2006. The plan, soundly based on both actuarial models and other successful programs, projected total program costs of $20 million (depending on benefits), supported by a $0.005 sales tax. Annually, it

Box 3.3 *Continued*

would provide about 10,000 of the almost 20,000 uninsured low-income county residents with primary care, preventive screenings, specialty care, and mental health and basic dental health care. Low-income participants would be required to pay a moderate co-payment.

While there was opposition among county commissioners, TEAM organized community support, and the commission approved the plan in May 2006. Approval of the plan, however, was only an interim step. Since funding involved adoption of a tax, the measure would have to receive public approval through a referendum. The county voted to place it on the November 2006 ballot and provided funds for community education.

TEAM members assisted the county in organizing the public education campaign, and several congregations hosted open community meetings around the county to present the plan to the public, including a question-and-answer session. The local business community did not back the plan because of the negative economic impact it felt that higher tax rates would have on the local economy. TEAM provided publicity packets in support of the plan, including health-care FAQs, a myths-and-facts sheet, background on the health-care initiative, and suggested homily and sermon materials for local faith community leaders. Several TEAM board members acted as a speakers bureau and visited civic organizations and other groups to advocate the initiative. In the weeks leading up to the November referendum, articles and letters about the issue appeared in the local newspaper almost every day. In addition, target precincts were selected

and canvassed door-to-door by TEAM volunteers to raise voter participation and support. In all, hundreds of hours of TEAM volunteer time were spent in bringing awareness of the issue to the voting public.

When the final votes were tallied, the tax referendum failed by an approximate margin of 60–40. Lower- and moderate-income neighborhoods tended to vote for the proposal, whereas most of the traditionally conservative neighborhoods opposed the adoption of the sales tax. Opposition to the tax increase had been fueled by higher-than-expected local property tax increases and midyear increases in homeowner insurance (a delayed result of the hurricane damage losses incurred by the insurance industry). There were some bright spots. The one candidate who campaigned on an anti-health-care tax platform was soundly defeated in the county commission elections, and the majority of the county commissioners remained committed to health care for the uninsured—if not specifically in support of funding it through a sales tax.

TEAM continues to support efforts to address the needs of the uninsured and took a markedly upbeat approach in the weeks following the referendum defeat, planning to keep health care for the uninsured as a priority for 2007. Health care for the 20,000 uninsured residents in the community is now a front-burner issue for the county and will remain so until it is adequately addressed.

Rev. Marcus Hepburn, TEAM member
Good Shepherd Catholic Church
Adrian Davis
TEAM Organizer

and the gaining of power on behalf of and with community members and are concerned with changing societal structures perceived to exclude some citizens (R. Fisher, 2005; Valocchi, n.d.; Weil, 2005; Weil & Gamble, 2005). They are referred to by a variety of names, including neighborhood and community organizing, organizing of functional communities, political and social action, political social work, progressive social work, radical social work, social movements, and coalitions (Weil & Gamble, 2005). These social change approaches use skills similar to those used in political activism and labor union organizing. Social workers in this area may coordinate voter registration drives, organize labor unions, synchronize groups protecting women's reproductive health services, or direct groups protesting the location of toxic waste dumps. Community organizing and political social work have several common threads. Social workers help individuals and groups find a common interest around an issue of concern. The issue negatively affects the participants' quality of life or that of those with whom they have a personal or philosophical allegiance, such as family members with cancer or individuals facing the death penalty. The individuals and groups are usually marginalized; that is, they are outside the usual social structures of power, influence, and decision making. Permanent new empowering structures may evolve out of these efforts. Practitioners are involved in tasks such as identifying social problems, analyzing factors that create or cause these problems, formulating plans, developing strategies, mobilizing resources to take action, strengthening bonds among community members, training and enabling indigenous community members to assume leadership positions, and getting allies to take action. Community organizing and political social work often involve challenging what is perceived to be the acceptable social order through dissident actions, and sometimes even civil disobedience, though not all social workers are willing to engage in unlawful acts.

Community practitioners generally distinguish themselves from other helping professionals for several reasons. They believe that most professional social work practice is based on erroneous assumptions concerning both the nature of social problems and appropriate strategies for problem resolution. They perceive most nonradical social workers as relying on a single methodological skill (such as casework or group work) that incorrectly identifies variables within the client as the focus of problem resolution. Community practitioners assume the problems of at-risk populations can be traced to political or economic relationships that exist in the larger social system (Longres, 1996). Their primary focus is on political and economic variables as explanations for social problems. They define the problems of individual clients in terms of the social forces that shape their circumstances. Dysfunction is defined as having been thrust purposely on less powerful individuals or groups as a way of reinforcing the power of a dominant group within the political system. They see the arena of struggle as falling outside the social work agency and within the larger social environment. Community practitioners rely on political skills and ties to larger social movements as opposed to technical knowledge in direct practice or clinical methods.

The newest form of community practice entails e-organizing, or cyberorganizing, which requires technical and interactional skills. Because the interactional skills depend on technology, information and communications technology skills assume both a social and a technical function for cyberorganizing. Unlike a community built on spatial boundaries, a cybercommunity is a nonplace-based conscious community that is totally voluntary and built upon shared interests (Chaskin, 1997; Palloff & Pratt, 1999).

Like traditionally organized groups, cyberorganized groups are built on group interaction. Because the written word rather than face-to-face interaction is the general medium of communication, cyberpractitioners must be adept at creating a common experience through written discourse. The cyberpractitioner's challenge is creating a community with a traditional sense of benefit for participating through interaction, negotiation, and conflict resolution, but in a novel environment with weak ties, low exit barriers, and a lack of personalized, physical interaction. Therefore, the cyberpractitioner must be skilled not only in facilitating group interaction and processes but also in written communication and the use of information and communications technology employed for Listservs, chat rooms, and electronic mail.

Common Skills for Community Practice

Whether they are planners, developers, community organizers, or political social workers, community practitioners need interactional skills and technical skills. In actual practice, however, one skill set usually dominates. The hallmark of the skilled community practitioner is the ability to balance interactional and technical skills, know when to use each set, and mix and match the skills necessary to solve the problem.

Technical skills are essential for social planning and policy practice. These skills are an amalgamation of data management (evaluating information; analyzing data; and developing, evaluating, and measuring outcomes), translating data into work (identifying and analyzing issues, converting data into action or strategies), and understanding the policy process (knowing how the process works and how to influence it).

Interactional skills, which focus on deliberate human interaction through the artful and purposeful "use of self," are often overlooked in community practice (McNutt, 2000; Wernet, 2002). Like other social workers, community practitioners must understand their own strengths and weaknesses in facilitating communication and cooperation. They must be genuine but temper their personal reactions and desires to help the group or community achieve its goals. The skilled community practitioner is interested in building community capacity by creating and sustaining both weak and strong ties (Gilchrist, 2000). Interventions focus on groups and organizations as well as on creating consortia and community. Practitioners should be skilled in process facilitation (i.e., building relationships among individuals around common issues of concern). They must be able to exert leadership and recruit, engage, and support people while creating a sense of common interest by bridging groups and individuals, building gateways for intergroup interactions, and eliminating barriers to involvement (Mizrahi & Rosenthal, 1993).

Policy Practice

Some aspects of policy practice are closely related to community organizing and political social work. In fact, some social workers use the terms *political social work* and *policy practice* interchangeably. Government interventions for addressing social problems are referred to as social policies and include taxation or fiscal policy, regulation or legislative policy, and social welfare policy (Midgley, 2000). The question of how involved or detached government should be in influencing human well-being through public policies foments vociferous debate and commentary among people across the political spectrum.

Social workers' long history of involvement in public policy dates back to the Pittsburgh Survey of 1909–1914 and the settlement house workers (Midgley, 2000). In the 1950s, the study of social policy evolved as an academic discipline, but policy practice is much more than the study of laws. With the Great Society legislation and the war on poverty, policy practice blossomed into the full-fledged and exciting field of social work practice. Social workers specializing in social welfare policy may have jobs as program planners and evaluators or as legislative committee staff or policy analysts in the governor's (or mayor's) office, public interest groups, advocacy groups, and client or consumer organizations. They may work as lobbyists or as aides to legislators or other elected officials. They may even be elected officials. Among the social workers who have served in elected positions is Senator Barbara Mikulski (D-Maryland).

Policy practice involves both technical skills and political activity (DiNitto, 2007; Midgley, 2000; Midgley, Tracy, & Livermore, 2000). It typically involves the following steps:

- Identification of policy problems through publicized demands for government action
- Formulation of policy alternatives or proposals through political channels by policy-planning organizations, interest groups, government bureaucracies, and the president and Congress
- Legitimization of public policy through Congress, or courts, including executive orders and budgets, laws and appropriations, rules and regulations, and decisions and interpretations, which have the effect of setting policy directions
- Implementation of public policy through the activities of public bureaucracies and expenditure of public funds
- Evaluation of policies by government agencies, outside consultants, interest groups, the mass media, and the public (DiNitto, 2007; Jones, 1984)

Evaluation of policy alternatives is based on rational econometric criteria of efficiency, effectiveness, cost-effectiveness, and cost-benefits, but whether government should intervene is a political choice (DiNitto, 2007). Citizens and their representatives make their preferences for intervention known during public debate. The fundamental task of policy practice (i.e., defining a public problem such as poverty or child abuse) is by its very nature a political act. Therefore, policy practice entails influencing decision makers. This work is the art and political side of policy practice. It requires many of the same external control skills needed by the social work administrator—communication or interactional skills, advocacy, and values clarification.

Every social worker is a policy practitioner. Each social worker directly providing client services is implementing social policy. Social workers are at the forefront of identifying social needs and must share information regarding social need with legislators and policy practitioners in the service of policy formulation. To strictly define policy practice as a technical skill is to neglect its political, disputational, and value components. Policy practice is both science and art—technical skill and political activity (Wildavsky, 1979). As policy practitioners, social workers must be involved in drafting and advocating legislation, testifying at legislative hearings, and gathering evidence about the prevalence and impact of social problems and their solutions (see box 3.4).

Box 3.4   Combining Technical Skills and Policy Practice

Rick is a program planner in a large state welfare agency. His unit is responsible for planning child welfare programs. He spends a great deal of his time collecting data. When he started this job five years ago, no one really knew what kinds of programs were needed to serve the children of this state. He now has a fairly reliable database from which he can predict needs for such services as foster homes, juvenile detention, and programs for teenage parents. Rick works directly with the individuals who operate these programs in proposing budgetary requests to the state legislature. Although public employees in this state are technically prohibited from lobbying, he spends much of his time during the legislative session providing invited testimony before the House and Senate subcommittees on children's services. Hoping for opportunities to score points for his agency's program proposals, he also has lunch with friendly legislators and makes a point of attending many social functions with other legislators. Rick is well acquainted with all of the state's major human services lobbies, and he has worked hard to influence their agendas. During the legislative session, he has twice-weekly meetings with the executive director of NASW, the president of the League for Human Services, the director of the local Urban League, and officials of several other small organizations. He has been very active in the state NASW chapter and has served in several elected positions; this has given him an opportunity to help determine the organization's agenda.

SUMMARY

Social work macropractice remains a hallmark of the profession. Macropractice social workers focus on public issues. Social work administration, community practice, and policy practice are concerned with solving and preventing social problems at organizational, community, and societal levels. Social work macropractitioners work in a variety of settings and use an array of skills. The common goal of the various macropractice approaches is to move society toward social, economic, and political justice. Macropractice social workers seek a civil society. Through voluntary associations and communities, they help people learn the importance of cooperation and mutual assistance as well as build common interests and trust. These webs of relationships help people meet the human need for affiliation and intimacy and learn the necessary skills for political activity and civic engagement.

Each macropractice method involves a somewhat different approach to solving social problems. Social work administrators see themselves as managers or implementers of social programs working through the social system to effect social change. Social work administration continues to grow as a career option because of the outsourcing, privatization, and load shifting of public services. The use of government funds for social services creates jobs in for-profit, nonprofit, and government settings.

Community practitioners see themselves as agents for social change and social action who struggle to empower the disenfranchised, who are outside the system. Social workers in community practice help individuals coalesce to address social problems that negatively affect a community. They help people help themselves by building the collective power of the citizenry through participation and, ultimately, strengthening and building a democratic society.

Policy practitioners seek change specifically in the political arena. Some policy practitioners focus on analyzing social policies and their intended and unintended consequences, particularly as they affect underserved and disenfranchised groups. Others focus on advocacy through education or lobbying. Some run for elected office—and win!

SUGGESTED READING

Hammack, D. (1998). *Making the nonprofit sector in the United States: A reader.* Indianapolis: Indiana University Press. This collection of works written over approximately two hundred years of American history presents an excellent perspective for understanding the development of the nonprofit sector.

Hick, S. F., & McNutt, J. G. (Eds.). (2002). *Advocacy, activism, and the Internet: Community organization and social policy.* Chicago: Lyceum Books. This work discusses the advocacy approach to community organizing in the information age. Contributions present both domestic and international perspectives and approaches to the use of the Internet for advocacy, community organizing, and electronically based government.

Lohmann, R. A. (1992). *The commons: New perspectives on nonprofit organizations and voluntary action.* San Francisco: Jossey-Bass. This classic work discusses the philosophical basis for community and administrative practice. It presents an excellent alternative understanding to the predominant economic analysis of public and nonprofit sectors and services.

Midgley, J., Tracy, M., & Livermore, M. (Eds.). (2000). *The handbook of social policy.* Thousand Oaks, CA: Sage. This work consists of pieces discussing contemporary thought about and approaches to social policy from a social work perspective. Domestic and international perspectives on social policy are included.

Patti, R. (2000). *The handbook of social welfare management.* Thousand Oaks, CA: Sage. This work contains the definitive array of works on social work administration. Chapters discuss theoretical as well as practical issues concerning social work administration in both public and nonprofit organizations.

Salamon, L. S. (1999). *America's nonprofit sector: A primer* (2nd ed.). New York: Foundation Center. This book provides an overview of the nonprofit sector in the United States, including historical, descriptive, and analytic information about the nonprofit sector and its various subsectors.

Weil, M. (Ed.). (2005). *The handbook of community practice.* Thousand Oaks, CA: Sage. This volume contains the authoritative array of works on community organization practice. The chapters present theoretical and practice perspectives on community organizing, community development, and policy practice.

THE WORLD WIDE WEB OF SOCIAL WORK

Association of Community Organizations for Reform Now http://www.acorn.org

ACORN is the nation's largest community organization of low- and moderate-income families working together for social justice and stronger communities. ACORN pioneered multiracial and multi-issue organizing among the poor and powerless to develop democratic and grassroots leadership. ACORN has been involved in electoral organizing, innovative housing development, community media, and labor organizing. It is made up of more than 175,000 member families organized in 850 neighborhood chapters in seventy-five cities across the United States and in cities in Canada, the Dominican Republic, and Peru.

Institute for the Study of Civic Values http://www.iscv.org

The ISCV was established to build a new politics of community focused on the fulfillment of America's historic civic ideals. It seeks to strengthen democracy as set forth in the country's founding documents. ISCV demonstrates how to build community and revitalize grassroots democracy through youth civic engagement and get-out-the-vote campaigns, examine public policy within the framework of America's civic values, and negotiate social contracts between citizens and government, thereby allowing the two to work together to build better neighborhoods and schools.

National Network for Social Work Managers http://www.socialworkmanager.org

The National Network for Social Work Managers is a membership organization composed of social workers in management and leadership positions. It is dedicated to effective management that combines the leadership expertise of a superior manager with the people-centered focus of social work practitioners. The Network has developed a set of practice standards that describe the competencies and best practices expected for social workers in management and leadership positions. It has also established a credential, the Certified Social Work Manager, for social workers practicing as managers. It offers training, resources, and networking opportunities. The Network sponsors an Annual Management Institute as well as national and regional conferences for social work professionals.

Neighborhood Funders Group/Community Organizing Toolbox http://www.nfg.org/cotb

The Neighborhood Funders Group seeks to improve the economic and social fabric of low-income urban neighborhoods and rural communities. The Community

Organizing Toolbox is a resource that explains community organizing and illustrates how to galvanize low- to moderate-income people, their neighborhoods, and their communities to achieve a higher quality of life through neighborhood and community revitalization and better housing, employment, education, health, and environment.

OMB Watch http://www.ombwatch.org

OMB Watch is a nonprofit research and advocacy organization dedicated to promoting government accountability, citizen participation in public policy decisions, and the use of fiscal and regulatory policy to serve the public interest. It seeks to improve access to decision makers and energize citizen participation to strengthen civil society and make government more just, equitable, and accountable. OMB Watch focuses on budget, taxation, and government performance issues; information and access; nonprofit action, advocacy, policy, and technology; and regulatory policy.

United Way of America http://national.unitedway.org

United Way is among the nation's largest private charities. Its mission is to improve lives by mobilizing the caring power of communities. In addition to fundraising, United Way uses unique partnerships and approaches to bring diverse people and resources together to address the most urgent issues their communities face. The United Way system consists of approximately 1,350 community-based organizations. Each is independent, separately incorporated, and governed by local volunteers.

4 Culturally Competent Social Work Practice

Rowena Fong

This chapter defines culturally competent social work practice, addresses the evolution and importance of this practice, and provides demographics of the U.S. population and diversity within and between ethnic and other cultural groups. The kinds of problems that social workers are likely to help clients address are discussed in the context of culturally competent assessment and interventions skills. Issues, opportunities, and challenges that may arise in working with clients of different cultural backgrounds are also highlighted.

As we begin this discussion, imagine you are a social worker in an elementary school. A teacher brings a ten-year-old girl who appears to be of Asian background to your office. Apparently the girl is having problems in the class, and the teacher asks you to find out what her family situation is. Because there are great variations in ways of thinking and behaving among the many Asian groups, and differences in philosophies of raising children between American- and foreign-born individuals, one of your first tasks is to determine the child's ethnic background and where she was raised. Is she American-born Vietnamese? Is she from the People's Republic of China? Merely asking her where she's from might get you an answer. But how do you then go about understanding her social environment and how growing up Asian in America might make her different from the rest of her elementary school classmates? Social workers involved with ethnically diverse clients are expected to consider these questions and seek answers to them.

Should you choose to become a social worker, children and adults coming to you for help might speak a language different from your own or wear clothes that are not familiar to you. You would soon discover that their customs and practices are strikingly different from your own and those that you observe in your office, neighborhood, and even the state in which you reside. To begin to understand and work effectively with people from different ethnic and cultural backgrounds, you need the tools of *culturally competent social work practice.*

Culturally competent practice is a must for working with ethnically diverse clients. It encompasses learning about historical, political, social, and cultural events; the significance of ethnic families and communities; the role of language in creating meaning; and honoring ethnic rituals in everyday life. It also acknowledges experiences of racism and discrimination, especially in the lives of many people of color. Acquiring the skills and knowledge associated with culturally competent social work practice is challenging but necessary because large multicultural populations are becoming increasingly commonplace in the United States.

Culturally competent practice has generally been thought of as working with people of color. Much of this chapter is devoted to working with populations of color, identified as African Americans or blacks, Asian and Pacific Islander Americans, Mexican Americans, Latinos, and American Indians or First Nations people. Often overlooked are interracial individuals and families, and some of the diverse populations of immigrants (documented and undocumented), refugees, and asylees. They, too, are discussed in this chapter. Culturally competent practice also has a broader connotation encompassing all distinctive ethnic and cultural groups, such as those of various white European heritages (e.g., Irish, Italians, Portuguese) and religious groups (e.g., Jews, Christians, Muslims). In an even broader sense it encompasses groups defined by social class (e.g., poor and rich; see chapter 13); geography, such as those residing in rural areas (see chapter 15); and sexual orientation (see chapter 6), as well as some groups of individuals with disabilities (see chapter 10).

DEFINITIONS AND TERMS

Culturally competent practice can be thought of in three parts: (1) helping people of distinct cultural groups solve problems by incorporating their personal, family, and community strengths and resources; (2) understanding their social and environmental contexts, especially in reference to racism, oppression, and discrimination; and (3) using bicultural interventions that focus on cultural values and integrate them as strengths, and incorporating indigenous methods as well as Western ones.

To be culturally competent, one must have some understanding of the terms *culture, race, ethnicity, racism, discrimination*, and *oppression*. Culture is broadly defined as a way of life and behavior based on norms, values, and skills (Gordon, 1978) or elements of history, traditions, and social organizations (Green, 1999). Culture is associated with race, ethnicity, gender, sexual orientation, abilities, religious beliefs, socioeconomics, geographical location, and political beliefs. Lum (2000) asserts, "Culture reflects the lifestyle practices of particular groups of people who are influenced by learned patterns of values, beliefs, and behavioral modalities" (p. 89). Thus, cultural values are reflections of people's race and ethnicity and many other characteristics and contexts of culture.

Race and ethnicity are closely related but different concepts. Some sociologists, cultural anthropologists, and social and cultural historians argue that race is a socially constructed phenomenon because physical phenotypes based on genetic or biological differences among people are not sufficiently distinct to classify a person as being of one race and not another. Thus it is argued that race is a social construction that gives one group of people more or fewer opportunities and resources than others. Historically and currently, people of color receive fewer opportunities and resources than whites.

Ethnicity, on the other hand, is usually associated with cultural identity. Ethnicity is "a sense of identity based on loyalty to a distinctive cultural pattern that is related to common ancestry, nation, religion, and/or race" (Lum, 2000, p. 85). Ethnicity also intersects with a person's identity based on cultural variables of gender, age, sexual orientation, abilities, social class, and/or geographic location.

Race and ethnicity are the usual or primary factors based upon which people experience racism, discrimination, and oppression. Social workers who practice cultural competency have opportunities to address these issues with many of their clients.

EVOLUTION OF CULTURALLY COMPETENT PRACTICE

Europeans who immigrated to the United States faced considerable discrimination, especially as their numbers increased early in the twentieth century. They usually did not speak English. They brought their own traditions that were often not accepted in their new environments, and they often performed menial jobs. Even today, immigrants and refugees from European countries may be looked at with suspicion, but culturally competent practice derives largely from the experience of working with people of color rather than with white ethnic groups.

In the 1970s, Norton (1978) proposed that the worldviews and experiences of people of color are not the same as those of the white population. She coined the term *dual perspective*, which implies that people of color, be they American Indians, African Americans, or Latinos, may see situations differently than whites do. Norton argued that people of color experience life differently than whites due to different historical experiences and cultural values; thus, social workers working with people of color, be they other professionals or clients, have to accept alternative ways of viewing the world. Among other things, social workers have to recognize that people of color face racial discrimination and oppression that whites seldom experience, and this knowledge needs to be factored into professional assessments of clients as well as the design and implementation of social welfare policies and programs.

Ethnic-Sensitive Practice

In the 1980s Devore and Schlesinger (1999) began to write about ethnic-sensitive social work practice. Effective social workers, they maintained, had to be sensitive not only to minority clients' race or ethnicity but to social class as well. They coined the terms *ethnic reality* and *eth-class* to emphasize that not all people of color are poor, and not all poor people are people of color. Certainly, not all African Americans are poor, nor are all Asians well-to-do, and there are whites in every socioeconomic stratum. Ross-Sheriff and Husain (2004) note that the South Asians who have settled in the United States are distributed among early immigrants, who often became professionals, and later immigrants, who have tended to become small-shop owners. The culturally competent practice literature of the 1980s strongly emphasized the ethnic reality of racial discrimination and stereotyping. Social workers were called upon to fight these injustices.

Process-Stage Approach

In 1986, Lum (2000) published the groundbreaking book *Social Work Practice with People of Color: A Process-Stage Approach*, which established the necessity of cultural awareness, knowledge acquisition, skills development, and inductive learning (forming ideas or principles from repeated observations). His process-stage approach involved contact, problem identification, assessment, intervention, and termination and emphasized culturally diverse social work practice with people of color. Lum called for assessments and interventions to be conducted with an understanding that people of color are not all the same. Even within the same race, each individual's unique cultural attributes should be recognized and factored into assessments and interventions tailored to him or her.

Until the late 1980s, culturally competent practice centered primarily on the social worker's need to be culturally sensitive, aware, informed, and skilled. Lum's attention to the cultural values of people of color remained unnoticed until the 1990s, when others began to emphasize ethnic minority clients and the role of cultural values as strengths and the importance of indigenous interventions (practices grounded in the client's own culture) (Fong & Mokuau, 1994; Mokuau, 1991).

Cultural Values as Strengths

A paradigm shift in the 1990s brought the client of color to the center, in the role of expert. This shift occurred as others recognized that minority cultural values are often strengths and that indigenous interventions could play an important role in helping clients. For example, Fong, Boyd, and Browne (1999) note that the purpose of culturally competent practice is to help the social worker "start with the client" and use the client's cultural values as strengths in both assessments and interventions. They believe that everyone affiliated with an ethnic community has positive, important, and meaningful cultural values. Cultural values give clients strengths and resources to cope with and adapt to stressors.

Most of these cultural values are carried from geographical locations where ethnic roots originate. For example, although there are significant exceptions, people from Asia tend to place a high value on educational endeavors and achievements. A culturally competent social worker needs this knowledge in order to draw on the value of education as a strength and resource when helping Asian immigrant families become more familiar with their new environment.

There is a caveat here. Social workers do not view every cultural value or cultural practice as a strength. For example, some cultures do not value the education of girls or place less value on female children than on male children. Cultural values can also be sources of tension in families. For example, traditional Asian families place a high priority on filial piety and the primacy of familial relations. They may not appreciate the desire of younger generations to spend a great deal of time with friends, and, like many whites, they may disapprove of or forbid their children from dating or marrying outside their ethnic group.

Biculturalization of Interventions

One undeveloped or underdeveloped aspect of the paradigm shift of culturally competent practice is combining indigenous ethnic treatments or interventions with Western treatments or interventions. For example, in Nicaraguan, Salvadoran, and other Latino cultures, spirituality is important and is manifested through "organized religion or most commonly though domestic rituals and practices such as *altares* (altars) and *curanderismo* (traditional healing practices)" (Marsiglia & Menjivar, 2004, p. 263). When appropriate, social workers incorporate traditional healing practices in helping individuals and families.

The biculturalization of interventions is more than combining indigenous and Western interventions (Fong et al., 1999). It is a systematic way of assessing the appropriateness of Western interventions to see if they are compatible with the cultural values and the indigenous interventions of the client's ethnic group. Operating from a strengths perspective, both types of interventions can support, rather than contradict, clients' cultural values. For example, acupuncture, a treatment commonly used by Asians, has been incorporated into many chemical dependency programs as a procedure used in detoxification (though evidence of its effectiveness in detoxification is not consistent). Social workers who do family therapy may call in native healers to participate in sessions, or they may participate in rituals conducted by spiritualists, medicine men or women, or other indigenous healers.

Culturally Competent Contextual Practice

Clients' backgrounds and cultural contexts continue to receive attention in the literature (Brave Heart, 2001; Fong, 2004; Guadalupe & Lum, 2005; O'Melia & Miley, 2002). In its current expanded form, culturally competent practice means helping people of color solve problems by incorporating their personal, family, and community strengths; understanding their social and environmental contexts; and using bicultural interventions. This framework recognizes that the Western model (generally the traditional medical model with the professional in the role of expert) is not always sufficient or appropriate for clients of color. It assumes that indigenous interventions exist and are effective with clients of color and should be included in treatment planning. There may, of course, be exceptions since some practices can cause harm. For example, Cambodian women have reported being encouraged to drink alcohol in the months immediately before or after giving birth in order to strengthen the blood (D'Avanzo, Frye, & Froman, 1994). The U.S. Surgeon General advises women not to drink during pregnancy because of the potential to cause birth defects. Drinking alcohol while breast-feeding also results in alcohol being delivered to the child.

Culturally competent contextual social work practice assumes that people behave differently depending on their social environment experiences. For example, a Liberian refugee woman may behave differently in America than she did while living in Liberia because of the trauma she experienced in the refugee camps before she reached America. Culturally competent contextual social work practice dictates that special attention needs to be paid to the individual's social context, especially the multiple social environments that the individual has experienced. In doing assessments, social workers collect information on all of the client's relevant experiences and utilize culturally competent practice skills to understand the client's cultural contexts and the meanings of these experiences.

Fong's (2004) work on immigrants and refugees addresses culturally diverse social environments and the importance of understanding cultural contexts. She encourages social workers to become proficient in applying the four components of culturally competent contextual practice, many of which were discussed in chapter 2: (1) an ecological and person-in-environment model; (2) a strengths-based orientation using cultural values in assessment and intervention planning; (3) the intersectionality of macro values and the application of differential assessments; and (4) an empowerment approach reflecting the biculturalization of interventions, such as solution-focused therapy. This approach is especially valuable for refugees and asylees who have gone from their home country to refugee camps before coming to the United States. Some individuals spend only a few days in such camps; others remain there for significant parts of their lives. As box 4.1 indicates, camp life can be dangerous, and clients' experiences there should be considered by social workers in assessing their well-being and functioning. Another assumption of culturally competent contextual practice is that good social work practice integrates cultural values, cultural contexts, and indigenous treatments into a unified framework through a process that may be called intersectionality. Intersectionality joins such variables congruently by considering clients' characteristics holistically rather than as single variables in isolation. For example, a woman from South America cannot ignore her traditional values concerning gender when living in the United States, just as a Nigerian man in the United States cannot ignore his religious values. The holistic approach to culturally competent practice with immigrants and refugees is to discern how variables

---

Box 4.1   The United Nations High Commission for Refugees and Refugee Camps

The United Nations High Commission for Refugees, located in Geneva, Switzerland, and founded in 1950, was established to protect and support refugees. It strives to ensure their right to find safe refuge in another place. Often there is a gap between the time the refugees leave their home countries and are allowed to enter their host countries. During this time, refugees, whether they are adults or children, usually stay in refugee camps. Built by governmental agencies and nongovernmental agencies, these camps are intended to be short-term residences, but some refugees live in camps for years because they cannot return to their home countries for fear of death or persecution or because they cannot find refuge in another country. Refugees must remain in these makeshift facilities until a host country is willing to accept them. More than 9 million official refugees fall under the United Nations High Commission for Refugees' mandate, but some estimate that as many as 35 million people live as refugees or internally displaced persons (Doctors Without Borders, 2000).

Poor sanitation conditions affecting hygiene and water supplies are common problems in the camps and result in severe illnesses. Social workers in refugee resettlement agencies may help clients practice methods to avoid health problems or obtain health care because of infectious diseases in the camps. Women and children are especially vulnerable populations in the camps and often need mental health services when they arrive in host countries. Social workers provide much of this mental health care. Social workers also offer culturally competent services as they help refugees learn the customs and habits of their new homelands. Knowledge about the refugees' home countries and the kinds of trauma endured during camp residence helps social workers better serve this oppressed population.

such as race, ethnicity, gender, social class, religion, place of origin, cultural values, and cultural contexts all intersect to affect the client's well-being (see box 4.2 for a case example of a Muslim family).

Box 4.2   Case Example of a Muslim Family

Jameela is a fifty-two-year-old South Asian Muslim woman from Pakistan. She came to the United States when she was in her twenties to attend a university. She met her husband, Ali, now a successful engineer, and has three children. Recently, Jameela has been having problems with her sixteen-year-old son, Bar, who is beginning to question his Muslim faith. Bar doesn't understand why the family has to believe only in Allah, the creator, and follow the teachings of the Prophet Mohamed. His American peers at school speak of Christianity and the teachings of Jesus. They have challenged his Muslim faith, and he is tired of defending himself. He is beginning to feel confused and isn't sure what he believes in.

Jameela desperately wants to help her son because he is the oldest and she fears he will become depressed and set a poor example for his younger siblings. She seeks help from her Muslim friends, but they are not sure how to help her. Her friends, too, fear that their children might abandon their Muslim faith.

Because they have been unable to solve the problem, Jameela and Ali finally decide to go to family counseling with Bar, who has become more depressed. His grades have dropped, and he is less and less interested in going to school because of peer ridicule. You are a social worker skilled in family therapy, but you do not know much about the Muslin faith. You are, however, very aware that this is a core issue for this family. Having grown up a deeply religious Christian in a Southern Baptist church, you begin to wonder if you have the knowledge necessary to help this family. As a social worker, should you keep this case or refer it to another worker? The National Association of Social Workers' Code of Ethics requires social workers to practice only in their areas of competence. You consider whether you can apply the principles of culturally competent practice to help this family reach an optimum solution or if you should refer the family to another practitioner.

Source: Adapted from Ross-Sheriff, F., & Husain, A. (2004). South Asian Muslim children and families. In R. Fong (Ed.), *Culturally competent practice with immigrant and refugee children and families* (pp. 163–182). New York: Guilford Press.

Standards and Specializations

In 2001 the National Association of Social Workers established *Standards for Cultural Competence in Social Work Practice*, ten guidelines and goals for culturally competent practice. The standards emphasize the need to value diversity; the importance of self-awareness, being knowledgeable of the client's culture, and the adaptation of skills; and the challenges of processing the dynamics of differences when cultures interact. Texts such as *Culturally Competent Practice* (Lum, 2003), *Culturally Competent Practice with Immigrant and Refugee Children and Families* (Fong, 2004), and *Multidimensional Contextual Practice* (Guadalupe & Lum, 2005) emphasize these guidelines and promote contextual practice and intersections that incorporate clients' spirituality.

While the movement toward improving culturally competent practice has been the focus of seminal books published to further models and frameworks applicable across ethnic and racial groups, there is also a wealth of literature on culturally competent practice for specific ethnic groups. Mokuau (1990), for example, has reported on *Ho'oponopono*, a Hawaiian family decision-making process (see box 4.3); Jung (1998) has promoted Chinese American family therapy; Brave Heart (2001) describes historical trauma intervention for Native Americans; Harvey (2001) has written of the Africentric approach with African Americans; and Falicov (1998) addresses Latino families in therapy. Cultural competence has also been incorporated into such topical areas as child welfare, family violence, and substance abuse (Fong, McRoy, & Hendricks, 2006); mental health (Hernandez & Isaacs, 1998); and health, social, and human services (Lecca, Quervalu, Nunes, & Gonzales, 1998).

Box 4.3 *Ho'oponopono*: An Example of Biculturalization of Interventions

In the Hawaiian culture, social workers may use a family conflict resolution intervention known as *Ho'oponopono*, which means "setting to right" (Mokuau, 1990; Pukui, Haertig, & Lee, 1971). It is based on the Hawaiian cultural values of *o'hana* (extended family), *laulima* (cooperation), *kokua* (help), and *lokahi* (balance). *Hóoponopono* is used when there are conflicts among extended family members and resolution is sought to regain balance and cooperation through the help of a Hawaiian elder.

Ho'oponopono involves several steps. It starts with an opening prayer, called *pule*. There is a statement of the problem and "setting to right," and a discussion of the presenting problem.

Individual conduct and thoughts are then examined, followed by questions posed by the Hawaiian elder, who monitors discussion and emotions. Honest confession for wrongdoing is then expected, as well as repentance. Finally the family members work toward restitution, restoring harmony and cooperation in the family. Forgiveness is offered. A closing prayer ends the process, and everyone shares a meal. In this intervention, the Hawaiian cultural values and practices of prayer and "setting to right" are combined with Western family therapy techniques. A culturally competent social worker would need to respect and work with a Hawaiian elder to effectively use *Ho'oponopono*.

Culturally competent practice is closely linked to all areas of practice with people of color (Fong & Furuto, 2001). Social justice issues are also closely tied to culturally competent practice as they manifest themselves in the effects of American Indians' struggles against colonization (Weaver, 2005; Yellow Bird, 2001) or in the frustrations of immigrants and refugee families from Mexico, Cuba, and Central and South America as they adapt to life in the United States (Galan, 2001; Webb, 2001). Discriminatory and racist practices toward African Americans and other minorities in the United States continue to exist. After September 11, 2001, the war on terrorism increased hostility and threats to individuals of Middle Eastern backgrounds—not only those abroad or in the United States illegally, but also those who are American born, naturalized citizens, or otherwise residing legally in the United States. Social workers engaged in culturally competent practice are encouraged to consider their obligations to engage in macro-level skills of advocacy and activism in fighting the injustices that people of color face.

DEMOGRAPHICS OF A MULTICULTURAL SOCIETY

That the racial and ethnic demographics of the United States are swiftly shifting as the multicultural population flourishes is hardly news. The 2000 U.S. Census Bureau reported that people of color numbered nearly 70 million, or 25 percent of the total population. Hispanics, a term the federal government uses instead of "Latinos," are the fastest-growing ethnic group in the United States. In June of 2003, the U.S. Census Bureau reported that Hispanics were the largest ethnic minority group in the nation, now outnumbering African Americans. Table 4.1 shows the racial and ethnic composition of the U.S. population.

Of the approximately 281 million people in the United States, 31 million, or 11 percent, are foreign born. Slightly more than half (52%) of the foreign born come from Latin America, a quarter (26%) come from Asia, 16 percent were born in Europe, and 6 percent were born elsewhere. Thus, one

Table 4.1   Racial and ethnic composition of the U.S. population, 2000

Race/ethnicity	Population (in millions)	Percent of total population
White	211,460,626	75.1%
Hispanic or Latino	35,305,818	12.5%
Black or African American	34,658,190	12.3%
Asian	10,242,998	3.6%
Native Hawaiian and other Pacific Islander	398,835	0.1%
American Indian and Native American	2,475,956	0.9%
Another race	15,359,073	5.5%
Two or more races	6,826,225	2.4%
Two races	6,368,075	2.3%
Three races	410,285	6.0%
Four races	38,408	0.6%
Five races	8,637	0.1%

Source: U.S. Census Bureau. (2000). *Census briefs and special reports: Overview of race and Hispanic origin*. Retrieved September 8, 2006, from http://www.census.gov/prod/2001pubs/c2kbro1-1.pdf

out of four people in the United States is a person of color, and one out of ten is foreign born. These figures have important implications for social work practice.

DIVERSE POPULATIONS
People of Color

People of color are often referred to as ethnic minorities since they are fewer in number than the white population. The word *ethnic* also implies having a distinctive culture, norms, food, and language, while *minority*, in addition to being the opposite of majority, suggests an imbalance in power. The term *minority* is quickly becoming outdated, as demographic data indicate that by the year 2050 people of color are likely to be the majority group in the United States.

Ethnic groups are themselves undergoing evolutions of identity. Asian and Pacific Islander Americans used to be referred to as Orientals, but as a result of Asian American awareness and activism, Asian Americans are now separated into Pacific Islanders (Hawaiian, Tongan, Samoan, Chamorro, etc.), East Asians (Chinese, Japanese, Korean, and Filipino), South Asians (Indian, Sri Lankan, Pakistani, etc.), and Southeast Asians (Vietnamese, Cambodian, Laotian, etc.). Lumping people of diverse cultural groups together is called *ethnic glossing* because it obscures differences among the groups. American Indians identify by tribe but also as Native People, Native Americans, Indians, and First Nations people. Mexican Americans have also been referred to as Chicanos, Latinos, and Hispanics, and there is still much debate within this ethnic group about name and identity. When assessing a client, it is critical for the social worker to determine how the client self-identifies, and the best way to do this is to ask him or her. This is especially important to persons who are from mixed-blood backgrounds and identify as bi- or multiracial.

Each ethnic group has unique struggles in living in or adapting to the United States. They also share common struggles with members of other ethnic groups. Social workers in child protective services address the disproportionate number of African American children in the child welfare system (see box 4.4), a problem that has attracted national attention with a series of Race Matters forums. The National Indian Child Welfare Association holds an annual Protecting Our Children conference to discuss ways to ensure the well-being of American Indian children and preserve their cultures. Asian Americans deal with the stereotype of being the "model minority" group that works hard and rarely experiences problems of any kind, and families of undocumented Mexicans share concern about personal safety and deportation. A culturally competent social worker has the opportunity to address these issues with multicultural clients.

Box 4.4 Disproportionality in Foster Care and Project HOPE

African American children are overrepresented in the public child welfare system, constituting about 40 percent of all children in foster care in the United States (Green, Rodriguez, & Fong, 2005). In light of the nationwide attention to the subject, social work practitioners, administrators, researchers, policy makers, and community agencies have come together to find solutions to decrease the number of African American children in foster care and to improve the outcomes for those who are in care. Disproportionality has been a concern of the Casey Family Programs, a private foster care agency, and Texas Child Protective Services and has resulted in a community-based collaboration model called Project HOPE. It is part of the Texas State Strategy to reduce the disproportionate representation of and disparate outcomes for

African American children in the child welfare system. In addition to the Casey Family Programs and the Texas Department of Family and Protective Services, Project HOPE involves community stakeholders from local government agencies, nonprofit agencies, community members, and African American children and families. A collaborative community-based process preceded the opening of the center for Project HOPE. Casey Family Programs and Child Protective Services are now reaching out to Texas communities so that the needs of African American families can be identified and community resources can be gathered to meet them. New initiatives like Project HOPE are examples of successful social work collaborations aimed at meeting the needs of poor and oppressed populations.

Immigrants, Refugees, and Asylees

Historically, and predictably, culturally competent practice first focused on those ethnic minorities born and raised in the United States. Eventually social workers recognized that foreign-born individuals are not just variations of people of color born in the United States. Their needs are different. In addition, immigrants may have different needs than refugee populations (Fong & Mokuau, 1994). The documented immigrant population has entered the United States legally, and they presumably left their home countries voluntarily. The expectation is that they will eventually apply for citizenship. Refugees have left their home countries not because they wanted to do so, but because conditions in the home country have become intolerable and unsafe. They typically seek to relocate permanently to the United States, recognizing that a return to their home countries is unlikely. Asylees come to the United States to escape political persecution, determine that they cannot return to their home countries, and seek political asylum either in the United States or elsewhere.

The foreign-born population that has unquestionably drawn the most controversy is illegal, also called undocumented, immigrants. They do not have permission (legal documentation) from the U.S. government to live or work in the United States. These individuals and families often need services nonetheless, and social workers may have ethical and moral obliga-

Representatives of a farmworkers' aid organization provide water to immigrant workers from Mexico.
© A. T. Willett/Alamy

tions to serve them (see the National Association of Social Workers' Code of Ethics). This can present both an ethical and a legal dilemma when law or public policy prohibits such services.

Section 1 of the Fourteenth Amendment to the Constitution declares that any person born in the United States is a citizen entitled to the rights of all other citizens, but what might happen when a social worker attempts to serve a citizen whose family includes undocumented immigrants? For example, a child born in the United States, and therefore a U.S. citizen, is referred to a school social worker. The child's parents are undocumented. The social worker sees that the family could benefit from help with grocery bills and health care. While the child may be entitled to governmental food and health benefits, the parents, who are undocumented, are not eligible. They want services for their child but fear that applying may expose them to authorities. How can the social worker serve this family? Legislation that has been proposed to the U.S. Congress would make it illegal to render nearly all types of help to undocumented immigrants. This would pose additional dilemmas for social workers, who frequently see undocumented individuals in schools, hospitals, church-sponsored programs, and many other settings.

Multiracial Individuals and Families

The U.S. population is becoming more diverse in yet another way. Biracial and multiracial individuals are becoming a more prominent part of the population as interracial marriages and relationships become more common. The U.S. Census Bureau now allows respondents to identify themselves on census forms as mixed race (biracial or multiracial). The terms *biracial* and *multiracial* are generally applied to individuals born to interracial or interethnic couples, though they may also be used to describe individuals born to intraracial couples (e.g., the child of a Chinese and Japanese couple can be multiethnic but monoracial).

Historically, the white community, and sometimes communities of color, shunned individuals of mixed race because of the threat to hegemony (the domination of one group by another) (Dhooper & Moore, 2001). Winters and DeBose (2003) address the dilemmas that biracial and multiracial people face as they seek self-definition and validation, though today many individuals of mixed race take pride in their multiple-ethnic heritages. With regard to social work practice, Fong (2005) writes about the need to do biological, psychological, social, and cultural assessments that acknowledge that a person of mixed races may have experiences that individuals of a single race do not share. Box 4.5 presents a case example of turmoil in the life a biracial gay youth. Social workers generally clarify with mixed-race

---

Box 4.5   Case Example of a Biracial Gay Youth

Twenty-year-old José grew up in a biracial family with a Spanish-speaking Mexican father and a second-generation Chinese mother. The oldest of three children, José is aware of his mother's expectations that he be a good Asian son and honor the ancestors because he is male. His father's cultural value of machismo also dictates that as a male, he provide for and protect the family. While both cultural values of filial piety and machismo prescribe what a male is to do and how he is to behave in the Asian and Mexican cultures, José feels caught because he is not pleasing either parent. He is feeling a lot of pressure to do better and not make his family "lose face."

José wants to come out and tell his family he is gay but fears their ridicule, scorn, and possible rejection. He feels he can't share this with his mother because in the Asian culture males are suppose to have sons to carry on the family name and honor the ancestors. His Asian family members would be distressed because as a gay person he would not have male heirs. Although he is biracial, his mother still expects him to closely follow Asian cultural values and practices. On his father's side, his Mexican relatives have always made fun of his mannerisms and interests and have said he does not display machismo or follow traditional male gender roles. He dares not tell any family members about his boyfriend, with whom he has had a relationship for the past three years while away at college.

A college friend has been seeing a social worker at the counseling center at the college they attend and encourages José to see him. José makes an appointment and confides that he is gay. He seeks understanding of his situation and advice on how to handle the pressures he feels from his family. Based on the principles of culturally competent social work practice, how do you think the social worker will help José resolve his dilemma?

clients how they self-identify and the kinds of social supports they have that validate their ethnic identification.

CULTURALLY COMPETENT PRACTICE PRINCIPLES

Culturally competent practice focuses on values, knowledge, and skills that are grounded in social workers' examinations of their own cultural awareness. Students enrolled in social work degree programs spend a considerable amount of time studying cultural content and are asked to take stock of their attitudes toward their own cultural group and the cultures of others.

As this chapter emphasizes, social workers who practice in culturally competent ways assess clients' strengths, cultural values, and contexts and combine Western and indigenous treatments in treatment planning and implementation. In doing so, social workers consider three primary elements: the client in the context of family and community, similarities and differences in the client's cultural values and broader societal values, and the client's cultural values as strengths.

Every individual is part of some type of family constellation and a community whose cultural norms and pressures frequently override the individual's needs and desires. Client assessment therefore generally includes consideration of the family's functioning. In assessing clients of color or those with strong ethnic and cultural identities, it is also important to assess their involvement with the ethnic community. Even if the client is estranged from family members, has no remaining family members, or is the only family member residing in the United States, there is still usually some affiliation with the ethnic community. In some cases, social workers help clients strengthen ties to their ethnic community. For example, those American Indians who have little knowledge of their tribe's or tribes' language or customs may find it useful to connect or reconnect with their cultural heritage. A number of substance abuse prevention programs on reservations and in other communities help American Indian youths learn how tribal values and culture can lead them to happier, healthier, and more productive lives. In African American communities, Afrocentric values and traditions are used to achieve the same ends.

Every ethnic group has particular cultural values that social workers must consider. For example, Christmas and Easter are widely celebrated Christian holidays. While it is useful for schoolchildren to learn about many cultural traditions, school social workers who support a teacher's mandate that all students participate in class celebrations of these holidays may be doing an injustice to Muslims, Jews, and people of other faiths.

Clients of various ethnic groups routinely depend on indigenous interventions such as the services of native healers and religious practices, which are part of their resources or support systems. Indigenous interventions should be included in the treatment plan whenever appropriate for the client. Practitioners of Western interventions have frequently monopolized treatment planning and excluded bicultural interventions or assumed that Western interventions should be dominant, and indigenous interventions secondary. For example, American Indians may prefer the use of vision quests, sweat lodges, or other purification rituals to the "Minnesota model" inpatient alcoholism rehabilitation treatment programs typically used in the United States, where group therapy is the main form of treatment, or twelve-step programs like Alcoholics Anonymous, where the Our Father is recited and emphasis is placed on admitting in meetings that one is an alcoholic. Others may wish to use both these indigenous and Western interventions.

If a client is Latino, the assessment stage would surely require the social worker to identify his or her personal, family, and community strengths. This approach assumes that the client has strengths that stem from Latino culture, such as *compradazgo* (fictive kin, i.e., those who are not blood relatives but are considered family members) whose support can be counted on (Zuniga, 2004). Some assessment of level of acculturation is also necessary if the client is foreign born or if the family has not been in the United States for many generations. As families reside in the United States for increased generations, they may become removed from their ancestors' cultural traditions and values. Under those circumstances, personal strengths may be individualized and not as vigorously intertwined with traditional cultural values.

A further consideration for clients who have grown up in the United States is that they may themselves be quite acculturated but have immigrant relatives who live with them or influence how the extended family functions. These social contexts and environments affect both the individual's and family's functioning. Working with clients who are different from you, with different customs, attitudes, and beliefs, requires knowledge about where and how they grew up. What were their ethnic communities like? How did the social environment of the larger ethnic community influence how the individual or family client system functions? These are the types of questions a culturally competent social worker would ask the client.

It is unlikely that anyone doing social work or thinking about becoming a social worker would be thoroughly informed of and proficient in the interventions or treatments that are indigenous, familiar, and ethnically relevant to every client. Often treatments based on a Western, Americanized philosophy of helping and problem solving are recommended without regard for cultural practices. Good social work incorporates elements of the approach of the client's ethnic community. For instance, Asian medicine like acupuncture and herbal remedies has become popular among Americans, but for some traditional Asian clients, acupuncture would not be just one option but would be the preferred method of treatment.

Sometimes the illnesses clients present are unfamiliar to Westerners. For example, Mexicans or Mexican Americans may present with *susto*, an ethno-specific illness caused by a frightening experience in which the soul is thought to leave the body. Indigenous healers and rituals may be needed to cure the client.

Culturally competent social work practitioners should have solid knowledge of a client's community, both locally and nationally. Knowing the community's size, its past, and the historical and contemporary issues that have marked the community's experience in its homeland and in the United States is important for being accepted and respected and for working effectively with the ethnic population.

CHALLENGES AND OPPORTUNITIES FOR SOCIAL WORKERS

Some issues that arise in culturally competent practice are old, and some are new. The old ones are related to the new ones—racism and discrimination continue to be problems. However, some have intensified since the September 11, 2001, bombing of the World Trade Center and the Pentagon. The threat of terrorism has heightened tensions about who does and does not belong in the United States and who is a threat to public safety.

As the U.S. government considers how to address immigration—both legal and illegal—debate about how these individuals should be treated in the social service arena has intensified. Since government resources are finite, social workers are forced to examine their own moral and ethical positions on immigration and to determine what policies will result in fair treatment of immigrants, refugees, and asylees.

In working with non-English-speaking clients, social workers often use the services of interpreters. Problems can occur when the client's language is not widely spoken in the United States. Just finding an able interpreter poses obstacles. In addition, relaying highly personal or complicated material through an interpreter can be difficult. For example, when victims of human trafficking are discovered, interpreters may need to be located quickly to determine what has happened. Many of these victims expected a safe trip to America only to experience a harrowing journey after having paid their fee, which has often cost them dearly. They may have even expected to receive a visa and a legal job upon entering the United States. Upon arrival, many are told that the passage money was insufficient and are forced into unwanted jobs or situations without hope of relief or release. In other cases, husbands or fiancés bring women to the United States and then abuse them. These women may fear deportation and fail to call the police. Social workers get involved in many of these cases and may help individuals in these situations find resources and avoid deportation, perhaps under provisions of the Violence Against Women Act.

While the challenge to understanding cross-cultural issues and advocating for oppressed and marginalized populations is sometimes daunting, social workers reap many rewards. Below are some examples:

- In working with immigrants and refugees, especially those who have just arrived and need a great deal of help, social workers provide essential services and significantly influence the futures of those who may have few other resources and alternatives. Just imagine how much you would appreciate the help of a capable social worker if you had just taken up residence in a new land where you did not speak the language, knew no one, and had little or no money.
- By working with various ethnic groups, social workers acquire new knowledge, values, and skills and learn about many cultures.
- Social workers have the opportunity to challenge their own sensitivity and competence in working with clients from backgrounds different from their own.
- Social workers can engage in cross-disciplinary and international social work with opportunities to network and arrange creative multicultural collaborations.
- Social workers working with an international population learn about cross-cultural protocols and improve their verbal and nonverbal communications skills.
- Since many people of color experience racism, social workers in the United States have many opportunities to utilize their advocacy and political action skills to fight against oppression and social and economic injustices.

Most enduring, though, are the intrinsic rewards. As a social worker working with immigrants, it would not be uncommon for you to sit in an audience with a client's family as they wait to learn if their loved one has passed the naturalized citizenship test. You listen with the others to hear the name of your client, Mrs. Ramirez. At the announcement that she has passed, a thunder of applause erupts because Mrs. Ramirez is sixty-five years old, and her family desperately wants her to be able to remain with them in the United States. As a social worker, you have learned a great deal about Mrs. Ramirez's culture and you played a significant role in her citizenship by helping her find English-language tutors and transportation to practice test sessions over the past six months. The family hugs you and invites you to their home for a family meal next Saturday night. You arrive and are greeted like a dignitary and patted on the back, the recipient of smiles and more warm embraces. You know how grateful the family is to you for helping their mother remain in the United States without fear of being deported—what's more, Mrs. Ramirez is now very proud to be a real American. She looks forward to voting in the next presidential election.

FUTURE DIRECTIONS

As the U.S. population becomes more culturally diverse, social workers will be required to be more knowledgeable about clients' cultural backgrounds, since cultural competence will increasingly be a part of social workers' education and more emphasis will be placed on knowledge of culturally diverse human behaviors and social environments. South Asians, for instance, are a growing population, and social workers need to know the differences between Muslims and Hindus and their regional cultures. Those working with Hispanics will be expected to differentiate among the situations of Cubans, Puerto Ricans, and other populations with origins south of the U.S. border.

Labels that imply weakness, such as *ethnic minority* or *refugee*, will fall into disuse because they too easily obscure clients' strengths. More effort will be made to appreciate and utilize cultural values as strengths in assessments and indigenous approaches in treatment planning. Social workers will more fully embrace strengths-based and client-focused interventions, like solution-focused therapy—helping clients determine how they coped successfully before problems developed. Solutions come from within clients, and the social worker's role is to help clients find those solutions. This kind of therapy is very compatible with the emphasis on client strengths based on cultural values and the biculturalization of interventions.

SUMMARY

Culturally competent practice has evolved over the past thirty-five years to become increasingly client, context, and indigenously focused because of the complexities of the nation's population and the treatments needed to serve the myriad constituents. Social workers are called upon to be self-aware and strengths and solution focused with an emphasis on the client's cultural values and indigenous treatments. Working with people of racial and ethnic groups different from one's own is inevitable, given that the United States is becoming an increasingly multicultural society. This work offers the committed social worker the promise of extraordinary challenge, opportunity, and reward.

SUGGESTED READING

Fong, R., & Furuto, S. (Eds.). (2001). *Culturally competent practice: Skills, interventions, and evaluations.* Boston: Allyn and Bacon. This book is a compilation of writings about skills, interventions, and evaluations of culturally competent practices with Asian American, African American, Native Americans/First Nations people, and Latino/Mexican American individuals, families, groups, communities, and organizations.

Lum, D. (Ed.). (2005). *Cultural competence, practice stages, and client systems: A case study approach*. Belmont, CA: Brooks/Cole. This book suggests a culturally competent framework based on client intersectional systems. It has chapters on practice with First Nations people; African Americans; Latino Americans; Asian Americans; multiracial/multiethnic clients; women of color; lesbian, gay, bisexual, and transgender people; immigrants and refugees; people with disabilities; and older adults of color.

McGoldrick, M., Giordano, J., & Garcia-Preto, N. (Eds.). (2005). *Ethnicity and family therapy* (3rd ed.). New York: Guilford Press. This book discusses family therapy with white, Asian, African, Mexican and Latino, and native families.

THE WORLD WIDE WEB OF SOCIAL WORK

Association of Multiethnic Americans http://ameasite.org

AMEA is an international organization dedicated to advocacy, education, and collaboration on behalf of the multiethnic, multiracial, and transracial adoption community. Most of its activities occur at the local level.

Bridging Refugee Youth and Children's Services http://www.brycs.org

BRYCS is a national technical assistance project facilitating information sharing and collaboration among a diverse group of service providers, including child welfare, health and mental health, juvenile justice, education, refugee-serving, and refugee community agencies, in order to improve services to refugee youths, children, and their families.

National Latino Behavioral Health Association http://www.nlbha.org

NLBHA's mission is to provide national leadership for the advancement of Latino behavioral health services and to bring attention to the great disparities that exist in areas of access, utilization, practice-based research, and adequately trained personnel.

National Indian Child Welfare Association http://www.nicwa.org

NICWA provides public policy, research, and advocacy; information and training on Indian child welfare; and community development services to a broad national audience including tribal governments and programs, state child welfare agencies, and other organizations, agencies, and professionals interested in the field of Indian child welfare.

National Research Center on Asian American Mental Health
http://psychology.ucdavis.edu/nrcaamh

NRCAAMH was established in 1988 with a grant from the National Institute of Mental Health. The center aims to contribute theoretical and applied research that will have a valuable impact on mental health policy and service delivery to Asian Pacific Americans.

5 | Gender and Social Work Practice

Beverly Black and Janet M. Joiner

Issues that are unique to women arise in every setting in which social workers practice, but some agencies and programs have been developed specifically to address women's needs. These include women's advocacy organizations, women's shelters, rape crisis centers, women's health centers, women's fitness centers, and family service agencies. Social workers in these settings provide a variety of services, including counseling, therapy, education, advocacy, and case management, to meet women's needs and maximize their strengths. It should not be surprising that social work, a profession made up of so many women, is committed to gender equality. This chapter addresses issues that inhibit gender equality and approaches that social workers use to promote equality for women and men and bring an end to sexism and gender discrimination.

SOCIAL CONSTRUCTION OF GENDER

Jahquan and Jillian just celebrated their fifth birthday. The twins play on the floor in the family's living room. Jahquan pushes the new fire engine he got for this birthday. He wants his mother to read him his book about becoming a firefighter. After hearing the story, Jahquan builds a tower with his blocks. Jillian cradles the new doll she was given. She pretends to feed and bathe the baby doll. Jillian takes one of Jahquan's blocks and pretends it is food she is cooking on the stove of her kitchen set.

Jahquan's sex as a male and Jillian's sex as a female were determined at birth based on their genitalia. The twins' genders have been constructed gradually, consciously and unconsciously, over their five years of life. Gender and sex are not the same. Sex is biologically determined; gender is socially constructed. Gender is related to society's definition of what it means to be a male or female; it is created and re-created out of human interactions and the society in which we live (Lorber, 2000). Gendered patterns begin early in life. Adults interact with babies in a manner that enables others to infer their sex. Jahquan's and Jillian's sex categories became their gender status through their names, the clothing they wear, the toys they play with, their activities, and the relationships they form with others.

Although definitions of gender vary, gender can be viewed as a person's socially constructed identity along a culturally defined continuum of masculinity and femininity. Gender roles also vary over time. Male and female roles are very different today from what they were just fifty years ago. In the 1930s, only one-fourth of women worked for pay; today half of women work for pay (Institute of Management and Administration, 2003). Fathers have become more active in the care of their children and increasingly share in household chores. However, there is much variation in gender roles within and between cultural groups in the United States. African American women have historically worked outside the home. In many Mexican American communities, females are permitted to venture outside the home in only limited ways, while males are permitted much greater freedom (Ramirez, 1998).

There is also a great deal of variation in gender roles around the world, and these roles are changing as well. Although women in Saudi Arabia are still not permitted to drive, they are now issued ID cards and have the right to interact with other women on the Internet (Upadhyay, 1999). Few women in Arab countries are formally employed in the labor force; however, many women perform unpaid work in agriculture or family-owned businesses. In contrast, women in most developed countries work outside the home in large numbers. The rates of working women in China and Russia even top those in the United States (Beisie, 2000). Social workers in the United States are increasingly paying attention to the situations of women all over the globe and recognize that women everywhere can help each other.

Gender roles serve both social and economic functions. Socially, gender provides an organizing framework in which we operate and live our lives (Lorber, 2000). When an individual's gender is unclear due to unisex attire or an ambiguous hairstyle, we might be uncomfortable if we feel we are missing vital information needed to relate effectively to that individual. Gender also serves economic purposes. Historically, women were encouraged to join the workforce when they were needed—for example, during wartime—and asked to exit the workforce when men needed jobs. Nations also emphasize gender roles when they wish to increase or decrease their population for economic growth. Particularly important from an economic standpoint is that much of the work women contribute to society—from child care to elder care—is vital but low paid or not paid at all. Social workers are very concerned about how gender affects human well-being. This information affects how social workers work with individuals, couples, families, communities, and larger social systems.

SEXISM

Sexism is discrimination, prejudice, or stereotypes based on sex or gender. Sexism's negative effects are manifested through attitudes, behaviors, laws, and policies that disproportionately affect women. Sexism maintains the current social construction of gender and exists in a variety of forms in all societies. The social work profession is committed to ending sexism and all forms of discrimination, and social work education is committed to preparing students to practice social work free of sexism (National Association of Social Workers, 2005). Various mechanisms in society contribute to the preservation of sexism. For example, pornography explicitly perpetuates sexism, while the media more subtly perpetuates sexism.

Pornography

Pornography is a multibillion-dollar industry primarily targeted at males. Pornography generally depicts women in demeaning and degrading positions, enjoying passivity, victimization, and pain, and incapable of being independent and assertive. These negative images of women influence the way men see and relate to women. Although many men deny that pornography negatively affects their relationships with women, repeated exposure to pornography can condition men to treat women as sexual objects rather than as whole, unique, complex, and intelligent individuals (Katz, 2000). The right to free speech protects pornography depicting adult subjects, though community standards are used to define what constitutes obscenity.

The relationship between pornography and sexual violence is a subject of debate. In 1985, the Attorney General's Commission on Pornography announced that both clinical and experimental research showed a causal relationship between men's exposure to pornographic material and aggression toward women. Kernsmith and Kernsmith (2005) found that females' use of pornography was positively related to sexual coercion, extortion/bargaining, sweet talk, and emotional manipulation, but not to physical force or intimidation. While pornography is associated with sexually coercive behaviors for both genders, only men's use of pornography is linked to sexual violence. Social workers help women and men address the negative effects of this violence.

Media

The media perpetuates women's inequality in ways that are often not obvious to most viewers. For example, the $180 billion advertising industry promotes gender stereotyping that is especially harmful to women. Average Americans spend three years of their lives watching TV commercials and see about 3,000 advertisements each day (Green, 1999). Despite improvements over the last couple of decades, women are more likely to be portrayed in passive, frivolous, and degrading roles, while men are more likely to be portrayed in active, strong, and domineering roles. Artz, Munger, and Purdy's study (1999) of advertisements found that male characters were twice as likely as female characters to be portrayed as employed outside the home. Hansen and Osborne (1995), who studied sexism in drug advertisements, found that females are twice as likely as males to suffer from depression, but that five times as many antidepressant ads in the *American Journal of Psychiatry* depict females as they do men.

One of the most damaging consequences of the negative portrayal of women in the media and advertisements is the poor body image that females of all ages have. Body image is an especially important issue for female adolescents. Girls tend to be less satisfied with and more critical of their physical appearance than boys; 85 percent of girls express concern about their weight, compared to 30 percent of boys (Newman & Newman, 1999). It should be no surprise that girls make up the vast majority of those with eating disorders. Ninety percent of individuals with anorexia nervosa and bulimia nervosa are females (American Psychiatric Association, 2000). Some social workers specialize in treating women with eating disorders, and social workers should be proactive in assessing clients', especially female clients', views of their bodies to prevent eating disorders or intervene early.

WORKING TO END SEXISM

Ending sexism will take the effort of many and must occur on several different levels. On the individual level, social workers can actively challenge the attitudes, comments, and behaviors of clients and colleagues that suggest males must always be strong and that females are naturally more nurturing than males. They can encourage males and females to express themselves as androgynous whole human beings, rather than adhere to restrictive traditional male and female roles, and to challenge sexist images of females in the media and advertising. Social workers can also encourage fathers to become equal parenting partners. Children who grow up seeing nurturing men (and women) and successful women (and men) will no longer have to categorize their human qualities as masculine or feminine (Steinem, 2000).

It is important for social workers to model the use of nonsexist language. In using words that are inclusive of both men and women, social workers recognize the influence and power of language. Rather than saying *mankind*, social workers often prefer the word *humankind*. Men are usually called *Mr.*, which does not connote marital status. Women are often called *Mrs.* or *Miss,* titles that announce whether or not they are married. Calling women *Ms.* eliminates this categorization and can reduce stereotyping. Social workers must also be at the forefront of challenging and interrupting sexist remarks and jokes that reinforce stereotypes about women. These jokes and remarks are hurtful, not funny. Social workers must also recognize the interrelatedness of all forms of oppression and speak out against them. For example, homophobia is a key mechanism used to maintain sexism. The sexual orientation of individuals—both men and women—who speak out against sexism or homophobia is often challenged.

On the macro level, social workers must confront discriminatory laws, regulations, and practices. Social workers advocate and lobby for laws that provide harsher penalties for the perpetration of violence against women and other forms of oppression and discrimination, like violations of the Equal Pay Act. Social workers can initiate campaigns to support businesses that do not engage in discrimination and have pro-family policies, and they can invest in companies that have fair hiring practices and in which women are fairly represented in managerial positions. Social workers are sometimes involved in more controversial practices of organizing boycotts of businesses known to be sexist or discriminatory. Ending sexism will take concerted individual and group efforts. Social workers are an important part of this effort (see box 5.1).

Box 5.1   Advocating Gender Equality

Social workers use their advocacy and political skills to advance women's status in society and eliminate gender discrimination. One way the National Association of Social Workers does this is through its educational and lobbying efforts on Capitol Hill. NASW also supports political candidates and public appointees who support women's issues and gender equality and opposes those who do not. Another mechanism NASW uses is amicus curiae, or "friend-of-the-court," briefs, in which a party or organization interested in an issue files a document with the court even though it is not a litigant in the case being considered. The brief may offer additional information the organization or party wishes to have considered. For example, in 2005, NASW and its Pennsylvania chapter joined an amicus curiae brief in support of young people's right to reproductive health services and contraception without parental involvement. In 2005, NASW also filed a brief involving Title IX of the Education Act Amendments of 1972 to the Civil Rights Act of 1964. The Civil Rights Act prohibits sex discrimination in educational institutions receiving federal funds. Title IX applies specifically to athletics and requires that girls and women have equal access to athletic programs, scholarships, coaching, equipment, facilities, and other resources. Many people believe that the goals of Title IX have never been realized. The brief supported a high school basketball coach in Birmingham, Alabama, who argued that he was removed from his position as coach in retaliation for complaining about sex discrimination—that is, that the girls' basketball team was not being treated equally with regard to funding, facilities, and equipment. The U.S. Supreme Court ruled 5–4 that Jackson could bring a retaliation suit under Title IX.

Source: National Association of Social Workers. (2005). *Decision favorable in Title IX case*. Retrieved on November 15, 2005, from http://www.socialworkers.org/pubs/news/2005/06/titleix.asp

WORKING WITH WOMEN

Throughout history, women across the world have been disproportionately affected by poverty, economic discrimination, inadequate mental and physical health care, infringement on reproductive rights, and domestic and sexual violence. Remedying these situations is an important part of the work of social workers.

Poverty and Economic Discrimination

Women in the United States are more likely than men to be poor. In 2004, nearly 13 percent of women and 10 percent of men ages eighteen to sixty-four lived in poverty, and 12 percent of women and 7 percent of men over sixty-four lived in poverty (U.S. Census Bureau, 2004). Female-headed households make up most of the nation's poor, and the gap between female-headed households and married-couple households is widening. Women who are separated, divorced, or widowed are at especially high risk of living in poverty. Many parents fail to make the child support payments ordered by the court. Of all mothers who did not live with their child's father in 2003, 77 percent received a child support payment, and only 45 percent received everything due (U.S. Census Bureau, 2006). As chapter 13 discusses in greater detail, lack of economic resources is associated with many social problems, including mental and physical illness. Social workers play important roles in assisting women and children living in poverty by advocating policy reform in welfare legislation and child support laws.

One reason more women than men live in poverty is economic discrimination. In the United States, women earn about 76 percent of what men earn (U.S. Census Bureau, 2005). College-educated women earn only 72 percent as much as college-educated men, and women of color earn significantly less. The gap between men's and women's earnings has remained about the same over the last twenty years. Sex discrimination in the workforce can be both subtle and overt (Swim & Cohen, 1997). Employers' negative responses to requests for pregnancy and maternity leaves are often signs of discrimination. Because family responsibilities often disrupt their job or career tracks, women receive lower wages and occupy lower-status jobs. So-called glass ceilings prevent women from advancing to higher levels of financial remuneration and power, and glass walls limit their access to particular professional specialties and higher-paying blue-collar jobs (Landrine & Klonoff, 1997). The military still prohibits women from occupying some positions—ones that are often high paying and important steps for career advancement. About one-third of positions in the U.S. Army and the Marine Corps are still not open to women, and only about 15 percent of army and navy officers are women (Women's Research and Education Institute, n.d.).

Social workers often work with women who have experienced workforce discrimination and listen to their anger and frustration. In addition to advocating changes in law and policies that prohibit workforce discrimination and promote economic equality, social workers have formed partnerships with women's organizations to pressure businesses to pay employees based on the amount of education required, years of experience, and levels of skill and risk needed to perform each job satisfactorily. Though paying women equally would have repercussions for the U.S. economy, social workers believe that women deserve to be paid fairly and that society must take steps to achieve this goal.

Mental and Physical Health Care

An understanding of the relationship between health problems and economic problems is important in social workers' work with women. The lack of economic resources can lead to or aggravate health problems, and health problems can deplete economic and social resources and leave women in dire straits. Although these factors also affect men, women's higher risk for economic discrimination can create greater challenges in addressing physical and mental health problems.

This chapter has noted that twice as many women as men in the United States are depressed, and this holds true across racial and ethnic backgrounds and economic status. The same ratio has been reported in ten other countries (National Institute of Mental Health, 2000). In addition, low-income women are twice as likely as higher-income women to be depressed. Depression and mental health problems often lead to low-paying jobs and job loss. Since women are often relegated to lower-level jobs, their employers are less willing to hold their jobs for them after absences related to physical or mental health problems. Mental health problems also lead to physical health problems for women. Women with mental health problems frequently fail to adhere to medical regimes and access the health-care services they need, especially prenatal care.

As chapters 1 and 7 indicate, many social workers provide mental health services. While depression is one of the most common reasons women seek mental health services, social workers must identify gender bias in the recognition and treatment of depression and other mental health problems. Primary-care physicians are more likely to diagnose women with depression than men who report similar levels of symptoms (Bertakis, Helms, Callahan, Azari, Leigh, & Robbins, 2001). Social workers recognize that gender socialization may be one of the reasons why women are more likely to be diagnosed with depression than men. Social workers in mental health settings must be particularly cautious in distinguishing between a woman's reasonable response to environmental stressors and clinical symptoms of depression.

Though traditionally fewer women than men are diagnosed with substance abuse and dependence, the gap has been closing in younger age groups (Davis & DiNitto, 2005). Women may find it especially difficult to access treatment for alcohol and drug problems because of child-care responsibilities. Many outpatient programs do not offer child care, and residential programs generally do not allow mothers to bring their children with them, nor do they usually accept pregnant women, for fear of liability issues. Women more often than men find themselves in difficult situations due to a spouse or partner's alcohol or drug problems.

Physical health-care issues also differ for men and women. Although women live longer than men, women have more physical illnesses and use more medications (Kasle, Wilhelm, & Reed, 2002). Heart disease is a leading cause of death for both men and women in the United States, but women are less likely to receive an accurate diagnosis of heart disease and aggressive treatment. Two challenges that many women face in relation to their health are increasing their physical exercise and preventing obesity. Social workers educate clients about these issues and help them engage in healthier lifestyles.

Reproductive Rights

Abortion became illegal in the United States in the mid- to late 1800s, after which states rarely permitted abortion except when the mother's life was in danger. Women often made desperate and dangerous attempts to induce their own abortions or sought help from untrained individuals to terminate their pregnancies. In countries where it is still illegal, abortion is the leading cause of death among pregnant women. An estimated 68,000 women die each year from unsafe abortions (World Health Organization, 2005).

In 1973, the U.S. Supreme Court changed the abortion policy in the United States. In its landmark *Roe v. Wade* decision, the court ruled that the right to privacy extended to the decision of a woman, in consultation with her physician, to terminate her pregnancy. After *Roe v. Wade*, the number of legal induced abortions in the United Stated increased until 1990. The introduction of numerous regulations and restrictions on abortions at both the state and federal levels led to a gradual decline in the number of abortions between 1990 and 1997. From 1998 to 2003, the abortion rate remained relatively constant (Center for Disease Control, 2006). For example, some states have enacted a mandatory waiting period, which many view as an effort to restrict abortions. Women are required to wait anywhere from eight to twenty-seven hours after their first appointment before an abortion can be performed. Such restrictions present a hardship for women, especially low-income women who must take time from work or travel long distances to obtain an abortion. In rural communities, access to abortions can be limited because there are few abortion providers. Social workers may be asked to assist women in locating abortion providers and finding the resources for low-income women to obtain abortion services.

About one million American teenagers become pregnant each year, and about 35 percent of them choose to have an abortion (National Abortion Federation, 2003). Social workers play a critical role in working with pregnant teens who are experiencing increasing restrictions on their access to abortions. Parental notification laws require medical personnel to notify a minor's parent of her intention to obtain an abortion, and parental consent laws require medical personnel to obtain written permission from the parents before performing an abortion. Laws in forty-six states allow mothers who are under eighteen to relinquish their child for adoption without involving their parents, but many of those states require parental notification or consent for an abortion. Social workers can assist teens in making the difficult decision whether to seek an abortion or place their child for adoption. They can also assist teens in talking with their parents about their pregnancy and their decision about the pregnancy. A policy statement of the National Association of Social Workers (2003) affirms the organization's commitment to making abortions accessible to all women, but not every social worker holds this value. The social work principle of client self-determination calls on social workers who are not pro-choice to put their personal views aside since abortion is legal in the United States. Some social workers, including some who believe in the right to choose, work for religiously affiliated agencies that oppose abortion. In these cases, social workers are obligated to refer clients who desire information about abortion or abortion services to agencies that can help them.

Violence Against Women

Social workers were involved in the early days of the battered women's movement and remain active in shelters for battered women and rape crisis centers across the country. This section addresses several types of violence: domestic violence, dating violence, sexual assault, sexual harassment, and stalking. Males are also victims of these acts of violence, but victims are overwhelmingly female. The language used to discuss violence against women is often controversial itself. Wife beating and wife battering are now called spousal abuse, domestic violence, and family violence. Rape is now referred to as sexual assault. The renaming of violent acts against women in recent decades has generalized the phenomenon of violence directed at women and has masked the fact that most victims are women.

Domestic Violence Conservatively speaking, 22 percent of women in the United States will experience domestic violence during their lifetimes (Tjaden & Thoennes, 2000). The FBI estimates that a woman is beaten, raped, or abused by her husband every seventeen seconds (Cho, 1996). Although domestic violence can affect men, 95 percent of heterosexual victims of spousal abuse are women (Letellier, 1996). Immigrant women may experience domestic violence at high rates; a coalition for immigrant and refugee rights and services found that 25 percent of Filipinas and 35 percent of Latinas are victims of spousal abuse (Cho, 1996). Most domestic violence research focuses on white, poor, and heterosexual women; social workers must be cautious in generalizing this research to women of other races, ethnicities, socioeconomic classes, and sexual orientations (Bent-Goodley, 2005).

Social workers employed in family service settings, mental health treatment settings, and child welfare agencies see many domestic violence victims. Recognizing that women may remain in violent relationships because they fear that they cannot support themselves and their children, social workers help women develop safety plans and options that will allow them to escape the violence. Psychological abuse generally accompanies physical abuse. Over a period of time, the battered woman begins to believe she is at fault and has little value. Many battered women also fear that leaving

Domestic violence causes both physical and psychological harm; social workers often intervene to help victims of abuse leave violent relationships.
© Jeff Smith/Alamy

will result in further abuse and may endanger their children. Evidence indicates that leaving may increase the risk of harm. The abuser may stalk the woman and even try to kill her.

Social workers serving victims of domestic violence are at risk for vicarious trauma (trauma experienced from working with individuals who have suffered terrible experiences) (Iliffe & Steed, 2000) or other long-term psychological effects. Working with people whose victimization is human induced, premeditated, chronic, and progressive (all of which may characterize domestic violence) is especially difficult (Courtois, 1993). Effective social work practice with victims of abuse requires both knowledge of domestic violence and a repertoire of professional coping strategies. Social workers must make time for themselves, and they need support and consultation from colleagues to deal with vicarious trauma and maintain perspective on their work.

Today all states have some type of legislation to protect victims of domestic violence. Although there is no uniform federal legislation for legal intervention in cases of abuse, Congress passed the Violence Against Women Act in 1994, recognizing the extent of violence against women in the United States. It established penalties for offenders and provides funding for programs to reduce domestic violence. Social workers often make up a large proportion of the staff in the more than 2,000 domestic violence shelters across the country, which offer short-term housing, counseling for women and their children, and job placement services (see box 5.2). Most shelters are unable to meet the demand for housing. In communities without shelters (often rural areas), social workers may work with motels or community residents willing to temporarily house domestic violence victims. Anticipating the length of time it takes women to start a new life, some programs provide transitional housing for women (e.g., apartments, group living arrangements).

Dating Violence Violence or the threat of violence in interpersonal relationships has emerged as a significant social problem and public health concern, and one to which American youths are especially vulnerable. Studies suggest that about one-third of high school students experience dating violence (Molidor & Tolman, 1998). Dating violence occurs among youths of all racial and ethnic backgrounds. Being a perpetrator and being a victim are often correlated. Youths who perpetrate dating violence are also often victimized by dating violence (Black & Weisz, 2003). Girls are particularly at high risk of victimization, as they are more likely than boys to experience emotional or physical injury from dating violence. Girls, in particular, fail to recognize the seriousness of the injuries and harm inflicted upon them, and their desire to have a dating partner may outweigh their health and safety concerns (Banister & Schreiber, 2001). Adolescents who

---

Box 5.2   Helping a Victim of Domestic Violence

Police were called to the house where Nancy, Mike, and their three children have been living with Mike's parents. Nancy had been punched in the face, and the couple's three young children were screaming and crying. Nancy said this was not the first time Mike had hit her. Mike was arrested. Nancy declined medical attention. She did not want to remain in her in-laws' home. A police officer asked if he could call the victim assistance unit for her. A victim assistance social worker arrived and, after talking with Nancy, arranged for her and the children to go to the local battered women's shelter. Nancy packed some clothes and a few toys for the children.

A social worker at the shelter talked with Nancy, got her and the children something to eat, and helped them get settled in a room. The social worker helped Nancy assess her options. She helped Nancy file for a restraining order, since she wanted no further contact with Mike. Nancy participated in the shelter's group and individual counseling sessions and educational sessions about the cycle of battering. Nancy had no job and no place to live in the community. She wanted to make a plan for herself and the children, but she was depressed and scared.

Mike got out of jail on bail. He found out from friends that Nancy was at the shelter. He began sending messages begging her to come home. Nancy was torn about what to do. She did not want Mike to hit her anymore, but he kept sending notes asking her to forgive him and promising he would change. Nancy struggled with whether to return to Mike or move out of state to her mother's home. Though the social worker had her own feelings about Nancy's situation, she kept the principle of client self-determination foremost in her mind. When Nancy decided to return to Mike, who had served a short jail sentence and was enrolled in a program for batterers, she helped Nancy consider ways to keep herself and the children safe should problems emerge. She also encouraged Nancy to continue participating in groups at the shelter and to get her GED.

---

experience dating violence are at increased risk for physical and psychological harm and serious health risk behaviors, including eating disorders, alcohol and drug use, and suicide (Callahan, Tolman, & Saunders, 2003).

Adolescents rarely seek help from social workers, parents, law enforcement, teachers, guidance counselors, or crisis lines. Instead, they turn to friends, who may inadvertently offer unhelpful and victim-blaming advice. To address this problem, domestic violence programs around the country have begun dating violence prevention programs in middle schools and high schools to reduce dating violence and provide resources for victims and perpetrators. Social workers play an integral role in the prevention programming offered in schools today (Weisz & Black, in press). Many colleges also offer education and prevention programs.

Sexual Assault   Sexual assault is another form of violence most often perpetrated against women. Rape and other forms of sexual assault can be defined as one person forcing or attempting to force another to engage in unwanted sexual activity. It includes touching or grabbing private body parts for sexual gratification. Rape and sexual assault are not just sex crimes; they are crimes of power and control in which sexual activity is used to dominate, humiliate, and hurt the victim. Many people think that the typical rapist is a stranger who randomly assaults a woman; however, more than 70 percent of rapes and sexual assaults are committed by someone the victim knows (Rape, Abuse and Incest National Network, 2006). Victims may endure greater psychological suffering when they know the perpetrator. Many victims are shocked and invariably hurt that someone they knew and/or cared about could have done something like this to them. They may begin to question their ability to judge and trust others. Male perpetrators of acquaintance or date rape often do not perceive the situation as rape. Reasons women are reluctant to report a rape include embarrassment, fear of revenge from the rapist, and concerns about poor treatment from the criminal justice system.

Based on data from the U.S. Department of Justice, the Rape, Abuse and Incest National Network (n.d.) estimates that in the United States a rape or sexual assault occurs every two-and-a-half minutes, and that one in six women and one in thirty-three men have been sexually assaulted. However, the actual incidence of sexual assault is unknown because most victims (more than 60%) never report the assault (Rape, Abuse and Incest National Network, 2006). Rates of sexual assault among college students are particularly alarming. According to Fisher and Cullen's (2000) nationally representative survey of 4,446 college female students, 15.5 percent had experienced some type of sexual victimization during a seven-month time interval, and 2.8 percent had experienced an attempted or completed rape. Among college men who acknowledge committing sexual assault, at least two-thirds have committed more than one assault (Zawacki, Abbey, Buck, McAuslan, & Clinton-Sherrod, 2003). Abbey and McAuslan (2004) surveyed 197 male college students and found that 35 percent had committed at least one sexual assault since the age of fourteen. Men who assaulted more than once were significantly more hostile toward women, consumed more alcohol in sexual situations, expressed less remorse, and held the woman more responsible for the assault than did men who committed only one assault. This type of information may help social workers design more effective prevention and intervention programs.

Social workers often work in rape crisis programs (see box 5.3). Those who counsel sexual assault victims help them understand that they are not to blame. Some counsel sexual assault perpetrators to help them take responsibility for their crimes or work with men to prevent sexual assault. Many social workers advocate changes in the laws addressing sexual violence, such as legislation that does not victimize rape victims further when they press charges against offenders.

Box 5.3   Developing a Community Task Force to Assist Sexual Assault Victims

Social workers and community members in a medium-size southeastern town developed a hotline and outreach program for rape victims, but they were frustrated because police and hospital personnel rarely called when they encountered rape victims. The social workers realized it would take time to develop a relationship with law enforcement and hospital personnel, who might be concerned that they would interfere with or criticize their work with victims. The social workers developed written materials describing the hotline and outreach services and mailed them to the police chief, sheriff, emergency department physicians and nurses, and the prosecutor's office. They followed up, asking to meet with these individuals to find out how they could help them in their work with rape victims. They explained that they could support victims who wished to report the crime and help them proceed through the stages of the legal process so that they would be less likely to drop the case.

They could also stay with the victim throughout the hospital rape exam and provide support so that hospital social workers could tend to other cases. They could bring clothes for the victim since the victim's clothes are generally kept as evidence, and they could transport her home or to another destination after the exam.

Eventually, the social workers won the trust of law enforcement and hospital personnel. Today, law enforcement and hospital protocols require that victims be asked if they would like the help of the rape crisis advocate. Victims who choose to speak with a rape crisis advocate are better apprised of the status of the case as it proceeds through the legal system. In addition, the rape crisis program organized a sexual assault task force, which meets monthly to discuss cases and how services to rape victims can be improved. Thanks to the social workers' community organization skills, victims are being better served by all the agencies involved.

Sexual Harassment   Many people think of sexual harassment as simply catcalls, suggestive whistles, and crude and annoying remarks. Today, sexual harassment is generally considered sexual advances or other conduct of a sexual nature that is unwelcome, hostile, offensive, or degrading. Like sexual assault, sexual harassment is used to control or degrade another person. It can substantially interfere with an individual's employment, education, or housing and can also have long-lasting psychological effects. Fineran and Bennett's study (1999) of sexual harassment among high school students found that an amazing 87 percent of girls and 79 percent of boys reported being targets of sexual harassment, and 77 percent of girls and 72 percent of boys reported perpetrating sexual harassment. Sexually harassing behaviors among adolescents generally include unwanted sexual jokes, comments, gestures, name-calling, written notes, and graffiti on lockers; antigay put-downs; pinching or grabbing; the spreading of sexual rumors; and sexual touching.

Sexual harassment can be quid pro quo harassment, in which a person in a position of power or authority demands sexual contact in exchange for a favor or the granting of a particular status. More commonly, it takes the form of hostile environment harassment, in which ongoing physical, verbal, or nonverbal conduct of a sexual nature creates an overall school or work climate that is offensive and intimidating. Social workers often serve as advocates for those victimized by sexual harassment at work or school. They help victims report the behavior, counsel those experiencing distress and trauma, and help them access resources to put an end to the behavior. Social workers employed in human resource departments may educate employees about sexual harassment as well as aid victims.

Stalking   Stalking is repeated or continuous harassment that causes a person to feel frightened, intimidated, threatened, harassed, terrorized, or molested. It is another form of violence primarily directed at women that often requires social work services to address psychological effects or meet safety needs. About three-quarters of stalking victims are women, while 87 percent of stalkers are men (Tjaden & Thoennes, 1998). Stalking occurs when the perpetrator continuously follows or appears within the sight of the victim, approaches the victim, or contacts the victim by phone, mail, or e-mail. College women are especially likely to be stalked. Fisher, Cullen, and Turner (2002) found that 13 percent of college women were stalked during a single period of six to nine months; 80 percent of the victims knew their stalkers. Over two-thirds of female murder victims were stalked by their assailant (McFarlane, 1999).

WORKING WITH MEN

Although many issues discussed in this chapter disproportionately affect women, some issues disproportionately affect men. Social workers often work with men who feel pressure to conform to the strong and macho stereotypes of masculinity and who narrowly measure their success as husbands and fathers by the amount of money they earn. Many social workers also work to change policies that discriminate against men, especially in the area of child custody.

As discussed at the beginning of the chapter, gender is socially constructed. Thus, what it means to be a man is socially constructed. For example, young boys are taught not to show their feelings. If a little boy is hurt and cries, he is often admonished not to cry "like a girl." When men express feelings, especially sad ones, they run the risk of being called feminine, which challenges their gender identity. The fear of being perceived as gay, as not a real man, encourages men to exaggerate traditional masculine traits

Although the majority of social work clients are women and children, men such as this homeless veteran also benefit from social work services.
© Janine Wiedel/Alamy

and expend time and energy trying to prove that they are not feminine, passive, weak, soft, or sensitive (Kimmel, 2000).

Around the world, men are known as the family breadwinners. A man's identity often derives from his work. A man who fails to provide financially for his family is deemed a failure. Although women face many financial pressures, society does not view women who cannot provide for their families as failures in the same way that it views men. Unemployment is often devastating for men. Men who cannot find work often feel worthless. Men also are less likely than women to seek professional help for their mental health concerns (Mansfield, Addis, & Courtenay, 2005). Social workers' awareness of and sensitivity to these issues enable them to work with men to overcome their reluctance to seek help and to address gender stereotyping (see box 5.4).

There is perhaps no place where men experience more discrimination than in child custody disputes. Mothers are the primary custodial parent in 85–90 percent of all divorces involving children (Stamps, 2002). Studies suggest that when child custody conflicts must be settled in court, judges prefer to grant custody to mothers, especially when there are younger chil-

---

Box 5.4   Dealing with Infertility

Brian and Beth have been married for seven years. They both want a child but decided to wait until they could purchase a home and get on solid financial footing. For two years they have been trying to conceive, but they have not yet been successful. Recognizing that there might be a fertility problem, Beth undergoes testing. When no abnormalities are found, Brian decides to be tested. He is shocked to find that his sperm quality is likely the reason that Beth has not gotten pregnant. Though Brian knows intellectually that his sperm quality is not an indicator of his masculinity, he is having trouble dealing with this news and with alternatives to the traditional means of conceiving a child. Beth is sympathetic to Brian's concerns but wants them to move beyond this and decide whether to use another means of conception or adopt.

As the months go by, Brian becomes less communicative with Beth, and they begin arguing over many small things. Beth is also feeling increasingly stressed and worries that their marriage in on the line. She wants to seek marital counseling. Brian is reluctant, but Beth insists. After talking with several licensed professionals on the phone, Beth and Brian select a social worker and go to see him. The social worker recognizes the effect infertility has had on Brian and suggests some individual sessions with Brian as well as couples counseling. The social worker provides supportive counseling to Brian and an opportunity for him to discuss his feelings about infertility and alternative ways of becoming a father. Brian has had no experience with social workers and is surprised that this social worker could identify his feelings and address his concerns so quickly. Beth and Brian's marriage is now on stronger footing. The social worker helped them map out a strategy to investigate all their alternatives for becoming parents. After learning about the many children languishing in foster care, they have decided to adopt.

---

dren involved (Stamps, 2002). Social workers are active in political action groups proposing legislation that would end discrimination against men in child custody cases. Social workers also lead support groups for men dealing with child custody issues.

GENDER ISSUES IN THE SOCIAL WORK PROFESSION

Social work is an exciting and challenging profession that has grown exponentially since its inception in the late nineteenth century. Like nursing and education, social work has attracted mostly women to its ranks, and increasingly so over the last forty years. Thus, many view social work as a profession for women only. Since most social workers are women, the profession faces many gender-related issues. Social workers must continue to address discrimination in the profession and at the same time increase the number of qualified males entering social work programs in the United States and other countries in order to diversify the profession and appeal to a broader range of constituents.

Discrimination in the Social Work Profession

Women in social work, like women in other professions, particularly female-dominated professions, face discrimination. Sex discrimination in social work first became an issue over thirty years ago, when Kravetz (1976) pointed out that female social workers were paid less than male social workers. The situation remains much the same today. A study conducted by NASW of male and female licensed social workers working full-time in a single job revealed that the women earn about $7,000 less per year than the men, even when factors such as age, highest degree, work experience, and practice area were taken into account (Clark, 2006).

Gender inequality is also evident in the positions male and female social workers occupy. Although fewer than 25 percent of all practicing social workers in the United States are men, they hold nearly half of all administrative and leadership positions in social work practice (Gibelman & Schervish, 1995). The gender gap in income is greater in administrative positions than in direct practice positions. In higher education, the proportion of women in faculty and administrative positions in schools and departments of social work has greatly increased over the last thirty years (DiPalma & Topper, 2001). In fact, more women than men are now employed as faculty members in schools of social work; however, women are more likely than men to hold lower academic ranks and to work at less prestigious institutions (Lie & O'Leary, 1990).

Traditional gender roles may still be apparent among social work students. Hyde and Deal (2003) explored student communication styles at one school of social work and found that female students displayed more stereotypical female behaviors, such as passivity and subjugation, than their male counterparts. Female students tended to defer to authority in discussion groups, while male students were more assertive. The male students felt, however, that they were "oppressed" as men because they were outnumbered by female students.

Recruiting Males into the Profession

While social work employment opportunities are expected to grow steadily, the profession is experiencing difficulty increasing its numbers as well as gender and ethnic diversity (Bowie & Hancock, 2001). Greater diversity will help social workers reach a broader cross-section of those in need of services. Many schools of social work make sincere efforts to recruit ethnic minority faculty and students. Few schools make explicit efforts to recruit male students. Discussions about strategies to increase the number of men in the profession have been virtually nonexistent, and there is little research relative to gender and social work practice. Some argue that the lack of research in these areas stems from a general lack of interest in bringing more males into the profession.

What would happen if more men entered the profession? Would salaries and prestige increase for all social workers, or would women experience even greater economic discrimination than they currently face? Would men secure the majority of high-level administrative positions? Would the profession maintain its commitment to gender equality? Social work students have traditionally been a somewhat homogeneous population of white, middle-class females. The challenge to enlarge and diversify the profession economically, socially, and ethnically may rest in part on the profession's ability to increase the number of male social workers.

FEMINIST SOCIAL WORK PRACTICE

When one of the authors of this chapter asks students to raise their hands if they are "feminist," generally two or three hands slowly rise. Asked why they do not consider themselves feminists, students frequently say, "I'm not one of those radicals who hates men."

What is feminism? Most people only have a vague, often-distorted notion of what feminism is. Few realize that males can be feminists. Succinctly put, feminism is the belief that men and women should have equal rights. Feminists are those who work to eliminate discrimination and oppression of women and promote equality between men and women. Many people are surprised by these definitions, and although they support equal rights for women, they do not consider themselves feminists. Feminist bell hooks (2000) expands on the definition of feminism:

> Feminism is the struggle to end sexist oppression. Its aim is not to benefit solely any specific group of women, any particular race or class of women. It does not privilege women over men. It has the power to transform in a meaningful way all our lives. . . . Feminism as a movement to end sexist oppression directs our attention to systems of domination and the inter-relatedness of sex, race, and class oppression. (p. 240)

There are many branches of feminist theory. Liberal feminists believe that society has prevented women from achieving their potential and equality with men by providing them with limited opportunity. Radical feminists believe that males have a need to dominate and that they benefit from oppressing women. Socialist feminists believe women's inequality is based in the class structure of capitalism and the patriarchy (Nes & Iadicola, 1989). Other kinds of feminists are gender feminists, who believe that women should receive some special privileges due to years of discrimination, and ecofeminists, who draw parallels between men's domination of women and their domination of the environment (Besthorn & McMillen, 2002).

Feminism is a model that social workers can apply when working with various populations in social work (e.g., women with substance abuse problems, women who are homeless, women with AIDS) and to all methods of social work practice (e.g., casework, group work, community practice, administration, research, and policy) (Van Den Bergh, 1995). A feminist problem-solving style is participatory, not top down. A feminist leadership style empowers others in an organization, whereas a traditional leadership style is used to command and control (Chernesky, 1995). As a social worker, you may prefer to work in a feminist organization, which expects all employees to be involved in management and is therefore considered a "flat" organization, unlike the typical hierarchical top-down bureaucracy. Feminist organizations value the decision-making process as much as the product.

Feminism also influences social work practitioners to change larger systems. For example, liberal feminist social workers focus on addressing not only an individual's strengths and weaknesses but also deficits in social structures like educational systems that limit opportunities for women and inhibit their growth. Radical feminist social workers make clients aware that their problems are rooted in patriarchy and mobilize women to effect change in the larger systems, such as laws and policies. Socialist feminist social workers take actions similar to those of the radical feminist social workers but also try to increase awareness of the relationship between class and patriarchy so that individually and collectively people can change systems that promote domination and oppression (Nes & Iadicola, 1989).

Many social workers consider themselves feminists and support a feminist perspective in social work practice. Other social workers do not consider themselves feminists but support nonsexist attitudes and actions. Social work and feminist principles often mirror each other. For example, the NASW (2005) Code of Ethics stresses social action, not just passive support, to improve human welfare. Similarly, feminist principles stress action to raise consciousness and change discriminatory practices.

SUMMARY

Although some people suggest that women no longer face discrimination in the United States, many of the issues discussed in this chapter indicate that they do. Poverty, violence, and discrimination keep women from full and equal participation in society. Social work is committed to eliminating all forms of discrimination and oppression, including sexism, from the profession and society. Social workers must be aware of and take responsibility for their own attitudes and behaviors that contribute to sexism. Until the inequalities that women across the globe face are fully addressed, the richness of women's, as well as men's, diverse contributions to the betterment of society cannot be fully realized. Feminist social workers define and assess these issues and exercise leadership to develop interventions to address gender-related forms of oppression.

SUGGESTED READING

Abramovitz, M. (2000). *Under attack, fighting back: Women and welfare in the United States* (Rev. ed.). New York: Monthly Review Press. This book examines the impact of welfare reform on issues such as hunger, homelessness, and male-perpetrated violence against single mothers. The author proposes that social and welfare policy change aimed at improving quality of life for women can be achieved through grassroots actions.

Affilia: Journal of Women and Social Work. The journal addresses the concerns of social workers and their clients from a feminist point of view. It covers diverse topics and publishes research reports, empirical articles, commentaries, opinions, book reviews, news updates, fiction, and poetry.

Frieze, I. H. (2005). *Hurting the one you love: Violence in relationships.* Belmont, CA: Thomson Wadsworth. This book draws on a large body of empirical research on violence in relationships to offer an understanding of violence, aggression, and victims' responses to violence.

Gardella, L. G., & Haynes K. S. (2004). *A dream and a plan: A woman's path to leadership in human services.* Washington, DC: NASW Press. This book offers insight into how women in the human services can pursue advanced careers, the obstacles women face in human services work, and guidance on cultivating mentorship.

Hunter, S., Sundel, S. S., & Sundel, M. (2002). *Women at midlife: Life experiences and implications for the helping professions.* Washington, DC: NASW. This book examines issues relevant to social work practice with women in midlife. The authors discuss family, work, health, sexuality, personality, and well-being.

Sauliner, C. F. (1996). *Feminist theories and social work: Approaches and applications.* New York: Haworth Press. This book discusses the major feminist frameworks and clarifies their similarities and differences. It also applies feminist frameworks to social work practice, policy, administration, research, and education.

Van Den Bergh, N. (Ed.). (1995). *Feminist practice in the 21st century.* Washington, DC: NASW Press. The book addresses feminist social work practice in methods, fields of practice, and special populations. It promotes effective social work practice with women and leadership of women in the profession.

THE WORLD WIDE WEB OF SOCIAL WORK

About-Face http://www.about-face.org
About-Face is a nonprofit group based in San Francisco that is dedicated to promoting self-esteem in girls and women through media education, outreach, and activism. The organization aggressively challenges negative media portrayals of women. It seeks to empower women, encourage diversity, enlighten men on women's issues, and confront public images of sexism.

National Coalition Against Domestic Violence http://www.ncadv.org

NCADV works to end violence against women through collective efforts. Work at the local, state, regional, and national levels, including public education and policy development, is geared toward changing the social issues that contribute to violence against women. The Web site includes a hotline number that provides information on services across the United States, twenty-four hours a day, for victims of domestic violence and anyone calling on their behalf. This service provides support, safety planning, referrals to local agencies, and other information.

National Committee on Women's Issues
http://www.socialworkers.org/governance/cmtes/ncowi.asp

NCOWI is the committee within NASW responsible for developing, reviewing, and monitoring NASW's programs that affect women. The committee ensures that women's issues are addressed in all aspects of the organization, promotes the development of theory and knowledge of women's issues in social work, and monitors legislation that affects women.

National Organization for Women http://www.now.org

NOW is a broad-based national organization dedicated to ending sexism, racism, homophobia, violence against women, and all other forms of oppression. It seeks to make legal, political, social, and economic changes through direct mass actions, intensive lobbying, grassroots political organizing, and litigation to promote equality and justice in society.

National Women's Health Information Center http://www.4woman.gov

NWHIC offers information on women's health, including information on reproduction, women's health issues, and health issues faced by minority women and women with disabilities, through a free call center and Web site.

Society for the Psychological Study of Men and Masculinity: Division 51 of the American Psychological Association http://www.apa.org/divisions/div51/

Division 51 seeks to address the restrictive aspects of masculine gender roles in society through research, education, public policy, and improved clinical practice. Division 51 provides studies on how narrow interpretations of masculinity inhibit male development and contribute to the oppression of all people.

Women's Human Rights: Amnesty International's Human Rights Concerns
http://www.amnestyusa.org/women/index.do

Amnesty International is currently engaged in global campaigns aimed at stopping violence against women. This organization confronts international violence against women from a human rights framework to hold international governments responsible for stopping violence against women.

6 Social Work Practice with Gay, Lesbian, Bisexual, and Transgender People

Gary Bailey, Steve J. Onken, Catherine Crisp, and Lacey Sloan

In recent decades, much has changed in society regarding gay, lesbian, bisexual, and transgender (GLBT) communities. Twenty years ago, one spoke only of the gay and lesbian community, largely ignoring bisexual and transgender individuals. AIDS was considered a gay disease rather than a disease affecting the larger population. The term *queer* had negative connotations and had yet to be adopted by younger and often more radical gay and lesbian youths. The representation of gays and lesbians in the media was sketchy at best, and when they did appear, it was as caricatures. Television shows such as *The L Word*, *Noah's Ark*, *Queer As Folk*, and even *Will and Grace* were nowhere on the horizon. Much of this is changing. Today, already-strong GLBT advocacy movements continue to gain strength, and human service professionals have become more aware of how they can meet the needs of those who are gay, lesbian, bisexual, and/or transgender.

The inclusion of a separate GLBT chapter in this textbook is not meant to imply that individuals who are gay, lesbian, bisexual, and/or transgender require the assistance of social workers. It does mean that some GLBT individuals may see social workers because they are members of an oppressed group, or because they encounter the psychological and social problems that people from all walks of life face. In order to assist clients, social workers must examine their own feelings toward people of different sexual orientations and understand practice principles for working with each of these groups. This chapter discusses issues important to effective social work practice with GLBT individuals, but it should only be considered a beginning in the process.

TERMINOLOGY AND DEFINITIONS

The terms *gay* and *lesbian* are generally used to refer to men and women who are attracted to and/or have sex with people of the same gender. Although the term *gay* is generally used to refer to gay men, lesbians may also use that term to describe themselves. The term *bisexual* is generally used to refer to men and women who are attracted to people of both genders. GLB individuals generally use the term *sexual orientation* rather than *sexual preference,* because people do not choose to be gay, lesbian, or bisexual any more than they choose to be heterosexual. In addition, sexual orientation is a relative rather than absolute concept. Researchers such as Kinsey, Pomeroy, and Martin (1948) have demonstrated that an individual's sexual orientation falls along a continuum running from totally heterosexual to totally lesbian or gay and may change over the course of the individual's lifetime (Savin-Williams, 1998). Furthermore, it is important to distinguish between *identity* and *behavior.* Some individuals may identify as gay, lesbian, or bisexual but not engage in sexual behavior with others of the same gender (e.g., a lesbian who chooses to be celibate), while others may have same-sex contact but do not see themselves as gay, lesbian, or bisexual (e.g., a married man who has sexual contact with other men but does not identify as gay or bisexual).

Sexual orientation is different from gender identity and gender roles. As chapter 5 noted, gender identity is an individual's perception of him- or herself as male or female. *Gender role* refers to the behaviors generally expected of males and females and is often fraught with stereotypes. Sexual orientation and gender identity are also different from sexual lifestyle. People who identify as heterosexual, gay, lesbian, bisexual, and/or transgender lead a variety of lifestyles and may be single, celibate, monogamous, or polygamous.

Transgender individuals are those whose gender identity differs from their genital characteristics. They generally acknowledge being born one gender but feel they should be the other gender. To reconcile this conflict, they may take steps to make their physical body match what they feel they are through the use of hormones, limited surgical work (for example, having breasts removed but not having a penis constructed), or more extensive reassignment surgery. Other transgender individuals forgo all medical interventions. These interventions can be arduous processes and must be considered carefully. They can also be expensive, precluding some who desire them from undergoing the process (Bailey, 1996). Transgender individuals should be distinguished from cross-dressers, who wear clothing associated with the opposite gender but do not want to change their gender identity or be the opposite gender.

SOCIAL WORK'S RESPONSE TO SEXUAL ORIENTATION

The Code of Ethics of the National Association of Social Workers (1999) states that "social workers should not practice, condone, facilitate, or collaborate with any form of discrimination on the basis of . . . sexual orienta-tion." Though this statement focuses on what social workers should not do rather than what they should do to improve GLBT individuals' lives, the profession has strengthened its commitment to GLBT rights. NASW has issued policy statements on GLB-related issues and gender identity and has taken a position against reparative therapies that claim to help a person change his or her sexual orientation (National Committee on Lesbian, Gay, and Bisexual Issues, 2000), and against a proposed amendment to the U.S. Constitution that would outlaw marriage between members of the same sex (National Association of Social Workers, 2007). In 2006, the Delegate Assembly, NASW's policy-making body, voted to add "transgender" to the terminology "lesbian, gay, and bisexual" in relevant policy statements and publications.

The Council on Social Work Education (2004) requires baccalaureate and master's programs to teach students to practice with respect, knowl-edge, and skill regarding clients' sexual orientation but does not mandate that content on GLBT individuals be included in the curriculum. Furthermore, although colleges and universities generally have a written affirmative action policy governing the entire institution, and many such policies prohibit discrimination against GLB individuals, neither federal law nor Council on Social Work Education standards require universities and colleges to enact policies prohibiting discrimination based on sexual ori-entation.

DIVERSITY AND DISCRIMINATION

The rainbow flag is a symbol of gay and lesbian pride as well as diversity. GLBT people may be of any ethnicity, socioeconomic status, age, religion, and political persuasion. One thing that all GLBT people have in common is the experience of oppression and discrimination. Those who are women and people of color face additional bias. Bias against lesbians and bisexu-al women occurs due to sexism and heterosexism. Many lesbians feel that the gay liberation was insensitive to them because it did little to challenge patriarchy and sexism, and that the feminist movement did little to support the rights of lesbians. Lesbians and bisexual women have expanded the objectives of the GLBT rights movement to include women's issues, and of the women's movement to include lesbian issues. Lesbianism is an impor-tant component of feminism's response to sexism because it challenges the idea that women must remain in subservient (hetero)sexual roles in relation to men (feminism is also discussed in chapter 5).

GLBT people of color also face many challenges that are compounded by their membership in particular ethnic groups, because "growing up in a racist, sexist, and homophobic society, [they] must deal not only with their sexual identity but with their racial or ethnic identity as well" (Hunter & Schaecher, 1995, p. 1057). They may be rejected by members of their own ethnic group and may face racism within GLBT communities. In recent years, GLBT people of color have been breaking their silence and affirming their sexual orientation and/or gender expression through organized groups and activities such as the National Black Justice Coalition, the National Black Lesbian and Gay Leadership Forum, Black Pride Weekend (celebrated in many cities across the United States), the GALAEI Project, and the Gay Asian Pacific Alliance.

The stigma attached to being bisexual often leads to the rejection of bisexual men and women by both the heterosexual and gay/lesbian communities. For example, bisexual men have been blamed for carrying AIDS from the gay population to the heterosexual population. Some lesbian groups accuse women who identify as bisexual of refusing to give up their "heterosexual privilege." When bisexuals date or marry individuals of the opposite sex, their participation in GLBT communities may be regarded as even more suspect. Though gay and lesbian organizations are becoming increasingly inclusive of bisexual and transgender people, some give this inclusion little more than lip service, and some still overtly exclude them. Due to the differences among lesbian, gay, bisexual, and transgender populations, issues of inclusiveness and exclusiveness are more complicated than they may seem at face value, and GLBT individuals and communities are struggling with them.

There is much debate as to whether issues being confronted by GLBT communities are analogous to those African Americans confronted during the civil rights movement. For social workers, these debates offer an opportunity for dialogue about race, class, power, and privilege and a chance to clarify that the Civil Rights Act of 1964 and its amendments still fail to protect people from discrimination based on their sexual orientation. It also provides an opportunity to address the limits of the law and the need for broader attitudinal change.

The discrimination and oppression that all GLBT people encounter result from homophobia, biphobia, transphobia, and heterosexism. Homophobia is a fear of lesbians or gay men that is sometimes manifested in expressions of hatred toward them. Biphobia and transphobia are similar reactions to individuals who are bisexual or transgender, respectively. Heterosexism can be defined as "a set of values and structures that assumes heterosexuality to be the only natural form of sexual and emotional expression" (Zimmerman, 1992, p. 342). These attitudes cause problems for GLBT people in virtually all areas of life. GLBT individuals may internalize these negative messages, which can result in a negative self-image, self-hatred, and self-destructive behaviors.

HATE VIOLENCE

Hate violence is violence carried out against an individual due to the aggressor's hatred of the group to which the victim is presumed to belong and may be based on the victim's expressed or perceived sexual orientation or gender identity. Hate violence can take many forms, including harassment, vandalism, arson, terrorism, assault, sexual assault, and murder. Accurate estimates of the extent of hate violence against GLBT people are lacking because there is no central reporting resource, these acts are not always classified as crimes or hate crimes, and such crimes are underreported. Hate violence affects the whole community. It is a form of terrorism that creates fear in those who identify as part of the targeted group (LAMBDA GLBT Community Services, 1997–2005).

The National Coalition of Anti-Violence Programs (2006) reports on hate violence against GLBT people in order to bring attention to the issue and reduce this violence. Hate violence is generally perpetrated by male adolescents and young adults who do not know the victim and frequently attack in groups. The coalition has reported that the number of serious injuries resulting from GLBT hate crimes continues to rise. In particular, violence frequently takes place against transgender people and tends to be extreme; homicide of transgender individuals often takes the form of dis-

Demonstrators at a rally protest hate violence against GLBT people.
© Frances Roberts/Alamy

memberment (Patton, 2005). Violent homicides of transgender people rarely receive media coverage. Many people feel that these hate crimes are socially condoned since no federal laws ban discrimination against GLBT individuals, and historically, GLBT behaviors have been condemned. Cases such as the murder of Matthew Shepard, a young gay man who was left to die on a roadside in Wyoming in 1998, are harsh reminders of the depth of hatred based on sexual orientation that some people harbor. Such violence has promoted increased activism among GLBT individuals, their families, and other Americans who recognize that it must be stopped.

THE STRUGGLE FOR RIGHTS

Laws and court decisions protecting GLBT people are slowly being enacted. For example, certain sexual acts between consenting adults of the same sex were still illegal in over half of the states until June 2003, when the Supreme Court finally struck down sodomy laws in the landmark case of *Lawrence v. Texas*. However, since few states have laws that prohibit discrimination based on sexual orientation, discrimination against GLBT people in jobs, housing, education, and other areas of life continues to be sanctioned by law.

Benefits that heterosexual couples take for granted are generally denied to GLBT people in same-sex relationships, but some employers, including Fortune 500 companies like Anheuser-Busch, Bank of America, and Campbell Soup; state governments like New Jersey and New Mexico; municipal governments like those in Bloomington, Indiana, and Anchorage, Alaska; and colleges like Agnes Scott College in Georgia and the University of California, Berkeley, extend health insurance or other benefits (also known as domestic partnership benefits) to the same-sex partners of employees (Human Rights Campaign Foundation, 2007a). Lesbians and gay men are asserting their right to marry in religious or private noncivil ceremonies, and the state of Massachusetts has recognized the legal right of same-sex couples to marry. Several states recognize civil unions, and numerous cities, towns, and municipalities recognize domestic partnerships between individuals of the same sex (Human Rights Campaign Foundation, 2007b). At the same time, political backlash has led most states to pass constitutional amendments that give only opposite-sex couples the right to marry and, in some cases, ban domestic partnerships, even among heterosexual couples. Without the right to marry or commit to a civil union, same-sex partners are denied many rights that married couples take for granted, such as making medical decisions or funeral arrangements for each other (unless they plan ahead and arrange for a power of attorney or a medical directive). Social workers must ensure that GLBT individuals take full advantage of existing laws to protect themselves, their property, and their families, as they define family. Since laws vary by state, it is important to be aware of strategies and legal documents (e.g., advanced directives, legal wills, and durable legal power of attorney) that can protect GLBT couples and families regarding inheritance, custody, and other legal decisions (Howard, 2006). Even then, advocacy may be required to ensure that authorities honor such legal documents. There is still a long way to go before GLBT individuals enjoy the full benefits society offers others. Many social workers have joined with GLBT groups to pursue these rights and empower GLBT individuals, their families, and other supporters to do the same.

COMING OUT AND SEXUAL IDENTITY FORMATION

Coming out is a lifelong process that involves sexual identity formation and disclosure of this identity to others. In the past three decades, a growing body of scholarship on coming out and sexual identity development has emerged. Since this work has focused on lesbians and gay males, it should not be generalized to bisexual and transgender people.

Several scholars have conceptualized gay and lesbian identity formation in stages (e.g., Cass, 1984; Coleman, 1982; Lee, 1994; Troiden, 1993). The stage model characterizes coming out as a process in which individuals respond to their feelings of attraction to others of the same gender and determine how to disclose those feelings to other people. At various points in the process, people may have a variety of reactions, including confusion, despair, self-doubt, denial, pride, and acceptance.

The first two stages of Cass's (1984) six-stage model are identity confusion and identity comparison, during which a person begins to wonder if he or she is different from heterosexuals and considers the possibility that he or she may be gay or lesbian. If a negative feeling develops, the individual may reject the notion that he or she is gay or lesbian. If instead a more positive sense of self develops, the person moves from tolerating the possibility that he or she is gay or lesbian to the stages of identity acceptance, identity pride, and identity synthesis, where one begins to fully integrate a gay or lesbian identity into one's self-concept.

Stage models may describe the general experiences of many older gay and lesbian individuals, but quite a few gay men and lesbians, especially gay and lesbian youths (who may refer to themselves as queer or questioning), do not experience many of these stages or do not proceed through them in the same way. Stage models also do not fully consider the impact of characteristics such as race/ethnicity, sex, gender, and socioeconomic class; one's home, family, work, and community life; and the timing of sexual identity formation (see Hunter & Hickerson, 2003). For example, the process of sexual identity formation for gay men has been characterized as more abrupt and more frequently associated with psychological stress than it is for lesbians (Gonsiorek, 1995). Additionally, people of different sexual orientations may experience sexuality and emotional intimacy differently. Stage models also "do not account for the fluidity and changing nature of sexual identities, or for nonlinear processes of coming to terms intellectually with one's felt and embodied experiences" (Brown, 1995, p. 17).

Onken (1999) has introduced the use of states, rather than stages, to describe sexual identity formation. The notion of states—which Onken describes as the states of pre-awareness conformity, contact, denial, exploration, confusion, dissonance, tolerance, connection, immersion and resistance, acceptance and pride, introspection, and synthesis—regards identity as multidimensional: sexual identity formation is understood to be a continuous process, and the boundaries between states are seen as fluid and constantly influenced by an individual's biopsychosocial experiences. In such a model, a person may move back and forth between states and may experience more than one state at a time, though individuals generally wish to achieve a steady state (a sense of stability or equilibrium). Social workers can use stage or state models to help clients understand the process of sexual identity development and achieve a more positive and consistent sense of self.

Little research has been conducted on the sexual identity formation of bisexual and/or transgender individuals. There is a greater stigma attached to bisexuality and transgenderism than to being gay or lesbian, and such individuals have fewer role models for sexual identity formation (see Hunter & Hickerson, 2003) but may have some of the same reactions as gay men and lesbians to the realization that they are bisexual and/or transgender. Factors that complicate the process of bisexual identity include the lack of an agreed-upon meaning for the term *bisexual,* the lack of an independent bisexual community, and the misguided belief that bisexuality is a stage of sexual orientation formation, not an orientation unto itself (Wishik & Pierce, 1995). Some people mistakenly believe that bisexuality is a transitional period through which a person may progress as he or she develops a gay, lesbian, or heterosexual identity; another common misconception is that bisexuals are in denial "or have not come out all the way and are trying to avoid the stigma of a gay identity" (Fox, 1995, p. 57).

People who initially identify as heterosexual, gay, or lesbian and later discover they are bisexual face difficult issues. For example, those who have always identified as heterosexual might be married and have families when they recognize their bisexuality. These individuals risk losing their already-established primary relationships and families. Gay and lesbian individuals who come to identify as bisexual may face a second coming out.

Disclosure of a GLBT identity occurs throughout the identity formation process. GLBT individuals often first disclose to another GLBT person with whom they have some type of relationship. They may then identify themselves to others in the GLBT community, often by socializing with other GLBT people. Because of the fear of rejection by loved ones, disclosure to parents and family is often the most difficult. Though some GLBT individuals disclose to many people in their social and work environments, others are very guarded. Constantly concealing one's sexual identity can be very stressful, but each individual must decide when and to whom to come out. Figure 6.1 depicts the Human Rights Campaign Foundation's model of and commentary on the process of coming out on a continuum. Social workers provide an important service in helping individuals who are questioning their sexual identity or moving from one sexual identity state to another. They also help GLBT individuals with decisions concerning disclosure.

Figure 6. 1   The Human Rights Campaign Foundation's guide for coming out

Coming out and living openly aren't something you do once, or even for one year. It's a journey that we make every single day of our lives. There are three broad stages that people move through on the coming out continuum. For each person it is a little different, and you may find that at times you move backward and forward through the phases all at once.

Opening Up to Yourself. The period when your journey is beginning— when you're asking yourself questions, moving toward coming out to yourself and perhaps the decision to tell others.

Coming Out. The period when you're actively talking for the first time about your sexual orientation or gender identity with family, friends, coworkers, classmates and other people in your life.

Living Openly. The ongoing phase after you've initially talked with the people closest to you about your life as a GLBT person and are now able to tell new people that come into your life fluidly—where and when it feels appropriate to you.

Source: Human Rights Campaign Foundation. (2007). *The coming out continuum.* Retrieved May 15, 2007, from http://www.hrc.org/Content/NavigationMenu/Coming_Out/Get_Informed4/Coming_Out3/ The_Coming_Out_Continuum/The_Coming_Out_Continuum.htm

When GLBT individuals come out, those to whom they disclose often experience their own coming out process. Tuerk (1998) suggests that parents often go through a period of resistance and experience shock, despair, and shame when they learn their child is gay, lesbian, or bisexual (also see Saltzburg, 2004). They may worry that others will shun or ridicule their child. They may grieve because they will never have grandchildren conceived in the traditional manner or they fear that life in general will be more difficult for their child. Some parents try to change the child by taking him or her to psychotherapy, hope for a religious conversion, or sever the relationship with their child (Tuerk, 1998). The parents of GLBT people often do not progress through the coming out process at the same rate or in the same way; some reach a consolidation phase, during which they become an ally to their child (Tuerk, 1998). Parents and other family members must also decide to whom to disclose that their child, sibling, grandchild, or other relative is gay, lesbian, bisexual, and/or transgender. Parents and other family members may need the help that social workers or support groups can provide as they adapt to a new reality and new understanding of their loved one. Parents today are often enlightened about sexual identity and may wonder if their child is gay, lesbian, bisexual, and/or transgender before the child comes out to them. Some may have approached the child to discuss the possibility, and some parents become true advocates for their child and other GLBT individuals.

Adolescents

Some unique aspects of coming out for adolescents warrant attention. Many GLB people recognize their sexual orientation before age twenty, and many young men do so before they are fifteen (Savin-Williams, 2005). According to *The New Gay Teenager*, young people are disclosing their sexual orientation with unprecedented regularity and are doing so at much younger ages than previous generations, and many are coming out just before or after graduating from high school (Savin-Williams, 2005). However, GLBT adolescents are frequently given the message that it is not all right to discuss their sexuality; consequently, they have no factual information or emotional support and are likely to develop negative self-images as a result. Helping professionals should help adolescents identify safe ways to learn about sexuality, explore their feelings, and develop behaviors and an identity with which they are comfortable (see box 6.1).

Adolescence is a time when conformity is stressed, and GLBT youths may find little solace or support from heterosexual peers or family members who struggle to accept the adolescent's identity as a GLBT person. Support groups for GLBT youths help those who are questioning their sexual orien-

---

Box 6.1 Working with GLBT Students

When Tom began his social work education as an undergraduate student, he didn't think he knew many people who were gay, lesbian, bisexual, and/or transgender. As a BSW student and later as MSW student, Tom learned about sexual orientation and sexual identity. He came to know gay and lesbian students in his program who were out, and he had to examine his own beliefs and feelings about people who are gay, lesbian, bisexual, and/or transgender. Tom decided to become a school social worker because he enjoys working with youths. Little did he know that as a school social worker he would be helping youths questioning or struggling with their sexual identity,

counseling their parents, and addressing harassment and hate violence at the high school where he works. He has also worked with the national office of the Gay, Lesbian and Straight Education Network to develop a Gay-Straight Alliance at his school. Tom has come to recognize that he can never assume that he knows a student's sexual identity. On occasion he has had to deal with parents and other community members who don't share his views about helping GLBT youths, but this has further convinced him that he must be a strong advocate for GLBT students at his school and for GLBT people everywhere.

---

tation or recognize that they are gay, lesbian, bisexual, and/or transgender. The National Youth Advocacy Coalition and the Gay, Lesbian and Straight Educators' Network maintain lists of support groups for GLBT youths. There is also a wealth of information and chat groups on the Internet.

The Gay, Lesbian and Straight Education Network (2003) suggests that due to the possibility of being ejected from their homes, youths may wish to consider waiting to disclose a GLBT orientation unless they are sure their parents will be supportive or they have alternative means of support (financial, housing, etc.). Social workers may help families work things out by assisting them in separating fact from fiction and dispelling the myths about GLBT individuals that many people believe. When youths are rejected or forced to leave home, social workers can help them find instrumental supports elsewhere.

Older Adults

Today's GLBT elders grew up in a very different time and may still not feel safe or comfortable being out. They may not define themselves as GLBT or may still be in the closet (i.e., they have disclosed to few others). For most of their lives, GLBT elders faced discrimination and the possibility of incarceration. Health and mental health professionals considered them maladaptive, and religious institutions considered them immoral; families often severed ties with their GLBT relatives, and employers terminated GLBT employees. Many were aware of their sexual orientation early in life, but it was not unusual at this time for GLBT people to marry and have families (Boxer, 2007; see box 6.2). In working with GLBT clients, social workers must take into account generational cohorts and norms as they relate to sexuality in general and GLBT issues and lifestyles in particular. Social workers help clients weigh the pros and cons of coming out and support clients when their decision is not to disclose.

Box 6.2   A Husband Comes Out

Tim and Beth, married for twenty years, and the parents of two children, viewed each other as good partners, and their family as a happy one. Despite this, Tim had always felt different, as though something was missing and he wasn't really living his own life. At forty-three, after much thought and research, he came to the realization that he had been attracted to men throughout his life. Might he be gay? He felt torn about this realization. Tim and Beth had an honest relationship and Tim felt it was important to share these realizations with his wife. He no longer felt honest. But how would she react? Might she reject him? What about the children—how would they react, and might they reject him? He became more and more tense, struggled to stay on task at work, and began distancing himself from his family. During a particularly difficult conversation with Beth, who was struggling to understand what was going on, Tim opened up. After much shock, confusion, anger, confrontation, pleading, tears, and talking, they decided that although it would be best for them to separate, they would also seek help. They found a social worker, who was able to help Beth identify and voice her anger, and her sense of rejection and betrayal, but also acknowledge the love and partnership that existed. Beth gained a sense of relief in realizing that she wasn't the one causing Tim's distancing behavior; the struggle was in Tim, not between them. The social worker helped Tim work through his sense of betrayal not only to his wife and children, but also to himself. Together Tim and Beth explored their feelings regarding each other and the children, and how they would share with the children the changes going on in their relationship and their family. The social worker linked Tim and Beth to PFLAG, and the other families they met helped them normalize many of the things they were experiencing. Ultimately, the social worker helped Tim and Beth redefine their relationship as friends who care deeply for each other and as co-parents. Tim began exploring his sexuality and, with guidance from the social worker, started to find safe ways to meet and interact with gay men. Two years later, now divorced, Beth has started to date. She feels she has come to terms with Tim's sexuality though at times struggles with his new life. Tim feels more at home with himself, more connected inside. He openly acknowledges that he is gay to an increasing number of people, but that isn't all that he is. "I'm a father, gay, and Beth's friend and co-parent."

People of Color

Coming out for GLBT people of color poses its own challenges. GLBT people of color often face heterosexism and homophobia in their ethnic communities, and they may also face racism in the GLBT community. Issues that members of various racial/ethnic groups must confront include the influence of religion and faith in African American and Latino communities (Crisp, Priest, & Torgerson, 1998; Greene, 1996), values such as machismo and women's traditional roles in Latino cultures (Morales, 1996; Ramos, 1994), and the expectation of conformity in Asian cultures (Chan, 1992). Because of the negative attitudes that many people have and the discrimination against GLBT people that often occurs within these communities—as well as the internalized homophobia that can result—coming out may be more difficult for people of color than for others (see, e.g., Stokes & Peterson, 1998).

GUIDELINES FOR CULTURALLY COMPETENT PRACTICE WITH GLBT CLIENTS

Several approaches that build on social workers' generalist practice skills have been proposed for assisting GLBT clients. Gay affirmative practice "affirms a lesbian, gay, or bisexual identity as an equally positive human experience and expression to heterosexual identity" (Davies, 1996, p. 25) and has been expanded to practice with transgender individuals (Hunter & Hickerson, 2003). Culturally competent social work practice, which was originally developed to improve practice with people of color, has also been expanded to practice with other cultural groups and affirms a GLBT identity. To be a culturally competent practitioner with GLBT clients, social workers can adopt the following principles in their work (Crisp & DiNitto, 2005; Van Den Bergh & Crisp, 2004).

- Do not assume you know a client's sexual identity. In many situations, social workers can better assist a client if they know whether the client is heterosexual, GLBT, or unsure of, or struggling with, his or her sexual identity. Practitioners may use nouns or pronouns that imply an assumption that a client is heterosexual, for example, by referring to a male client's partner as "she," or a female client's partner as "he," or by asking if the client has a husband or wife. This may convey to the client that the social worker does not value those who are GLBT. When a client is not comfortable sharing his or her sexual identity, he or she may find it difficult to develop a trusting relationship with the social worker and to provide information that may be vital to the helping process.

- Create a safe environment for all clients. Employers must require that all staff and clients respect others and must make it clear that derogatory comments about characteristics such as race, gender, appearance, physical and mental ability, religion, and sexual orientation will not be tolerated. Placing brochures or literature about GLBT-affirmative organizations and resources in clear view in waiting areas and offices also demonstrates the agency's commitment to serving GLBT clients. The organization's policies should prohibit discrimination on the basis of sexual orientation or gender expression, and agencies that offer therapeutic services should state that they do not offer reparative or conversion therapies, which purport to help people change their sexual identity (since sexual identity is not a choice, it cannot be changed).
- Address the client's presenting concern, not the client's sexual orientation. Though a client may come to see a social worker due to concerns about his or her sexual orientation, the presenting problem is usually not related to the client's sexual orientation. It is the presenting problem that the social worker must address. Focusing on the client's sexual orientation may lead to distrust or suspicion about the social worker's motives.
- Consider the client's presenting concern within the context of his or her sexual orientation. Culturally competent practice requires that clients be seen in the context of their biopsychosocial characteristics, and this includes sexual orientation and any relationship it may have to the client's presenting concern.
- Support clients who are questioning or struggling with their sexual orientation. When sexual orientation is the client's presenting concern, or if it emerges while the presenting concern is being addressed, culturally competent practice requires that social workers provide a supportive environment that facilitates the client's exploration of his or her feelings and concerns. Social workers should be knowledgeable about resources that can help clients in this process.
- Recognize and address internalized homophobia, biphobia, and transphobia. Internalized negative feelings about one's sexual orientation and gender identity are highly destructive to one's sense of self and well-being and may complicate the resolution of other concerns in an individual's life. Internalized negative feelings may take many forms, including depression, an inability to attain personal and professional goals, and expressions of hatred toward GLBT people. Social workers help clients identify, challenge, and change these negative feelings when this is the presenting problem or in the context of helping clients address other concerns.
- Determine to whom GLBT clients have come out and the support they have from others. Doing so helps social workers address any additional support the client may want or need and also helps them deter-

mine if others should be included in the therapeutic process. Social workers may also assist clients in determining the extent to which they want contact with unsupportive family members or help them as they consider forming families of their own choosing.

■ Include significant others in treatment when appropriate. Social workers recognize that significant others (e.g., family members, partners) may be useful sources of information in client assessments. The family unit may also be the appropriate target of the social work intervention. During the initial assessment, the social worker should ask the client about those who are significant in his or her life, recognizing that clients may or may not wish to be involved with members of their families and may have formed families of their own choosing. When helping GLBT clients address issues that involve family members, the social worker must be aware of whether or not the client has come out to them.

■ Refer clients to GLBT-affirmative resources. When referring clients to other agencies and resources, social workers must take care to determine whether these resources are affirming of GLBT individuals. For example, do they welcome clients regardless of sexual orientation, provide services specifically for GLBT clients, and have pro-GLBT personnel policies? When a community lacks GLBT-affirmative resources, social workers may help develop these resources or assist clients in identifying resources in other communities or online.

■ Address your own negative feelings toward GLBT clients and help other professionals do so. Practitioners must work to recognize negative feelings they have about clients, including those related to the client's sexual orientation. Social workers experiencing these feelings are responsible for obtaining education that may help correct misperceptions and requesting assistance from supervisors or colleagues to address these feelings. Social workers must also be prepared to provide supervision or consultation to help other professionals address negative feelings or intervene when colleagues or supervisees do not recognize their negative attitudes.

■ Support GLBT rights. Social workers have an obligation to be politically active, and supporting GLBT rights is another facet of culturally competent practice. Social workers involved in supporting GLBT rights serve as role models for others.

Culturally competent practice involves many other considerations as well. For example, it must be established whether a transgender client wants to be addressed as "he" or "she" and prefers to use the men's or women's restroom (Leslie, Perina, & Maqueda, 2001). Alternatively, a clearly marked unisex bathroom for individual use can render some of these questions moot. When there are separate therapy groups for men and women, transgender clients must be consulted about their preference.

Since few social service resources are designed specifically for transgender or bisexual individuals, social workers must also determine the best referral resources for these clients. For example, it is necessary to determine whether bisexual clients prefer to be referred to support groups specifically for gay men and lesbians and whether they are comfortable in support groups in which the majority of participants may be heterosexual (see, e.g., McVinney, 2001). Social workers utilize culturally competent practice principles as they assist GLBT clients with issues related to intimate relationships, parenting, mental health and alcohol and drug problems, health care, and other concerns.

INTIMATE RELATIONSHIPS

Whether GLBT or heterosexual, most people have concerns about intimate relationships. Social opportunities for GLBT individuals who wish to meet potential partners have grown tremendously. Lesbian and gay bars are still common meeting places for singles, but a plethora of social, civic, professional, political, and religious organizations have emerged specifically to meet the needs of GLBT individuals and provide avenues for meeting others. Though the Internet makes it much easier for GLBT individuals to identify such opportunities, in order to assist clients—especially those who are beginning to come out—social workers must be aware of these organizations, as well as online communities and how to explore these opportunities safely.

Relationship violence has begun to receive increased attention in GLBT communities, and social workers are involved in efforts to prevent and intervene in this violence (e.g., Fisher-Borne, 2006). Studies suggest the same incidence of domestic or partner violence among those who are GLBT as among heterosexuals (e.g., Fisher-Borne, 2006). In addition, the types of violence experienced in GLB and heterosexual relationships are thought to be similar. For example, about one-third of both battered lesbians and battered heterosexual women are sexually assaulted by their partners (see, e.g., Sloan, 1992). However, GLBT individuals face barriers in addition to the ones typically encountered by heterosexual women in seeking help and leaving violent relationships. GLBT individuals who are not out to family members and friends may be threatened with outing by their abusive partner or may fear being outed if they report the abuse. Due to homophobia and heterosexism among staff and clients, services designed for battered women may not be supportive of battered lesbians and rarely offer services for men who have been battered, regardless of their sexual orientation. However, some antiviolence task groups—such as the Lesbian and Gay Anti-Violence Project in New York City, the Montrose Counseling Center in Houston, the Gay Men's Domestic Violence Project in Massachusetts, and the Rainbow Project in Virginia—address battering in lesbian and gay relationships.

PARENTING

A growing number of GLBT people are becoming parents through adoption, artificial insemination, and surrogacy, and many have children from a previous heterosexual relationship (see box 6.3). In the United States, an estimated 39 percent of gay and lesbian couples are raising children; 60 percent of them are females and 40 percent are male couples (Sears, Gates, & Rubenstein, 2005). In a few states, lesbians and gay men with children

---

Box 6.3 Lesbian Parenting

My Mom Is a Lesbian by Sarah (Age 15)

My mom told me she was a lesbian before I was in kindergarten. It seems like something I have always known. It is no different from normal. It does not come up in most conversations, although lately with all the talk about whether or not gays and lesbians should be allowed to marry, it has come up. I told my friends that I am in favor of gay marriage because I think my mom should have the right to get married (as long as it is not one of my teachers). The first time anyone asked me if my mom was a lesbian, it was because they saw the rainbow sticker on her car. I was in seventh grade then. When I told them she was a lesbian, they thought it was cool. I thought that was a bit weird that they thought it was cool, but I am glad they were accepting. When we were talking about gay marriage in school and I told my classmates my mom was gay, they were okay with it, too. My mom is just like other moms. She loves me. She feeds me, takes care of me, and listens to me. I talk to her about the boys I like. She might be a little bit more of a free spirit than other moms. Like, she challenges authority. And she keeps a bowl of condoms and dental dams in a bowl in the kitchen. She will answer any question that my friends or I have about sex (she used to teach human sexuality at the university). I love my mom very much and I would not change anything about her.

I Am a Lesbian Parent by Sarah's Mom

I will never forget the day I had to tell my daughter that I am a lesbian. As a single mom, I wondered if I would actually have to tell her, or if she would just figure it out. But one day Sarah came home from day care and repeated something homophobic she had heard. I was shocked and asked her if she didn't realize that we had many friends who were lesbian or gay. She did not, so I then asked her if she realized I was a lesbian. She did not, so I told her that I am a lesbian.

Now that my daughter is in high school, many of her friends know that I am gay. I still have to figure out if and when to come out to her friends' parents, but I do not come out to her friends. I will answer any questions they have, but living in a rural area, I feel I need to be a bit cautious. When we lived in Arkansas, I worried that if the neighbors knew I was a lesbian, they would never let their children visit (fortunately, they had no idea what the rainbow flag on my car meant). I am lucky that we now live in a much more progressive community.

I try to be very open and honest with my child. I love her more than I ever realized was possible. She is a great person who loves to share her live with me. I am honored. She has a great sense of self. Like all moms, I hope she will grow up to be a happy adult.

can utilize existing adoption laws or rely on appellate court decisions to allow their same-sex partner to execute a second-parent adoption, thereby guaranteeing the child and the partner the legal protection and benefits afforded by adoption (Human Rights Campaign Foundation, 2002). In some areas, lesbians and gay men have been approved as foster and adoptive parents, especially for youths who identify as gay and children with disabilities, for whom homes may be difficult to find (Arnup, 1999; Hartman, 1999). Organizations such as Children of Lesbians and Gays Everywhere (n.d.) work to "make the world a better place for children of lesbian, gay, bisexual, and/or transgender parents and families." Through legislative advocacy and support of pro-GLBT agency policies, social workers support the child custody rights of GLBT parents in same-sex relationships and GLBT individuals and couples who wish to be adoptive or foster parents. They may also testify on behalf of those who have lost custody because of their sexual orientation or are engaged in fights for custody of their children in which their sexual orientation has been made an issue.

HEALTH CARE

Stigma and discrimination may make it difficult for GLBT people to access health-care services and be open and honest with their health-care providers about their sexual orientation or gender expression. Separate health and mental health agencies for GLBT individuals developed because traditional social service agencies and helping professionals were often unresponsive to these clients' concerns and could be more harmful than helpful to them. For example, Senior Action in a Gay Environment in New York City and Stonewall Communities and Ethos in Boston are innovative programs that respond to GLBT elders' special health and social needs and help them live independently.

Transgender people in particular have been subjected to discrimination in all sectors of the medical establishment (see, e.g., Currah & Minter, 2000). The discomfort caused by these situations, which may also be experienced by GLB people, often leads people to postpone seeking health care, and when one is already ill, such delays can create more serious health problems. Social workers must help educate health-care providers about transgender individuals' unique needs and address the hostility and insensitivity that are often directed at transgender people who have undergone sexual reassignment (Lombardi, 2007). Hormone therapy and sexual reassignment surgery complicate health-care management and require extra sensitivity. There is a growing underground market for hormones, as hormone therapy can be prohibitively expensive, especially for young transgender people. The self-administration of drugs secured illegally can cause a host of medical and health complications, including infectious diseases, and can lead individuals to resort to desperate means, such as the sex trade, to get the money to pay for the drugs.

HIV AND AIDS

Twenty years ago some health-care professionals were unwilling to treat people with AIDS. Many others responded to it as they had to other serious communicable diseases—by taking necessary precautions when treating patients. Approximately 50 percent of people in the United States with AIDS are men who contracted the disease through sex with other men (Centers for Disease Control and Prevention, 2007). The percentage of new AIDS cases contracted in this manner is leveling off, but most gay and bisexual men have experienced the AIDS-related deaths of close friends or loved ones and have friends who are living with HIV or AIDS. Though AIDS affects all segments of the population, helping professionals must be aware of the inordinate toll it has taken on gay men and the implications of this for the gay community. Gay communities still address AIDS deaths on a regular basis, and many gay men are active in AIDS information and support groups.

Social workers are employed in agencies dedicated to serving people with HIV/AIDS. They provide supportive counseling to people with HIV/AIDS and help them obtain medical care; housing; and disability, Social Security, and public assistance benefits and fight discrimination. Due to the loneliness and isolation that can pervade the final stages of life for those who do not have caring family and friends, they may assist with social supports. Social workers also provide support to the friends and loved ones of people with AIDS. The arrival of protease inhibitors has changed the face of HIV/AIDS by prolonging the lives of those living with the disease, but these medications can also take a heavy toll on one's health. Social workers have had to develop new skills to address what has become for many people a long-term chronic, but still fatal, disease.

MENTAL HEALTH AND SUBSTANCE ABUSE PROBLEMS

Studies of mental health and substance abuse problems among GLBT individuals suffer from methodological problems. Many utilize samples consisting only of subjects who self-identity as gay or lesbian, thus excluding those who engage in sexual activity with members of the same sex but do not consider themselves gay or lesbian. Few studies include those who identify as bisexual or transgender; when they do, they are generally grouped with lesbians and gays. Some studies rely on behavioral indicators, such as whether a person has had a sexual relationship with a person of the same gender, but many study samples are small, not randomly selected, or otherwise biased; for example, a study might use bars to recruit GLBT subjects to study alcohol intake and then compare these rates to those of the general population rather than similar populations of bar patrons in the general community.

There is no evidence to indicate that the majority of individuals who are gay or lesbian differ in social adjustment and psychological functioning from heterosexuals. Some studies suggest that the risk of substance abuse and some mental health problems may be higher in lesbian and gay populations. For example, Morrow (2006), in reviewing the literature, notes studies suggesting that approximately 30–40 percent of GLBT youths have attempted suicide, which is five times higher than the rates of their heterosexual peers. There have also been indications that substance use and related problems may be higher among gay men than among heterosexual men and that the difference between lesbians and heterosexual women may be even greater (see Crisp & DiNitto, 2005). Using data from the National Comorbidity Survey, a large and highly regarded study of the occurrence and co-occurrence of mental health problems among people ages fifteen to fifty-four in the United States, Gilman, Cochran, Mays, Hughes, Ostrow, and Kessler (2001) found that having one or more same-sex sexual partners in the past five years was "associated with a general elevation for risk for anxiety, mood, and substance use disorders and for suicidal thoughts and plans" (p. 933).

The psychological distress that arises as a result of discrimination, oppression, homophobia, biphobia, transphobia, hate violence, and struggles with one's sexual identity due to stigma are frequently suggested as explanations for what may be higher rates of depression, suicidal behavior, and alcohol and drug problems among GLBT individuals (e.g., Gilman et al., 2001). However, the studies that have been conducted do not discern whether it is sexual orientation or other factors associated with it that contribute to mental health problems.

Knowing the incidence and prevalence of mental health problems and alcohol and drug problems among GLBT populations is important in developing prevention programs and public awareness campaigns. Substance abuse and mental health professionals must also be aware of the unique stressors that GLBT clients may face in addressing mental health problems and substance abuse. Coming out may go hand-in-hand with recovery from alcohol and drug disorders because being clean and sober provides an opportunity to more clearly consider sexual orientation (Crisp & DiNitto, 2005).

Some communities have mental health and alcohol and drug treatment programs specifically for lesbians and gays that may also be more sensitive to the needs of those who are bisexual and/or transgender. GLBT individuals may feel more comfortable in specialized or separate programs, but it should not be assumed that they would prefer them (see Crisp & DiNitto, 2005, for a discussion). Some believe that specialized programs promote separatism rather than acceptance of GLBT individuals. Others feel that specialized programs may be preferable when individuals are struggling with coming out at the same time that they are addressing alcohol and drug problems. Twelve-step programs such as Alcoholics Anonymous and Gay Alcoholics Anonymous and other mutual-help groups with different philosophies and approaches can be important resources for those recovering from chemical dependency. Social workers are always mindful of the principle of self-determination and the need to present clients with all treatment options.

ORGANIZATIONS FOR GLBT COMMUNITIES

GLBT clients who see social workers often need outlets that provide them with an opportunity to interact with other GLBT individuals. The number of organizations that fit this description—political, religious, social, sports oriented, professional, and volunteer—has grown rapidly over the past few decades. The Internet also provides opportunities for individuals who are isolated due to geography or fear of exposure to interact with other GLBT individuals.

The best known of the political organizations are the National Gay and Lesbian Task Force and the Human Rights Campaign, both headquartered in Washington, D.C. There are also many state and local groups. These organizations are concerned with issues such as preventing discrimination in employment and housing, extending health insurance and other benefits to domestic partners, and expanding civil rights protections for GLBT people. In addition to local, state, and federal legislation, these groups address the presentation of GLBT people in the media and the ways in which social service agencies and human rights agencies address GLBT concerns.

Religious organizations specifically for GLBT people include the Metropolitan Community Church, which was founded in the 1960s in an effort to meet the spiritual and religious needs of lesbians and gays who were not embraced by other churches. Other organizations like DignityUSA for Catholics; Integrity for Episcopalians; and the World Congress for Gay, Lesbian, Bisexual, and Transgender Jews represent GLBT individuals who espouse these religions. Although a discussion of the opinions of various religions on GLBT issues is beyond the scope of this chapter, GLBT individuals are finding more ways to meet their needs in religious and spiritual communities.

The lives of GLBT individuals are also being enriched by GLBT recreational and sporting organizations, book clubs, travel groups, and music and art events. Social groups for GLBT people can often be found on college campuses, or they may be affiliated with a community political organization. The number of gay-straight alliances, clubs for GLBT and GLBT-friendly youths on U.S. high school and middle school campuses, has grown to over three thousand (Gay, Lesbian and Straight Education Network, 2005).

The number of professional organizations has also burgeoned. Among them are groups ranging from the Association of Gay and Lesbian Psychiatrists to the National Gay Pilots Association and the Association for Gay Seminarians and Clergy. Other professional organizations, such as the National Association of Social Workers and the Council on Social Work Education, have GLBT task forces or committees to address GLBT issues.

GLBT community organizations may operate information and referral hotlines and distribute publications with information about local resources as well as GLBT-friendly businesses, health-care providers, and other services. Two publications for GLBT communities are the *Advocate* and the *Gay Yellow Pages*.

SUMMARY

This chapter has addressed a number of topics, including what it means to be gay, lesbian, bisexual, and/or transgender. We have attempted to offer information that normalizes the experiences of GLBT individuals and explains the covert and overt forms of prejudice, discrimination, and oppression they face. Opportunities for social workers to respond in creative ways to meet the needs of GLBT people abound. We have the ability both as individuals and through social work organizations to work with this population by developing policies and programs to eliminate the oppression of and discrimination against GLBT people and promote their rights; assisting GLBT families to meet their unique needs; ensuring social parity for GLBT people; and promoting social, recreational, and political activities for GLBT individuals that further enrich their lives. Social work can support GLBT people in being who they are meant to be and in expanding community life to incorporate those who have been left on the fringes.

SUGGESTED READING

Appleby, G. A., & Anastas, J. W. (1998). *Not just a passing phase: Social work with gay, lesbian, and bisexual people.* New York: Columbia University Press. This carefully researched book provides information on topics such as life-span issues, family relationships, the work environment, and health and mental health issues.

Hunter, S., & Hickerson, J. C. (2003). *Affirmative practice: Understanding and working with lesbian, gay, bisexual, and transgender persons.* Washington, DC: NASW Press. This volume focuses on practice issues with GLBT individuals, couples, and families and larger systems such as institutions and communities. It addresses coming out and life-span issues.

Morrow, D. F., & Messinger, L. (Eds.). (2006). *Sexual orientation and gender expression in social work practice.* New York: Columbia University Press. This edited volume discusses the context for social work practice with GLBT people, identity development and coming out, family relationships, and aspects of society and culture, such as religion and health, that are especially relevant to GLBT people.

Van Den Bergh, N., & Crisp, C. (2004). Defining culturally competent practice with sexual minorities: Implications for social work education and practice. *Journal of Social Work Education, 40*(2), 221–238. This article applies the framework of culturally competent practice to assisting GLBT individuals. It addresses the knowledge, values, and skills one must have to be an effective practitioner.

THE WORLD WIDE WEB OF SOCIAL WORK

Children of Lesbians and Gays Everywhere http://www.colage.org
COLAGE is the only national organization for children of GLBT parents. It has chapters in several communities across the United States and offers a variety of programs, including a pen-pal program and a newsletter.

Human Rights Campaign http://www.hrc.org
The HRC, founded in 1980, promotes the civil rights of gay, lesbian, bisexual, and transgender people by educating the public, supporting candidates, and lobbying. The HRC Web site provides a great deal of information on the status of GLBT populations.

National Gay and Lesbian Task Force http://www.thetaskforce.org
The NGLTF, founded in 1973, promotes equality by building the political power of the GLBT community. It also conducts research and provides policy analysis in the pursuit of equality for GLBT people.

Parents and Friends of Lesbians and Gays http://www.pflag.org
PFLAG is a support, education, and advocacy organization for GLBT people and their families with affiliates in over 500 communities across the United States and abroad.

Mental Illness and Social Work Practice

Linda Openshaw, Ara Lewellen, and Catheleen Jordan

This chapter describes the history of the response to mental illness and focuses on social workers' roles in helping people with mental illness and their families. Broadly defined, the mental health field includes everything from programs for the prevention of mental health problems to marriage and family counseling and the treatment of depression and schizophrenia. Alcohol and drug problems also fall under the umbrella of mental illness; they are addressed in more detail in chapter 8. Today the treatment of mental health, alcohol, and drug problems is called *behavioral health services*.

Thirty-seven percent of licensed social workers in the United States call mental health their primary practice area (National Association of Social Workers, 2006). Mental health is the largest area of social work specialization, and social workers are the largest group of mental health practitioners in the United States (National Association of Social Workers, 2006).

DEFINITION AND SCOPE OF MENTAL HEALTH PROBLEMS

One reason so many social workers are in mental health practice is that nearly half (46%) of all Americans experience some form of mental illness in their lifetime (Kessler, Berglund, Demler, Jin, Merikangas, & Walters, 2005). The most common mental disorders are anxiety disorders, impulse-control disorders, and mood disorders; respectively, 29, 25, and 21 percent of the U.S. population will experience these problems at some point in their lives (see box 7.1). These diagnoses are defined in the fourth edition text revision of the *Diagnostic and Statistical Manual of Mental Disorders* (*DSM*), published by the American Psychiatric Association (2000). Since conceptions of the terms *mental disorder, mental illness,* and *mental health* vary according to cultural norms, values, and research criteria, the *DSM's* authors must be specific about the biopsychosocial criteria for each mental disorder. A *DSM* diagnosis requires that the mental disorder cause "clinically significant distress or impairment in social, occupational, or other important areas of functioning" (American Psychiatric Association, 2000,

p. 7). The *DSM* has been criticized for lacking scientific evidence to support some diagnostic categories (Corcoran & Walsh, 2006), but it is the most widely used diagnostic tool in the United States, and mental health practitioners must be familiar with it.

Box 7.1   Examples of Mental Disorders

Anxiety disorders cause anxiety serious enough to interfere with work and lead to avoidance of certain situations and an inability to enjoy life. Examples are phobias, which cause people to focus on specific objects or on social or public situations. Post-traumatic stress disorder can occur after exposure to a terrifying event or ordeal in which grave physical harm occurred or was threatened. Generalized anxiety disorder is chronic exaggerated worry, lasting at least six months, about everyday routine life events and activities. Other anxiety disorders are separation anxiety disorder, panic disorder, and obsessive-compulsive disorder.

Impulse-control disorders include conduct disorder, a repetitive and persistent pattern of behavior in children and adolescents that causes them to violate the rights of others or basic social rules. Another impulse-control disorder is attention-deficit/hyperactivity disorder; one type is characterized by a child's inattentiveness, and one by a child's hyperactive or impulsive behavior, and in the third, characteristics of both types occur. Symptoms may persist into adulthood.

Mood disorders include various forms of depression, in which people do not experience pleasure from daily life; these can be serious enough to lead to suicide. Bipolar disorder, also known as manic depression, is another mood disorder in which a person's mood swings from excessively high and/or irritable to sad and hopeless, with normal periods in between.

Personality disorders (e.g., antisocial personality disorder, borderline personality disorder) must fulfill several criteria. They are characterized by a deeply ingrained, inflexible pattern of relating, perceiving, and thinking serious enough to cause distress or impaired functioning.

Psychotic disorders include schizophrenia, a serious disorder that affects how a person thinks, feels, and acts. Someone with schizophrenia may have difficulty distinguishing between what is real and what is imaginary, be unresponsive or withdrawn, and have difficulty expressing normal emotions in social situations.

Source: Mental Health America. (2007). *Disorders and treatment*. Retrieved January 7, 2006, from http://www.nmha.org/go/information/get-info/disorders-and-treatment

---

Serious Mental Illnesses

Some mental disorders, such as depression related to a personal loss, are temporary (acute) problems. Others, such as schizophrenia, bipolar disorder, and some types of depression, are termed *serious mental illnesses* (SMI) because they are chronic (long term) or persistent, rather than acute, and have no known cure. SMI also may be defined by the severity of problems a mental disorder causes rather than solely by diagnosis. Approximately

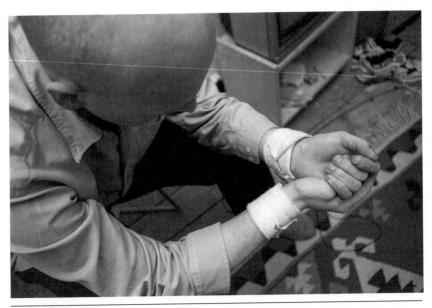

Severe untreated depression can become a debilitating condition and increases the risk of suicide. This man, who suffers from depression, attempted suicide by cutting his wrists. He is now being helped by a multiprofessional interdisciplinary professional team that includes a social worker.
© David Hoffman Photolibrary/Alamy

5–7 percent of adults have an SMI, and 5–9 percent of children have a serious emotional disturbance (President's New Freedom Commission on Mental Health, 2003). Social workers in public mental health agencies work primarily with clients (also called consumers) who have an SMI.

Co-occurring Disorders

Individuals may have more than one mental disorder, or they may have a mental disorder and a substance use (alcohol or drug) disorder. Mental health professionals refer to those with a mental disorder *and* a substance use disorder as having co-morbidity, dual diagnoses, or, more commonly today, co-occurring disorders. About half of individuals with a mental disorder also have a substance use disorder (Kessler, Nelson, McGonagle, Edlund, Frank, & Leaf, 1996). One theory as to why some individuals with a mental disorder develop a substance use disorder is that they use alcohol and other drugs in an attempt to self-treat uncomfortable psychiatric symptoms such as hallucinations, depression, and anxiety (Mueser, Drake, & Wallach, 1998). However, alcohol and illicit drug use can further impair the functioning of people with mental illness. Co-occurring disorders can also include physical illnesses and intellectual disabilities (mental retardation).

HISTORY OF MENTAL HEALTH SERVICES

Early Greek philosophers and physicians debated the causes of mental illness. Over two thousand years later, debate continues over whether mental illness is a result of physical (biological or brain chemistry) problems, morally corrupt behavior (illicit drug use or sexual promiscuity leading to disease), or unfit social environments (poverty and degradation).

The Moral Treatment Movement

Initially, mental illness was thought to arise from causes such as demonic possession or sin, and people with severe mental illness were treated brutally; some were accused of being witches and were burned at the stake. Even in the early twentieth century in the United States, individuals with severe mental illness were treated horrifically; they were often shackled and left in filth, and sometimes subjected to psychosurgery and other damaging procedures to control their conditions.

The modern evolution of mental health treatment can be divided into four reform movements (Goldman & Morrissey, 1985; Grob, 1994; Morrissey & Goldman, 1984). The first reform era began in the nineteenth century, when treatment reflected both moralistic and biological explanations of mental illness. The French physician Phillipe Pinel introduced "moral treatment," a kind and considerate approach to care that encouraged clients to discuss their personal problems and lead active lives. Dorothea Dix, a nineteenth-century social reformer, also sought to improve the lives of people with mental illness by encouraging their separation from criminals and other societal outcasts and institutionalizing them for treatment in a controlled environment (Grob, 1994). Moral treatment was important for its promotion of more humane and compassionate care of those with mental illness; however, scientific knowledge of mental illness was still lacking, and people with SMI continued to suffer tremendously. Many who were homeless, poor, or of color remained confined in asylums, jails, and prisons.

During this period, Sigmund Freud had a major influence on social workers and others aiding people with mental illness (Austin, 1986). Freud's work led many social workers away from their social reform efforts to an emphasis on intrapsychic factors and psychotherapy. The prominent social worker Mary Jarrett presented a paper at the 1919 National Conference of Social Work that discussed the relationship between social casework and Freudian concepts such as the inner self, the unconscious, and infantile sexual desires. Freud reinforced the medical model as the desired form of mental health practice. The medical model focused on isolating a physical or mental cause of bizarre behaviors, thoughts, and feelings and largely ignored the person-in-environment considerations currently emphasized by social workers.

The Mental Hygiene Movement

The mental hygiene movement emerged in the late 1800s in response to the quality of care in asylums (mental institutions), which had deteriorated abysmally because of overcrowding and lack of financial support from local governments. State care acts of the late 1800s and early 1900s vested in state governments the responsibility for treatment of those with mental illness. Psychiatric units were built in conjunction with hospitals, and outpatient care was introduced in the hope that early treatment could prevent chronic mental illness. However, mental health treatment programs were still in their infancy and remained largely ineffective.

Beginning in the 1930s and 1940s, two schools of thought shaped mental health training for social workers. The diagnostic school emphasized internal psychological processes as the primary focus of intervention. Mental disorders were diagnosed based on categories, and social workers counseled the individual to change his or her attitudes, feelings, and behaviors associated with the mental disorder. Treatment involved long-term social casework. The functional, or Rankian, school focused on the environmental problems of those with a mental disorder. Functional social workers made assessments based on functional or daily living needs, rather than diagnoses; facilitated access to community resources; and relied on time-limited, task-oriented interventions. Today, most individuals with an SMI are treated by social workers educated to integrate both diagnostic and functional approaches.

During World War II, routine mental health screenings caused large numbers of young men to be rejected for military service for psychiatric reasons. Although these screening procedures have been criticized, they brought renewed attention to mental health. This concern was reflected in Congress's passage of the Mental Health Act of 1946. The act created the National Institute of Mental Health and established the federal government's role in mental health care. The National Institute of Mental Health is the largest funding agency of mental health research in the world.

Deinstitutionalization and the Community Care Movement

The community mental health movement began in the 1950s. It was heralded by the discovery of new psychotropic drugs, also called antipsychotics, antidepressants, and neuroleptic medications. These drugs reduced many of the distressing symptoms of mental illness, such as hallucinations, aggressive behavior, and severe depression, making it easier for people with mental illness to reside in the community. Symptom control also made communities more accepting of people with mental illness.

Psychotropic drugs, which allowed those with mental illnesses to control their symptoms and function in society, helped lay the groundwork for a second major national event during this era, the passage of the Community

Mental Health Centers Act of 1963. The act emphasized increased community-based care and greater federal involvement in this care. It provided federal funding for establishing community mental health centers, and state and local support in order to expand care. Amendments provided additional funding and defined service categories. In 1965, Congress enacted Medicare (health insurance for older Americans) and Medicaid (health insurance for some Americans living in poverty), which included coverage for some mental health care.

The goal of deinstitutionalization—to prevent the unnecessary confinement of patients—was humane, but the allocation of resources to allow patients released from mental hospitals to live with adequate means in the community never followed. In addition, greater emphasis on civil rights meant that fewer people with SMI would be hospitalized for initial treatment or that they would be quickly released. Landmark court decisions have held that individuals may not be committed to a mental institution unless they are harmful to themselves or others, and they cannot be held unless they are provided appropriate treatment. For all its merits, desinstitutionalization has been associated with increases in the number of individuals suffering from an SMI who are homeless and left to fend for themselves on the streets.

The Community Reform Movement

The community reform era began around 1975 and stressed that people with mental illness can lead productive lives if they are provided treatment, medications, and necessary supports such as housing, vocational assistance, and medical care. The combination of these services, designed to promote optimal client functioning, is often called *psychiatric* or *psychosocial rehabilitation*. Congress passed the Mental Health Systems Act in 1980 to extend the Community Mental Health Centers Act. It added special provisions for adults with SMI, children and adolescents with severe disturbances, and other underserved groups, such as the elderly and people of color. However, the Reagan administration quickly worked to rescind its major provisions. In 1981, the Alcohol, Drug Abuse, and Mental Health Block Grant was instituted in its place, cutting mental health funding by over 25 percent. The block grant made no mention of the specific mandates contained in the Community Mental Health Centers Act amendments and gave states greater latitude to determine the services they would provide. However, with less funding, community mental health centers increasingly looked to Medicaid, Medicare, and private insurance companies to pay for services. Unfortunately, insurance policies often excluded care for major mental illnesses or provided only limited coverage. The federal Mental Health Parity Act of 1996 prevents certain group health plans from placing annual or lifetime dollar limits on mental health benefits that are lower or less favorable than the annual or lifetime dollar limits for medical and surgical benefits offered under the plan. Many Americans, however, still lack adequate coverage for mental health care or have no coverage at all.

During the 1990s, the Comprehensive Community Mental Health Services Program for Children and Their Families advanced children's mental health services by emphasizing individualized, family-focused, and culturally competent services (Walthrap, Petras, Mandell, Stephens, Holden, & Leaf, 2004). In 1992, the U.S. Department of Health and Human Services agency responsible for substance abuse and mental health services became the Substance Abuse and Mental Health Services Administration (SAMHSA). SAMHSA is now made up of three centers—the Center for Mental Health Services, the Center for Substance Abuse Prevention, and the Center for Substance Abuse Treatment—as well as offices that address AIDS, women's services, and applied studies. This restructuring has not changed the responsibilities and program offerings of state mental health and substance abuse services. States and communities still bear the major responsibility for funding and providing care. Service types and quality continue to vary widely depending on each state's investment and commitment.

The Recovery Movement

The first four periods in the history of mental health care are being followed by what may be called the recovery movement, which is increasingly consumer driven. In 2002, George W. Bush formed the President's New Freedom Commission on Mental Health (2003) to recommend improvements to the U.S. mental health service system. The commission envisions a future when mental illnesses will be prevented, detected early, or cured; everyone will have access to effective mental health treatment and supports; and everyone with a mental illness will recover. The commission also identified obstacles to obtaining adequate mental health care, including the stigma surrounding mental illness; private insurers placing unfair treatment limitations and financial requirements on mental health services; and the fragmented mental health delivery system, which is composed of poorly coordinated public, nonprofit, and private service providers and is difficult for many clients and their families to navigate.

The New Freedom's Commission's goals are that Americans will understand that mental health is essential to overall health; mental health care will be consumer and family driven; disparities in mental health services will be eliminated; early mental health screening, assessment, and referral to services will be common practice; and excellent mental health care will be delivered and research will be accelerated. These goals stress the need for easily accessible, "seamless," high-quality services and are closely aligned with the social work principles of respecting the dignity and worth of the individual and client self-determination.

MENTAL HEALTH PRACTICE AND CONSUMERS IN NEED

As box 7.2 illustrates, social workers hold many jobs in the mental health field, and they work in many mental health practice arenas—emergency psychiatric services, hospitals, residential programs, partial hospital (day) programs, and outpatient services. Examples of consumer groups that social

---

Box 7.2   Social Work Practice in the Mental Health Field

Mary Yu is a social worker employed at the micro level in a private inpatient mental health program that serves adolescents and their families. Mary has five years' post-BSW experience and is currently enrolled in a part-time MSW program. When Mary arrives at the center each morning, she reviews the charts to see how many new clients have arrived and consults with the nursing staff about the clients' situations. Mary does brief intake interviews with all the new clients then conducts a peer support group with clients before lunch. The group may discuss problems with family members or teachers, concerns about hospitalization, or difficulties in getting along with peers at the center. After lunch, Mary meets with clinical staff to discuss clients' treatment and discharge plans. Depending on the recommendations of each client's clinical treatment team, she may arrange for referrals to a group foster home, intensive inpatient treatment, or outpatient treatment at a family service agency. One night a week, the center has a family night at which Mary may provide clients' families with information on adolescent development, parenting or communication skills, or referrals to community resources. Mary also provides community education at schools and churches.

Joyce Powers is the executive director of a community mental health center. Joyce is responsible for a staff of sixty employees, including six supervisors who report directly to her. Four of the supervisors are responsible for clinical services; one is responsible for all support staff activities, including clerical and accounting functions; and one is responsible for building maintenance. Joyce has a master's degree in social work and fifteen years' experience in mental health services. She no longer treats clients. Today, she spends most of her time working on grant proposals to support the center's programs, meeting with city and county commissioners to encourage their continued financial support, and working with supervisors to ensure that client services are being delivered in accordance with standards.

John Velasquez is the assistant deputy commissioner for mental health services in a northeastern state. He has an MSW and a PhD in social work. John practices macro-level social work. His job involves making policy recommendations and planning decisions for the entire state. The staff in John's office monitors the expenditures of public funds that support services for mental health clients. Staff from his office conduct annual reviews of the programs it funds to determine whether they are in compliance with state and federal regulations. Periodically, John's staff conducts studies of services provided to clients. Two staff members recently completed a study of adolescents treated in state mental health hospitals to determine what happens to them after discharge. A major finding of the study was that there is an inadequate number of community-based programs to assist adolescents when they leave the state hospital. As a result, more are returning to the state hospital. This study has been forwarded to the state legislature in the hope that it will appropriate more money for adolescent mental health treatment during its next session.

workers help are discussed below. (Mental health services to groups such as older adults and incarcerated individuals are discussed in later chapters.)

Children and Adolescents

Since half of mental disorders manifest by age fourteen, and three-quarters by age twenty-four (Kessler et al., 2005), youths should be a primary concern of mental health practitioners. However, mental health services for children are not presently available in the same quantity and quality as those for adults. Though many mental disorders also have a biological basis, children at high risk for mental disorders are those who have histories of physical or sexual abuse, substance abuse, running away from home, or sexually abusing others. Other factors that increase children's risk are having a history of family violence; caregivers who have felony convictions, substance abuse problems, or histories of psychiatric hospitalization; or a sibling in foster care or an institutional setting (Walthrap et al., 2004). Youth suicide has also become an increasing concern (see box 7.3).

Box 7.3   Preventing Suicide

The aftermath of suicide is devastating for family and friends, who must deal with their loss and often feel guilty that they did not recognize the warning signs and intervene to prevent the suicide. Most social workers in mental health practice and other fields deal with a client's suicide sometime over the course of their careers.

Adult Suicide

Among adults, deaths from suicide outnumber those resulting from homicides at a ratio of five to three. Suicide is the eleventh-leading cause of death (National Institute of Mental Health, 2003). Age, gender, and ethnicity are related to suicidal behavior, and suicide risk increases when there is a mental illness such as depression or substance abuse. Three times as many men as women die from suicide; however, more women than men attempt suicide. Individuals age sixty-five and older accounted for 18 percent of the deaths from suicide in the year 2000. Prevention programs should be based on identifying and providing treatment for risk factors such as severe depression, substance abuse, and adverse life circumstances.

Youth Suicide

Suicide is the third-leading cause of death for people between the ages of fifteen and twenty-four (Mental Health America, 2007a). Of every 100,000 individuals in this age group, 10.4 commit suicide annually (National Center for Injury Prevention and Control, 2004). This rate has nearly tripled since 1960 (Mental Health America, 2007a). Four of five teens who attempt suicide have given clear warning. Warning signs may include:

- Suicide threats (direct and indirect)
- An obsession with death
- Poems, essays, and drawings that refer to death
- Dramatic changes in personality or appearance
- Irrational, bizarre behavior
- An overwhelming sense of guilt, shame, or reflection
- Changed eating or sleeping patterns
- A severe drop in school performance
- Giving away belongings (Mental Health America, 2007b)

As a result of federal laws requiring school districts to serve disabled children, many social workers now work in early childhood intervention programs. They screen and identify children with mental and developmental problems as early as possible. Early childhood intervention services may begin at birth, and school districts must serve children with disabilities from age three to twenty-two. Social workers also serve children with emotional disturbances in child guidance centers, correctional facilities, and many other settings.

Consumers with Co-occurring Disorders

Treatments for mental illness have gradually been extended to co-occurring disorders, including substance use disorders and the medical problems that frequently accompany them (e.g., heart disease, HIV/AIDS, cirrhosis, hepatitis B, alcoholic hepatitis). Social workers are concerned about consumers with co-occurring SMI and substance use disorders because of the multiple difficulties they must overcome. Ideally, treatment agencies provide integrated treatments that address SMI, substance abuse, and medical problems simultaneously, but in many states, integrated programs are in their infancy, and consumers must go from agency to agency in what is a fragmented service delivery system. Integrated programs usually employ a multidisciplinary team of clinicians that consists of a physician, nurse, social worker, and others who provide services tailored to the consumer's needs. Team members may take turns visiting clients at their homes, which may be a board-and-care home or other community residence. Home visits are a mainstay of social work services because they provide practitioners with a better understanding of clients' biopsychosocial functioning.

In addition to medications, the techniques that seem most effective in helping consumers with co-occurring conditions are education, cognitive-behavioral interventions, and peer support (Lambert, 2004). For this reason, social workers frequently use psychoeducational interventions, which combine education, behavior therapy, and peer support. Outreach to engage reluctant clients with SMI in treatment and interventions appropriate to the client's motivation to change problematic behaviors are also common features of effective programs.

Consumers Who Are Homeless

Between 20 and 25 percent of individuals who are homeless have SMI (Sullivan, Burnam, & Koegel, 2002). About half of these individuals also have alcohol or drug abuse disorders, and many have substantial health problems. Homeless individuals with mental illness also have greater problems with social and family relationships, employment, and the criminal justice system than do homeless individuals without mental illness (Shern, Tsemberis, Anthony, Lovell, Richmond, Felton, et al., 2000). Homelessness is more likely to follow the onset of mental illness than vice versa, and schizophrenia and bipolar disorder are the most common diagnoses of homeless individuals (Sullivan et al., 2002). Many communities use the assertive community treatment (ACT) team model to seek out individuals living on the streets and deliver services to them (Stein & Test, 1980). Social workers are often key members of ACT teams. Research indicates that the ACT approach can increase these individuals' contact with service providers and reduce psychiatric hospitalizations and may improve housing and employment outcomes (Marshall & Lockwood, 2007).

The number of families among the homeless population has increased. Homeless mothers have higher rates of SMI and substance abuse than domiciled low-income mothers (Hoffman & Rosenheck, 2001). Seventy-six percent of homeless children have a mother who has major depression, schizophrenia, a substance use disorder, or high distress (Hicks-Coolick, Burnside-Eaton, & Peters, 2003). Nearly half of the children in homeless shelters show symptoms of depression and anxiety, and one-third meet the criteria for clinical depression (Hicks-Coolick et al., 2003). In addition to providing many social services, homeless shelters may employ social workers to provide mental health services to adults and children, or social workers from mental health agencies may come to shelters to assist them.

Military Personnel and Their Families

Military personnel and their families can face a pileup of stressors that puts them at risk of dysfunction, including moving often; adapting to living in other countries; episodic or long separations; and, during wartime, the fear of death or disability (Black, 1993). Military personnel in combat may also experience mental health problems like post-traumatic stress disorder. Substance abuse is another problem that may emerge. In addition, early military retirement often results in dramatic lifestyle changes (e.g., role adjustments) for family members. Social workers may themselves be military personnel serving in the United States or abroad, sometimes in combat zones. They provide many services to military personnel and family members, addressing problems such as child abuse, spousal violence, alcohol and drug problems, and post-traumatic stress disorder. The Department of Veterans Affairs is also a major provider of mental health services that employs a substantial number of social workers.

Addressing Diversity, Reducing Disparities

Gender   Most health and mental health research is performed with male subjects, but "women's high risk status is reflected in their greater likelihood to suffer from severe depression" (Wetzel, 1994, p. 232). Biological differences between men and women do not adequately explain the greater incidence of depression among women. Societal factors suggest that women may be diagnosed as mentally ill as a result of socialized behaviors such as submissiveness, dependency, lack of assertiveness, and conceit about appearance, indicating a double standard for what constitutes mental health for males and females (Tarvis, 1991). In order to avoid gender stereotyping in the mental health field, it is critical that professionals be educated about women's gender roles and overdiagnosis. It is also important that professionals do not underdiagnose men, who fail to report symptoms because being depressed flies in the face of stereotypical male characteristics, such as being strong and being able to take care of one's own problems.

Ethnicity   Increased attention is being paid to mental health disparities between whites and people of color (President's New Freedom Commission on Mental Health, 2003; U.S. Department of Health and Human Services, 1999). For example, although African Americans and whites residing in the same community have similar rates of mental illness, African Americans are more likely to face the stressors associated with being incarcerated, homeless, poor, and victims of violence. African Americans with the same symptoms as whites are more likely to be diagnosed with schizophrenia, but less likely to be diagnosed with depression and, therefore, less likely to receive prescriptions for the treatment of depression. Research indicates that African Americans metabolize psychotropic medications more slowly than whites but often are prescribed higher doses, resulting in increased side effects that may cause them to stop taking medication. African Americans are half as likely as whites to receive mental health treatment. They are underrepresented in outpatient treatment but overrepresented in inpatient treatment and are more likely to get care from an emergency department or primary health-care provider than from a mental health specialist.

The suicide rate for Hispanics is about half that of whites, and Hispanics and whites residing in the same community seem to have similar rates of mental health problems. Hispanics are, however, far less likely to have health insurance and to use mental health services. Hispanics may also suffer from ethno-specific or culture-bound illness, such as *susto* (fright), *nervios* (nerves), and *mal de ojo* (evil eye). Mental health providers may be unfamiliar with these illnesses and how to treat them.

Asian Americans and Pacific Islanders generally have very low rates of mental health service utilization. When they do seek help, their symptoms tend to be severe, indicating that treatment has been significantly delayed. American Indians experience high rates of poverty, homelessness, alcohol-related deaths, and suicide. In addition to the lack of attention to the mental health needs of people of color, knowledge gaps exist because of the diversity among ethnic groups (e.g., there are hundreds of American Indian tribes and many Asian subgroups).

Growing immigrant populations in the United States have fled their homelands to escape extreme poverty, political upheaval and the scourges of war (including torture), and famine. The added struggle to start a new life in this country makes them vulnerable to mental health problems. Paradoxically, their utilization of mental health resources remains low, perhaps because of the desire to save face or because they are unfamiliar with mental health services or cannot obtain services in their native language.

An emerging trend in social services involves the promotion of awareness of ethnic biases through diversity training (Smith, 1990). Diversity training recognizes that behaviors that appear abnormal to one ethnic group, race, religion, or culture may be culturally appropriate for another ethnic group, race, religion, or culture (for example, white American mental health professionals may misinterpret African Americans' emotional expressions as blunted or lacking in normal affect, one of the symptoms of schizophrenia). Behaviors that seem strange may be appropriate for clients who have experienced racism and unfair treatment in other institutional settings.

Racism and sexism remain major barriers to the accurate assessment, treatment, and long-term management of mental health problems. Concern for culturally competent practice has led social workers to examine societal values and how they affect clients and mental health professionals. This is a crucial step in reducing mental health problems and disparities in prevention and treatment among ethnic groups. It is also critical that the number of mental health practitioners of diverse backgrounds increase so that all groups can be better served.

SOCIAL WORK SERVICES IN MENTAL HEALTH

Among the most common direct services that social workers in the mental health field provide are case management, evidence-based treatment, strengths-based services, motivational interviewing, and family psychoeducation. These practice models can be applied to the full array of mental health problems, from personality disorders to anxiety and mood disorders and schizophrenia.

Many social workers provide therapy to people with mental illness, like this young woman who is being stabilized in a psychiatric hospital.
© Janine Wiedel/Alamy

Case Management

Many baccalaureate-level social workers provide case management. According to one model drawn from the state of Texas, case management (sometimes called care management) is a system in which a single accountable individual ensures, to the extent possible, that a client has access to and receives all resources and services that can help maintain his or her optimal functioning. A case manager's duties generally include:

- Reaching out to each client and establishing a relationship in which the client views the case manager as a positive helper
- Performing a comprehensive life needs assessment that covers the views of the client, case manger, significant others, and present service providers
- Developing a comprehensive service plan to meet clients' needs, including transportation
- Making all necessary service referrals
- Coordinating the activities of all service providers so the client experiences an integrated service system
- Maintaining regular contact with each client in order to monitor response to services and identify any problems

- Providing informal counseling to clients as needed, including supportive conversations about daily problems, use of resources, and basic coping strategies
- Participating in scheduled rotation (night, weekend, holiday) coverage so that twenty-four-hour support from staff familiar with the client's needs is available, and informing other rotation staff of problems that surface
- Documenting services according to current recording policy and procedures

Social work case managers provide valuable services designed to prevent the many problems that occur in mental health service delivery systems. These include situations in which the client gets lost in the system or fails to get all the services he or she needs. The philosophy of case management and the skills needed for one to be an effective case manager have long been an integral part of social work education and reflect a systems perspective of social work practice. The National Association of Social Workers has set standards for practice for social workers who are case managers.

Evidence-Based Practice

Social workers and other mental health practitioners who utilize evidence-based practice make case decisions based on information gleaned from high-quality scientific studies (Janzen, Harris, Jordan, & Franklin, 2006). When social workers use best practices, they are selecting the approaches that research or, where sufficient research has not been conducted, clinical evidence has shown to be the most effective. Insurance companies and government agencies are increasingly requiring service providers to use evidence-based approaches. The trend toward greater scientific justification has encouraged social workers to use brief, often behaviorally focused, interventions with empirical evidence to justify their selection. Social workers are increasingly conducting their own research studies and contributing to the evidence-based practice literature. In addition to scholarly journals, the Campbell Collaboration and the Cochrane Collaboration provide systematic reviews of treatment effectiveness studies to help practitioners select interventions. The information that SAMHSA provides on evidence-based practice approaches also makes it easier for practitioners to select interventions. Practitioners must also monitor treatment services and measure client outcomes with established tools that have good validity and reliability, such as depression inventories, family functioning indexes, and quality-of-life measures (e.g., the Global Assessment of Functioning Scale, found in the *DSM*).

Strengths-Based Framework

Many social workers combine the problem-solving and strengths-based approaches (see chapter 2). Both are person-in-environment or ecosystem approaches. The strengths-based framework is a unique social work paradigm. It depends on collaboration between clients and their helpers. Clients and their families, rather than the social worker, are seen as the authorities on the individual's mental illness (Poulin, 2005). Rather than focusing on what is wrong in a person's life, the strengths approach focuses on when and how the client has used effective coping skills. The optimism of this approach helps to promote clients' health and well-being. The social worker's interpersonal relationship is based on a warm, accepting belief in the client. In fact, the relationship itself may be as important as other treatment considerations.

Psychosocial rehabilitation clubhouses are a unique reflection of the strengths or empowerment approach (International Center on Clubhouse Development, 2002). Participants are members (not clients) who direct clubhouse operations with staff assistance. The focus of services is on members' strengths and abilities and on leading productive lives in the community.

Motivational Interviewing

Motivational interviewing is a counseling approach that social workers have embraced to gain clients' trust and help them move in a positive direction. The principles of motivational interviewing are:

- Express empathy. Acceptance facilitates change. Skillful reflective listening is fundamental. Ambivalence is considered normal in making decisions to change.
- Develop discrepancy. Clients are encouraged to recognize (or explore) the discrepancy between their goals and hopes for the future and their current behavior. Change is motivated by a perceived discrepancy between one's present behavior and important personal goals or values. The client, not the social worker, should present arguments for change (such as the benefits of keeping therapy appointments, participating in mutual-help activities, or taking prescribed medications).
- Roll with resistance. Accept client reluctance to change; don't oppose resistance directly. Resistance is a signal to respond differently. New perspectives are invited but not imposed; the client is a primary resource in finding answers and solutions.
- Support self-efficacy. The client's belief in the possibility of change is an important motivator; the client, not the social worker, is responsible for choosing and carrying out change. The social worker's own belief in the person's ability to change becomes a self-fulfilling prophecy (Miller & Rollnick, 2002, pp. 36–41).

Empathy builds rapport between social worker and client. In using empathy effectively, a social worker expresses respect and positive regard for the client's feelings, listens rather than tells, and is supportive and non-judgmental. Social workers act as knowledgeable consultants who persuade gently and compliment and reinforce clients as often as possible (Center for Substance Abuse Treatment, 2005; Miller & Rollnick, 2002).

Relapses of mental illness can occur because of neurobiological conditions over which clients and practitioners have no control. In other cases, social workers can help clients take steps to prevent symptoms from reoccurring. The changes needed to prevent relapse and promote recovery may come in incremental steps, and recovery is often a nonlinear process (McHugo, Drake, Burton, & Ackerson, 1995). A relapse is neither the client's nor the social worker's failure, but a natural part of recovery and an opportunity for learning to prevent future problems. To avoid relapse, social workers encourage clients to participate in psychosocial treatment and support groups, take any prescribed medications as directed, and make needed lifestyle changes, such as engaging in work and meaningful social activities and developing healthy interpersonal relationships.

Family Psychoeducation

Family psychoeducation, a social work intervention, has been used extensively in addressing schizophrenia but recently has been used with other conditions, such as depression and attention-deficit/hyperactivity disorder (Janzen et al., 2006). Psychoeducation for mental disorders and substance abuse "typically focus[es] on the signs and symptoms of mental disorders, medication, and the effects of mental disorders on substance abuse problems" (Center for Substance Abuse Treatment, 2005, p. 140). Family psychoeducation is particularly important in the treatment of schizophrenia because the levels of expressed emotion and degree of criticism, hostility, and overinvolvement in families of individuals with schizophrenia are related to relapse. Lower expressed emotion is associated with lower relapse rates. This knowledge has led to the development of family psychoeducation interventions combining education, social skills training, and behavioral family therapy (Jordan, Lewellen, & Vandiver, 1995). Social workers generally deliver family psychoeducation in four phases:

1 Connection involves joining with the family to form a therapeutic alliance. Offering support and suggestions for coping is important in this phase.

2 The survival skills workshop is the information or educational phase of the treatment. Families learn about their relatives' illness and about stress reduction.

3 The phase of reentry and application focuses on increasing skills in areas such as family communication and problem solving.

4 Maintenance aims to reintegrate the patient into the community with the family (Anderson, Reiss, & Hogarty, 1986).

Research has shown that family psychoeducation interventions reduce but do not prevent relapse, behavioral interventions are superior to other treatment modalities or education only, and long-term intervention is necessary (Lambert, 2004). Thus, psychoeducation is more effective when combined with behavioral interventions and long-term treatment.

MUTUAL-HELP AND VOLUNTARY ASSOCIATIONS

In addition to religious or faith organizations that can help clients to cope, heal, grow, and change (Richards & Bergin, 2002), mutual-help groups and voluntary associations are also important adjuncts to professional mental health services. Social workers often refer clients and family members to them.

In mutual-help organizations, members share problems and receive help from others with mental illness. One such group is Emotions Anonymous. Emotions Anonymous is patterned after Alcoholics Anonymous, which also recognizes the importance of spirituality in recovery. A major emphasis of mental health consumer groups such as Emotions Anonymous is client empowerment. Individuals in recovery generally lead mutual-help groups, though professionals may be involved in helping to start local groups and may encourage and support their work. Other support groups for people with mental illnesses are led by mental health professionals. For example, Good Chemistry groups, designed for people with co-occurring mental illness and substance use disorders, are co-led by a professional and an individual in recovery (Webb, 2004). Groups especially for individuals with co-occurring disorders are important because members often have needs that are not addressed in other groups. For instance, medications may need to be distinguished from street drugs that should be avoided.

Among the best-known voluntary organizations is Mental Health America, formerly the National Mental Health Association. Clifford Beers, a former patient who is considered the father of the mental hygiene movement, founded the National Mental Health Association in 1909. This broad-based citizens' organization is dedicated to promoting mental health, preventing mental disorders, and achieving victory over mental illness through advocacy, education, research, and service. Another important voluntary association is the National Alliance on Mental Illness (NAMI). This advocacy organization brings together families and friends of people with mental illnesses to eradicate mental illness and improve the quality of life of all people affected by these diseases. NAMI's local affiliates and state organizations identify and work on the issues that are most important in each geographic area. Social workers are often active members of groups like Mental Health America and NAMI; their involvement in these organizations is a natural outgrowth of social work's commitment to advancing policies and programs that promote improved prevention and treatment services for those with mental illness and their families.

ISSUES IN MENTAL HEALTH PRACTICE

Interdisciplinary Cooperation or Competing Professions

Social workers, psychiatrists, psychologists, and psychiatric nurses have long traditions as mental health service providers. Other mental health professionals are called counselors or therapists; they focus on marriage and family concerns, vocational issues, and other topics. Although their services overlap, each profession has different educational requirements and makes unique contributions. Psychiatrists can prescribe medications, psychologists administer and interpret psychometric tests to assess mental health problems, and social workers use a systems perspective by incorporating family members in the treatment process and use community resources to improve client functioning. Many mental health programs use multidisciplinary treatment teams, the members of which cooperate with each other to ensure that the client receives the services needed for recovery.

Clients seeking the services of a public or nonprofit mental health authority (an organization designated by the state to provide services or contract with service providers in a given locality) often have little opportunity to select the mental health professionals who will treat them. For example, certain staff members may specialize in treating children or adolescents or in treating depression or schizophrenia. In the private sector, selecting a treatment provider can be quite different. Individuals seeking outpatient services often have many choices. A large number of private practitioners representing various helping professions may all offer similar services. Clients seeking private inpatient treatment may also have several options. Clients should be encouraged to determine if individual practitioners are licensed or are otherwise qualified or to check with licensing agencies to investigate whether a facility has had deficiencies.

In this era of health-care cost containment, insurance companies often determine which professionals or programs patients or clients will use if they wish to be reimbursed for services. Social workers have made substantial progress in obtaining third-party (insurance) reimbursement for their services. Because of increased competition for patients, private facilities and individual practitioners may advertise their services.

Social workers seeking jobs in mental health care should keep in mind the problems of defining social work and distinguishing its services from those of other professions. This concern is complicated because the newer helping professions have borrowed heavily from social work in this area of practice (e.g., case management). As demarcations among the mental health professions become less well defined, social workers must demonstrate that their services result in measurable improvements for clients.

Private Practice and Privatization

Social workers in mental health practice are increasingly employed by for-profit organizations. Privatization is based on an entrepreneurial rather than benevolent spirit. The for-profit sector focuses more on the bottom line (profit) than on traditional social work values of accessibility and best care. In many states, services are brokered out to the private sector, generally nonprofit mental health authorities. Because public funds for mental health services are scarce, these nonprofits must act more like for-profit enterprises. Public and private insurers and treatment facilities have established strict criteria for the time frame, medications, and costs allowed to treat many mental illnesses. Social workers who must apply these standards frequently face ethical dilemmas when they disagree with the type or duration of treatment prescribed by insurers or cannot get insurers to cover services. Social workers rely heavily on their advocacy skills to see that consumers get the services they need, and on their political skills to promote better insurance coverage for mental health care.

Despite the dissatisfaction social workers often express with privatization, growing numbers have opened their own private solo or group practices. Social workers may enter private practice for a number of reasons, including lack of stable funding in public and private agencies, little choice over working hours and cases, lack of professional autonomy, and pay that is not commensurate with ability (Wallace, 1982). Jayaratne, Davis-Sacks, and Chess (1991) found that the personal well-being of social workers in private practice was better than that of those in agency settings. These factors make private practice sound like an attractive option, but some social workers worry that it adversely affects access to services for people who cannot afford private treatment. Those who support the increased interest in private practice argue that social workers, like members of other helping professions, have a right to be paid competitive fees for their work. Many social workers charge lower fees than psychiatrists and psychologists or use a sliding scale, making their services a more economical and accessible alternative.

The majority of students pursuing master's degrees in social work choose concentrations in direct client services (see chapter 1). Schools of social work usually discourage new graduates from opening their own private practices until they have had considerable supervised social work experience, and some states have laws restricting which social workers can engage in private practice. The prerequisites for private practice established by these laws may include possession of a master's degree, required coursework, a certain number of years of practice experience, and prior supervision.

Protecting Consumers' Rights

In the last several decades, mental health consumers have gained substantial recognition of the civil rights protecting them from inappropriate institutionalization and forced treatment. The federal and state governments are responsible for protecting these rights. Today, social workers aid many patients with serious symptoms through mobile crisis units designed to quickly reach people in need, and in community-based short-term crisis stabilization units. When appropriate, an individual mandated to receive additional treatment may be committed to outpatient rather than hospital care. These services may avert the need for longer-term hospitalization and reduce costs.

In some cases, mental health providers, particularly those in the private sector, may be too quick to opt for hospitalization. For example, congressional investigations have exposed practices such as the use of finder's fees for patient referrals and other abuses of inpatient mental health care. On the other hand, public facilities often come under attack for failing to provide hospitalization when family and community members think it is needed. The line between protecting individuals with mental illness and community members and the civil rights of people with mental illness is often difficult to draw.

Consumers committed to treatment have the right to know the reasons for their admission and what must happen before release will be granted. They must be provided access to mental health laws and legal assistance. Those in inpatient facilities should be afforded privacy when they have visitors, and visits should not be denied unless there is reason to believe this might be harmful to the patient or others. Hospitalization in state facilities located far from the patient's home makes it difficult for family members to visit or for the patient to visit them on short leaves of absence from the hospital. In remote areas, it may be especially difficult to recruit and retain qualified staff, yet decisions about patient care and activities are generally made by staff members. A patient may have little influence over these decisions, short of refusing to participate. Moreover, patients who refuse to participate are often considered uncooperative and resistant, which may prolong their stay.

At the urging of Congress in 1980 and again in 1986, a number of states have adopted a bill of rights for mental health consumers, which specifies:

- The right to appropriate treatment and an understanding of what it includes
- The right to an individualized treatment plan
- The right to refuse treatment
- The right to freedom from restraint and seclusion
- The right to maintain the confidentiality of one's records
- The right to see one's records
- The right to file a grievance (Mental Health Systems Act, 1980; Protection and Advocacy for Mentally Ill Individuals Act, 1986)

The Americans with Disabilities Act of 1990 protects individuals with a physical or mental impairment from discrimination in employment, public accommodations, transportation, telecommunications, and state and local government services. Some of the rights of the mental health consumer may be compromised if he or she is declared incompetent by a judge. In these cases a legal guardian is assigned to handle the individual's affairs, such as financial management. Many guardianship programs lack oversight, so there is potential for client exploitation, and social workers must be extra vigilant that clients are not being exploited. Some social workers are employed as patient or client advocates by treatment facilities, independent agencies, or organizations whose mission is to promote better services and see that clients' rights are not violated.

Accountability and Program Evaluation

Social workers are responsible for ensuring that services are accessible, available, and appropriate. Funding agencies like SAMHSA and NIMH generally require evaluation of program processes and outcomes. Program processes are evaluated according to the program's success in meeting its goals, for example, the number of clients served or treatment fidelity (is the treatment being delivered in the way in which it was intended to be delivered?). Another aspect of evaluation is quality management—the process of measuring program goals and objectives and continually making changes in the program to improve it. Outcomes to be measured are tied to client goals, such as reduced depression, decreased number of relapses, and fewer hospitalizations.

The profession's value base requires that social workers explore all avenues of help for clients. One study found that 41 percent of American adults who had anxiety, mood, impulse-control, or substance disorders lasting twelve months received treatment; however, most of those who received services did not receive an adequate level of care (Wang, Lane, Olfson, Pincus, Wells, & Kessler, 2005). Children, the elderly, people of color, and those who are poor or uninsured are among those most likely to have unmet treatment needs (Wang et al., 2005). Social workers may be alarmed that the vast majority of Americans in need receive no care or inadequate care, but given the barriers to services, this should not be a surprise. SAMHSA (2006) has found that the primary reasons people do not seek services are cost or lack of insurance, followed by failure to perceive a need for treatment, stigma, and lack of knowledge about where to go for help.

Can social workers remain responsible to and for clients when services are grossly inadequate? Social workers are grappling with ways to expand prevention and treatment services so that they are universally available. For instance, employee assistance programs are designed to help employees and their family members obtain services before their problems become so severe that they result in unemployment or homelessness. Perhaps most importantly, social workers advocate health insurance that provides mental health benefits for all Americans.

SUMMARY

Social workers' expertise in providing case management services and using evidence-based treatments, family psychoeducation, a strengths-based approach, and motivational interviewing makes them well equipped to work with mental health clients, especially those targeted through state and federal legislation to receive community-based services. Many people with a serious mental illness live in the community, making meaningful contributions to their families, friends, schools, and the workplace. Unprecedented strides are being made in identifying the neurochemical and genetic underpinnings of mental illnesses of all types. Research has expanded practitioners' capabilities to diagnose, treat, and prevent mental illness. Ironically, in the midst of this knowledge explosion, support of publicly funded programs serving people with mentally illness has decreased. Nevertheless, trends in social work practice and education indicate that social workers' interest in mental health practice will continue to grow. There is tremendous satisfaction to be gained from helping clients overcome mental health problems. Social workers' primary challenge is to increase the number, types, and quality of services to prevent and treat mental health problems among all segments of the population.

SUGGESTED READING

American Psychiatric Association. (2000). *Diagnostic and statistical manual of mental disorders* (4th ed., text rev.). Washington, DC: Author. This book contains the standard classification of mental disorders used by mental health professionals in the United States. It provides clear descriptions of diagnostic categories so that clinicians and investigators can diagnose, communicate about, study, and treat people with mental disorders. It also contains diagnostic codes that can be used to satisfy record-keeping and reimbursement needs.

Bentley, K. J., & Walsh, J. F. (2001). *The social worker and psychotropic medication: Toward effective collaboration with mental health clients, families, and providers* (2nd ed.). Belmont, CA: Wadsworth. This book gives an overview of the different medications used in treating mental illness and helps social workers understand some of the issues related to medications. Bentley and Walsh present relevant facts about psychotropic medications, provide an understanding of the basics of psychopharmacology, and help social workers to be active with regard to their clients' medication-related concerns.

Gray, S. W., & Zide, M. R. (2006). *Psychopathology: A competency-based treatment model for social workers.* Belmont, CA: Thomson Brooks/Cole. This book explains different kinds of treatment modalities that fit with *DSM* diagnoses. It provides clear overviews of *DSM-IV-TR* disorders and background information to help the reader understand the disorders. It also includes detailed case examples for each class of disorders.

Morrison, J. (2001). *DSM-IV made easy: The clinician's guide to diagnosis.* New York: Guilford Press. This book explains each of the diagnoses in the fourth edition of the *DSM* and gives case examples. It helps professionals learn how to apply the diagnostic criteria of the *DSM-IV* to patients. It explains how to arrive at a complete diagnosis by taking the reader step-by-step through the diagnostic process for every *DSM-IV* category.

Sands, R. G. (2001). *Clinical social work practice in behavioral mental health: A postmodern approach to practice with adults* (2nd ed.). Needham Heights, MA: Allyn and Bacon. This book summarizes some practice approaches used to address mental health problems that affect adults. It focuses on community mental health services in the United States and discusses chronic diseases and the psychological aspects of illness.

Social Work in Mental Health. Published by Haworth Press, *Social Work in Mental Health* is the journal of behavioral and psychiatric social work. Past contents, information on submitting articles, and related links can be found at http://www.haworthpress.com/web/swmh.

Sue, D., Sue, D. W., & Sue, S. (2006). *Understanding abnormal behavior* (8th ed.). Princeton, NJ: Houghton Mifflin. This book gives an introduction to the various types of abnormal behaviors. It discusses the nature of psychological problems and the pathology of mental illness.

THE WORLD WIDE WEB OF SOCIAL WORK

About Mental Health http://mentalhealth.about.com/od/professional
    This site provides resources for mental health professionals as well as links to sites about mental health and mental illness.

Mental Health InfoSource http://www.mhsource.com/disorders
This is the mental health Web site for continuing medical education. It provides education, resources, and support for addressing mental health problems. Under each mental disorder, links connect to related sites on the Web.

Mental HelpNet http://www.mentalhelp.net
This site promotes mental health and wellness education and advocacy. It contains summaries of the characteristics of several mental disorders. The site provides news, articles, reviewed links, interactive tests, book reviews, self-help resources, therapist and job listings, and videos that educate the public about mental health and wellness issues.

Mental Health America http://www.nmha.org
Mental Health America, formerly the National Mental Health Association, is the nation's oldest and largest nonprofit organization addressing mental health and mental illness. With more than 340 affiliates nationwide, the organization works to improve the mental health of all Americans, especially the 54 million people with mental disorders, through advocacy, education, research, and service.

National Alliance on Mental Illness http://www.nami.org
NAMI describes itself as "the nation's largest grassroots organization dedicated to improving the lives of those living with serious mental illness and their families through advocacy, research, support, and education." NAMI organizations operate in every state and over 1,100 U.S. communities.

National Institute of Mental Health http://nimh.nih.gov
The NIMH offers publications and other educational resources to help people with mental disorders, the general public, mental health and health-care practitioners, and researchers better understand mental illnesses and NIMH research programs.

***Schizophrenia Bulletin* http://www.schizophreniabulletin.oxfordjournals.org**
This Web site provides reviews of recent developments and empirically based hypotheses on the etiology and treatment of schizophrenia. The *Bulletin* publishes new knowledge on subjects ranging from the molecular basis of schizophrenia to social and cultural factors. It carries unsolicited manuscripts of high quality that report original data related to theme issues and can provide a special venue for a major study.

**Substance Abuse and Mental Health Services Administration
http://www.samhsa.gov**
This U.S. Department of Health and Human Services agency provides assistance and resources on mental illness and substance abuse prevention and treatment. This site offers information about the agency's programs, grants, and policies.

8 | Addictions and Social Work Practice

Diana M. DiNitto and C. Aaron McNeece

According to the National Association of Social Workers (2006), just 3 percent of licensed social workers in the United States call addictions their primary practice area, but nearly three-quarters of NASW members report having helped a client with an alcohol or drug problem in the last year (O'Neill, 2001). Social workers play vital roles in assisting individuals, families, schools, workplaces, and communities to address addictions. Addictions affect people from all walks of life, and social workers in virtually all practice areas see people with these problems. This chapter discusses addictions, broadly defined, and methods that social workers use to address these problems. It also considers policies that social workers may wish to promote to better address addictions. You may decide to specialize in addictions practice, but even if you don't, you will be a more confident practitioner if you know how to screen for addictions and intervene, no matter where you work.

Alcohol and drug problems are not the only problems commonly called addictions. Though helping professionals argue about what constitutes an addiction, the public uses the term to describe impulse-control disorders or compulsive (repeated) behaviors that can cause psychological, social, and sometimes physical harm, such as gambling, overeating, sex, Internet use, and shopping. Some strongly object to calling all these problems addictions. Despite common features that these behaviors share, such as escalation of the behavior in order to get the same high, or relief, and the life problems that result, these individuals see substance use (alcohol and drug) disorders as distinctly different from these behavioral disorders.

Addictive disorders, broadly defined, often co-occur. For example, many pathological gamblers have alcohol use disorders (Center for Substance Abuse Treatment, 2005). In addition, a person trying to control one addictive disorder may develop another in its place. Addictive or impulse-control disorders also often co-occur with depression or other mental disorders.

Social workers see individuals with addictions or impulse-control disorders in many settings. For example, social workers help parents with alcohol and drug problems in the child welfare system, and they often treat individuals who gamble pathologically as a condition of deferred adjudication for

171

writing bad checks. Social workers employed as supervisors or agency administrators are also responsible for employees who come to work intoxicated or have other addictive disorders that interfere with their work. Social workers may also see colleagues impaired by these problems. In all these situations, social workers need to be able to identify problems and intervene.

HISTORY OF SOCIAL WORK IN ADDICTIONS

Social workers in the United States have assisted individuals with addictions and their families since the earliest days of the Charity Organization Societies and the settlement house movement in the late 1800s (Straussner & Senreich, 2002). The public generally considered alcoholism a sin or moral problem. Mary Richmond, a notable Charity Organization Societies leader, had a more enlightened view. She referred to "inebriety" as a disease, encouraged early identification and treatment, and developed an alcoholism assessment instrument that contains items that social workers today continue to use. In these early days of the profession, social workers often addressed alcohol problems through the temperance movement and their work in public welfare, child welfare, and the workplace, but few alcoholics received direct help. Many died early or were confined in mental institutions, jails, or prisons because professionals knew little about how to treat them or had little interest in helping them.

During social work's early years, pathological gambling was also considered a moral failing rather than a treatable mental illness. Compulsive overeating was not the problem it is today. The processed food and fast food industries had not blossomed, and the Great Depression limited many individuals' access to food. In fact, many Americans were poorly nourished and were encouraged to eat more (see DiNitto, 2007).

Though the mutual-help group Alcoholics Anonymous was founded in 1935, there was little focus on specialty alcoholism treatment programs until the mid-1950s. Among social workers' most notable accomplishments during the mid-1900s was the work of Gladys Price, Margaret Cork, and Margaret Bailey, particularly in helping families of alcoholics (Straussner & Senreich, 2002).

Developments in the 1970s led more helping professionals to enter the field of addictions. The federal government established the National Institute on Alcohol Abuse and Alcoholism, the National Institute on Drug Abuse, and the agency now known as the Substance Abuse and Mental Health Services Administration (SAMHSA). These agencies lent legitimacy to work on alcohol and drug problems, and federal financial aid became available to students to prepare for careers in the field. The number of hospital- and community-based alcohol and drug treatment programs grew rapidly.

Mental health professionals also began recognizing impulse-control disorders. In 1980 pathological gambling earned a place in the American

Psychological Association's *Diagnostic and Statistical Manual of Mental Disorders (DSM)*.

Eating disorders like anorexia nervosa and bulimia nervosa are considered mental disorders that social workers also treat, but they are beyond the scope of this chapter. Rather than a mental disorder, obesity is considered a general medical condition. Social workers often address compulsive overeating as well as nicotine dependence in their work with clients who are dealing with depression, stressful events, or other problems.

Today's social workers have a growing interest in addictions. In 1995, NASW established a specialty practice section for its members in the alcohol, tobacco, and other drug field and now offers a specialty clinical credential in this field. The first social work journal on addictions, the *Journal of Social Work Practice in the Addictions*, was established in 2001. Social workers hold some of the top positions in government agencies like SAMHSA. With initiatives like the National Institute on Drug Abuse–funded social work research development programs begun in 1999, social workers have become increasingly involved in conducting alcohol and drug research, especially on preventing and treating these problems.

THE MANY PROBLEMS CALLED ADDICTIONS

Conceivably, an individual could become addicted or habituated to almost anything that seems to make him or her feel better or assuage pain. We now consider some behaviors commonly referred to as addictions.

Substance Use Disorders

The American Psychiatric Association (2000) does not use the term *addiction*; instead, it refers to alcohol and drug problems as *substance use disorders*, and more specifically, *substance abuse* or *dependence*. These diagnoses are determined by the effects alcohol and drug use have on an individual's functioning, *not* how much alcohol or drugs one uses or how often. Individuals diagnosed with substance abuse have experienced one or more of four symptoms related to their alcohol or drug use within the past year: (1) failure to meet obligations at work, school, or home; (2) use of alcohol or drugs in hazardous situations, such as driving; (3) legal problems, like arrests for public intoxication; and (4) interpersonal problems, like fights. In order to be diagnosed with substance dependence, one must have three or more of seven symptoms: (1) use of more of the substance to get the same effect, (2) withdrawal symptoms when one is not using the substance (e.g., shakes, delirium tremors), (3) use of more of the substance than one intended, (4) unsuccessful efforts to cut down, (5) increasing amounts of time spent using and recovering, (6) decrease in usual activities, and (7) continued use despite persistent physical or psychological problems. Substance

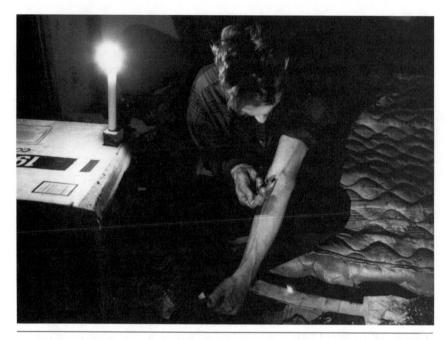

Social workers intervene to prevent drug problems and help clean up neighborhoods such as the one where this shooting gallery is located.
© Steve Liss

abuse may seem like a lesser problem than dependence, but abuse can result in serious problems like disabling or lethal motor vehicle accidents. You probably know someone who has met the criteria for abuse or dependence and suffered consequences like the loss of his or her family or job, serious health problems, or incarceration. Even misuse of alcohol (sometimes called risk drinking) or drugs that does not meet diagnostic criteria can result in life-threatening problems like overdoses or accidents. Social workers are also concerned about alcohol and drug misuse.

Alcohol problems are far more common than problems with illicit drugs. Commonly used illicit drugs that can result in abuse or dependence are marijuana; stimulants, or uppers (e.g., cocaine, including crack cocaine; amphetamines; and methamphetamines); depressants (e.g., heroin and quaaludes); opioids (e.g., heroin, morphine, and codeine); and hallucinogens (e.g., LSD and psilocybin, or magic mushrooms). Many prescription drugs and over-the-counter drugs can also lead to misuse, abuse, or dependence. Young people are more likely than older people to experience problems from using inhalants, so-called designer drugs such as Ecstasy, or anabolic steroids. Older adults are especially susceptible to problems associated with prescription drug use because they take more prescribed medications than other segments of the population, and as people age, they generally do not metabolize medications as efficiently as they once did. Medications may have negative interactions with each other, and alcohol can exacerbate this problem. A recent trend is for young people to abuse prescription drugs that are usually obtained illegally, a practice known as "pharming." They mistakenly believe that this is safer than using illicit substances.

Approximately 9–10 percent of the U.S. population currently meets the criteria for substance abuse or dependence; about 15 million have an alcohol use disorder, about 4 million have a drug use disorder, and about 3 million have both alcohol and drug disorders (Office of Applied Studies, 2005). Most do not receive treatment because they cannot afford it or do not recognize that they have a problem (Office of Applied Studies, 2005). A majority of parents in the child welfare system and incarcerated individuals have alcohol or drug problems, as do about half of individuals with a mental illness and those involved in domestic violence, and nearly a third of those with disabilities (see Straussner & Senreich, 2002). It is no wonder that social workers assist so many people affected by alcohol and drug problems.

The Betty Ford Clinic in California, perhaps the most famous alcohol and drug rehabilitation program, was named after President Gerald Ford's wife. This First Lady was addicted to alcohol and prescription drugs. Her courage in going public—and that of many others—has encouraged others to get professional help. Social workers work in inpatient rehabilitation programs, residential programs like therapeutic communities and halfway houses, outpatient treatment programs, and addiction programs located in many jails and prisons.

Dependence on nicotine—cigarettes and other tobacco products that are smoked, chewed, placed between the cheek and gum, or sniffed—generally does not cause legal problems, but it causes great human suffering. The Centers for Disease Control and Prevention (2007) cite tobacco use as the nation's leading preventable cause of death, close to a half million per year. Few social workers are employed in smoking cessation programs, but all social workers should help their clients quit using tobacco products.

Pathological Gambling

The American Psychiatric Association (2000) criteria for pathological gambling include a preoccupation resulting in illegal acts to obtain money for gambling (embezzlement, forgery); loss of family, friends, and jobs; increasing amounts of time spent gambling; lying about gambling; having to gamble more money to achieve excitement; and failed efforts to control gambling, and irritability when trying to do so. The increase in gambling venues—casinos, state and multistate lotteries, and the Internet—has made gambling easier and has also increased social workers' need to be aware of problem gambling and to intervene when necessary. An estimated 1.5 percent of adults in the United States (0.9% in the past year) have met the criteria for pathological gambling. More adolescents than adults gamble pathologically (National Research Council, 1999).

Compulsive Eating

Needless to say, Americans have easy access to fattening foods that many do not eat in moderation. Approximately 61 percent of adults in the United States are overweight or obese, and 13 percent of children and 14 percent of adolescents are overweight (the number of overweight adolescents has tripled in the last two decades) (U.S. Department of Health and Human Services, 2001). Excessive weight may result in increased risk for type 2 diabetes and coronary heart disease and may exacerbate conditions such as hypertension (high blood pressure).

Compulsive Shopping or Spending

Compulsive shopping and spending are not listed it in the *DSM*, but some criteria for substance use disorders and pathological gambling can be applied to these problems. Individuals may experience excitement or euphoria from purchasing items even if they do not need or even want them. They may promise to stop buying but fail to do so, incur large debts, and try to cover them with illegal activities (Engs, 2004). Excessive spending can result in financial ruin and break up families. Social workers may see clients specifically for compulsive shopping, but such problems often come to light during marital therapy or through court-mandated education and treatment following legal proceedings for writing bad checks, stealing from an employer, or other charges.

Compulsive Sexual Behavior

The *DSM* describes disorders such as pedophilia, but not compulsive sexual behavior or sex addiction. The Society for the Advancement of Sexual Health (2007) says that sexual addiction is difficult to define and takes many forms but involves loss of control over some form or forms of sexual behavior, negative consequences, and constant involuntary preoccupation with the behavior. Sexual Compulsives Anonymous (n.d.) has devised twenty questions to help people determine if they are sexually compulsive; these criteria include feeling guilt or shame over sexual behavior and having sex with prostitutes, others one has just met, or people with whom one would not otherwise associate. Individuals who have sex compulsively may engage in abusive or painful sexual activities and practice unsafe sex, putting themselves and their sexual partners at risk for sexually transmitted diseases. Others may restrict sexual activity to masturbation or other solitary sexual behavior. The construct of sexual compulsivity or sexual addiction needs more study, but many social workers see clients whose behavior indicates that they have some form of this problem.

Excessive Internet Use and Other Excessive Behaviors

Some people use the Internet to engage in illegal activities such as viewing child pornography or soliciting sex from minors. Internet use may also lead to extramarital relationships that may be confined to emotional infidelity or result in sexual infidelity. Excessive Internet use itself can become a problem. People may spend inordinate amounts of time online searching for news, sports, or other harmless information. Internet use becomes problematic when it interferes with relationships, work, and other aspects of everyday life. The same can occur with watching TV or engaging in sports or other activities.

WHAT CAUSES ADDICTIONS AND OTHER COMPULSIVE BEHAVIORS?

The causes of addiction or impulse-control disorders are widely debated (McNeece & DiNitto, 2005). Many people have strongly held views about what causes these problems. Social workers should carefully examine their personal views of these problems before proceeding to help clients.

Some people see addictions as moral problems that result from a lack of willpower or the wanton acts of individuals unwilling to change and become responsible citizens. Others see them as a lifestyle or conscious choice and believe that if individuals choose to engage in these behaviors, they can choose to stop.

Many individuals with alcohol or drug disorders have a family history of these problems, suggesting a genetic predisposition. Growing evidence indicates that genetics and abnormal neurotransmitter systems (brain chemistry) play a part in substance use disorders (National Institute on Alcohol Abuse and Alcoholism, 2000). Many report that using alcohol and drugs makes them feel "normal." Alcohol and drug consumption in sufficient quantities and over a period of time can alter brain chemistry and promote continued use. Abnormal brain chemistry has also been identified in some pathological gamblers (American Psychiatric Association, 2000). Social workers need information about brain chemistry and medication use in treating these problems.

Having parents, grandparents, or other relatives who have had alcohol or drug disorders may suggest a biological predisposition to these problems. It may also mean that using alcohol or drugs to deal with life is a learned behavior. In addition to learning theory, personality theories have been used to explain substance use and other impulse-control disorders. Some people are thrill seekers, behave impulsively or antisocially, or have unresolved insecurities or immature personalities. Such psychological conditions have all been used to explain why some people develop substance use disorders, gamble pathologically, overeat, or shop compulsively, though proof is lacking.

Culture may also play a role in people's development of or protection from addictive behaviors. Alcohol and drug problems vary across countries and among cultural groups. For example, the French and Irish reportedly have higher rates of alcohol problems than Italians and Jews (Levin, 1989). Though members of some American Indian tribes do not drink, other tribes have high rates of alcohol dependence and fetal alcohol spectrum disorders (physical abnormalities and/or mental retardation in newborns) (National Institute on Alcohol Abuse and Alcoholism, 2000). SAMHSA (2006) reports that Puerto Ricans are more likely to be treated for opiate (heroin) problems than other ethnic groups in the United States. Since genetics or other biological factors do not seem to account for these differences, culture may be an explanation.

Gender and sexual orientation may also be factors. Women are reportedly less likely to have substance use disorders. This may be due to the ways problems are identified or measured (e.g., women are less likely to get into fistfights after drinking). Pathological gambling is also more common among men. Research suggests that lesbians have higher rates of alcohol problems than straight women (Crisp & DiNitto, 2005).

Poverty may play a role in alcohol and drug problems. Residents of poor communities have greater exposure to alcohol advertising, bars and liquor stores, and illicit drugs; this, combined with feelings of hopelessness about the future, might promote substance use. Culture may also affect gambling and eating habits. Social workers take into account gender, ethnicity, culture, and class in order to make more accurate diagnoses and better referrals and to improve treatment.

Social workers view many problems of the human condition as having a biopsychosocial basis. Thus, social workers consider whether and how biological, sociological, and psychological factors may contribute to an individual's addictive or impulse-control disorders. Social workers generally reject simple moral explanations for these problems. They believe that human beings prefer to act morally, but due to biopsychosocial risk factors, they may need help in doing what they believe is right. Social workers also generally believe that people should be held responsible for poor judgment or illegal acts, but they are compassionate toward those struggling with addictions or other problem behaviors. Social workers understand that overcoming addictive behaviors is usually a difficult task and often requires professional help. Just think of a behavior you have tried to change and how difficult it was.

Social workers typically take detailed social histories to learn more about factors that may cause, contribute to, or exacerbate a problem. But without proof that biological, psychological, or socioenvironmental factors cause addictive behaviors, social workers utilize what seems to work best for helping people with these problems.

EVIDENCE-BASED ADDICTIONS PRACTICE

There is a growing number of evidence-based approaches for preventing and treating addictive behaviors. Most are behavioral or cognitive-behavioral interventions designed to change the addictive or compulsive behaviors and cognitions (thoughts and feelings) that precede these behaviors. Social workers try to discern which may be most useful in their practices.

Prevention

Many social workers enjoy working with children. Children are the focus of many efforts to prevent addictive behaviors, and school social workers are often involved in delivering prevention programs. For example, SAMHSA offers information on evidence-based prevention programs targeted to children of different ages and ethnic backgrounds.

Adults also need prevention or health promotion programs. Social workers in public health practice and other medical and social service settings help adults recognize early indicators of alcohol and drug problems or overeating before they develop into full-blown problems, encourage them to adopt healthier habits, and instruct them on how to do so. Social workers have become increasingly involved in developing adult prevention programming that is culturally relevant and age appropriate.

Screening and Diagnosis

Social workers in nearly all practice areas need skills to screen for the problems discussed in this chapter and refer to treatment providers. Screening tools are generally short questionnaires administered by the social worker or completed by the client. There are many alcohol- and drug-problem screening tools. For example, the CAGE is a four-item screening device for alcohol problems that social workers can administer in less than a minute (Ewing, 1984). But helping requires more than asking clients questions about whether they have tried to reduce their drinking or have felt guilty about their drinking. Developing rapport, asking questions in a nonjudgmental way, and ensuring confidentiality (to the extent possible) are also important. Social workers also use questionnaires or inventories based on *DSM* criteria, such as the South Oaks Gambling Screen, to help screen clients for gambling problems (Lesieur & Blume, 1987).

Social workers assess the validity and reliability of screening and diagnostic tools and select those appropriate for their clientele based on age, gender, ethnicity, and whether the client has a disability. For example, the South Oaks Gambling Screen has adult and adolescent versions. The Problem Oriented Screening Inventory for Teenagers screens for alcohol and drug problems as well as social, behavioral, and learning problems (Winters, 1999). The Alcohol Use Disorders Identification Test is available in several languages and can be adjusted for drinking norms in different cultures (Babor, Higgins-Biddle, Saunders, & Monteiro, 2001). You can search the Internet to learn about tools for helping people consider whether they are overeaters, sexually compulsive, or have other problems, but they may not have been subjected to reliability and validity testing.

Screening may suggest an individual has a particular problem, but the social worker needs additional knowledge and skills to support or confirm a diagnosis. Social workers must usually have a master's degree and credentials such as a clinical license to make diagnoses. A clinical license may also be required to obtain payment for making diagnoses and providing treatment.

Brief Interventions

Brief interventions can take many forms, such as having clients attend one or several short counseling sessions, asking clients to read educational materials and keep logs to monitor their behavior (e.g., number of drinks consumed; cigarettes smoked; amount of time or money spent gambling, shopping, or using the Internet), and providing cards to remind clients what to do should alcohol or drug cravings or urges to gamble, eat, or engage in compulsive sexual behavior occur. Research indicates that brief interventions are often, but not always, effective in reducing risk drinking (National Institute on Alcohol Abuse and Alcoholism, 2000). It may be a sign of the times and current insurance policies that brief interventions are now used to address many problems discussed in this chapter, particularly those that have not reached very serious proportions.

One framework for brief interventions is the FRAMES approach, which stands for giving *feedback* to the client on his or her problem behavior (such as exceeding safe drinking limits or screening positively on the South Oaks Gambling Screen), *recognizing* the individual's personal responsibility to change, providing clear *advice* about how to alter the behavior of concern, offering a *menu* of choices about how to change, counseling in a warm and *empathic* way, and emphasizing *self-efficacy*—that the client can do it (Miller & Sanchez, 1994). Social workers delivering brief interventions also help clients establish goals for behavior change, follow up to assess progress, and provide ongoing encouragement. Of course, some clients need interventions that are more intense or of longer duration.

Effective Treatment

The National Institute on Drug Abuse (2000) has identified "principles of effective drug addiction treatment" that overlap with social work principles, like individualizing treatment to clients' needs and addressing multiple problems. Social workers may need to help clients do more than stop using drugs or gambling. They may provide marital and family counseling or help clients obtain legal aid and find a job, child care, or other assistance to rebuild their lives due to the destruction that addictions or compulsive behaviors have caused. Social workers also monitor progress. They might check urine screen results for those with drug problems, review clients' logs of problem behaviors and healthy behaviors, and with the client's permission, contact "collaterals" such as family members, teachers, or probation officers to ask how the client is doing. Social workers also monitor attendance at counseling sessions. They want to ensure that clients follow through with referrals and remain in treatment long enough to see positive results, and they follow up when clients have missed sessions. Monitoring is often the job of social workers employed as case managers. Social workers also discuss clients' feelings about their progress, difficulties they are having, and gains they have made.

Motivational Enhancement Therapy

Approaches more consonant with social work practice have replaced the heavy confrontation once used in alcohol and drug treatment programs. Research suggests that alcohol and drug therapists' interpersonal skills are key factors in treatment effectiveness (Najavits & Weiss, 1994). Among the approaches that stress a supportive, empathic counseling style are motivational interviewing and motivational enhancement therapy (Miller & Rollnick, 2002). Motivational enhancement therapy is usually short term and can be applied to a variety of problem behaviors (Center for Substance Abuse Treatment, 2005). The therapist helps the client weigh the advantages and disadvantages of changing (decisional balance) in order to resolve the client's ambivalence about changing.

Motivational approaches can help move clients along the stages of change, from *precontemplation*, where they may not recognize a problem ("I drink like everyone else," "I can control my gambling") or its cause ("I wouldn't drink like this if my work weren't so stressful"), to *contemplation*, where they recognize the problem and consider changing, to *preparation*, where they make plans to change, to *action*, where they make behavioral changes, and *maintenance*, where they continue to change and prevent relapse (Prochaska, DiClemente, & Norcross, 1992). Depending on the stage of the intervention and the individual client, social workers may use education, consciousness-raising, role-playing, positive reinforcement (e.g., rewards), community involvement, and many other techniques to help clients move on in the process of change.

Treating Adults with Substance Use Disorders

It takes skilled and dedicated social workers to keep up with the increasing numbers of evidence-based treatments for addictions. One such method for treating adults with substance use disorders is the community reinforcement approach, which seeks to alter the client's environment in order to reduce substance use and increase well-being (Meyers & Miller, 2001). Social workers may find it appealing because of its comprehensiveness. The community reinforcement approach involves the client's spouse or partner and provides assistance finding employment, social skills training, social and recreational counseling, relaxation training, and help complying with medication regimens. Network therapy is another multimodal cognitive-behavioral approach (Galanter, 1997). A network usually consists of two or three family members or friends who provide support and work with the client and therapist to help the client reach his or her goals. Clients participate in individual sessions with the social worker (or other therapist) as well as sessions with other network members. Some clients either have alienated family and friends or have none available locally. Social workers may need to be creative in finding others who can be incorporated into the treatment, such as clergy members or other service providers assisting the client. Behavioral marital or behavioral couples therapy may also appeal to social workers because it involves the client's significant other (Fahls-Stewart, O'Farrell, Feehan, Birchler, Tiller, & McFarlin, 2000).

Social workers may work in shelters and missions, like those operated by the Salvation Army, where they provide many services to clients who have lost everything as a result of addictive behaviors. They may help clients locate more permanent shelter in a halfway house or other residential program, find a job, apply for food stamps, and get health care from a free clinic and substance abuse treatment and mental health care from a community mental health center or similar program.

Treating Adolescents with Substance Use Disorders

Behavioral therapy seems effective with adolescents who have substance use disorders (National Institute on Drug Abuse, 2000). In this approach, social workers utilize techniques like assignments, rehearsals, logs, progress reviews, urine screens, and rewards as the client moves toward goal achievement (Azrin, Donohue, Besalel, Kogan, & Acierno, 1994). Adolescents learn to avoid risky situations; increase the amount of time they spend engaging in healthy activities; and recognize and redirect thoughts, feelings, and plans that lead to drug use. Family members and others are included in the treatment. Also promising is multidimensional family therapy, which involves individual and family sessions (Schmidt, Liddle, & Dakof, 1996). The adolescent gets help with life skills, and the parents with parenting skills. Consistent with social workers' systems perspective, this approach sees drug use in terms of individual, family, peer, and community influences and requires intervention in each system.

Treating Pathological Gambling and Other Compulsive Behaviors

There have been few randomized clinical trials of pathological gambling treatments. Some evidence indicates that behavioral or cognitive-behavioral interventions can be useful (Oakley-Browne, Adams, & Mobberley, 2004). These approaches help clients address irrational beliefs, for example, that they are able to increase their odds of winning (see Center for Substance Abuse Treatment, 2005). Psychodynamic treatment may also be used in combination with cognitive-behavioral therapy to help clients understand the negative emotions, conflicts, or defenses that may underlie the need to engage in pathological gambling (Center for Substance Abuse Treatment, 2005) or other compulsive behaviors. Box 8.1 describes a social worker helping a client cease pathological gambling.

The most common approaches to addressing overeating and obesity are helping the client to eat a healthier diet and engage in more physical activity. For severely obese adults, gastrointestinal surgery may also be an option when traditional approaches are not effective or there are serious obesity-related health problems (National Institute of Diabetes and Digestive and Kidney Diseases, 2004). The advantages and disadvantages of the different types of surgeries must be weighed. Social workers can provide emotional support to clients as they consider these choices with their physicians and help ensure the client's questions are answered. Overeating and obesity in children are generally addressed through diet, physical activity, and parental involvement (Steinbeck, 2005).

Box 8.1   Helping a Pathological Gambler

A social worker at a community mental health center was assigned the case of Michael B. Screening with the South Oaks Gambling Scale and an interview based on the *DSM* criteria for pathological gambling made it clear that Michael had a gambling problem. During the first few sessions, Michael was reluctant to express his feelings. The social worker focused on using an empathic counseling style and motivational interviewing skills, and eventually, Michael began to realize that she was truly interested in helping him. As Michael began to talk more about his gambling, he described how he relished the competitiveness of card playing and had developed a reputation as a tough player and a winner early in his gambling career. His gambling gradually got out of control, and he was unable to stop until he lost all his money. However, when he attempted to stop gambling, he would feel depressed. In treatment, he acknowledged that he felt increasing anxiety when he was winning and felt relief only when he lost everything.

The social worker learned that Michael's father had been a successful business executive who had been very demanding and critical of Michael throughout his life. Michael had been determined to "beat my father at his own game" and become even more successful. Michael had developed many businesses, but they always collapsed after an initial success, a pattern that mimicked his gambling. In therapy, the social worker saw that Michael felt guilty about his thoughts of "beating" his father, which contributed to the destructive pattern of his gambling and his unsuccessful business ventures.

The social worker helped Michael weigh the pros and cons of continuing to gamble. Eventually the balance was tipped, and Michael stated that he wanted to stop gambling entirely. The social worker also helped Michael let go of his guilt-producing fantasy of spectacular success and focus on how he could enjoy life without feeling a need to compete with his father. At the social worker's suggestion, Michael identified hobbies he was willing to pursue, including activities with his wife. Michael was able to set more realistic goals to achieve a sense of accomplishment without gambling. After several sessions in which Michael's progress was evident, he and the social worker developed a relapse prevention plan. Michael identified triggers he feared would continue to prompt his gambling, like coming into extra money or feeling particularly lucky. He pursued his newly found hobbies and agreed to call the social worker if he needed booster sessions.

Michael B had two relapses within a six-month period. He did recontact the social worker. Eventually, Michael was able to abstain from gambling for longer periods without feeling depressed and inadequate. Today, he holds a job he enjoys, continues to engage in hobbies, and has not gambled in three years.

Source: Adapted from the Center for Substance Abuse Treatment. (2005). *Substance abuse treatment for persons with co-occurring disorders*. (DHHS Publication No. SMA 05-3992). Rockville, MD: Substance Abuse and Mental Health Services Administration.

Relapse Prevention

Individuals usually make more than one serious attempt before they successfully abstain from alcohol or drugs, quit smoking, stop gambling, or reduce other behaviors to nonproblem levels. Those in recovery from alcohol dependence often say, "It is easier to get sober than to stay sober." People who have lost weight know how easy it is to regain weight. Lifelong work is often needed to remain free of an addictive or compulsive behavior. Lifestyle changes are generally needed. Many individuals do not sustain the desired change indefinitely, but social workers continue to help them achieve progressively longer periods of abstinence or other desired behaviors.

Some professionals may be dissuaded from specializing in addictions practice because they perceive clients' resistance to be strong and relapse rates to be high. Treatment compliance and relapse in clients with alcohol disorders are similar to treatment compliance in individuals with other chronic illnesses like type 2 diabetes, hypertension, and asthma (McLellan, Lewis, O'Brien, & Kleber, 2000). Helping clients prevent relapse is an important task. Social workers use relapse prevention approaches to help clients identify triggers, or high-risk situations, for problem behavior and ways to avoid or defuse these situations and adopt healthier lifestyles (Marlatt & Gordon, 1985). For example, socializing with old buddies may be a trigger for drinking for one client, or failed relationships with men may be a trigger for shopping sprees for another. Social workers help clients avoid triggers and make plans to adopt other behaviors in their place—counting to ten and going for a walk, exercising, talking with friends, or engaging in other healthy and rewarding behaviors.

Medications

Social workers cannot prescribe medications, but they can listen to clients' concerns about medication use and help them discuss these treatment options with psychiatrists or other physicians. The Federal Drug Administration has approved a few medications for the treatment of alcohol and drug dependence, but they seem to lack acceptance (i.e., few use them) (McNeece & DiNitto, 2005). Disulfiram, or Antabuse, has been used to help alcoholics refrain from drinking for several decades, but it may be unappealing because individuals know that they will become violently ill if they drink while taking it. Naltrexone prevents the drinker from experiencing the euphoria produced by opiate drugs; it may also inhibit the euphoria produced by alcohol and may help reduce gambling cravings and behavior (Center for Substance Abuse Treatment, 2005). The use of methadone to treat heroin dependence remains controversial. Although it helps individuals lead more productive lives because it reduces drug cravings and this results in less illegal activity to obtain heroin, patients become addicted to methadone. Patients generally obtain methadone from an approved clinic, where social workers may provide counseling and other social services. More recently, buprenorphine has been approved for treating heroin and other opioid dependence. It differs from methadone, as it seems to create a milder dependence, is taken less frequently than methadone, and can be obtained from approved physicians in private practice, which may make it more attractive to clients than methadone (see Center for Sustance Abuse Treatment, n.d.). Many individuals who have substance use disorders or gamble pathologically suffer from depression, and antidepressants may help them (Center for Substance Abuse Treatment, 2005).

Social workers are obligated to discuss the range of treatment options with clients to help them make informed choices. To do so, social workers need to stay abreast of information on psychopharmacological agents (medications). The services that social workers provide remain the mainstays of addiction treatment, because medications to treat addictions are recommended only in conjunction with psychosocial services.

Social Workers and Mutual-Help Groups

Some individuals recovering from addictive disorders utilize professional assistance; others utilize mutual-help groups; some use both. In 1935, a stockbroker and a doctor both struggling with alcoholism founded Alcoholics Anonymous. The number of AA groups has grown tremendously. Narcotics Anonymous, Cocaine Anonymous, Marijuana Anonymous, Gamblers Anonymous, Overeaters Anonymous, Sexual Compulsives Anonymous, and Debtors Anonymous are all patterned after AA. These are all twelve-step programs that have a spiritual orientation and make reference to God. The Lord's Prayer is generally recited at meetings. Atheists, agnostics, and those of non-Christian religious persuasions have recovered through twelve-step programs, perhaps due to the camaraderie and support. Those who do not want a spiritually based program may prefer programs like Secular Organizations for Sobriety or Rational Recovery.

The loose organization and emphasis on voluntary participation and anonymity make studying mutual-help groups' effectiveness difficult, but many individuals attribute their recovery to these programs. Some clients need a relatively short course of professional treatment and use one or more of the many mutual-help groups for longer-term assistance. Others report that they do not find these groups useful. While many social workers embrace these groups, others have a more reserved view of them and for whom they may be most helpful. Since little hard research is available, social workers need to learn about mutual-help groups and attend meetings before they make their own judgments. Many groups have open meetings where professionals and other visitors are welcome.

Social workers generally educate clients about mutual-help groups; suggest they attend; and consider which, if any, they might find useful. Social workers also keep group literature and Internet addresses handy for clients. Mutual-help group members may offer help that professionals do not provide and may be available at times when professionals are not. Some AA groups operate clubs that are open twenty-four hours a day, seven days a week. Many mutual-help groups have twenty-four-hour phone lines or answering services. Continued attendance at meetings may help avert relapse.

Impaired Employees and Colleagues

Social workers may supervise an employee who is not performing adequately at work. The reason may be an addictive disorder. In these cases, the supervisor does not screen or diagnose but may make a referral to an employee assistance program, where social workers are often employed to identify the problem and provide necessary services. In other cases, a social worker may recognize a colleague is impaired (cannot perform adequately at work) because of an addictive disorder. The social worker may be responsible for discussing the concern with the colleague or reporting to a superior, licensing board, or group designated to intervene by a professional organization.

ADDICTION POLITICS

The Office of National Drug Control Policy reports that the federal government's annual drug control budget is about $12 billion. For the fiscal year 2006, about 39 percent went to demand-side efforts (treatment, prevention, and related research), and 61 percent to supply-side efforts (law enforcement and interdiction). However, there is really no evidence that supply-side efforts reduce drug abuse and dependence (McNeece & DiNitto, 2005). No matter how many drugs are confiscated, drug trafficking continues and drug supplies continue to flow. Since there is evidence that one dollar spent on treatment results in twelve dollars saved in money spent on criminal justice, health care, and other services (National Institute on Drug Abuse, 2000), social workers will continue to make a case for allocating more funds to treatment.

Social workers support efforts like community drug courts and Proposition 36 in California, which divert drug possession offenders to treatment rather than incarceration (see box 8.2). Other aspects of decriminalization also warrant social workers' consideration, such as reduced penalties for possession of small amounts of drugs and permitting the use of marijuana for medical purposes. Crack cocaine offenses are treated much more harshly than powdered cocaine offenses, which discriminates against poor people and African Americans, who are more often arrested for offenses involving crack cocaine (see U.S. Sentencing Commission, 2002).

Box 8.2   Proposition 36 Helps Cynthia M

Cynthia M had been in the grip of alcohol and drugs since she was sixteen. She says she doesn't know why she went down that path. No one else in her family did, but for her, things were different. She was in and out of programs for many years but never stayed sober for long. "I stopped believing I could change my life," she says. "I used to talk about what I was going to do in my next life. Because I was convinced I was going be an addict for the rest of this life." But in 2003, after a second round of legal problems related to her drug use, she says she received a "gift": Proposition 36.

She says she didn't realize at the time what an opportunity she was being given, but after seven months in treatment, she began to make changes in her life. Now she is sober, attends college, and sees a future without drugs and alcohol. "I used to dream of a life not controlled by my addiction, and it is happening for me now, thanks to so many who care."

Source: Adapted from California Proposition 36. (n.d.). *Success stories*. Retrieved May 28, 2006, from http://prop36.org/successStories_Cynthia M.php

---

Action may also be needed in public benefit programs (DiNitto, 2002). Alcohol and drug problems are the only disabilities that can keep otherwise-qualified individuals from receiving publicly supported disability benefits. Felony drug convictions can keep parents from receiving public assistance and food stamps. Public housing tenants may be evicted if any household member is using drugs. A college student with a drug conviction as an adult is ineligible for federal financial aid for a designated period of time. In addition, the Americans with Disabilities Act does not provide employees who currently use illegal drugs or whose job performance is impaired by alcohol use with the same employment protections as individuals with other disabilities. Children may be removed from homes where a parent is using drugs even if there is no evidence of child abuse or neglect. Women have been arrested and incarcerated for using drugs while pregnant even though a fetus has no legal standing as a person. Such practices and policies may violate the Constitution's equal protection and due processes clauses and require social workers' vigilance to prevent civil rights infringements and promote social justice.

Work is also needed on health insurance parity. Insurance coverage for alcohol and drug treatment lags behind coverage for mental health treatment, and both lag behind physical health coverage. Managed care has taken a toll by limiting access to the type and amount of alcohol and drug treatment (Hay Group, 2001). Even worse, millions of Americans have no health insurance coverage at all. These situations affect individuals' access to treatment and social workers' and other providers' opportunities to treat them and to be paid for their work. Social workers will continue to press for ways to ensure that all Americans have health insurance, including full parity for addictions treatment.

Many alcohol and drug treatment programs espouse a goal of abstinence for clients. Harm reduction approaches make no such demands, focusing instead on reducing the harm that may come from drug use. Harm reduction is consistent with the social work principles of starting where the client is and respecting the dignity and worth of the individual. Some harm reduction strategies (e.g., heroin replacement therapy) are too radical for the U.S. government to consider. More moderate approaches have also been ignored. For example, the federal government has refused to fund needle-exchange programs despite its acknowledgment that they can reduce HIV transmission and do not promote injection drug use (U.S. Department of Health and Human Services, 1998). To save more lives, social workers who support needle exchange or other harm reduction approaches are seeking to make them more palatable to elected officials and the public.

FUTURE OF ADDICTIONS PRACTICE AND SOCIAL WORK

Social workers specialize in addictions practice for many reasons, including the challenge of the work (DiNitto, 2007). The field needs social workers' systems and strengths perspectives to develop new and improved approaches that will prevent people from developing addictions, motivate those with addictions to enter treatment, and produce better treatment results. Social workers are also needed to press for policy changes that will increase treatment access and promote more rational and effective approaches to drug offenders and others with impulse-control disorders and compulsive behaviors.

The expanding definition of addictive disorders provides new employment opportunities for social workers. Addictions practice is also growing because professionals in child welfare, criminal justice, and other fields recognize that many clients have addictive disorders and need simultaneous (integrated) treatment for their problems. Many insurance plans cover treatment for addictive disorders, and the public has come to understand that these problems are treatable, resulting in increased demand for social work services. Increased treatment demand, also resulting from measures like Proposition 36, may overload the system, especially if more social workers are not prepared for addictions practice (McNeece, 2003).

Demographic trends are also increasing addiction practice opportunities (DiNitto, 2007). There has been a general population growth due to factors such as increased life spans, and baby boomers are the first generation with wide exposure to illicit drugs. Thus, a growing portion of the older population may need services for illicit drug use as well as alcohol use disorders and prescription drug misuse. Younger people can obtain drugs with increased ease, meaning that more youths are being referred to services for drug offenses and drug treatment. More youths are overweight due to life-long habits of drinking too much soda and eating too much high-calorie processed and fast foods. Youths' familiarity with the Internet fuels gambling and shopping habits.

Another demographic consideration is the many immigrants who were victims of war, genocide, extreme poverty, and other horrific conditions before coming to the United States (Amodeo, Robb, Peou, & Tran, 1996). They may turn to alcohol and drugs, including substances indigenous to their homelands, to assuage the pain from these ordeals. Social work's attention to culturally relevant definitions of addictions and models of practice can be useful in identifying and treating these problems.

The addictions workforce of the future may go to the lowest bidder—those willing to do the work at the lowest cost—as often seems to be the case today (DiNitto, 2007). On the other hand, highly skilled professionals commanding larger salaries may be needed to address the complex problems of individuals with addictive disorders and those with co-occurring mental disorders and health problems. Though there are no data indicating that any particular profession is best suited to treat clients with addictions, social workers, with their person-in-environment and biopsychosocial perspectives, may be ideal professionals for addictions practice (Straussner & Senreich, 2002).

Since the number of specialty addictions programs will not be sufficient to meet treatment demands, professionals in many settings must be able to incorporate addictions treatment in their work (Miller & Weisner, 2002). To do so, social work students should take courses on addictions, even if they are not required by their degree program. As members of the various helping professions vie for jobs and prominence, social workers can help secure their place in addictions prevention and treatment by demonstrating that they can help clients successfully address addictive behaviors.

SUMMARY

Social workers play important roles in addressing addictions. Some do this by specializing in addictions prevention or treatment. Others work in settings like probation, corrections, child welfare, emergency rooms, and college campuses, where alcohol and drug problems are prominent and interventions must be conducted or service referrals made. Others are employed in medical settings where patients present with conditions like diabetes related to being overweight and with lung cancer, emphysema, and other health problems caused by smoking. Many of them need social work services as well as health care. In addition to developing skills in screening, intervention, and treatment, social workers can work to ensure that everyone with an addictive disorder, broadly defined, has access to affordable and effective treatment. More social workers are needed to address the growing problem of addictions.

SUGGESTED READING

Abbott, A. A. (Ed.). (2000). *Alcohol, tobacco, and other drugs: Challenging myths, assessing theories, individualizing interventions.* Washington, DC: NASW Press/National Association of Social Workers. This book describes theories of substance misuse, provides a problem-solving model for intervention, and offers information on assessment, engagement, and interviewing. It also addresses culture, race, ethnicity, and gender.

McNeece, C. A., & DiNitto, D. M. (2005). *Chemical dependency: A systems approach* (3rd ed.). Boston: Allyn and Bacon. This textbook relies on social workers' systems perspective to address alcohol and drug problems and their effects on individuals, families, communities, and the broader society. It provides information on epidemiology, screening, diagnosis, prevention, treatment, gender, culture, sexual orientation, age, co-occurring disorders, and public policy.

Straussner, S. L. A. (Ed.). (2001). *Ethnocultural factors in substance abuse treatment.* New York: Guilford Press. This book aids helping professionals in learning about various cultural groups and provides information to help address the substance abuse problems these groups face.

Straussner, S. L. A. (Ed.). (2004). *Clinical work with substance-abusing clients* (2nd ed.). New York: Guilford Press. This book discusses many models of intervention and approaches to treatment to help clinicians choose those best suited to the client. There are chapters on adolescents; older adults; women; homeless individuals; individuals with borderline personality disorder; people who are HIV positive; and gays, lesbians, and bisexuals. The book contains many clinical case examples.

Van Wormer, K., & Davis, D. R., (2003). *Addictions treatment: A strengths perspective.* Pacific Grove, CA: Brooks/Cole. This book addresses addictions treatment using the biopsychosocial framework and strengths perspectives widely embraced by social workers. It discusses alcohol and drug problems, eating disorders, compulsive gambling, and other behavioral addictions as well as particular population groups and public policy.

THE WORLD WIDE WEB OF SOCIAL WORK

Join Together http://www.jointogether.org/home/

This is a national resource center for communities working to reduce substance abuse through policy, prevention, and treatment. The organization provides timely information in condensed form through newsletters and alerts on topics of interest to social workers and those they assist.

National Addiction Technology Transfer Center http://www.nattc.org/

The NATTC, a project of the federal government's Substance Abuse and Mental Health Services Administration, is dedicated to rapidly translating scientific information on addictions prevention and treatment for practitioners' use. Its Web site offers links to the regional addiction technology transfer centers.

National Institute on Alcohol Abuse and Alcoholism http://www.niaaa.nih.gov

The NIAAA is a federal agency dedicated to promoting research on alcohol problems. The Web site contains a wealth of information on alcohol disorders of interest to social workers.

National Institute on Drug Abuse http://www.nida.nih.gov

The NIDA is a federal agency dedicated to promoting research on drug problems. The Web site contains a wealth of information on drug disorders of interest to social workers.

**Substance Abuse and Mental Health Services Administration
http://www.samhsa.gov/**

This federal agency includes the Center for Substance Abuse Prevention, the Center for Substance Abuse Treatment, and the Center for Mental Health Services. SAMHSA provides an abundance of practice-relevant information on mental and substance use disorders, including its Treatment Improvement Protocol Series manuals (compilations of practice information and tools to help serve clients).

Social Work Practice in Health-Care Settings

Robin Kennedy

The hospital social service movement aims to throw new light on medical practice in our institutions. It seeks to understand and to treat the social complications of disease by establishing a close relationship between the medical care of patients in hospitals or dispensaries and the services of those skilled in the profession of social work. It strives to bring to the institutionalized care of the sick such personal and individual attention to the patient's social condition that his recovery may be hastened and safeguarded.

The goal of medical social work has changed little since Ida Cannon, the first person identified as a medical social worker, wrote these words almost a century ago. However, advances in medical technologies, the proliferation of practice arenas for medical social work, the growth of public and private health insurance, and the advent of managed care have broadened the scope of social work in health care well beyond what Cannon could have imagined. This chapter examines today's changing health-care environments and medical social work's role in those environments.

THE HISTORY OF MEDICAL SOCIAL WORK

During the 1800s there were two popular beliefs regarding disease: it was retribution from God for errant behavior, and it resulted from residing in unsanitary living conditions. Eventually, Louis Pasteur and other scientists formulated germ theory and discovered that the real cause of disease was bacteria, leading them to conclude that neither God nor cleanliness alone could fend off illness (Trattner, 1994). This medical breakthrough and the identification of the relationships among a concentrated urban population, poverty, and disease brought social workers into public health practice. As one reformer of the day put it, "Social workers and health officers met because their work brought them to the same place, namely, the home in which there was both communicable disease and poverty" (qtd. in Trattner, 1994, p. 146).

Medical social work originated during the Progressive Era in the late 1800s, when settlement house workers began offering public education on personal hygiene, providing medications through drug dispensaries, and

193

requesting the assistance of visiting nurses (Leiby, 1978). In 1903, social workers employed by the Charity Organization Society conducted the first comprehensive study of tuberculosis, in which the disease's social aspects were examined (Trattner, 1994).

At first, the terms *medical social work* and *hospital social work* were used interchangeably, in part because medical care outside an individual's home was almost always delivered in a hospital (Trattner, 1994). Even outpatient health clinics were located in hospitals. In 1907, the medical reformer Dr. Richard Cabot hired Ida Cannon, the pioneer of medical social work, to work at Massachusetts General Hospital. In a clinic in the hospital, Cannon began to illuminate the connection between health and social conditions. As medical care was increasingly delivered in hospitals, physicians' familiarity with patients in the context of their homes, families, and neighborhoods was lost, and the need for hospital social workers grew. Cabot wrote:

> I found myself constantly baffled and discouraged when it came to treatment. Treatment in more than half of the cases . . . involved an understanding of the patient's economic situation and economic means, but still more of his mentality, his character, his previous mental and industrial history, all that brought him to his present condition in which sickness, fear, worry and poverty were found inextricably mingled. . . . Facing my own failures day after day[,] . . . my work came to seem intolerable. I could not . . . face the patients when I had so little to give them. (Qtd. in Dodds, 1993, p. 149)

From the beginning, medical social workers have recognized the interface between patients' biological, psychological, and social conditions. Cabot and Cannon shared concerns for patients' social circumstances, but they disagreed on the tasks medical social workers should perform to meet patients' needs. Cabot (1928/1955) expected medical social workers to act as liaisons between the hospital and community resources in order to "connect the hospital with all the social forces and helpful agencies outside its walls" (p. 260). Today, this is called case management, and those who perform this service are case managers. Cannon (1913) wanted to expand social work's role to include the treatment of psychological and social problems, problems that may be a cause or effect of illness. Even recently in a study of medical social work, one physician reported using social workers as "psychotherapists," while another saw social workers as "connectors, [who] connect to transportation, . . . home health, meal programs," and the like (Netting & Williams, 1996, p. 221). Some of the struggles social workers experience in the medical field can be attributed to the various ideas other medical professionals have concerning what constitutes medical social work.

Reacting to political and professional forces, over the past century, social workers themselves have emphasized either social or psychological care. In the beginning, medical social work reflected the social concerns of the day, emphasizing the social roots of disease. During the 1920s, social work embraced Freudian thought, and the profession became more psychologically focused. In the 1930s the Great Depression put the spotlight back on social interventions. During the 1950s, returning World War II veterans suffering from shell shock (now called post-traumatic stress disorder) brought renewed attention to psychological interventions. And in the 1960s and 1970s, the civil rights movement and President Lyndon Johnson's Great Society social reforms, which included the establishment of government health insurance programs, influenced medical social work. Since the 1980s, medical social work has incorporated both a psychological perspective, which has been fueled by third-party (insurance) reimbursement for therapy and counseling, and case management and discharge planning, which have been driven by managed care and cost controls (Cowles, 2003).

THE CHANGING FACE OF HEALTH CARE
Medical Advances

Prior to the mid-twentieth century, the primary cause of death was infectious diseases (tuberculosis, cholera, malaria, leprosy, and typhoid), that is, diseases caused by bacteria. Once cures for those diseases were discovered, a new group of illnesses, chronic diseases that evaded cures, became the major cause of death. Today, the four leading causes of death in the United States are chronic illnesses (see box 9.1). Such diseases once rapidly resulted in death. Now they are often treated with prolonged and costly interventions.

Advanced medical technology has had positive outcomes, such as earlier detection of illnesses, increased life expectancy, decreased recuperation time, and increased quality of life. But technology also has social and eco-

---

Box 9.1   Leading Causes of Death and Sources of Health Disparities

Five leading causes of death in the United States, 2004

Cause	Number of deaths
Heart disease	654,092
Cancer	550,270
Stroke	150,147
Chronic lower respiratory disease	123,884
Accidents (unintentional injuries)	108,694

Death rates due to heart disease, cancer, stroke, chronic lower respiratory disease, and unintentional injuries increase with age. Death rates for African Americans exceed those for whites of the same gender for each of the five major causes of death, and socioeconomic factors are strongly associated with risk of death. The death rates of adult males and females with a high school education or less are more than twice as high as the rates for those with more than a high school education. Social workers work to reduce these health disparities by advocating universal health care, promoting healthier lifestyles, and helping individuals obtain preventive health care.

Source: National Center for Health Statistics. (2006). *Deaths—leading causes.* Retrieved February 28, 2007, from http://www.cdc.gov/nchs/fastats/lcod.htm

nomic drawbacks. Technology can extend an individual's life even while quality of life deteriorates. Social workers often help individuals and family members struggling with decisions to prolong or end care. They also serve on hospital ethics committees that address these difficult issues. In all health-care settings, adult patients who are mentally competent should be urged to complete a durable power of attorney for health care and advance directives so that their wishes will be clear should they become unable to participate in their own health-care decision making (see box 9.2).

Box 9.2 Advance Directives

As life spans increase due to advances in medical technology, social workers are concerned about the quality of those additional years. Advance health-care directives allow individuals to retain autonomy over their health-care decisions, including their right to refuse life-sustaining treatment and, ultimately, the right to die. The Patient Self-Determination Act of 1990 requires health-care providers who accept Medicare and Medicaid to discuss advance directives with patients. Each state has unique guidelines for drafting advance directives, but four features are common:

1 Instructions for health care state an individual's wishes for medical care should he or she have an incurable or irreversible condition that will result in death within a brief period of time, should he or she become unconscious and the chances of regaining consciousness are unlikely, and in cases where the risks of treatment outweigh the anticipated benefits. Individuals can state preferences regarding feeding tubes, hydration, ventilators, and other health-care interventions.

2 In most advance directives, individuals have the option of filling out a section on organ donation. Should an individual wish to be an organ donor, he or she may clarify which organs and tissues may be donated and for what purpose (transplant, research, or education).

3 Individuals have the option of designating a primary-care physician. This can be especially helpful when several specialists are caring for a patient.

4 A durable power of attorney for health care allows individuals to appoint a proxy to make health-care decisions for them in the event of their incapacitation. A durable power of attorney is usually a family member or close friend who understands the individual's health-care wishes and is willing to accept responsibility for making medical decisions when the individual cannot.

Once the document is completed, it is highly advisable for the individual to inform the durable power of attorney and family members of his or her decisions. It is important to make sure they understand the individual's wishes. Copies of the directive should be given to the durable power of attorney, all physicians providing care, and the hospital each time an individual is admitted. The directive should be kept in a readily accessible place in the home, *not* in a safe-deposit box. Should an individual wish to change his or her advance directive, all interested parties should be notified, and a new advance directive executed and distributed. When possible, old advance directives should be destroyed.

Psychosocial Illnesses

Psychosocial problems that social workers often treat, such as alcohol, drug, and nicotine dependence; domestic violence; eating disorders; and a high-stress lifestyle, have created a new group of health-care consumers. These conditions are not amenable to cures in the way that infectious diseases are, and many of them lead to health problems that require medical treatment (e.g., emphysema and lung cancer due to smoking, cirrhosis due to alcoholism), but in earlier stages, the mainstays of treatment are the cognitive and behavioral treatments (interventions designed to change thoughts, feelings, and behavior) that social workers deliver. These conditions are often called public health problems because they require public education and community efforts to prevent and treat them. Many of them are discussed in chapter 8.

Cost Containment and Managed Care

In 2004, health-care spending in the United States (public and private) totaled $1.9 trillion (Centers for Medicare and Medicaid Services, 2006). Health-care costs have increased dramatically over the past forty years. National health-care expenditures rose from 5.3 percent of the gross domestic product in 1960 to 15 percent in 2003, making the United States the country with the largest share of the GDP being spent on health care (see table 9.1). The United States also spends far more per capita on health care than any other country. The percentage of total health-care costs paid out-of-pocket by patients has declined, while that paid by private health insurance companies has risen (see table 9.2). Health care is an expensive commodity, as anyone who has recently received a medical bill can confirm.

Table 9.1   **Total health expenditures as a percent of gross domestic product and per capita health expenditures in U.S. dollars for selected countries**

Country	Percent of GDP	Per capita expenses
Australia[a]	9.3	$2,699
Canada[b]	9.9	$3,003
Germany[c]	11.1	$2,996
Sweden[a]	9.2	$2,270
United Kingdom[a]	7.7	$2,594
United States[c]	15.0	$5,635

[a]2002
[b]Estimate, 2003
[c]2003

Source: Organization for Economic Cooperation and Development. (2005, July). *OECD in figures, 2005: Statistics on the member countries*. Paris: Author.

Table 9.2   Percent of personal health-care expenses by type/source of funds: 1960, 1980, and 2002

Sources of funds	1960	1980	2002
Out-of-pocket	55.2	27.1	15.9
Private health insurance	21.4	28.3	35.8
Other private funds	2.0	4.3	4.2
Government	21.4	40.3	44.2
Federal	8.7	29.3	33.6
State and local	12.6	11.1	10.6

Source: National Center for Health Statistics. (2004). *Health, United States, 2004 with chartbooks on trends in the health of Americans*. Hyattsville, MD: U.S. Department of Health and Human Services.

During the mid-1960s, Congress passed Medicare and Medicaid legislation as part of the Social Security Act. These public health insurance programs were introduced to address the increasing medical needs of older and indigent individuals. As health-care costs escalated and the number of people covered by these programs grew, expenditures for these programs rose dramatically. Both state and federal governments have controlled Medicaid spending for outpatient and inpatient medical care by severely limiting reimbursement rates to medical providers (many physicians do not accept Medicaid payments due to low reimbursement rates, and both this and the paperwork involved make it difficult for Medicaid participants to obtain care).

In the mid-1980s, Congress took a major step toward cost containment when it introduced diagnosis-related groups (DRGs) in Medicare. Under the DRG system, hospitals receive a flat fee depending on the patient's diagnosis, not the patient's length of stay in the hospital. Hospitals' financial success, therefore, depends on the timely and efficient discharge of patients. The use of DRGs has resulted in shorter hospital stays and in patients frequently being discharged before they or their families can independently provide care. Medicare's use of DRGs has also influenced private health insurers to shorten hospital stays in an effort to reduce costs. DRGs spurred the rapid growth of a health-care delivery system outside the hospital that has revolutionized the role of the hospital social worker, who often plays a key role in discharge planning. The hospital social worker's expeditious assessment of biopsychosocial needs, family circumstances, housing needs, economic circumstances, and aftercare needs can foster a patient's safe transition from hospital to subacute or home care.

Managed Care

Managed care is a generic term that refers to a number of arrangements insurers and health plans use to control health-care utilization and costs. In these systems, care managers often determine whether third parties (i.e., public or private insurers) will pay for a service. Some managed care systems reimburse based on *capitation*: each year the insurer pays the health-care provider a set amount to serve a patient, regardless of how much health care the patient requires. Managed care's overarching goals are to control health-care costs and provide responsible, high-quality care (Wernet, 1999). These goals can be at odds. Sometimes social workers find themselves helping patients obtain services that a health insurer has denied. Managed care has transformed medical care by affecting decision making, providing standardized treatment, and relying on community-based care (Wernet, 1999).

Decision making   Prior to the 1980s, patients and physicians exercised a great deal of autonomy in health-care decisions. Individuals chose their primary-care physician or specialists based on personal preference. Physicians operated independently; they worked in private offices and saw their own patients in the hospital. They ordered tests, diagnosed illnesses, and prescribed medical procedures and medications as they saw fit. Health-care providers billed patients and insurance companies after services were rendered. In this fee-for-service system, insurance carriers had little voice or veto power in health-care decision making (Robinson, 1999). Managed care has sought to constrain the autonomy of both patient and physician in an attempt to stabilize as well as standardize health-care costs (Wernet, 1999). Today, in many cases, a patient's care manager, who either is employed by or contracts with an insurance company, must be consulted to approve the procedure as well as the physician who will do it.

Standardized treatment   Perhaps the most frequently criticized aspect of managed care is standardized treatment—the belief that eliminating idiosyncratic treatment decisions can ensure quality care while reducing costs (Wernet, 1999). Under this system, patients and physicians may request a particular medication or surgical procedure only to have the insurance carrier deny it and recommend another form of treatment in its place. Critics claim that standardized treatment infringes on the intimate relationship between patients and their health-care providers. Social work is often at odds with such standardization because it impinges on the social work principles of client self-determination and confidentiality.

Community-based care   Managed care policies restrict needed hospital stays not only by limiting the length of patients' stays but also by utilizing new modes of health delivery such as outpatient surgery centers, subacute care units, home health care, and hospice care. Social workers help by directing patients to resources that facilitate prevention, early detection, and comprehensive service delivery, which not only increase the quality of life but also reduce health-care costs (Cook, Freedman, Freedman, Arick, & Miller, 1996). Social workers have become increasingly involved with health promotion activities in the areas of women's health, chronic pain management, smoking cessation, and stress management, as well as support services such as caregiver support groups, psychoeducational cancer groups, and grief support groups for women who have experienced miscarriages and stillbirths. Although managed health care can challenge social work values, it has the potential to improve health-care quality, lower costs, and offer new opportunities (Schneider, Hyer, & Luptak, 2000), perhaps by extending coverage to more individuals without insurance.

Declining Health-Care Coverage

The Medicare program covers virtually all Americans age sixty-five and older, but the percentage of uninsured adults under age sixty-five increased from 15.6 percent in 1987 to 20.6 percent in 2004. Furthermore, 11.6 percent of U.S. children are uninsured (Kaiser Commission on Medicaid and the Uninsured, 2005). The U.S. Census Bureau reports that most uninsured adults in the United States work part-time or full-time, earn moderate incomes, and have dependent family members (DeNavas-Walt, Proctor, & Lee, 2006). Due to the costs involved, some employers do not offer employees health insurance. Other employers have shifted increased insurance costs to their employees. Low- to moderate-income workers who find it difficult to absorb the additional costs may decline coverage. It is also likely that they cannot afford to pay large medical bills out-of-pocket. Medical bills are the leading cause of bankruptcy in the United States (Himmelstein, Warren, Thorne, & Woolhandler, 2005), and lack of insurance contributes to the health disparities described in box 9.3. In general, people of color are much more likely to be uninsured than whites, and Hispanics are most likely to be uninsured. The National Association of Social Workers (2003) is working to see that all Americans have "access to a continuum of health and mental health care to promote wellness, maintain optimal health, prevent illness and disability, treat health conditions, ameliorate the effects of unavoidable incapacities, and provide supportive long-term and end-of-life care" (p. 172).

MEDICAL SOCIAL WORK PRACTICE

Medical social work incorporates three theoretical perspectives that are the foundation of all social work practice: the biopsychosocial model, a strengths perspective, and multilevel practice.

Box 9.3   Organ Donation

The current supply of organs and tissue is not keeping up with demand. Most organ donors are accident or trauma victims. Medical social workers often help families as they face the imminent death of a loved one. Social workers' skills in grief work, cultural sensitivity, and family conflict resolution can all play a vital role in helping families in shock and grief decide whether to donate a loved one's organs.

Before a transplant can occur, psychological assessment and counseling are required for the recipient and family. Transplants affect individuals and their families emotionally, socially, financially, and spiritually. Social work's advantage is in viewing the whole family as the patient. After transplant, social workers help patients and their families cope with fears of organ rejection, relationship and lifestyle issues, medication side effects, and the emotions involved in living with another person's organs (Geva & Weinman, 1995).

Transplant demand is particularly high among African Americans and Asian Americans, who are three times more likely than whites to have end-stage kidney disease. Four times more American Indians than whites have diabetes, and African Americans have the highest hypertension rates of all races. These disorders may result in the need for organ transplantation. Medical social workers serve as educators and advocates in communities of color, where donations lag well behind need. Donors and recipients often need to be genetically similar in order to prevent infection. While 23 percent of the individuals on the kidney waiting list are African American, only 12 percent of donors are African American. People of color wait longer for an organ, are sicker when they receive a transplant, and are more likely to die before an organ can be located (U.S. Department of Health and Human Services, 2005). Social workers often head organ procurement (donation) teams and work on legislative initiatives that support organ donation and transplantation.

Biopsychosocial Approach

The World Health Organization (1947) defines health as "a state of complete physical, mental and social well-being and not merely the absence of disease or infirmity" (p. 225). This definition was not written by a social worker, but it could have been. It succinctly summarizes social work's interest within the medical model, but the social work perspective differs from the medical model in critical ways. The medical model focuses on disease and the treatment of disease. The biopsychosocial model sees the patient holistically, acknowledging the connections among the patient's health, psychological state, family situation, employment, financial status, culture, religion, and neighborhood conditions. Cowles (2003) explains:

> A social situation or life change event (such as marital dysfunction, social isolation, loss of one's job, or death of a loved one) can produce emotional distress that can lead to changes in physical functioning that increase vulnerability to disease. On the other hand, a physical health problem can erode self-confidence or

interfere with the ability to perform customary activities, which can affect work, marriage, or other social roles and relationships and, in turn, lead to emotional distress. (pp. 12–13)

In other words, social work is just as concerned with how the patient and his or her environment affect the disease and the healing process as they are with how the disease affects the patient. Although both physicians' and nurses' training has begun to move away from a strict medical model by incorporating a psychosocial perspective, this holistic view of the patient remains the focus of medical social work.

Strengths Approach

The strengths perspective is an important counterbalance to the medical model's preoccupation with pathology and deficits. Saleebey (1997) recognized that "trauma, abuse, illness, and struggle may be injurious but they may also be sources of challenge and opportunity" (p. 14). The strengths approach acknowledges the resources within the individual and in his or her environment. It invites each patient's participation in his or her own treatment plan. Instead of viewing patients as victims of their disease or disability, the focus of the strengths approach is on their inherent ability to survive and perhaps even thrive in the face of adversity (Johnson & Yanca, 2001).

Multilevel Approach

In taking a multilevel approach, social workers apply the biopsychosocial model and the strengths perspective at all levels of practice. *Micropractice* focuses on the individual patient and family system and requires knowledge of the client population being served, including common health problems and frequently used treatment approaches. For example, an oncology social worker is knowledgeable about various types of cancers, including those that are more common among different segments of the population; the generally recognized treatments; and the side effects that often accompany these treatments (Cowles, 2003).

Mezzopractice refers to work with organizations and communities. In health care, social workers often deliver an intervention in a host setting such as a hospital or community-based agency. Mezzopractice requires knowledge of organizational settings (public; nonprofit; and for profit, or proprietary); range of health-care services provided; the mission or vision statement; and authority structure, policies, and rules. It also requires the use of interdisciplinary teams and an understanding of how social work fits within the organization (Cowles, 2003). For example, a nursing home social worker understands the facility's ownership, auspices, and corporate structure, and how the voice of social work affects decision making in that system. Mezzopractice also involves an understanding of communities and the problems they face, such as environmental hazards that may negatively affect residents' health or barriers to health-care services such as limited health-care providers. Social workers work with community groups to address these problems.

Macropractice involves policy analysis and development, program planning, and political advocacy for adequate and equitable health-care services for all Americans. It requires thorough knowledge of national, state, and local health-care systems, including the rules governing eligibility, participation, and services provided (Cowles, 2003). Medical social workers are expected to stay informed of the latest health-care issues and advocate care that best meets clients' needs in all areas of the health-care system.

MEDICAL SOCIAL WORKERS' DUTIES

The medical social worker's duties vary across work settings and populations. Even within a hospital setting, social work responsibilities differ depending on the facility, the unit in the facility, the culture of the unit, and the culture of the social work department within the facility. A pediatric unit social worker's duties, for example, will differ from an emergency department social worker's duties. In addition, social workers' duties in the same hospital on the same unit may differ depending on the shifts they work. Social workers on the night shift need to be well acquainted with community service providers; however, they generally make few referrals other than for emergency psychiatric or drug treatment. Cases may be handed over to the incoming day-shift social worker, or the patient could be discharged with referrals for follow-up care. In contrast, day-shift social workers may spend a great deal of time on the telephone making referrals, meeting with patients and family members, and talking with the treatment team. Box 9.4 lists many responsibilities of medical social workers, and box 9.5 provides an example of culturally competent social work practice in the event of a patient's death.

Medical social work was the first specialization area in the social work profession. Medical social workers were also the first members of the profession to work in what has come to be called a secondary setting, where providing social work services is not the organization's primary function (Cowles, 2003). Secondary settings where social workers are employed or provide services on a contract basis include hospitals, schools, prisons, and corporations. Effective practice in a secondary setting demands that differ-

---

Box 9.4   Medical Social Work Responsibilities

Micropractice (Individual and Family)

Assess biopsychosocial needs of patients

Provide counseling services to patients and families

Offer health education for patients and families

Provide case management

Provide information and referral services for patients and families

Advocate for patient within family

Provide treatment and care planning

Discharge planning

Provide home assessment (determining if the housing structure needs modification or if special medical equipment is needed)

Assist with advanced directives

Mezzopractice (Organization and Community)

Participate in interdisciplinary treatment teams

Advocate for patient in the health-care organization or community

Ensure provision of quality services in the organization

Identify unmet health-care needs in the health-care organization or community

Act as liaison between organization and community

Plan community health-care services

Offer health education in the community

Macropractice (National and Global)

Advocate needed services within existing national health-care systems

Advocate adequate patient services in private insurance companies

Advocate national health-care plan that ensures health care for everyone

Advocate health-care research funding

Offer public education regarding current health-care issues (e.g., organ donation or physician-assisted suicide)

Seek funding to meet global health-care demands

Promote healthy environmental conditions (safe drinking water or reduction of industrial pollution)

Advocate an adequate level of health care for all people of the world

---

ent disciplines recognize and respect each other's theoretical perspectives and professional values. Formal education professionalizes individuals into their respective disciplines, and little time is devoted to exploring the values and ethical standards of other health-care professions. Interdisciplinary medical teams are the ideal vehicle for recognition and respect of other health-care professionals. With its emphasis on an ecosystems approach, social work is well suited for interdisciplinary work.

Depending on the setting and the patient's needs, medical interdisciplinary teams can include a range of professionals. Primary-care teams are usually the smallest; they generally consist of the patient, doctor, social worker, and any needed ancillary-care professionals, such as a physical or speech therapist. Nursing home interdisciplinary teams, which are often the largest, may also include the director of nursing, nurses' aides, family

Box 9.5   Mr. Vang's Death

Mr. Vang, a forty-five-year-old man of Hmong heritage, was brought to the emergency department with cardiopulmonary resuscitation in progress. He had collapsed on a popular jogging trail, and another jogger administered CPR on the scene until emergency medical services arrived. Mr. Vang's wife, mother, and father arrived at the emergency department shortly after he was brought in. The emergency department social worker, Jill Baker, met the family in the waiting area and quickly escorted them to a private room. She got a very brief medical history from the wife and mother that indicated no chronic or recent illness. Ms. Baker also learned that Mr. Vang was not taking any medications and did not use alcohol, recreational drugs, or tobacco. She returned to the treatment area and relayed this information to Elizabeth Johnson, the physician in charge.

Attempts to save Mr. Vang's life were unsuccessful; he was pronounced dead approximately thirty minutes after his arrival in the emergency department. Dr. Johnson and Ms. Baker delivered the news to his family. Dr. Johnson explained the patient's condition upon arrival in the emergency department and the efforts to save his life. The doctor stayed with the family for a short time before returning to the treatment area. Ms. Baker remained to provide emotional support and answer questions. She asked the family members if they would like to view the body. When they stated that they would, she prepared them for what they would see.

As an experienced emergency department social worker, Ms. Baker understands the effects a sudden and unexpected death can have on a family. In addition to understanding their grief,

she knows the challenges the family faces concerning their loved one's funeral and burial. It is a Hmong ritual to wash, clothe, and display the body in the family's home prior to burial. Ms. Baker had previously learned whom to call for permission to have a deceased person returned home prior to the funeral. However, because Mr. Vang was a relatively young and healthy man who died less than twenty-four hours after arriving in the emergency department, the body would have to be sent to the coroner for an autopsy, which involves cutting the body. Hmongs believe that the body should remain uncut and unscarred so that the individual will not be deformed when he or she is reincarnated. Due to the pending autopsy, Ms. Baker could not leave the family alone with the body. She explained to the family the criteria for an autopsy and provided a general overview of the process, while avoiding going into too much detail. She acknowledged the cultural conflict between the hospital's legal requirements and the family's religious customs and discussed how long the process would take and when the family could expect the body to be returned. Ms. Baker gave the family the telephone number of a local funeral director who had begun including Hmong traditions in the services offered. She also gave the family written step-by-step instructions for having the body delivered to their home.

The Vangs had suffered a devastating loss. Many of their customs could not be followed because of the circumstances of the death. The social worker's skills and cultural expertise at this tragic time were invaluable for the family and the emergency department.

members, and in some cases, the activities director and nursing home administrator.

Interdisciplinary team composition is also a product of organizational culture. While some institutions do not pay much attention to interdisciplinary meetings and do little in the way of thoughtful, inclusive care planning, others expect each professional to participate meaningfully and encourage patients' and family members' active involvement. When patients or family members cannot participate directly, it is usually the social worker's responsibility to ensure their wishes are considered in treatment and discharge decisions to the extent possible.

The concept of interdisciplinary teams requires that each team member complete an assessment according to the standards of his or her respective discipline, identifying tentative goals and the means of achieving those goals. Interdisciplinary team meetings bring all members together to share information and develop a treatment plan. Cowles (2003) suggests that "Perhaps the goal should be . . . an integration of theories and methodologies to reveal a clearer picture of how each is an integral part of a whole, like puzzle pieces that fit together to reveal an illuminating picture" (p. 123). Social workers are taught to place a high value on collaboration, whereas physicians are generally taught to assume leadership roles in interdisciplinary groups (Mizrahi & Abramson, 1985). Social workers use their systems-based strengths perspective to encourage all team members, from the nurses' aides to the physician, to learn from each other and contribute to treatment planning for each patient.

MEDICAL SOCIAL WORK PRACTICE SETTINGS
Primary Care

The term *primary care* means first contact with the health-care system. Many health-care delivery settings are forms of primary care: individual and group medical practices, emergency departments, public health clinics, outpatient clinics (often under the auspices of a teaching hospital), HIV/AIDS clinics, renal dialysis centers, and family planning clinics. Social work's integration in these settings varies depending on perceived need and available funding.

Although some private physicians include social workers on their practice team, group medical practices lag behind other primary health-care providers in social work collaboration (Badger, Ackerson, Buttell, & Rand, 1997). Emergency departments with trauma units usually have a full-time social worker, but many emergency departments share the social workers assigned to acute care (e.g., surgery, cardiac) units in the hospital. In public health settings such as HIV/AIDS or family planning clinics, social workers are firmly entrenched in the care delivery system.

Department of Veterans Affairs

The Department of Veterans Affairs established social work services in 1926. Although social workers initially focused on patients with tuberculosis or psychiatric illnesses, the VA pioneered social work services across the health-care spectrum. The Department of Veterans Affairs (2004) describes social workers as "responsible for ensuring continuity of care through the admission, evaluation, treatment, and follow-up processes" (para. 3). Special VA programs have focused on veterans who are homeless, elderly, or ex-POWs; have spinal cord injury or HIV/AIDS; or served in the Vietnam or Persian Gulf wars.

Renal Dialysis Centers

When a patient's kidney function fails, renal replacement therapy may maintain his or her life. Most patients eventually develop terminal kidney failure, for which the only treatment is a transplant. The increase in kidney disease over the last fifteen years has increased the wait for a kidney to four years or more (National Institutes of Health, 2000). Social work has a strong presence in nephrology (the medical specialization for kidney disorders), due to the life-altering nature of the disease. Nephrology social workers help patients address physical, emotional, and social stresses, including the financial burdens of services, interruptions in employment,

A veteran checks in for her appointment with a social worker at a veterans affairs hospital.
© Mary Whelens

changes in sexual functioning, demanding and time-consuming treatment regimens, and shortened life expectancy. Nephrology social workers support patients and their family members and caregivers by discussing with them the range of treatment options, arranging for treatment, and providing pre- and post-transplant counseling (National Association of Social Workers, 1994).

Gay, Lesbian, Bisexual, and Transgender Clinics

Negative attitudes held toward GLBT populations by the general public as well as physicians and health-care providers have spawned community-based primary-care clinics such as the Callen-Lorde Community Health Center in New York and the Fenway Community Health Center in Boston (also see chapter 6). These clinics were developed over twenty years ago to combat substandard care and stigmatization of the GLBT population. Social workers in these clinics offer a range of culturally sensitive services to support patients' physical and emotional well-being, including support groups that address the coming-out process and recovery from methamphetamine abuse, as well as groups for lesbians with cancer, partners of people with HIV, and partners of transgender individuals. In addition to group work, social workers provide individual counseling for transgender issues, alcohol and drug problems, and family planning (e.g., insemination, adoption, and surrogacy).

Hospitals

Hospitals (acute care facilities) emerged in the late 1700s as a result of the middle class's demands for clean and respectable places to obtain health care (Nacman, 1977). The number of hospitals in the United States grew steadily during the early twentieth century, peaking in 1984. Since then, the number of facilities and the number of beds have decreased, as many procedures are now done on an outpatient basis or require much shorter hospital stays. The increased costs of delivering inpatient care have also caused most independent hospitals to become part of large corporations, both nonprofit and proprietary (Gray, 1991). These trends and the restrictions imposed by managed health care have had considerable implications for social work practice in hospitals. Many hospital social work departments have decreased in size or have been eliminated and absorbed into case management departments. Nurse case managers have taken over many of the responsibilities of discharge planning (previously a social work domain).

Although the number of hospital social workers has decreased, social work remains a mainstay in acute care settings. As Ross (1993) notes, "there is more for social workers to do, because when admitted to the hospital, patients are often sicker than they were in the past, and when they are discharged they are barely well. Today patients have more needs and more social problems for which there are few resources" (p. 243). Medical social workers are the only hospital professionals prepared to assess patients' and families' psychosocial and economic needs, negotiate treatment plans, provide interpersonal counseling, make referrals for community-based treatment, and bring this information to the interdisciplinary care team to aid in discharge. Today's hospital social worker needs well-developed clinical skills to assess highly complex cases and resolve psychosocial dilemmas in a very short period of time (Humphreys & Falck, 1990).

Subacute Care

When patients no longer need the acute care that hospitals provide but are still unable to return home safely, social workers often arrange for their transfer to a *subacute* or transitional care unit. Subacute care units may be discrete units within a hospital; designated beds in a nursing home, usually referred to as a skilled nursing facility; or freestanding facilities such as rehabilitation facilities. Patients' needs might include complex wound care, cardiovascular accident recovery, infusion therapy (medication delivered through an IV), post-surgery recovery, orthopedic recovery, brain injury treatment, spinal cord injury treatment, tracheotomy care, ventilator care, or cancer treatment. Subacute care stays can range in length from one day to two years, but most are less than thirty days (Burns, 1993). The approach in subacute care units is generally outcome focused (e.g., helping a patient regain sufficient use of his or her limbs to return to independent living). The social worker's job often involves counseling individuals or families to address the physical and mental challenges that accompany the patient's condition.

Home Health Care

Nursing, social work, physical therapy, and occupational therapy delivered in the patient's home are referred to as home health care. The services of personal care providers such as home health aides and homemakers, who help patients with activities of daily living like bathing and toileting, and independent activities of daily living like meal preparation and housekeeping, are also a form of home health care. Anyone with significant impairments may need home health services, but the typical client is an elderly woman who lives alone, has a number of impairments that prevent her from carrying out activities of daily living, receives Medicaid, and has few family ties and little informal support (Kadushin, 2004).

Although the Visiting Nurse Association was organized in 1885, home health care as it is delivered today was virtually unknown prior to Medicare and Medicaid's enactment in 1965 (Cowles, 2003). From 1965 to 1985, the number of home health-care agencies grew slowly. These agencies were often affiliated with a hospital or a nonprofit agency like the Visiting Nurse Association. The nature of home care changed drastically in the mid-1980s. The introduction of DRGs led to earlier and earlier hospital discharges, which brought about the rapid growth of both nonprofit as well as proprietary home health-care agencies, but family and friends still provide most home care. Although patients generally prefer to recuperate in their own homes rather than in a hospital, they as well as their family members are frightened when they are sent home before independent ambulation or their ability to perform independent activities of daily living is restored. Home care can be seen as a humane response to the early (sometimes premature) discharge of patients from acute care units.

Even when they are clearly needed, home health patients are not necessarily referred for social work services. Under Medicare, such referrals are contingent on the physician's judgment that social work services are necessary to resolve the patient's medical problems. Some evidence indicates that nonprofit agencies that are supported by philanthropic sources and have altruistic community service values are more likely to provide social services for which they will not be reimbursed than for-profit agencies, whose income derives from third-party reimbursement or private-pay patients (Williams, 1994). In other cases, for example in rural areas, home health-care agencies do not offer medical social services because the community lacks social workers to provide them.

Nursing Homes

The term *nursing home* generally refers to two levels of care: intermediate (custodial) care facilities and skilled nursing facilities. Intermediate care entails a slightly lower level of care than skilled care and is not covered under Medicare. Medicaid is the largest payer of nursing home care. For Medicaid to pay for a nursing home, an older or disabled individual's income must generally fall below the poverty level. Medicare, the third-largest payer, generally covers only brief stays in skilled nursing facilities. Eligibility criteria are strict: patients must have severe physical limitations and enter the nursing home within thirty days of discharge from an acute or subacute care facility. Those who do not meet Medicare or Medicaid criteria must pay privately, either out-of-pocket (the second-largest source of nursing home payments) or with long-term care insurance (which accounts for only a small percentage of costs). Many residents pay for long-term care in intermediate care facilities out-of-pocket until they exhaust all their resources. Then they convert to (qualify for) Medicaid reimbursement. Nursing homes may operate under public, private nonprofit (often civic or religious), or private for-profit (corporate-owned) auspices. The for-profit nursing home industry receives billions of dollars in revenue (for example, in 2004, nursing home giant Beverly Enterprises reported netting $191 million, a 54 percent increase over its revenue for 2003).

A recent study of state nursing home inspection reports found that for-profit facilities averaged 46 percent more deficiencies per home than public facilities and overall "provided worse care and less nursing care than not-for-profit or public homes" (Harrington, Woolhandler, Mullen, & Himmelstein, 2002, p. 315). Despite their negative image, nursing homes serve a vital purpose. They care for those not sick enough to be in the hospital but too sick to be at home, those who cannot afford home care through public or private means, and those who do not have family or friends who can care for them. Medicare and Medicaid regulations require that social workers lead interdisciplinary teams of nursing home care providers in creating individual care plans for each nursing home resident. But when sick, frail, old people spend exorbitant sums for substandard nursing home care while corporations experience unprecedented earnings, a redesign of the system is clearly in order. This, too, is social work's domain.

Research shows that residents who have been involved in the decision to move to nursing homes and who take part in their own care plans have a greater sense of control, higher satisfaction, and decreased levels of aggression and depression (Ingersoll-Dayton, Schroepfer, Pryce, & Waarala, 2003). Since individuals entering nursing homes are often frail, it is easy for them to be overlooked in decision making. Social workers uphold the principle of self-determination by inviting residents to participate in their care planning to the extent they can do so. Residents without full mental capacities still have wishes and desires that should be incorporated in their treatment. If the patient has severe dementia, the social worker is responsible for enlisting available and concerned family members' participation.

Hospice

Hospice comes from the word *hospitality*, meaning to host and give comfort. Since about 300 CE, abodes called hostels or hospices (e.g., convents, monasteries, and private homes) have taken in the sick and dying (Kerr, 1993). Cicely Saunders, considered the mother of the hospice movement, opened the first modern-day hospice, St. Christopher's of London, in 1967. Saunders was a nurse working with World War II casualties in the early

1940s in London. In the mid-1940s she earned a degree in medical social work. Her work with terminally ill patients piqued her interest in analgesics (pain relievers). She received a pharmacological fellowship at St. Joseph's Hospice and later completed a medical degree and began conducting clinical trials on pain medication. Describing her work at St. Joseph's, Saunders (1996) later reported "having the time to sit and listen to a patient's story, [which] transformed the wards." She also said:

> It soon became clear that each death was as individual as the life that preceded it and that the whole experience of that life was reflected in a patient's dying. This led to the concept of "total pain," which was presented as a complex of physical, emotional, social, and spiritual elements. The whole experience for a patient includes anxiety, depression, and fear; concern for the family who will become bereaved; and often a need to find some meaning in the situation, some deeper reality in which to trust. (Para. 12)

The first U.S. hospice, the Hospice of Connecticut, opened in 1974 and was modeled after St. Christopher's (Hayslip & Leon, 1992), but hospice services in the United States evolved differently than those in Europe. The British model centered primarily on inpatient hospice care. In the United Stares, hospice care is generally provided in the patient's home (Center to Advance Palliative Care, 2002). Only 20 percent of hospice patients receive hospice services in nursing homes or freestanding hospice facilities. British hospice care evolved from its national health-care system, in which all individuals have equal access to medical care. Hospice care provided specialized knowledge of pain control and the dying process. U.S. hospice care developed outside the established health-care system due to the lack of specialized care for many terminally ill patients. To qualify for hospice services, patients' life expectancy must be six months or less and they must decline curative treatment (e.g., chemotherapy or radiation).

The hospice mission embodies the spirit of medical social work, which makes sense, given Cecily Saunders's background. Values of self-determination and the individual's dignity and worth are woven into the hospice philosophy. Emphasis is on quality of life, service to the patient as well as family and caregivers, recognition that each individual's dying process is unique, and providing the most sophisticated forms of pain relief as well as physical, emotional, spiritual, and social support and validation according to patients' and families' needs.

Palliative Care

The term *palliative care* means comfort care. Historically the term has described the services delivered by hospice workers, but over the last decade it has come to describe the care provided to a broader population of patients. Palliative-care recipients differ from hospice patients in two important areas: their life expectancy can exceed six months, and they may still receive curative treatment. For example, an individual with cancer would not have to give up chemotherapy to receive palliative-care services. Palliative-care and hospice patients receive similar services, including sophisticated pain evaluation and treatment and social work and spiritual counseling, if desired. The patient's family may also receive counseling before and after the patient's death. Public and private insurance may not cover palliative-care services. Most palliative-care providers work under the auspices of a hospital, nursing home, or hospice.

FROM THE PRESENT TO THE FUTURE

Health care in the United States continues to change rapidly. Despite health-care providers' and social workers' resistance to managed care, this paradigm continues to evolve in an effort to further contain costs, affecting all areas of health-care delivery. Hospitals and subacute care facilities have been pressured to reduce the length of patient stays. Publicly supported home health-care services have been cut, forcing patients to pay for more of the services they need. Criteria for Medicaid nursing home admissions have become stricter, and more individuals are denied nursing home placement, which places many frail individuals at risk. Caseloads are increasing in the emotionally demanding atmosphere of hospice care. These changes all contribute to the practice challenges and ethical dilemmas that social workers in health care face.

Vaghy (1998) has identified additional issues facing medical social work:

- As technology continues to increase the life span, social workers will be helping more individuals decide whether they wish to receive life-sustaining procedures.
- As more illnesses that once caused a quick death become chronic conditions, social workers will help more patients manage long-term care demands.
- As the amount of money available for health care needs to be stretched to meet the needs of a growing number of people, social workers will assist more informal caregivers (family and friends).
- Social workers will be helping more proprietary health-care providers weigh the notion of high-quality compassionate care against the need for profit.
- Social workers will be helping more individuals who have socioenvironmental illnesses.

In the international arena, social workers are helping to get services to those who do not have even the most basic health care or nutrition necessary for good health. They are also delivering family planning services and helping to stem the spread of diseases such as AIDS. Both in the United States and abroad, these services are fraught with controversy (e.g., debates over birth control and abortion and appropriate sexual behavior between consenting adults of the same or opposite sex) that increasingly tests social workers' political and policy-making skills.

As in other important areas of social welfare policy, social workers have generally not been at the table when government or proprietary health-care organizations have made important policy changes in health-care programs. Social work's multilevel perspective provides an important point of view that should be considered in any major policy shift.

SUMMARY

Medical social work helps patients and their families navigate the changing health-care environment. Specht and Craig (1985) define social work as a "profession with a dual purpose: to assist individuals and groups whose needs are not adequately met and to help change institutions so that they are more responsive to individual and group needs" (p. 11). Medical social workers are educated to maneuver within systems to advocate needed changes on a patient's behalf as well as substantial changes needed to address health care in national and international arenas.

The fundamental purpose of medical social work is to improve the health of all people through interactions with individuals, families, organizations, communities, nations, and global structures. Social workers work in many health-care settings, where they play a primary role in ensuring that patients' psychosocial and physical needs are met. Health-care issues and practice arenas continue to change, but medical social work's mission remains as it was one hundred years ago. In Ida Cannon's (1913) words, social work strives to bring "care of the sick such personal and individual attention . . . that recovery . . . may be hastened and safeguarded" (p. 1).

SUGGESTED READING

Cowles, L. A. (2003). *Social work in the health field* (2nd ed.). Binghamton, NY: Haworth Press. This comprehensive and well-organized medical social work text covers the history of the profession and highlights social work responsibilities in various health-care settings from historical, theoretical, diversity, interdisciplinary, and organizational perspectives. It also discusses social work duties and skill requirements, value and ethical conflicts social workers experience when practicing from the medical model, and the increasing conflicts associated with managed care.

Matcha, D. A. (2000). *Medical sociology*. Needham Heights, MA: Allyn and Bacon. This comprehensive and easy-to-read sociological view of medicine is a valuable foundation for medical social workers. It presents the history of medicine, the professions in medicine, hospitals, and U.S. health-care financing. A unique feature is the focus on "health and illness behavior." It also addresses mental illness, epidemiology, and alternative treatments.

Rothman, J. C. (2003). *Social work practice across disability*. Boston: Allyn and Bacon. This unique social work text addresses practice in the disability field. Chapters focus on assessment and treatment of individuals and families, working with communities, and social and political issues of disability, including advocacy. Chapters also cover theoretical and historical perspectives and look at how disability affects identity development. Special attention is given to the disability rights movement and the Americans with Disabilities Act.

THE WORLD WIDE WEB OF SOCIAL WORK

Centers for Disease Control and Prevention http://www.cdc.gov

The CDC, the U.S. Department of Health and Human Services' public health agency, is dedicated to protecting the health and safety of all people in the world. The CDC Web site offers a wealth of information on disease, treatment, and research, and public health issues such as epidemiology, vaccinations, environmental health, bioterrorism, natural disasters, and food safety.

National Hospice and Palliative Care Organization http://www.nhpco.org

This organization is dedicated to increasing the quality of and access to care for all individuals facing serious illness. Its Web site provides information on advance directives, end-of-life care, research and statistics, and public policy.

Society for Social Work Leadership in Health Care http://www.sswlhc.org

This is the national professional organization of medical social workers. Its Web site provides an overview of the national and international issues medical social workers are addressing through advocacy and inclusiveness.

World Health Organization http://www.who.int/en

The WHO is the United Nations agency devoted to the health and well-being of the world's citizens. This Web site has links to all countries and territories detailing the latest rates of disease and public health circumstances.

10 Disabilities: The Fight for Inclusion Continues

Kevin L. DeWeaver

Disability is a vast and growing area of social work practice. No longer is it focused solely on mental retardation, as some scholars believe it was two decades ago (Dickerson, 1981). The broadening definition of the field allows social workers to make positive contributions in the lives of many more individuals. Some social workers specialize in the disability field, while others help clients with disabilities in other fields of social work practice, especially child welfare, school social work, aging, health care, and mental health. This chapter discusses important definitions, landmark laws and court cases, practice models and issues, emerging opportunities, and future challenges and ends with a call for unity in the disability field.

DISABILITY

Disability is a term that is not easily defined, as the World Health Organization (1980, 1993) found when it issued and reissued *International Classification of Impairments, Disabilities, and Handicaps*. The World Health Organization considers a disability to be any restriction or lack of ability to perform an activity in the manner or within the range considered normal for a human being. The World Health Organization's classification system is once again under revision because conceptions of disability change over time. The Americans with Disabilities Act of 1990 uses this definition: "The term 'disability' means, with respect to an individual: (a) a physical or mental impairment that substantially limits one or more of the major life activities [i.e., employment, socialization, mobility, self-direction, education, self-care, and communication] of such an individual; (b) a record of such impairment; or (c) being regarded as having an impairment."

Social workers Romel Mackelprang and Richard Salsgiver (1999) note that professions define disability differently, as some recognize social and environmental factors in addition to individual problems. The Institute of Medicine (1991), for example, stresses risk factors, whether they are biological, environmental (social and physical), or lifestyle or behavioral characteristics associated with health-related conditions. The Institute of Medicine model is based on the premise that disability is not inherent in a person, nor is it solely determined by biology; rather it is a combination of factors that determine if a physical or mental impairment will progress from a functional limitation to a disability. The Institute of Medicine's model also recognizes that disability may not be a unitary condition and that an individual may have a secondary condition or multiple disabilities.

As definitions of disability continue to evolve and be debated, there has been a subtle shift from emphasizing cognitive disabilities to placing an emphasis on physical disabilities. This shift is reflected in public policy; the general public is acquainted with the concept of mobility impairment and is used to seeing people who use wheelchairs. As Rothman (2003) has so succinctly stated, "Mobility limitations personify disability in our society" (p. 126). Some wheelchair users were born with their disability (e.g., cerebral palsy, spina bifida, and dwarfism). Others acquire mobility disabilities later in life as the result of conditions such as complications resulting from a stroke, muscular dystrophy, rheumatoid arthritis, multiple sclerosis, myasthenia gravis, polio, and spinal cord injuries (Mackelprang & Salsgiver, 1999).

DEVELOPMENTAL DISABILITIES

The term *developmental disabilities* (DD) began appearing in federal legislation in 1970. Originally, the concept was embraced as being more functional than categorical in nature (i.e., considering a person's abilities and limitations rather than relying strictly on diagnostic categories). However, the passage of the Developmental Disabilities Services and Facilities Construction Amendments of 1970 resulted in the states focusing mainly on the needs of individuals with mental retardation, epilepsy, and cerebral palsy. Several subsequent amendments have made the definition much more functional, engendering great debate about who has and does not have a DD. This debate is not just academic; it can affect a state's allocation of federal funding and whether an individual will receive services. Graziano (2002) has synthesized the legislative amendments and defines a developmental disability as a severe and chronic condition that

  1 Is attributed to mental or physical impairment or their combination
  2 Occurs before the age of twenty-one
  3 Is likely to continue indefinitely (i.e., is permanent)
  4 Results in substantial functional limitations in at least three of the following major areas of life activities: self-care, receptive and expressive language, learning, mobility, self-direction, capacity for independent living, and economic self-sufficiency
  5 Requires professional services that are of lifelong duration, planned and coordinated on an individual basis, and drawn from many disciplines (p. 18)

Functional aspects are primary in this definition, yet the diagnoses or conditions that may or may not fit under DD are still being debated. Though this list is not exhaustive, some major conditions currently considered a DD are physical disabilities (e.g., cerebral palsy, muscular dystrophy), chronic illness (e.g., AIDS, epilepsy, diabetes), birth defects (e.g., spina bifida), sensory disorders (e.g., auditory and visual impairments like deafness and blindness), cognitive disorders (e.g., mental retardation, learning disabilities), behavioral/emotional disorders (e.g., autism, attention-deficit/hyperactivity disorder), and environmentally induced impairments (e.g., fetal alcohol syndrome, spinal cord injury, lead paint poisoning) (Graziano, 2002). Newly identified conditions are constantly being added. For example, in 1994, Asperger's syndrome, an autism spectrum disorder that occurs in children of normal intelligence, was added to the American Psychiatric Association's *Diagnostic and Statistical Manual of Mental Disorders*, the diagnostic tool used in many social service agencies.

Critics have argued that although the concept of DD was supposed to be less stigmatizing than the use of the names of specific conditions (e.g., mental retardation), the stigma remains. Definitions of DD tend to focus on severe disabilities; for example, mild forms of mental retardation are no longer considered a DD. Hence, legislators may not take into consideration the provision of services for people who have milder disabilities (DeWeaver, 1995). That was not the intent of the 1970 DD legislation.

MENTAL RETARDATION

The organization that has contributed most to definitions of mental retardation is the American Association on Intellectual and Developmental Disabilities, the oldest and largest interdisciplinary organization concerned with mental retardation. (Prior to 2007, the American Association on Intellectual and Developmental Disabilities was called the American Association on Mental Retardation.) Over the decades, the diagnosis of mental retardation has evolved from depending on a strict categorical system based on IQ; it now depends upon a more functional system focused on levels of support needed by the individual. No longer is it appropriate to classify a client's level of functioning by IQ alone (i.e., mild mental retardation for an IQ of 55–69, moderate for 40–54, severe for 25–39, and profound for an IQ of less than 25); however, some school systems and agencies still rely on this categorization.

According to the most current definition, "mental retardation is a disability characterized by significant limitations both in intellectual functioning and in adaptive behavior as expressed in conceptual, social, and practical adaptive skills. This disability originates before age 18" (American Association on Mental Retardation, 2002, p. 1). In other words, "individuals' behaviors are considered adaptive by the degree to which they manage their personal needs, display social competence, and avoid problem behaviors" (Drew & Hardman, 2004, p. 22). Five assumptions are critical when one is using this definition for the purpose of making a diagnosis:

1 Limitations in functioning must be considered in the context of community environments typical of the individual's age, peers, and culture.

2 Valid assessment considers cultural and linguistic diversity as well as differences in communication, sensory, motor, and behavioral factors.

3 Limitations often coexist with strengths.

4 Describing limitations helps to develop a profile of needed support.

5 With appropriate personalized supports over a sustained period, life functioning will improve (American Association on Mental Retardation, 2002).

Though IQ is still taken into consideration, community integration and adaptive behavior are also important in making a diagnosis and determining service needs. The American Association on Intellectual and Developmental Disabilities developed a scale to measure adaptive behaviors and skills, many aspects of which are appropriate regardless of the disability a person has.

Recently a movement urging that the term *mental retardation* be replaced with *intellectual disabilities* has emerged. While the latter term is appearing increasingly in the professional literature and may sound less pejorative, it has not been universally accepted, especially in social service agencies. As Mackelprang and Salsgiver note (1999), different professions tend to use different terminology. Nurses, for example, often combine the terms *intellectual disabilities* and *developmental disabilities* (I/DD) (Hahn & Marks, 2003). For the purpose of this chapter, the terms *mental retardation* and *intellectual disability* are used interchangeably.

PREVALENCE AND INCIDENCE

The word *prevalence* refers to "the number of persons in a population at a given time who exhibit a particular characteristic and is usually reported as the number of current cases per unit of population" (Graziano, 2002, p. 32). *Incidence* is the number of new cases over a period of time, usually one year. The overall prevalence of disabilities continues to grow due to an increase in population and medical technologies that save lives. The prevalence of DD is about 5 percent of the total U.S. population; the prevalence of mental retardation is about 3 percent (though some believe this estimate is too high) (Graziano, 2002). While the rate of growth of some disabilities has slowed, others have increased rapidly. For example, a child is diagnosed with autism every twenty minutes, and the number of cases has increased fifteen-fold since 1991 (Autism Speaks, 2007; Graziano, 2002). That year, companies began to add thimerosal, a mercury-based preservative, to vaccines given to very young children. Scientific and political battles are now being fought over whether there is a connection between thimerosal and autism.

HISTORY OF SERVICES FOR DEVELOPMENTAL DISABILITIES

Fishley (1992) reports that in the 1700s, people with mental retardation were viewed as a potential threat, and they were often jailed. In the mid-1800s, a different response became popular—segregation for the sake of educating or even curing these individuals, who were often labeled idiots and feebleminded. By the 1880s, people with mental retardation were often institutionalized and sterilized. Large state-run institutions remained the preferred method of care throughout much of the twentieth century as more people with retardation were identified. More humane treatment was made available in the 1970s and 1980s, as rehabilitation and community residences began to replace institutions that often simply warehoused residents.

The history of services to people with mental retardation and developmental disabilities and the development of social work traveled along parallel tracks until the 1950s (DeWeaver, 1995). Social work's convergence with the broader field of disabilities has occurred more slowly. In fact, Mackelprang and Salsgiver (1996) have argued that this is a partnership that still needs to be developed: "Social work can contribute decades of experience with the ecology of society and multiple systems. The disability movement can help social work enhance approaches to clients, better empower oppressed and devalued groups, and understand the needs of people with disabilities" (p. 13).

Though disability practice is a growing area for social workers, social work is only peripherally involved in the newer area of disability studies. Disability studies is an interdisciplinary field based on the liberal arts tradition whose importance major universities are beginning to recognize. At Syracuse University, the disabilities studies program is a joint effort between the schools of education and law, and at Georgetown University it is located in the humanities division. Two exceptions to social work's lack of involvement in this movement are the University of Texas at Austin School of Social Work, which is home to seven courses offered by the Texas Center for Disability Studies, and the interdisciplinary Center on Disability Studies at the University of Hawai'i, where students in the Disability Studies Certificate Program can choose a social work elective.

Legislation

Social policy, made up of legislation and judicial rulings, is critically important to the emergence of the disability field in society and social work. Some seminal pieces of legislation are noted here:

The National Rehabilitation Act of 1920 expanded vocational rehabilitation to all people with a disability, with a focus on job training and placement.

The Social Security Act of 1935 included an entitlement program that helped states provide financial assistance to low-income elderly individuals and the blind. In 1950, others with disabilities became eligible for this program. In 1972, the federal government established a basic payment program for participants. The program is now called Supplemental Security Income, and children with disabilities are eligible as well.

The Social Security Amendments of 1956 and 1960 made disabled workers eligible for Social Security payments, which were formerly available only to retired workers.

The Maternal and Child Health and Mental Retardation Planning Amendments of 1963 authorized funding for preventive programs focused on mental retardation and provided funding for students, including those in social work, to study and practice in this area.

The Mental Retardation Facilities and Community Mental Health Centers Construction Act of 1963 developed a mental retardation branch in the federal government and funded university-affiliated facilities to focus on research and training. The act also provided the impetus for deinstitutionalization.

The Social Security Amendments of 1965 added Medicare (for which people with a disability may qualify, depending on their work history) and Medicaid (which provides health care for some people with disabilities, depending on their income).

The Rehabilitation Act of 1973 prohibits discrimination on the basis of disability in federal programs and hiring. The act makes use of the concept of affirmative action in the hiring practices of federal contractors and requires that people with the most severe disabilities get priority in receiving rehabilitation services.

The Education for All Handicapped Children Act of 1975, now the Individuals with Disabilities Education Act of 1990, provides for the education of all children with disabilities from age three through twenty-one. A 1986 amendment provides an early intervention program for infants and toddlers with disabilities and their families.

The Rehabilitation, Comprehensive Services, and Developmental Disabilities Amendments of 1978 instituted priority services (e.g., case management, child development, alternative community living, and nonvocational social development services) that provided many jobs for social workers.

The Americans with Disabilities Act of 1990 focused on the rights of people with disabilities and made the federal government responsible for enforcing antidiscrimination legislation. The act covers rights in employment, transportation (e.g., use of buses and trains), private facilities (e.g., access to hotels, restaurants, theaters), and telecommunications (use of telephone relay services).

In 2005 Congress amended the Social Security Act to allow people with disabilities to keep Medicare or Medicaid while they are employed.

Judicial Rulings

The following are landmark court cases in the areas of DD and mental retardation:

Wyatt v. Stickney (1972) was a case in which the district court in Alabama ruled that people with mental retardation in institutions have a constitutional right to treatment.

Arc v. Rockefeller (1972) and *Halderman v. Pennhurst State School and Hospital* (1977) contributed to institutional reforms and the development of appropriate community resources.

City of Cleburne Texas v. Cleburne Living Center (1985) established that zoning laws cannot be used to prohibit group homes in residential areas (see box 10.1).

Box 10.1   Due Process and Social Work Macropractice

In July 1980, Jan Hannah bought a residence on Featherston Street in Cleburne, Texas, with the purpose of leasing it to the Cleburne Living Center for a community residence—then called a group home—for people with mental retardation. The plan was for thirteen people with mental retardation to live there with assistance from the center's staff. The center planned to abide by all federal and state regulations. The city of Cleburne decided this was a "hospital for the feebleminded," and by a vote of 3–1, the city council denied the center's application for a special permit, which it claimed the Cleburne Living Center needed.

The Cleburne Living Center was stunned but, with the encouragement of many people, decided to appeal the decision and filed suit in federal district court. Part of the center's argument focused on discrimination and equal protection under the law. The court upheld the city's ordinance and actions as constitutional.

Again social workers and other professionals in the intellectual disability field were outraged by the decision, which they felt constituted blatant discrimination. They worked together and appealed to the U.S. Supreme Court. On July 1, 1985, the Supreme Court justices reversed the decision in a stunning 9–0 vote. In writing the opinion of the court, Justice White made the point that the denial of the permit was based on irrational prejudice against people with mental retardation and hence was unconstitutional under the equal protection clause of the Fourteenth Amendment. This example of macropractice relied on the court system to address discrimination. This tactic has been used a great deal to enforce the rights of people with disabilities. As these decisions build on each other, it is becoming more difficult to discriminate overtly against people with disabilities. The community home finally opened later in 1985 after five years of legal battles.

Penry v. Lynaugh (1989) granted partial relief from the death penalty under some circumstances when there is evidence of mental retardation and/or child abuse.

These court cases and federal laws affirm important rights for all people with disabilities. Though they have resulted in less overt discrimination, covert discrimination remains a problem. Some of these laws and rulings set in motion the massive deinstitutionalization and community integration that began in the early 1970s. Some states, like New Jersey and Vermont, have closed all their public institutions. In other states, few individuals are admitted to institutions, and time limits are often put on the admission contract. People with intellectual disabilities now live and work in the community, promoting inclusion and reducing negative stereotypes. Social workers have made important contributions to these advances.

SOCIAL WORK PRACTICE MODELS

Social workers practicing in the disability, DD, and mental retardation fields are involved in direct (micro) practice, mixed or community (mezzo) practice, and indirect (macro) practice. There is, however, no unifying social work practice model that is used in the disability field. Gilson, Bricout, and Baskind (1998) offer one reason for this: "Social work literature, research, and practice on disabilities have lagged behind other topical areas dealing with oppressed groups. The social work literature remains 'expert focused' and generally fragmented into discussions of specific disabilities or subpopulations. A viable general model that deals with the personal experience of disability is not available" (p. 188). Other disciplines have done more to incorporate disabilities into their practice and research efforts. For example, one subfield of education is special education, which seeks to educate children with intellectual disabilities. Psychologists learn various models of behavioral interventions to assist people with disabilities. Disabilities is an important part of the curriculum in schools of public health, and a section of the annual conference of the American Public Health Association is devoted to disabilities. As social work seeks its place in the field of disabilities, social workers draw on both traditional (behavioral, crisis intervention, case management, and advocacy) and newer (strengths, empowerment, and independent living) models of practice.

Behavioral Model

The behavioral model is used in many practice areas of social work. This model, derived from social learning theory, focuses on conditioning and changing undesirable behavior. Underwood and Thyer (1990) offer an example of social workers using several different types of conditioning to reduce self-injurious behavior in individuals with mental retardation. The behavior model utilizes positive and negative reinforcement to obtain the desired behavior. Its focus is on the actual change in behavior rather than on the theory that explains why change occurs.

Crisis Intervention

Social workers in the mental health field often use short-term crisis intervention. In the general disability field, crisis often occurs when an individual learns that he or she has acquired a disability that is permanent (e.g., following an injury or illness). Sometimes the client is a family member of the person with the disability or the whole family system. An example is parents who have just learned that their newborn baby has Down syndrome. Their immediate fears and feelings must be addressed before long-term planning can begin.

Case Management

Another model, which combines elements of direct practice (e.g., assessment) and indirect practice (e.g., resource creation) is case management. This model is often used in the DD and mental retardation fields when the

"The most important thing in my life is to help other people. Before I started working with Gerry, people said he couldn't speak. Now he can say his name, the date, what classes he is taking." A quotation from a social worker who is a community integration specialist.
© Richard Bermack

client has multiple needs and the resources addressing those needs are scattered over the community. In this situation, coordination is needed, and social workers often provide this coordination. This model can create feelings of resentment when the case manager is seen as the expert and the locus of control and clients are not given enough opportunity to provide input in their service plans. In the DD field, the comprehensive model of case management that offers a continuum of services to meet the client's needs is most popular.

Advocacy

This model spun off from case management. The social worker performs tasks that clients cannot do themselves, or the client asks the social worker for assistance in a specific area. Clients who are nonverbal or have a very low IQ and low levels of adaptive behavior often need advocacy services, as might a client with an HIV flare-up who requests assistance. Thus advocacy entails working with the client to assess what he or she needs and then working with community agencies to determine where those services are available and how they can be attained for the client. Often the second part is difficult, and that is where the social worker must make sure the client gets the proper services and that services continue to be delivered without problems.

Strengths Model

Although it is new to the field of disabilities, the strengths model has been used in many practice areas. This model focuses "on identifying strengths of clients and the environment, viewing client motivation as developing from a focus on strengths, and developing a cooperative relationship between the client and worker" (Russo, 1999, p. 26). Russo believes this model works well with clients with mental retardation. It also works well in the general disability field, as it takes the focus off the deficits associated with disability and can be expanded for use at the community level. This model is gaining popularity.

Empowerment

While closely related to the strengths model, the empowerment model is broader and centers on the principle of client self-determination. This model "assists clients to achieve their potential and to promote changes in their environment and in social policy that will promote social justice" (Rothman, 2003, pp. 210–211). Like social work itself, the empowerment model has dual goals of helping clients achieve their full potential and improving society. It is highly appropriate for use in the general disability field, especially in situations where severe cognitive deficits are not present. Mackelprang and Salsgiver (1999) state that "practitioners do not empower clients; people empower themselves" (p. 233), a message that professionals need to remind themselves of often.

Independent Living

Of the models discussed here, the independent living model is perhaps the least known in social work. In this model, professionals do not manage cases; instead, the clients, sometimes called customers, are responsible for running their own lives. Tasks that individuals have difficulties performing are not the main focus; instead, societal barriers—physical and attitudinal—are the obstacles to overcome. Customers may use professionals as consultants but make their own decisions. This is the dominant model of practice in centers for independent living (CILs), which grew out of the disability rights movement that emerged in the early 1970s. A CIL is a place where people with disabilities live and attempt to run their own lives. People order services that they feel they need (e.g., contacting, hiring, and

Social workers help people with disabilities live "normal" lives. This man and woman both have disabilities and have been married for ten years. They work together as writers and artists.
© Mary Whelens

firing personal attendants is a major item). CILs are primarily for people with physical disabilities. Social workers need to understand how CILs operate and support them. Some ways to do this are to become a board member, volunteer for one of their community committees, or assist with fund-raising projects. Another way to support CILs is by learning more about the disability culture and sharing this information with legislators and lobbyists at events sponsored by professional organizations such as the National Association of Social Workers.

SOCIAL WORK PRACTICE TODAY

Micropractice

In micropractice, the social worker directly assists the client and often the client's family. Direct practice jobs in DD, once located in state institutions, have moved along with clients into the community. Most social work micropractice positions in the disability field are in community agencies. In addition to the public (governmental) sector, not-for-profit private agencies (e.g., centers for independent living) and for-profit agencies (e.g., sheltered workshops that do contract work for private industries) offer practice opportunities. Services offered in micropractice typically include assessment, planning, writing service plans, implementing interventions, and evaluating the results of interventions. Sometimes the social worker provides supports for families so they can continue caring for their son, daughter, or sibling at home (Freedman & Boyer, 2000). The social worker may provide considerable counseling from time to time as family members of individuals with DD experience chronic sorrow, or the feelings of loss that arise when a child does not achieve a milestone typical for his or her age group (Wikler, 1981). This can be particularly difficult when a child's siblings are achieving these milestones. In addition to working with elderly individuals who are caring for adult children with developmental disabilities, social workers are also seeing more older clients with disabilities as advances in medical technology are made. Finally, the services that social workers provide and the models they use may vary depending on location. For example, in rural areas, social workers often provide more direct services and fewer referrals, due to a lack of community resources (DeWeaver & Johnson, 1983).

The use of interdisciplinary teams is common in the DD and mental retardation fields. Briggs (1997) describes team building in early childhood interventions, an increasingly popular area of social work practice (Malone, McKinsey, Thyer, & Straka, 2000). Beginning social workers must learn about the different disciplines, what they can offer, and their value base. Learning to negotiate team meetings and convey the social work point of view takes skill and practice. Meetings can become exercises in group dynamics, power struggles, and negotiations. Social workers must effectively communicate what they think the client needs and how best to proceed.

Mezzopractice

Some social workers obtain mezzo-level practice positions directly out of school; however, most of these jobs are reserved for social workers with direct practice experience. At the mezzo level, social workers often supervise newly hired direct line social workers and provide staff development and education. Social workers also provide clinical consultation in their employing agency and sometimes for clients served by another agency. They may also provide programmatic consultation to another agency on how to set up an innovative program, thus saving that agency time and money. For example, a substance abuse treatment agency may need consultation to develop services for clients with DD. Many social workers enjoy mezzopractice because it allows them to experience client contact while engaging in a variety of other activities. One area in mezzopractice in the intellectual disability field is consultation on how to open a community residence, formerly called group homes. This skill set can be very useful, especially as more public institutions are being targeted to close.

Macropractice

Other social workers prefer to work through macropractice, which might involve holding managerial and administrative roles in organizations or engaging in strategies such as policy making, lobbying, and legislative and court advocacy in order to end disability discrimination (May & Raske, 2005). Still others do research on disabilities. While these social workers may be invisible to clients and their families, and many people may not even recognize them as social workers, their work is extremely important. Another macropractice role that has recently become critical as agencies seek multiple income streams in the competitive social service funding environment is fund-raising. Box 10.2 provides examples of social workers working in the disability field.

TERMINOLOGY

The terminology used in the disability field is rapidly evolving. Many terms, like *crippled, wheelchair bound,* and *special needs,* are considered insulting. The word *handicapped* has also fallen into disfavor, though it is still used for designated parking. Some people also reject the words *disabled* and *consumer,* arguing that these terms perpetuate the labeling process (Jones, 1999) and that the word *consumer* can feel a bit impersonal. Many people have come to dislike the term *mental retardation* and prefer *intellectual disabilities,* a sensibility that is reflected in the American Association on Mental Retardation's recent name change. Others prefer the term *cognitive disability.* Sooner or later, you will use a term that someone finds objectionable; a quick apology and request for guidance

---

Box 10.2   Social Workers in the Disability Field

Immediately after earning her BSW, Kira began a position in which she provides direct services to clients as well as some mezzo functions such as resource location and creation. The nonprofit agency where she is employed serves people with intellectual disabilities who either are in high school or have just finished school. She is working hard to help clients achieve the goals they have set for themselves and loves it.

When Charlene completed her MSW program, she went to work at a center for independent living. An elective course she took on disabilities helped prepare her for this work and gave her an advantage over others who interviewed for the job. Charlene started in a case management position and is now taking on more managerial

responsibilities. She plans to make this field her career and become an administrator.

Gill, who has multiple disabilities, earned a PhD in social work and went on to work for a large urban rehabilitation center as a grant writer and researcher for about eight years. He is now a health scientist at the U.S. Centers for Disease Control and Prevention. Yael, also a PhD, is employed there as a behavioral scientist. She focuses on the general disability field and specializes in addressing the barriers women with disabilities face. While many students may not plan to enter the disability field when they begin their social work education, many who do find it rewarding.

---

usually are sufficient to defuse the situation. Person-first language, such as *a person with autism* rather than *an autistic person*, is usually recommended. Some individuals with disabilities, however, see themselves as a cultural group and reject person-first language, preferring disability-first language (see box 10.3).

LEAST RESTRICTIVE ENVIRONMENT

The least restrictive environment is defined in the Individuals with Disabilities Education Act, but applications of it have varied across federal courts. The act requires states to provide each student with a free, appropriate education in the least restrictive environment. If the child's local district or state of residence does not have what is determined to be the least restrictive environment for a particular child, the student is entitled to receive an education elsewhere at a private school or out of state at public expense (Palley & Van Hollen, 2000). This has become the subject of many court cases. When a family residing in one state moves to another state, the new state of residence may not provide the same types of services, prompting the family to go to court to secure what was already given or won in the first state.

Box 10.3   Hard-of-Hearing and Deaf People

About 1.35 million people in the United States are considered deaf (Mackelprang & Salsgiver, 1999). People who have acquired hearing loss, which can range in severity, rarely associate with the deaf community and usually view their condition as a medical one. The number of people who are hard of hearing is growing rapidly as the population ages, although hearing loss can occur anytime during the life span.

Terminology is very important to many deaf people. They generally reject people-first language as well as the term *hearing impaired*. Any label suggesting disability is also unacceptable. *Hearing loss* and *deaf people* are acceptable terms. A distinction is also made between *deaf* and *Deaf*. "The uppercase, Deaf, is used to describe Deaf people as a cultural group. The lowercase, deaf, refers to noncultural elements of deafness, such as medical conditions" (Mackelprang & Salsgiver, 1999, p. 107).

Deaf people have a distinct culture. The cornerstone of this culture is American Sign Language (ASL). As Rothman (2003) notes, "Deaf culture has all the distinguishing marks of a culture: a language, terminology and expressions, criteria for participation and membership, and an established way of interacting, as a culture, with other cultures. The growth of Deaf culture was dramatically enabled when the manualists won the communications war and created American Sign Language" (p. 135).

Few deaf people have pursued social work degrees, and few social workers have sufficient skills in ASL to serve deaf people. There are, however, notable exceptions. Martha Sheridan is a Deaf person and a professor of social work at Gallaudet University who mentors deaf and hard-of-hearing students (you can read more about her in Mackelprang & Salsgiver, 1999, pp. 118–121). Tara Alexander, a hearing person, is a social worker and professor in Texas who is fluent in ASL and developed a substance abuse screening video for deaf people called the Drug and Alcohol Assessment for the Deaf. The profession needs more social workers like Sheridan and Alexander.

ETHICAL DILEMMAS

Work in the disability field frequently presents ethical dilemmas. These dilemmas can involve decisions about life itself. For example, when an expectant mother has an amniocentesis and learns that her baby will have Down syndrome, a chromosomal form of mental retardation accompanied by physical abnormalities, she may struggle with whether to have the baby or have an abortion. For many women and couples, there is no easy answer. Social workers provide support and information and help expectant parents consider their options, and they continue to assist as long as they are needed. Social workers may also help individuals who have a high likelihood of passing on a serious genetic condition as they decide whether or not to conceive a child, and they help people with right-to-life and right-to-die decisions. Though social workers may have strong personal views about these situations, they are there to help patients and clients make fully informed decisions free of duress.

BUDGETS AND MANAGED CARE

Social workers must recognize the necessity of federal and state funding in meeting the needs of people with disabilities and use their advocacy and lobbying skills to keep funds flowing. Their efforts do not always succeed because the profession is spread too thinly, the definition of disability is constantly expanding and changing, and there are competing budget demands (e.g., national security and counterterrorism programs). Though managed care has reduced insurers' costs by seeing that patients or clients get only the services they need, patients or clients with disabilities may be denied services that the insurer does not consider medically necessary, even if the client or the client's family does. In other cases individuals are excluded entirely from health-care plans because their disability is deemed a preexisting condition. Most Americans get their health insurance through their employer, but many people with disabilities are not employed. Social workers are working to improve health-care provision for people with disabilities.

ADVOCACY: BATTLING DISCRIMINATION AND STEREOTYPING

Many people with disabilities are using their own advocacy and political skills to demand and expand their rights under the law, and they have made many gains. Social workers fill a vital advocacy role for those with intellectual disabilities who cannot advocate for themselves. This role involves raising the consciousness of professional colleagues and the public about disabilities. With the phasing out of federal categorical funding in favor of block grants to states, certain programs that serve people with one type of disability are often in direct competition for scarce dollars with programs serving people with other disabilities. For example, if the local center for independent living that serves people with mobility disabilities receives funding from a federal block grant, then the local program that serves people with mental retardation may not receive as much funding. Funding grows tighter each year, and one program's victory in securing funding is another program's defeat. Social workers must make sure that people with mental retardation receive their fair share and work to transform what has become a fierce zero-sum funding game into a system that works to meet the needs of all people with disabilities. Social workers help attorneys build cases to support the disability rights movement and extend services to people with disabilities who need and are entitled to them but are not receiving them.

Social workers can do much to battle stereotyping and discrimination against people with disabilities (Mackelprang & Salsgiver, 1999). One way is by fighting discrimination and stereotyping in other fields of practice, for example, when a person with a disability who wishes to adopt a child faces resistance. Another way is teaching advocacy skills so that people with disabilities can enhance their own self-determination whenever possible (Keigher, 2000). On a macro level, the National Association of Social Workers needs to be urged by its constituents to add disability rights to its legislative agenda.

FUTURE CHALLENGES

The disability field is a growing area of practice for social workers and is full of challenges. These challenges include considering disability as an aspect of human diversity and within the context of gender, race, and ethnicity; better preparing social workers for practice in the disability field; working to unify the field; and promoting greater inclusion of people with disabilities, especially in employment.

Disability and Diversity

There has been little research on disability and race and disability and gender; however, Thierry's (2000) work indicates that women with certain disabilities do not get regular breast and cervical cancer screening because many facilities do not have the equipment they need and because of the attitudes of health-care professionals, who, for example, may assume that women with disabilities are asexual. In addition, Han, Barrilleaux, and Quadagno (1996) found that in Florida, race and gender played a role in whether or not a person received a home and community-based services waiver, a Medicaid benefit, and that nonwhites and women were more likely to receive such services. Valentine, McDermott, and Anderson (1998) reported on racial differences among women caring for adult children with mental retardation and found that "regardless of in-home or out-of-home placement, . . . African American mothers reported greater satisfaction and more intimacy with their sons and daughters with mental retardation and less burden and conflict than Caucasian mothers" (p. 577).

There is tremendous interest in disabilities across the world, especially in countries with a more socialized approach to medicine and rehabilitation, such as Sweden and Canada. The Research to Practice meetings of the International Association for the Scientific Study of Mental Deficiency draw professionals and consumers from all over the world. Social workers are involved with international organizations and agencies in other countries that help children and adults who are disabled due to war (e.g., land-mine explosions) or poor health conditions and inadequate medical care. The disability field provides many opportunities to work in an area of international concern.

Social Work Education

DePoy and Miller (1996) found that only 22 percent of BSW and MSW programs offered DD courses, and only 4 percent offered a specialization in this area. After reading this chapter, you will know more about disabilities than many social workers, but social work education programs are beginning to offer more content on disabilities. DeWeaver and Kropf (1992) demonstrate how content on mental retardation can be infused across the foundation curriculum. Liese, Clevenger, and Hanley (1999) present a model for collaboration with university-affiliated programs that includes content on mental retardation, DD, and disabilities in general, which is highly unusual, as normally only one category is covered in such models. University-affiliated programs are federally funded initiatives that offer students education and training on disabilities. The term *university-affiliated program* is being replaced; for example, at the University of Georgia, the university-affiliated program is now the Institute of Human Development and Disability. In the last decade, the Council on Social Work Education has become much more interested in disabilities and has developed a Council on Disability and Persons with Disabilities. Now the challenge is to get the National Association of Social Workers interested and for these two major professional organizations to work together to promote this practice area so that a truly oppressed group can be better served.

Unification

Earlier sections of this chapter discussed mental retardation separately from DD, and both are often discussed separately from the concept of general disabilities. A movement is underway to incorporate all three into a unified practice field. The goal is to streamline services and professional education so that people with disabilities can get the services they desire more easily and more health and human service professionals can be prepared to work in the field. Beaulaurier and Taylor (2001) provide a framework for moving in this direction that begins with the general disability field and then looks at more specific conditions. With regard to social work practice in the disability field, Galambos (2004) has asked, "Are we doing enough?" The answer is a resounding no! Any of us can become a person with a disability. Social work practitioners and educators with disabilities are taking a leadership role in reconceptualizing this field into an integrated whole and promoting opportunities for social workers in this practice field.

Inclusion: How About a Job?

Finally, it is important that the social work profession promote employment for every person with a disability who wants to work. While employment is a major focus of the Americans with Disabilities Act, there is often a gap between the passage of a policy and its full implementation. Rothman (2003) elaborates:

> People with disabilities have a higher rate of unemployment and partial employment than the general public, and unemployment increases with the severity of the disability. At the same time, increased medical and health needs related to disability have a strong impact on disposable income. A greater proportion of people with disabilities are living in poverty, and, again, the more severe the disability the greater the number of people in poverty. (p. 295)

Employment discrimination is unacceptable and illegal. It prevents inclusion in the American way of life. Future social workers can help achieve the goal of ending employment discrimination. Recognizing that people with disabilities need jobs but are routinely screened out of the workforce, Mudrick (1991) proposed that occupational social workers, professionals who are generally employed by large corporations, can be key in promoting the inclusion of people with disabilities in the workplace. Social workers working in human resources departments are also instrumental in promoting the employment of people with disabilities.

SUMMARY

The field of disabilities offers many opportunities and challenges for the profession of social work, but social workers are frequently no more knowledgeable about disabilities than the general public. Definitions of disability have changed many times over the last two centuries, and they remain in flux. Disabilities cut across age, gender, and racial and ethnic groups. Many people with disabilities are active participants in the disability rights movement; however, some individuals, such as those with intellectual disabilities, need assistance in fighting for their rights and the programs and services they need. Professional social work organizations and educational programs should give more attention to practice in the disability field. This field offers tremendous potential for a rewarding career. With social workers' involvement, the dream of full inclusion can become a reality.

SUGGESTED READING

Mackelprang, R. W., & Salsgiver, R. O. (1999). *Disability: A diversity model approach in human service practice.* Pacific Grove, CA: Brooks/Cole. This work, written by two social workers, considers disability a form of human diversity. While the book is heavy on content about physical disabilities, developmental disabilities and, to a lesser extent, mental retardation (intellectual disability) are also covered.

Rothman, J. C. (2003). *Social work practice across disability.* Boston: Allyn and Bacon. This book is based on the ecological framework and discusses disability in the context of the social environment; individuals' experiences; micro-, mezzo-, and macropractice; and resources and support networks. Rothman's focus is mostly on physical disabilities, and the book has a nice review of social work models that might be used in a variety of settings for people with disabilities.

Schreiber, M. S. (Ed.). (1970). *Social work and mental retardation.* New York: John Day. This book is a classic in the field. It contains ninety-four articles that cover many aspects of mental retardation of interest to social workers.

Stone, J. H. (Ed.). (2005). *Culture and disability: Providing culturally competent services.* Thousand Oaks, CA: Sage. This volume discusses disability among various cultural groups. The book takes a rehabilitation and counseling approach to serving people with disabilities from a non-American cultural perspective. There are chapters on Chinese, Jamaican, Korean, Haitian, Mexican, Dominican, and Vietnamese people with disability service needs living in the United States.

Wikler, L., & Keenan, M. P. (Eds.). (1983). *Developmental disabilities: No longer a private tragedy.* Silver Spring, MD: National Association of Social Workers. This volume was one of the first books to discuss developmental disabilities and social work in general and is an important work in the history of social work's involvement in this field. The six articles on community are critically important, as they show the changing roles of social workers in the face of deinstitutionalization and as case management became a predominant community practice model in the 1980s.

THE WORLD WIDE WEB OF SOCIAL WORK

The Arc of the United States http://www.thearc.org
The Arc advocates the rights and full participation in society of all children and adults with intellectual and developmental disabilities. The members and affiliated chapters of the Arc work to improve services and supports and influence public policy. The Web site offers a great deal of legislative information for those who wish to become involved.

Caregiver http://www.caregiver911.com

This Web site provides information on a variety of topics to assist caregivers. This rather extensive site offers helpful aids such as an e-newsletter, a magazine, conference information, a book club, and various regional resources.

Consortium for Citizens with Disabilities http://www.c-c-d.org

The CCD is a coalition of approximately one hundred national disability organizations that advocates for national policy ensuring the self-determination, independence, and full inclusion in society of children and adults with disabilities. The Web site offers an important section on legislative issues as well as a media kit.

National Council on Disability http://www.ncd.gov

The NCD is an independent federal agency that makes recommendations to the president and Congress to enhance the quality of life for all Americans with disabilities and their families. The NCD is currently finishing several reports called *Investing in Independence* that focus on the president's plan for helping people with disabilities achieve more independence.

People First Language http://www.disabilityisnatural.com/peoplefirstlanguage.htm

This Web site discusses the terminology that people with disabilities prefer. It looks at disability as a natural part of the human experience and regards negative attitudes and environmental barriers as the problems that need to be addressed.

11 Social Work with Children and Their Families

Dorinda N. Noble and Angela Ausbrooks

Social work has a long tradition of helping children and families. This chapter describes how social workers shield children from abuse and neglect while strengthening their families and enhancing their lives through foster care, residential care, adoption, and school social services. Social workers labor to address the many life circumstances and events, such as violence, neglect, and poverty, that prevent children's needs for health, security, belonging, and self-fulfillment from being met.

CHILD ABUSE AND NEGLECT

Neglect (the failure of adults to meet children's physical, emotional, mental, educational, or social needs) accounts for 52 percent of the approximately one million cases of child maltreatment verified each year in the United States. About 25 percent of the cases involve physical abuse (nonaccidental injury inflicted by a caregiver), while approximately 12 percent of maltreatment cases involve sexual abuse (sexual intercourse, oral-genital contact, fondling, incest, or exploitation). The remaining cases involve emotional or psychological maltreatment (chronic denigration of the child's qualities and desires, isolation, terrorizing, excessive age-inappropriate demands, extreme parental violence and drug/alcohol abuse, and failure to procure services for seriously emotionally handicapped children). Most maltreatment perpetrators are parents (77% of perpetrators) or other relatives (11% of perpetrators). Women, frequently the primary caretakers of children, are responsible for about three-quarters of neglect and medical neglect cases, while men are responsible for about three-quarters of sexual abuse cases (Downs, Moore, McFadden, & Costin, 2000).

Social workers who investigate reports of child abuse and neglect consider many factors, such as the child's age. Shaking an infant can be life threatening, but shaking an eleven-year-old likely is not. Professionals also examine the location and pattern of injuries. Injuries to the head are more likely to cause permanent damage than injuries to the legs. Authorities consider what objects are involved in the abuse. Metal coat hangers, kitchen utensils, and fists are potentially more lethal than open-hand slapping. Social workers must distinguish between legitimate punishment, which shapes the child's behavior (such as denying access to TV), and abusive punishment (such as locking a child in a closet). Social workers consider the extent and causes of physical neglect; going hungry because the parent is unemployed is different from going hungry because the parent has spent all his or her money on drugs. Children may be educationally neglected (for example, a child who is regularly kept home from school to care for a sibling), or they may be medically neglected (denied medical care). Children sometimes suffer insufficient supervision (or even parental abandonment), but to determine the level of supervision a child needs, one must consider the child's age and the length of time a child is left alone. Children are morally neglected when parents encourage them to steal or to prostitute themselves (Glicken & Sechrest, 2003).

POVERTY AND MALTREATMENT

In the United States, 13 million or nearly 18 percent of children live in poverty, and children of color are at elevated risk of poverty (DeNavas-Walt, Proctor, & Lee, 2006). Child maltreatment occurs at all socioeconomic levels and in all racial and ethnic groups, but statistically, maltreatment happens more in poverty-stricken families. Money and social advantages can buffer families from stress, which often triggers child maltreatment. Wealthier families are less likely to come into contact with police officers, social workers, and other mandated child abuse reporters and thus are less likely to become statistics.

Poverty often leads to substandard housing, an issue that social workers address with families. Children living in crowded, unsanitary conditions are more susceptible to contagious diseases and injuries. Children exposed (even before birth) to radiation or to toxins such as lead, arsenic, mercury, or pesticides are at risk of serious developmental damage (Gracey, 2002). Homelessness is also devastating. Children who are homeless are often depressed and frightened. Homelessness interrupts children's schooling and makes life more dangerous for them.

EFFECTS OF MALTREATMENT

Traumatic experiences (for instance, witnessing or experiencing violence, being confined in closed spaces, or suddenly losing familiar caregivers) often leave permanent physical and emotional scars. Those scars may include cognitive dysfunction (such as impaired memory), hypervigilance (a heightened state of fear), recurrent memories of the trauma, emotional numbing, aggressive responses, or limited future orientation (Steele, 2004).

Traumatized children may find it difficult to trust others or to form healthy relationships. They may seek solace in alcohol or drugs. Abuse victims sometimes develop serious mental illnesses, such as clinical depression or post-traumatic stress disorder. Victims of long-term neglect may have health and academic difficulties. Children who witness abuse—between 3 and 10 million children witness domestic violence yearly—are more likely to be abused themselves and to abuse their own children and/or spouses in the future (Children's Defense Fund, 2000; Glicken & Sechrest, 2003). Children who suffer maltreatment or dangerous living conditions are also more likely to have intellectual deficits (Noble & Jones, 2006). Social workers offer a broad array of services to help children and families cope with and overcome mental and emotional difficulties and intellectual disabilities.

CHILDREN WHO FUNCTION AS PARENTS

Alcohol and drug abuse are highly related to child maltreatment and to situations in which children have to assume family duties inappropriate for their age. An estimated 67 percent of parents involved with the child welfare system abuse drugs and/or alcohol (Child Welfare League of America, 2001). When parents have drug or alcohol habits, children may be "parentified" by having to help their parents bathe, feed younger siblings and protect them from violence, and seek ways to earn money for the family (Winton, 2003). Numerous state laws define consuming high levels of alcohol or drugs during pregnancy as child maltreatment. Lack of appropriate child care also leads to parentification. Particularly in poor families, when adults are working and cannot purchase or otherwise provide child care, children may be left to fend for themselves while tending to siblings (see box 11.1).

Box 11.1   Helping Children Affected by Parental Drug Abuse

The parents of a five-year-old and a one-year-old taught the older child how to change the younger child's diaper and then disappeared for several days on a drug binge, leaving hamburgers and other food for the children. After several days, neighbors realized that the parents were not home. Social workers investigated and placed the children in foster care. Though social workers tried to help the parents get into drug rehabilitation and parenting classes, the parents did not cooperate with any of these efforts. Social workers and the court ultimately determined that the maternal grandparents could offer the children a more stable home, and they were granted custody. Social workers stayed involved with the family to help the grandparents ensure that the children's parents did not visit while under the influence of drugs, and efforts were made to encourage the mother to get drug treatment.

LACK OF HEALTH CARE

Child maltreatment sometimes involves lack of health care, which is often related to poverty. Twelve percent of American children have no health insurance (DeNavas-Walt et al., 2006). In 1977 Congress created the State Children's Health Insurance Program to help states insure children whose parents are too poor to buy insurance but are not poor enough to qualify for Medicaid (health care for segments of the population living in poverty). Some states, however, have not utilized the program to its full potential (DiNitto, 2007). Poor children are more likely to live and attend school in moldy structures that breed vermin and exacerbate respiratory illnesses. Though diseases such as measles and hepatitis can be prevented with vaccination, many poor children are not vaccinated. Children of color are less likely than white children to have completed their immunizations, and they are more likely than white children to get their health care in emergency rooms rather than medical offices or clinics (Moniz & Gorin, 2003).

Children with inadequate diets are more vulnerable to physical disease and emotional distress, and poverty exacerbates poor nutrition. Fast-food chains, which serve food high in calories and fats, are concentrated in low-income neighborhoods (Children's Defense Fund, 2005). In 2002, the U.S. Department of Agriculture reported that nearly 35 million Americans—including over 13 million children—are worried about how to secure their next meal (Children's Defense Fund, 2005). Poverty also affects children's options for exercise. Poor children cannot afford the fees and equipment for organized sports, and children living in dangerous areas may not be allowed to play outside.

Social workers help families develop health-care resources and healthier habits and lifestyles. Sometimes social workers intervene to help children who are not receiving necessary health care due to the family's beliefs or fears. For instance, a family that believes prayer alone is the answer to a child's cancer may need education and support about augmenting the power of prayer with traditional medical interventions. Children of undocumented immigrants may not get the medical help they need if parents are afraid of having their immigration status revealed at the clinic. Social workers also help them secure necessary health care for the child.

TEEN PARENTS

Statistically, three elements increase a newborn's risk of childhood poverty: being born to a teenager, being born to a woman who has not completed high school, and being born to a woman who has never married. On average, women who give birth as teens leave school three years before women who delay childbearing until after their teen years, and it is estimated that only a third of teen mothers go on to graduate from high school (*Kids Count*

Data Book, 2004). Teen parents are ill prepared to assume the financial costs of rearing children, and because poverty is often linked with neglect, children of teen parents are particularly vulnerable. Edin (2003) demonstrates that poor women desire marriage if it is accompanied by financial stability—but they view the many unemployed and underemployed men in poor neighborhoods as questionable marriage prospects. Schools and community agencies often operate programs for teenage parents; these are frequently staffed by social workers who teach young mothers and fathers parenting skills and support them in pursuing education and job training.

CUSTODY ISSUES

Children involved in highly emotional divorces may experience feelings of fear and anger and even physical danger when their parents fight. Social workers mediate between parents to make reasonable custody decisions during divorce. They also study the homes of the parties seeking custody and make recommendations to the court. Social workers also help find secure homes for children whose parents are incarcerated, and they help

The members of Girl Scout Troop 1500 are girls whose mothers are incarcerated. The troop is led by a social worker in Austin, Texas.
© Ellen Spiro

children understand and cope with the parent's crime and jail sentence. Social workers also intervene when there are custody (and bereavement) issues due to a parent's death.

HOW SOCIETY DEVELOPED A CHILD WELFARE SYSTEM

The colonies that became the United States recognized the need to provide "relief" (material aid) to poor families so that children could stay at home without starving. As the nation grew, however, many destitute mothers and children were housed in deplorable conditions in publicly funded poorhouses. By the mid-1800s, many citizens preferred another congregate facility for needy children: the orphanage. The first U.S. orphanage was established in New Orleans in 1727, and many orphanages sprang up after 1860 to care for Civil War orphans. Another option for children whose parents could not care for them was adoption. In 1851, Massachusetts instituted the first American adoption law. Many children were candidates for adoption because poverty and epidemics frequently left children without parents. In 1853, so-called orphan trains began carrying poor and homeless children south and west from the East Coast. Families could meet the train and choose children to take home. The orphan trains marked the beginning of the foster care movement.

Although traditionally fathers were awarded custody of children in cases of divorce, by the early 1900s, courts had begun to routinely award custody of children to mothers rather than fathers. This occurred in part because of the growing political power of women and in part because of the influential ideas of psychiatrist Sigmund Freud, who asserted that mothers and children had an elemental emotional relationship. In the early 1900s, women were also influential in convincing lawmakers to pass landmark legislation regarding children, such as laws to outlaw child labor and legislation to require schooling.

During the Great Depression, Congress passed the Social Security Act of 1935, which made survivors' benefits available to widows and their children. Another major provision of the act was Title IV-B, which provided federal grants to states to develop state child welfare agencies. Social workers have been deeply involved in shaping these agencies. Though states use federal funds for children's services, each state administers its own child welfare agency. The modern child welfare system has grown increasingly complex as more is learned about the grave effects and financial costs of maltreatment. Today, Title IV-E provides federal funds for foster care, while Title XIX, Medicaid (added in 1965), provides medical services for foster children and families who fall below an income threshold.

Due to growing public concerns about maltreatment, Congress passed the Child Abuse and Prevention and Treatment Act (CAPTA) in 1974. CAPTA created guidelines for states to follow in developing systems and increased mandatory reporting requirements for suspected child abuse and neglect, and it provided grants for abuse prevention programs. CAPTA also mandates that in every abuse or neglect case that goes to court, a guardian *ad litem* must be appointed to speak for the child's best interests. Today courts appoint either attorneys or special advocate volunteers to represent the child's best interests in court.

CAPTA's mandatory reporting provisions resulted in a steep rise in child abuse and neglect reports, but since services were not sufficiently funded, agencies were soon financially strapped. Increasingly, agencies gave priority to investigating life-threatening abuse cases over cases of neglect, even though neglect can have lifelong negative (and even deadly) effects. Consequently, the system became more of a child protection system than a child welfare system.

Laws to Protect Specific Groups of Children

Social workers have also helped shape legislation to assist specific groups of children, such as juvenile offenders, many of whom have suffered maltreatment. Beginning in Illinois in 1899, states established juvenile courts to ensure that children under eighteen who commit crimes are kept separate from adult offenders, based on the belief that juveniles can be rehabilitated more effectively if they are not exposed to people who have a history of criminal activity. Juvenile courts, however, deny children some rights (such as bail hearings) that are guaranteed to adults in criminal court. Over time, courts have determined that children should have more due process rights. At the same time, jurisdictions have increasingly certified children as adults for prosecution of serious crimes.

Congress passed the Indian Child Welfare Act of 1978 to preserve American Indian family unity. The act requires that American Indian children needing protection be placed with extended family, foster families in the child's tribe, or foster families in other tribes. Prior to this act, numerous American Indian children were placed outside the tribe, often in white families. This law ensures that more American Indian children are reared in their tribal traditions.

A few years later, in 1984, the National Institute of Mental Health formed the Child and Adolescent Service System Program to help states care for children with emotional and behavioral disorders. Anxiety disorders, attention-deficit/hyperactivity disorder, post-traumatic stress disorder, and depression are common among maltreated children and youngsters who have lost a family member or have witnessed violence (Noble & Jones, 2006).

Since 1999, forty-four states have adopted Baby Moses laws, which allow parents to legally relinquish custody of infants sixty days old or younger at a safe baby site, such as a fire station or hospital (Roussel, 2005). Such legislation provides parents with a way to leave the child with an emergency care provider rather than abandon the child in a dangerous or unprotected location.

Permanency Planning

Faced with alarming statistics about hundreds of thousands of children growing up in foster care, Congress passed the Adoption Assistance and Child Welfare Act of 1980, which mandated permanency planning for children. States are required to make "reasonable efforts" to prevent children from entering foster care or to reunite foster children with their parents. Placements that are made must be in the least restrictive (most family-like) setting. Permanency plans, which social workers frequently help develop, provide the following options, in order of perceived desirability: (1) to remain with the family of origin (assuming that the problems that put the child at risk are resolved), (2) to be placed with kin or in an adoptive home, (3) to live in foster care, or (4) to live in residential care or a group home (Administration for Children and Families, 1997).

A social worker in Alameda County, California, spends time with her clients on adoption day. Social workers play a critical role in the long and arduous process of adoption.
© Richard Bermack

The Adoption and Safe Families Act of 1997 extended many provisions of the 1980 legislation and requires that permanency plans be established within twelve months of the child's removal from his or her original family setting. This law emphasizes that the child's safety is paramount and encourages concurrent or dual planning, in which the agency works to reunite the child with his or her family while concurrently planning to place the child in adoption or with a legal guardian should reunification fail. The Adoption and Safe Families Act also expanded the role of the courts in deciding what family reunification activities should occur, setting deadlines for filing termination-of-parental-rights petitions, and establishing the rights of foster and adoptive parents to receive notice of court proceedings (Badeau, 2005).

The increase in child abuse reporting and the legal demands for timely permanency decisions have created greater workloads for courts. Courts control how and in what setting the child welfare system serves children, monitor the system's adherence to legal rulings, and in some states oversee the system, as the result of lawsuits requiring that the state remedy deficiencies. Judges and attorneys in the child welfare system generally carry large caseloads. Judges may hear one thousand cases per year—meaning that they often have as little as four minutes to devote to a particular child's hearing (Badeau, 2005). Courts, consequently, must depend heavily on the informed assessments of social workers regarding the child's best interests.

Permanency planning, and its emphasis on returning children to their families, generated interest in working with families in their homes so that parents can take better care of their children. Congress passed the Omnibus Budget Reconciliation Act of 1993, which established the Family Preservation and Support Program. Social workers help families learn skills such as cooking, budgeting, caring for and disciplining children, and keeping the home safe and clean.

How the System Works

Though the child protection system is guided by federal regulations, child protection is a state function and procedures vary by state. In general, social workers, police, and other professionals working with the public agency (or a private agency with which the state contracts) investigate suspected abuse or neglect. If the case is deemed to be unfounded, it is closed. Investigators may substantiate the report, and the court may hold a protective hearing to determine whether the child should be placed in an emergency setting or left in the home. Social workers testify to the facts and offer recommendations at such hearings. Depending on circumstances, the agency may (1) recommend to the court that the child be removed from the home; (2) leave the child in the home but provide supervision or support services, such as parent effectiveness training; (3) or leave the child at home and make no recommendations for services if it appears that the abuse or neglect will not continue (Pew Commission on Foster Care, 2005). If the child is removed from the home, social workers are involved in providing the least damaging transition for the child and in crafting future plans for the child. If the child is left in the home with supportive services, social workers often provide or oversee those services and reassess the home situation to ensure the child's safety.

If the court orders that the child be removed from the home, an adjudicatory hearing is conducted to determine if maltreatment actually occurred and a dispositional hearing in which the court determines where the child will live, who will have custody, and what conditions will apply (Badeau, 2005). The court may order that the child be placed with relatives or in a foster home, group home, or residential facility. Social workers help the family work toward reunification with the child while also developing an alternate permanent plan (such as kinship care or adoption).

The court conducts six-month periodic reviews to monitor the child's progress; social workers provide and testify to much of the review data. The court holds a permanency hearing after twelve months to approve a permanency plan. If the child's original family and the agency successfully complete the plan, the child returns home. When the permanency plan is not successful, the court holds a termination-of-parental-rights hearing. Parents may appeal a decision to terminate rights to a higher court of jurisdiction.

If the child is placed in a permanent adoptive, kinship, or guardianship home, the court conducts an adoption or guardianship hearing to make the child legally part of another family. Social workers do much of the work to identify the best placement and make it successful (see box 11.2). When a

---

Box 11.2   Permanency Planning for Siblings

Sixteen-year-old Ben, fifteen-year-old Jackson, nine-year-old Jared, and eight-year-old Harrison are brothers. The courts granted custody of the brothers to the state child welfare agency because of the death of their father and the mental illness of their mother. To keep the brothers together, the agency placed them in group foster care. While developing a permanency plan, social workers found no suitable relatives to take the children. Ben and Jackson were not interested in being adopted; they wanted to graduate from high school and get out on their own. Jared and Harrison, on the other hand, longed to be part of a family. Finding adoptive homes for teens or sibling groups is challenging. After much hard work, the social workers found a family to adopt the two younger boys, but this family lived several hundred miles away. This was difficult for Ben and Jackson, who felt they should stay very involved with their younger brothers. The new adoptive family, however, was amenable to including Ben and Jackson in their holidays and special occasions and even paid for the older boys to come visit the younger children. Ben and Jackson remained in the group home until they graduated from high school.

permanent home is not an option, the child remains in foster or residential care until he or she ages out of the system by reaching the age of eighteen, or, in some states, twenty-one (Badeau, 2005; Pew Commission on Foster Care, 2005).

FAMILY PRESERVATION

The notion that it is preferable for a child to live with his or her original family permeates public policy. The Promoting Safe and Stable Families Program of 1997, part of Title IV-B of the Social Security Act, allows states to use federal funds to keep the child safe at home while providing support services to the family, which may include programs to strengthen parental relationships. Another important facet of the law is that it supports transitional or independent living programs for youths who age out of foster care.

Each of the various models of family preservation seeks to help families overcome problems and stay together. Family preservation services are usually intensive and short term, though many families need periodic services for a long time. Social workers teach parents how to effectively parent their children and how to safely oversee their home. Also integral to family preservation is the provision of "wraparound services" by interdisciplinary teams of community professionals (such as social workers or clergy), which wrap services around the family to prevent the child's removal (Allen-Meares & Fraser, 2004; Downs et al., 2000).

Family group decision making is a model that brings together family members, friends, and other significant adults to create a permanency plan for a child. Family members and friends conference together and agree to tasks that will help the plan work, such as driving a child to therapy sessions. Family group conferencing helps to empower families and involve them in the complex task of seeing their children safely to adulthood (see box 11.3). It also can draw fathers into the process, a goal of the Fatherhood Initiative, launched in 2001 by the U.S. Department of Health and Human Services (American Humane Association, 2003).

Shared family care is another model for preserving families. An example is a faith-based residential center in which mothers at risk of homelessness are taken into specialized foster care. Several mothers and their children share a home with a foster family, and the foster parents help the mothers learn parenting, budgeting, and other skills. The mothers work or attend school and share the housework and cooking. As the residential center continues to offer them food and counseling, it also links the mothers with the local housing authority and other agencies, helping them become self-sufficient so they can find new housing for themselves and their children (Noble & Gibson, 1994).

Box 11.3   Family Group Decision Making

LaToya, a seriously diabetic sixteen-year-old girl, lived in a residential setting sponsored by a church. Her mother was addicted to drugs, and her father had just been released from prison after ten years of confinement. Social workers at the residential facility set up a conference with LaToya, her father, and other members of the family, and the social workers conducted a family group decision-making session to help LaToya plan for her future. One critical factor was the money and effort required to maintain LaToya's diet and health-care regimen. Various family members suggested what they could do to help meet LaToya's needs, but LaToya wanted her father, whom she had not seen in ten years, to take her home with him. Finally, the father turned to LaToya and said, "Baby, I love you, but I just can't take care of you right now." LaToya burst into tears, saying, "That's the first time you ever told me you love me!" This was a turning point for LaToya, who started coming to terms with her father's long absence from her life. LaToya continued to live in the residential facility, but family members became more involved in her life.

The Child and Family Program (Gibson & Noble, 2002), which is supported by the Presbyterian Children's Homes and Services, is another example of a family preservation effort. Churches give space and support to professional social workers who seek out families in need of help. The social workers then help obtain the items and support the families need in order to avoid placing their children outside the home. For instance, two young children lived with their grandmother during their mother's incarceration. The grandmother survived on a small Social Security check in a dilapidated and rat-infested home. One night a drunk driver plowed into the house. The family had to vacate while the house was repaired. During their absence, the house was vandalized and the family's possessions—including bedding, clothing, toys, and family mementos—were stolen. The children were heartbroken, and the grandmother was frantic with worry about how to take care of the youngsters. Social workers at the Child and Family Program found resources to clean up the debris and rewire and refurbish the house. Church members restored the inside of the house and donated household goods. Social workers provided counseling—and new toys (Gibson & Noble, 2002).

FOSTER FAMILY CARE

Foster care is full-time temporary substitute care in a family-like setting. On any given day, approximately 500,000 children (or about 800,000 per year) are in foster care in the United States. Children stay in foster care an average of thirty-three months, though 17 percent have been in care for five years or more (Pew Commission on Foster Care, 2005). Sixty percent of foster children enter care due to abuse or neglect, but they may also be in foster care because their parents are incarcerated, disabled, or deceased (Pew Commission on Foster Care, 2005). Foster care is sometimes used to help children who have committed juvenile offenses and children who require special care due to physical or mental health conditions.

Even when their home environments are miserable, children usually are traumatized and confused when they are suddenly removed from familiar settings and placed with strangers. Often they have to change schools and leave behind favorite toys and clothes and neighborhood playmates. Children may feel guilty and bereft about leaving their parents or siblings. Abused and neglected children often exhibit serious behavior problems, such as anger, cruelty to animals or younger children, eating disorders, depression, or inappropriate sexual awareness (Noble & Jones, 2006). They are often behind in school and feel unsuccessful in their personal relationships. Social workers work on the front lines to help foster children and substitute parents deal with these issues (see box 11.4).

Box 11.4   Foster Parenting Challenges

Terry, an eleven-year-old survivor of vicious physical abuse by his biological father, almost vibrated with anger, and his behavior was so difficult that four foster families were unable to help him. Terry's fifth foster mother, Verna, struggled to cope with Terry's behavior. She reported to Terry's social workers that he expressed his frustration with behaviors such as walking up to the toilet bowl but urinating on the floor. The social workers supported Verna in her determination not to reject Terry, and they helped her to come up with innovative strategies to alter Terry's behavior. Social workers helped Verna understand that Terry, who felt enormously betrayed by his father, was pushing the limits to see if Verna would stand by him, no matter what. Verna described her time with Terry as "tying a knot and hanging on."

Social workers help recruit, train, and oversee foster parents. To be licensed by the state, foster parents must undergo a home study to discuss how their children and associates will support them in fostering and identify their reasons for wanting to foster. Social workers conduct these studies and educate foster parents on such issues as understanding child development and managing child behavior, as well as addressing a child's cultural heritage, dealing with a child's loss and grief, and handling health problems and other emergencies that may occur. Payments for foster care are meant to help cover the foster child's basic needs. Some foster homes are classified as therapeutic homes; these are homes that are qualified to help children who have serious emotional, behavioral, or medical difficulties. Foster homes may be engaged directly by the public agency, or they may operate under the auspices of various faith-based, civic, or nonprofit entities. Public agencies often contract for housing from private entities for children. Families may also voluntarily place their children in private foster home agencies. Foster homes are not always safe havens. They can be dangerous if the foster parents are not well trained or not well suited to fostering. Social workers must be closely involved with foster parents, ensuring that they are emotionally able and sufficiently trained to provide suitable care.

Approximately 20,000 to 25,000 young people age out of foster care each year with no ongoing family support. Many become homeless (Allen & Nixon, 2000). They need transitional services, such as those authorized by the John Chafee Foster Care Independence Program of 1999, which gives funding to states to provide youths up to age twenty-one who are leaving foster care with educational, vocational, practical, and emotional support services. Numerous child-care agencies have developed transitional living programs for children aging out of foster care. They also reach out to children who need help transitioning to independence from living situations other than foster care.

For instance, Lily and Tim, ages seventeen and sixteen, awoke one day to find a note from their parents, who had left to join a traveling musical group; the note said that the children were now old enough to make their own way. Though the parents had left a little money, it did not cover the rent. A transitional services agency funded by a private foundation placed the children in a group living situation where social workers taught them such life skills as how to purchase groceries, find an apartment, locate community resources like emergency medical clinics, interview for a job, and deposit a paycheck. The social workers also helped the youngsters deal with the anger they felt toward their parents. The social worker encouraged both children to finish high school and arranged for tutoring services, but Lily dropped out. After eight months at the group home, the siblings got jobs in the food service industry and found an apartment. Though they lived close to the edge financially, they maintained their independence with occasional help from the agency to pay rent. The siblings avoided homelessness and were very supportive of one another.

ADOPTION

Like marriage, adoption is a legal avenue for building a family. Only state courts, and sometimes tribal courts, can grant adoptions, and that can happen only after the biological parents' rights to the child are legally severed—either voluntarily or because the parents are deceased or fail to perform parental duties for reasons such as incarceration or disability. When a child is adopted, he or she joins a new family, and the state rewrites that child's birth certificate so that the names of the adoptive parents appear on it. The adopted child enjoys all privileges of membership in the family, including inheritance rights.

An estimated 1.5 million children in the United States, about 2 percent of all American children, live in adoptive families (Downs et al., 2000). Adoption of infants is a small part of adoption activity, since only about 2–3 percent of mothers relinquish their infants for adoption (Mosher & Bachrach, 1996). There are, however, about 126,000 special-needs children—children who are older or who have physical, mental, or emotional difficulties—available for adoption, and finding suitable adoptive placements for most of these children is very challenging (U.S. Government Accountability Office, 2005). According to the Children's Bureau (2002), of those special-needs children who are adopted, about 61 percent are adopted by the their foster parents (a process often called "fost-adopt"), about 21 percent are adopted by relatives (kinship adoption), and 18 percent are adopted by nonrelatives. Special-needs children who are adopted may receive federal adoption subsidies and Medicaid insurance to help meet their special needs; however, these subsidies, which vary from state to state, often do not fully cover the costs of services needed (Barth, Gibbs, & Siebenaler, 2001). Because so many children with special needs are available for adoption, agencies often consider untraditional adoptive parents: single or older individuals, gays and lesbians, or those with health problems or limited incomes (see box 11.5).

Box 11.5   Adoption of a Special-Needs Child

Reymundo was a never-married gay man who had long wanted to be a father. During the adoption process, social workers studied Reymundo's home situation carefully and determined that he was emotionally and financially secure and had potential to be an effective, stable, and committed parent. The agency placed Ricardo, age thirteen, with Reymundo as a fost-adopt placement, which meant that Reymundo would act as foster parent for several months so that the agency could determine whether this adoption was in Ricardo's best interest. Ricardo had mobility and emotional problems due to early abuse; he had been through twelve different foster placements. Because Ricardo trusted no one, he and Reymundo had a few difficult months. Ultimately, however, Ricardo came to believe that Reymundo would set limits without hitting or fighting and would stand by Ricardo no matter what. Their relationship steadily improved, and Reymundo made sure that Ricardo got the physical therapy and emotional counseling he needed. The adoption was finalized a few months later.

Kinship adoption allows children to remain in their larger biological family. If the child is available for adoption because a parent has been violent or neglectful, it is critical that the kinship placement protect the child from the abusive parent.

Another growing segment of adoption is international adoption, which requires parents to comply with laws in both the United States and the child's country of origin. Some countries, notably Islamic countries, prohibit all adoptions. Other nations, such as Romania, have become increasingly restrictive in allowing children to leave their borders. Children adopted internationally often present special needs, since many have been abandoned, have unmet medical needs, or have spent most of their lives in institutions; these children must adjust to a radically different society, landscape, and language.

Adoption social workers recruit potential parents, thoroughly study potential parents' homes, and help determine the adoptive placements that best meet the child's needs. Many adoption agencies offer post-adoption services to help all members of the adoption triad—biological parents, adoptive parents, and child—deal with their emotions about the adoption experience and to help prevent adoption disruption or failure. They also help families address some adoptive children's needs to search for and reconnect with their biological families. Adoptions of infants and young children may be cloaked in confidentiality, or they may be cooperative or open adoptions, in which the biological family may participate in selecting the adoptive family and may interact with the adoptive family for years. Children who are no longer toddlers, however, remember their original families. Social workers help a child appreciate his or her past with activities such as developing "life books" of the child's history.

Like children from other countries, U.S. children awaiting adoption bring their original culture with them. In the United States, many children awaiting adoption are children of color. Historically, adoption agencies were hesitant to place children of one race or culture with adoptive parents of another race or culture. Since the 1970s, the National Association of Black Social Workers has argued that African American children should be placed in African American families so that they can appreciate their heritage and develop a secure racial or ethnic identity.

There is a strong tension between the desires to quickly find permanent homes for rapidly growing and developing children and to ensure that adoptive homes reflect the children's ethnic, cultural, and/or religious background. To prevent children from staying too long in foster care, Congress passed the Multiethnic Placement Act of 1994 and its amendment, the Interethnic Placement Act of 1996. These laws prohibit any adoption or placement agency that receives federal funds from delaying or denying a child's placement for reasons based solely on the child's or the foster or adoptive parents' race, color, or national origin. (A major exception is the Indian Child Welfare Act of 1978, which mandates that all efforts must be made to keep American Indian children with their tribes.) Social workers assist families in helping their adopted children learn about their heritage, participate in its traditions, and maintain relationships with others of the same heritage.

KINSHIP CARE

An increasing number of children are being raised by grandparents or other kin. Nationally, about 6 million children live in households headed by grandparents or other relatives. About 2.5 million of these children live in homes in which neither of the child's parents is present, so the relative is responsible for rearing the child (Children's Defense Fund, 2004).

Older relative caregivers may have limited energy to raise children, and many relative caregivers have modest incomes. Depending on the circumstances, the relative caregiver and/or the child may be eligible for financial assistance through Temporary Assistance for Needy Families or other public assistance programs. Some kinship care families may be eligible for state foster care payments, subsidized guardianship payments, or kinship care payments. If the relative wishes to adopt and the child is legally free for adoption, subsidized adoption may be possible. Children who are disabled, poor, and under eighteen may be eligible for Supplemental Security Income payments. Social workers play an important role in helping kinship care families find the resources they need.

GROUP AND RESIDENTIAL CARE

Many children enter foster care after being housed in emergency shelters, group facilities that accept children who suddenly must be removed from their homes for protection. Emergency shelters usually serve a child for no more than a few weeks while social workers and courts make other plans for the child.

Other types of group living arrangements, usually run by an agency or institution, serve particular groups of children, such as children who have run afoul of the law or children who are developmentally disabled. Group homes are staffed, based on the children's needs, either by live-in house parents or by shift workers (to ensure constant awake staff). Group homes use the services of social workers, psychologists, nutritionists, and other professionals.

Residential institutions may serve dozens of children who can benefit from a group environment that provides a variety of professional services. Such facilities, which vary widely in size and location within the community, offer residential treatment for children who are dependent and neglected or who have emotional, behavioral, developmental, substance abuse, or delinquency problems. Typically, residential centers provide many professional services as well as a structured environment with established routines and supervision. For children who are psychologically damaged by abuse and have difficulty forming relationships, residential care can offer a safe and homelike atmosphere without forcing children to form close family-like relationships. Some children need the opportunity to maintain emotional distance, something that is harder to achieve in foster family care. In other cases, large sibling groups that cannot be accommodated in a single foster home can stay together in residential facilities. Children living in facilities may be wards of the state, or they may be placed in the facility directly by their families.

American religious and civic institutions have always helped families in need, particularly in ethnic communities. Faith-based groups have long received federal money to help families, but they were required to separate religious functions from the federally funded services they offered. In 1996, as part of welfare reform legislation, Congress passed a Charitable Choice provision allowing faith-based groups to use public monies to provide social services that are openly religious in nature. A growing number of states are also contracting out public functions such as foster care to private nonprofit and for-profit organizations. Advocates of privatization argue that private services can be more innovative, rational, and accountable and less expensive and can provide more choices for consumers because the services are more removed from political decision making. In reality, privatization may simply be an expression of the American preference for capitalism. People who argue against privatizing public services claim that private organizations make choices based on costs and desire for profits; private organizations, they claim, provide low-quality care and less choice for consumers, and there is less cooperation and service integration among service providers (Petr, 1998). Regardless of the arguments, social services today are increasingly provided through partnerships between public and private entities. These partnerships can bring a broad array of people and organizations together to share ideas and resources to attack the problems that beset children and families.

SERVING CHILDREN IN SCHOOLS

The academic and social challenges that children face often prevent them from doing well at school. Social workers help children, their parents, and schools overcome barriers to learning and make school a more productive environment. Social workers in schools, for instance, help parents assist their children to learn outside school and to overcome family tensions so that children have more peaceful environments in which to study. Social workers help students with disabilities or other special needs access the educational services they need. They can help students overcome test anxiety or direct them to activities at which they excel. When students face a painful event, such as the death of a family member or a fellow student, social workers help them and their families cope with the situation.

To maximize learning, children need to feel safe in their schools and their neighborhoods. For example, when the school environment is disrupted by excessive bullying, social workers help students and faculty devise ways to reduce bullying and guard against its negative effects. In emergencies, school social workers can be invaluable. During traumatic events such as school shootings, social workers can help students stay calm and safe in the face of danger. Social workers also help children deal with having seen or heard about terrorist events.

Social workers often link community groups and schools to help children. A social worker, for instance, developed a partnership between a low-income high-need school and a church that trained mentors to work with children and their parents to improve educational outcomes. Through the social worker, the church secured a grant from a foundation to expand the program. Some school districts operate mental health units that use social workers to counsel children and families; others partner with community mental health clinics. School social workers also work with faculty and staff to identify potential abuse and neglect and instruct them on how to report cases.

Often social workers are involved with procedures related to the Individuals with Disabilities Education Act of 1990, often called IDEA. This legislation provides federal monies to states to augment education for children with mental, physical, or emotional disabilities (see chapter 10). Children with special educational needs are more likely than others to be disadvantaged and in need of social services (Oswald, Coutinho, Best, & Singh, 1999).

THE CHALLENGES OF SERVING CHILDREN

While the rewards of serving children are tremendous, the challenges can be daunting. Social workers serving disadvantaged children and families have the reward of knowing they help enhance children's lives. To do so, however, social workers deal with angry, frightened families in crisis, often in poor neighborhoods that may not be safe. They frequently have heavy workloads, get limited supervision, and earn less than the demands of their jobs warrant (Annie E. Casey Foundation, 2003). Child-serving agencies are also frequently the subject of negative media reports and legislative attention due to adverse publicity. When a child under the care of a child-serving agency is seriously harmed or killed, agency staff may hear threats of legal liability, though court cases have established precedents that may protect child welfare staff from liability (DiNitto, 2007). Because of stressful work circumstances such as these, child welfare staff turnover commonly exceeds 30 percent a year (Nissly, Mor Barak, & Levin, 2004).

High turnover has forced many child welfare agencies to hire child welfare workers who hold degrees in fields other than social work and then train them on the job. In fact, fewer than 15 percent of child welfare agencies require caseworkers to hold either a bachelor's or master's degree in social work, despite numerous studies demonstrating that staff who hold the BSW or MSW exhibit more effective job performance and have lower turnover rates (Child Welfare League of America, 1998).

Social workers in schools do not deal with acute life-and-death crises with the same regularity that child welfare workers do, but school social work nonetheless demands ingenuity, focus, and energy. Both child welfare workers and school social workers operate in large bureaucracies, which can create barriers to innovative and timely problem solving.

One key to success is developing partnerships that bring more people and organizations, with their ideas and enthusiasm, into the problem-solving process to create new approaches to help children and families. One successful partnership involves schools of social work and public child welfare agencies in more than forty states. Using Title IV-E dollars and state contributions, schools of social work have prepared thousands of students for child welfare careers by providing stipends in exchange for a commitment to work in child welfare agencies following graduation.

Some state child welfare agencies are striving to become accredited by the Council on Accreditation. The accreditation process helps agencies recruit and retain more and better-qualified staff; decrease caseloads; and ensure better supervision, work environments, and case outcomes. Illinois, Kentucky, Arkansas, and Louisiana currently have accredited state systems, and other states, such as Connecticut, are working toward accreditation (Council on Accreditation, 2005). Some states use competency-based interviews to screen job candidates in order to secure employees better suited for the work, and some use videos portraying child welfare workers doing their jobs in order to help candidates determine if they really want to do this work. In a few states, the agency offers bonuses to new child welfare workers or to workers who achieve an anniversary date; this strategy holds promise for helping agencies retain staff. In states such as Kentucky, experienced child welfare workers mentor new child welfare staff for three months to increase their confidence and prepare them for the challenges of the job (U.S. General Accounting Office, 2003). Strategies such as these help agencies find and keep effective staff to do the difficult work of serving children and their families.

SUMMARY

There are many challenges and opportunities in working with children and their families. Professional social work has played a unique role in creating strategies (such as laws and programs) and structures (such as child welfare systems, schools, and child-focused agencies) that aim to protect children and help families provide homes and relationships in which children can safely grow and prosper. As society deals with the serious effects of poverty and violence, social workers and other professionals serving children and families who are at risk for difficulties will continue to be called upon to study and develop avenues for intervening to help children. Working with and for children is an investment in the future of humanity.

SUGGESTED READING

Golden, R. (1996). *Disposable children: America's child welfare system*. Belmont, CA: Wadsworth. This book is a compilation of firsthand accounts of caseworkers, judges, and children who have been involved in the child welfare and juvenile justice systems. It explores the procedures and problems of the child welfare and juvenile justice systems and recommends strategies to resolve difficulties in each system.

Jones, B. J. (1995). *The Indian Child Welfare Act handbook: A legal guide to the custody and adoption of Native American children*. Chicago: American Bar Association. This book, a comprehensive source of information on American Indian children, is recommended for social workers, attorneys, counselors, and other professionals interested in American Indian children.

Karson, M. (2001). *Patterns of child abuse: How dysfunctional transactions are replicated in individuals, families, and the child welfare system*. New York: Haworth Maltreatment and Trauma Press. This work provides a systemic perspective on abuse and neglect and explores the patterns of maltreatment from generation to generation. It also identifies effective treatment approaches.

Myers, J. E., Berliner, L., Briere, J., Hendrix, C. T., Reid, T. A., & Jenny, C. A. (Eds.). (2002). *APSAC handbook on child maltreatment*. Thousand Oaks, CA: Sage. The American Professional Society on the Abuse of Children's handbook summarizes a great deal of literature, empirical research, and other information about child maltreatment, intervention, and prevention that is useful for professionals in child protective services, mental health, law, medicine, and law enforcement.

Petr, C. G. (2003). *Social work with children and their families: Pragmatic foundations*. New York: Oxford University Press. This book integrates policy and practice based on these perspectives: (1) combating adultcentrism, (2) family practice, (3) the strengths perspective, (4) respect for diversity and difference, (5) the least restrictive alternative, (6) ecological perspective, (7) organization and financing, and (8) achieving outcomes. It includes case studies that demonstrate practical applications of the perspectives and provides information on child welfare and children's mental health that is appropriate for students and professionals.

Saban, C. (2002). *50 ways to save our children: Small, medium, and big ways you can change a child's life*. New York: Harper Trophy. This book provides practical suggestions for individuals and organizations interested in making a difference in children's lives. It includes a list of relevant Web sites.

Smith, M. G., & Fong, R. (2004). *The children of neglect: When no one cares.* New York: Brunner-Routledge. This work defines neglect, explores its causes, and identifies its effects on children. It also discusses neglect as it relates to culture, substance abuse, and poverty.

Webb, N. B. (Ed.). (2006). *Working with traumatized youth in child welfare.* New York: Guilford Press. This book discusses a theoretical framework and practice suggestions for implementing interventions with traumatized youths. It explores the collaboration between child welfare and mental health professionals.

THE WORLD WIDE WEB OF SOCIAL WORK

Child Welfare Information Gateway http://www.childwelfare.gov

The Child Welfare Information Gateway, formerly the National Clearinghouse on Child Abuse and Neglect and the National Adoption Information Clearinghouse, provides access to information and resources useful for protecting children and strengthening families. The site contains links to information on understanding, preventing, and responding to child abuse and neglect; supporting and preserving families; and achieving and maintaining permanency, as well as information on out-of-home care, adoption and resources for adoption, statistics, conferences, and assistance with personal situations.

Child Welfare League of America http://www.cwla.org

The Child Welfare League of America is a nonprofit organization that provides services to aid children and families. CWLA's Web site offers information about child advocacy and empirical research and data on the status of children and families in the United States.

Focus Adolescent Services http://www.focusas.com/Abuse.html

This Web site provides information and resources relating to child abuse and neglect, specifically regarding adolescents. The site gives links to information that can help parents tell whether their child is exhibiting at-risk or self-destructive behaviors, and phone numbers that parents can call if they need assistance. The Web site also contains information about abuse and neglect, the use of technology to exploit adolescents, and dating violence. It gives links to resources such as books, events, speakers, and information for schools.

Prevent Child Abuse America http://www.preventchildabuse.org

Prevent Child Abuse America provides resources that individuals and organizations can use in their efforts to prevent child abuse. The site gives links for information on advocacy, research, publications, and conferences that focus on prevention efforts throughout the United States.

12 Gerontological Social Work

Allan Kaufman and Maggie Tang

This chapter discusses the older population and social work practice opportunities with older people and their families. We begin by defining gerontology as the "study of the biological, psychological, and social aspects of aging" (Hooyman & Kiyak, 2005, p. 3). This field of study examines the physiological and psychological changes that occur with aging and their effects on health, physical functioning, and psychological functioning (thinking, feeling, sensory functioning, and other mental capacities). It also looks at the ways that aging affects people's interactions with their social environments and the ways society and social institutions are affected by, and respond to, the circumstances and needs of people as they age (Atchley & Barusch, 2004).

BASIC CONCEPTS IN GERONTOLOGICAL SOCIAL WORK

What should social workers call the older clients to whom they provide gerontological services—older adults or senior citizens? Or is another term more appropriate? One factor to consider is that since the turn of the last century, the human life span has increased substantially so that what was once considered old or elderly may no longer apply. Furthermore, the minimum age for eligibility for social welfare programs may be fifty-five, sixty, sixty-five, or older, depending on the program.

In deciding on a name for this segment of the population, we might consider the following indicators of aging: chronological age, functional capacity, and life stage. A combination of chronological and social attributes is often used to categorize people as falling into a particular life stage, such as childhood, adolescence, young adulthood, middle age, and old age (Atchley & Barusch, 2004). The U.S. Census Bureau uses the word *older* to describe individuals age fifty-five and older, *elderly* for those sixty-five and older, *aged* for those seventy-five and older, and *very old* for those eighty-five and older. Others use the terms *young-old* and *old-old* to describe individuals at the ends of the continuum of older Americans, but it is often difficult to distinguish these groups by their functional capacity. Many older people remain active well into their seventies and eighties, or even later, while others begin to limit their activities much earlier due to poor health or other problems.

Functional age categories can also be difficult to assess since their definitions vary from one setting to another. For example, an athlete may become functionally old at thirty-five, whereas a university professor can be functionally capable at eighty or older. A functional category used to identify a subgroup of the older population is the *frail elderly*—those with severe limitations in activities of daily living, including "problems with walking speed, declining activity levels, weak grip strength, and chronic exhaustion" (Hooyman & Kiyak, 2005, p. 111). Many clients whom gerontological social workers see share these characteristics.

Harmful and damaging stereotypes about older people permeate contemporary society, perpetuating labeling and negative attitudes and beliefs about aging and old age. While advancing age does increase the risk of declining health, physical and cognitive functioning, and financial resources, most older people are in good health, have adequate incomes, live independently, and enjoy strong family ties and positive family relations. Aging is associated with many benefits. Increased age brings greater experience, knowledge, and skill in many areas. Compared to young and middle-aged adults, older people often have more freedom to pursue activities that increase life satisfaction (Atchley & Barusch, 2004).

To do their work effectively, gerontological social workers need particular values, knowledge, and skills. Among the essential values are positive attitudes toward older people, a desire to interact with older people in meaningful ways, and an appreciation of the contributions older people make to society. Social workers also need knowledge of the biological, psychological, and social processes associated with human aging that might require older individuals and their family members to be put in contact with human service and health-care providers. Social workers must also know about community programs and services that target older people and family systems. Among the skills that gerontological social workers need are the ability to perform thorough psychosocial and functional assessments, access a wide range of health and social services, and conduct evidence-based interventions designed to help older people achieve their goals.

THE GROWING NEED FOR GERONTOLOGICAL SOCIAL WORKERS

Where do social workers who assist older people and their families work, and what do they do? Some human service and health-care agencies serve a wide spectrum of the population, not just older people. These include acute care hospitals, outpatient health clinics, rehabilitation programs, inpatient and outpatient psychiatric programs, home health-care programs, hospice programs, prisons and other criminal justice programs, adult protective services, and long-term care facilities such as nursing homes and assisted living facilities that serve younger individuals with disabilities as well as older people. In contrast, some agencies—such as residential retirement communities, geriatric case management programs, senior adult volunteer programs, senior citizen centers, senior nutrition programs, certain information and referral programs, and geriatric psychiatry programs—have a specific mandate or mission to serve older people.

Depending on the agency's focus, social workers in direct practice, or micropractice, provide information and referral, discharge planning following hospitalization or other inpatient care, case management (service planning, acquisition, coordination, and management), counseling, protective services in cases of elder abuse or neglect, educational or recreational services, and advocacy. Boxes 12.1 and 12.2 illustrate some ways that social

---

Box 12.1   Helping a Widower

Mr. Walters is eighty-seven years old. He was married for forty-five years. His wife died three years ago. They had no children. Mr. Walters moved 250 miles to be near his elderly sister and middle-aged niece. They helped him find a small apartment. While he is able to live on his own and do some chores, he has glaucoma and arthritic knees. He walks with a cane.

Shortly after his move, Mr. Walters's sister was diagnosed with Alzheimer's disease. She died a year later. Being relatively new to the area, Mr. Walters has made few friends. He mostly listens to music or watches TV. He misses his wife very much.

Mr. Walters's niece helps him shop and get to medical appointments. He sometimes gets a ride with a neighbor to do errands, and they have lunch at inexpensive eateries. In good weather, they often chat in the complex's courtyard, and in bad weather in each other's apartments.

Mr. Walters's niece's husband lost his job unexpectedly. She took a second job to make ends meet. Another crisis struck when her father was diagnosed with cancer and moved in with her. Mr. Walters realized his niece no longer had much time to help him. She encouraged him to call the local aging services agency. He talked with a social worker but declined services other than home-delivered meals. Soon after, he had the meals stopped. He said the food was nothing like what his wife used to cook. He also told his neighbor, "I wasn't supposed to live this long."

Mr. Walters grew quite thin over the next few months. He simply had no interest in eating even though he had groceries. His niece called the aging agency and learned there was a service that provided meals for a fee. Mr. Walters could select what he wanted. He tried this service, but his niece was still concerned that he was not eating enough and was growing increasingly depressed. She again called the social worker, who arranged a home visit with Mr. Walters. Mr. Walters talked mostly about his late wife and how difficult it was without her. The social worker encouraged Mr. Walters to discuss this with his doctor, who prescribed a low dose of an antidepressant. He also encouraged Mr. Walters to participate in a bereavement support group. Mr. Walters said he couldn't imagine doing such a thing. One day Mr. Walters's neighbor mentioned that his cousin was attending such a group and that she really liked talking with people who understood what she was going

Box 12.1 *Continued*

through. Mr. Walters reluctantly said he would try it. When he attended, he was relieved to learn that others had the same feelings, and surprised at how nice everyone was.

The social worker arranged for other help. With Mr. Walters's permission, his niece and neighbor are checking in with him on a regular schedule. His doctor arranged for in-home physical therapy, and a home health nurse sees him monthly. The apartment manager installed assistive devices to help Mr. Walters. Rails were added to the walk leading up to the door of his apartment and to his bathroom walls so that Mr. Walters can pull himself up from the toilet and be safer in the shower. Medicare paid for a walker with a seat that Mr. Walters uses when he gets tired. The social worker helped Mr. Walters select a Part D plan so he can purchase his prescription drugs more economically.

Mr. Walters is doing better. He sounds more optimistic and is eating more. He has made friends with people in the bereavement group. They eat lunch at the senior citizens' center before meetings. A member gives him a ride to meetings. When Mr. Walters needs help, he knows he can contact the social worker at the aging agency.

Linda Vinton
Professor
Florida State University

Box 12.2 Ruling Out Physical Abuse

Ginger is seventy-nine years old. She was admitted to the hospital today after a fall at her home. She said she was reaching for a dish and lost her balance. Ginger sustained a broken arm. The doctor found bruises on Ginger's back and hips. She was also dehydrated. The doctor called the hospital social worker because he was concerned about abuse.

During Ginger's hospitalization, the social worker learns much about her situation. Ginger has lived alone since her husband, Warren, died ten years ago. They were married for fifty-one years and had one son and two daughters. Ginger and Warren married right out of high school. Warren found a civil service job as a mechanic and worked hard at that job all his life. He earned a good retirement for them. Ginger began work as a part-time secretary when all the children were in high school. She was always involved in her children's activities and was a long-time volunteer at the church she and Warren attended.

Ginger reported that her daughter, who lives thirty minutes away, helps her whenever she can and calls daily. Her other children and grandchildren live across the country and phone her weekly. The social worker asks Ginger for permission to talk with her daughter. Ginger's daughter confirms her mother's reports of her life history and current situation and expresses concern about her mother living alone.

Ginger has cardiovascular disease and hypertension. She had a heart attack about six years ago but has been able to take care of herself. She takes several medications. The social worker asks Ginger questions to check for cognitive or psychiatric problems and finds that none seem to exist.

Ginger explains that she loves living in her own place and loves her independence. She tells the story of her fall

Box 12.2 *Continued*

but is reluctant to talk about the bruising. She cuts off the social worker when she is asked about it. The social worker is unsure what to make of the injury and bruises. She calls adult protective services. Like the doctor, she is concerned about signs of possible physical abuse. During the visit with the adult protective services social worker, Ginger realizes that she must be forthcoming about the cause of the bruising. She shares that she can't keep up with her housework and admits that she has been falling about once a week. "I've been able to pick myself up. This time was different. I broke my arm."

In the multidisciplinary discharge planning meeting, the team discusses a plan for Ginger to return home and live independently. The social worker consults with Ginger for her agreement before plans are finalized. The plan includes referrals to home health for occupational therapy so that Ginger can learn adaptive techniques on how to dress and get around the house as her arm is healing, a home health aid to assist with bathing until Ginger can handle it on her own, homemaker services to do short-term housekeeping, and physical therapy to strengthen her arm after it heals.

During their last visit, the social worker reviews the details of the discharge plan with Ginger and her daughter and tells Ginger she will call to check on her and make sure the referrals have gone as planned. Ginger is happy that she will be staying in her home. Ginger's daughter is also glad that her mother will be able to continue living in her home. She offers to find her mother a part-time housekeeper and take care of the expense. Before leaving the hospital, both thank the social worker.

John Gonzalez
Doctoral Candidate
University of Texas at Austin

workers directly assist older clients, groups of elders, and families of older people. In all practice settings, social workers focus on enhancing quality of life and life satisfaction by helping older people maximize their physical and emotional well-being, their decision-making skills, and their independence. Social workers also assist those caring for functionally impaired and frail older family members. Their job is usually to help family caregivers maintain their caregiving role and to delay or prevent the need for the older person to enter an institutional setting like a nursing home or assisted living facility (Greene, 2000). Social workers also serve as administrators in public, not-for-profit, and private agencies that serve older adults, and as policy analysts and advocates who work to ensure that the needs of older people are addressed.

Gerontological practice is changing with the times. Social workers are engaging in many more preventive activities than they once did. For example, retirement planning services provided by many companies' human resources offices offer opportunities for social workers to educate individuals about the social and psychological challenges they may face as they move from the role of worker to the role of retiree, and the services that might help them. Case management services have expanded beyond tradi-tional health and human service agencies. Social workers may have private practices designed to provide these services to older people who desire them and can afford them, or adult children may purchase these services when they are not able to meet a parent's needs due to distance or time.

The need for gerontological services is expanding rapidly because those sixty-five and older are the fastest-growing segment of the U.S. population. Approximately 36 million people age sixty-five and older live in the United States, constituting just over 12 percent of the population (Administration on Aging, 2006). Since 1900, the percentage of people sixty-five and over has more than tripled. The Census Bureau estimates that by the year 2030, when all the members of the baby boom generation are age sixty-five and older, the older population will number about 70 million people, or approximately 20 percent of the population. The fastest-growing segment of the older population is people age eighty-five and older. This group is expected to number nearly 9 million by 2030.

The demand is strong, but there is a serious shortage of social workers to meet the staffing needs of the agencies and service programs that comprise the aging services network (see figure 12.1). This network consists of the Administration on Aging, a part of the U.S. Department of Health and Human Services dedicated to providing information and technical assis-tance to meet the needs of older Americans; state agencies that assess and address the needs of older people; area agencies on aging, which plan and coordinate services in communities; and local agencies, which provide many services to older people.

Increased demand for gerontological social workers also comes at a time when social work education programs are not encouraging sufficient inter-est in gerontology, in part, because many faculty lack training in aging or knowledge about the range of practice opportunities in aging services (CSWE SAGE-SW, 2000). A growing body of literature has begun to exam-ine the causes for this shortage and suggest steps to remedy it. Too often, social workers incorrectly presume that aging practice settings offer limited job opportunities and lower salaries. Some social workers hold negative attitudes and unflattering stereotypes about older clients, while others believe that social work practice with younger populations and in other practice fields offers higher professional status (Kosberg & Kaufman, 2002). To promote greater interest, social work practitioners, educators, and researchers are advocating more collaboration between social work educa-tion programs and aging service programs and more opportunities for stu-dents to gain practice experience with older clients. Social work researchers interested in gerontology are also encouraging more social work faculty and student affiliations with university-based interdisciplinary centers on

Figure 12.1   National aging services network

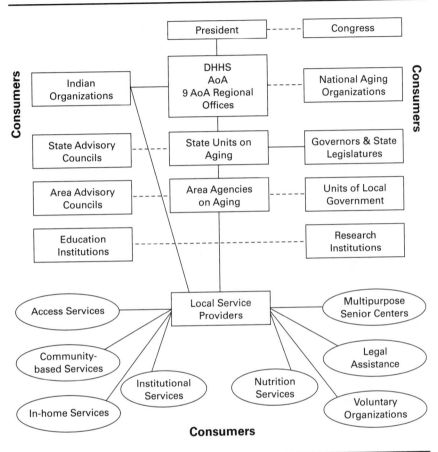

Source: Administration on Aging. (n.d.). *National aging services network*. Washington, DC: U.S. Department of Health and Human Services, Administration on Aging.

aging, like the Ethel Percy Andrus Gerontology Center at the University of Southern California and the Center for Mental Health and Aging at the University of Alabama.

In 1998, the John A. Hartford Foundation established the Geriatric Social Work Initiative to prepare future social workers to work with older adults. The initiative funds development of curricula and tools to facilitate the integration of aging content into undergraduate- and graduate-level social work courses. The Practicum Partnership Program is helping to create many agency-based social work field-training opportunities, including innovative aging-rich rotational field experiences for graduate students. Its Doctoral

Fellows Program supports promising social work doctoral students with a career interest in aging. The Hartford Foundation's initiative has greatly increased social work's involvement in gerontology.

SOCIAL WORK PRACTICE WITH OLDER PEOPLE AND THEIR FAMILIES

Generalist social work practice models like those described in chapter 2 are helpful tools for practitioners working with members of all age groups. In recent years, social work researchers and educators have complemented generalist models with ones specifically geared for gerontological social work practice. One example is Roberta Greene's (2000) Functional-Age Model of Intergenerational Treatment. This practice model provides a framework for conducting comprehensive psychosocial assessments of an older person within his or her family system. It helps social workers identify the variety of biological, psychological, and sociocultural factors that can help them understand an older person's physical and psychological functioning and the dynamics and functioning of his or her family system. The Functional-Age Model emphasizes the importance of understanding how functional changes experienced by an older person affect family members, and it encourages family participation in treatment planning and implementation. Greene recognizes the family as an important source of information for assessment and intervention planning. She emphasizes the value of considering the family as part of the treatment unit, and the necessity of addressing family members' needs in the treatment plan.

GENDER AND GERONTOLOGICAL PRACTICE

Some gerontological service programs, like Veteran's Administration facilities, serve many more men than women, but in most cases, gerontological social workers assist more women. Since the turn of the twentieth century, the human life span has increased dramatically for both men and women, but due in part to genetic and lifestyle differences between men and women, women live longer than men. There are seventy men for every one hundred women age sixty-five and older, and only forty-one men for every one hundred women who are eighty-five and older (He, Sengupta, Velkoff, & DeBarros, 2005). In 2004, about 42 percent of all women sixty-five and older were married, as opposed to 72 percent of men, and 43 percent of all older women were widows, while only 14 percent of older men were widowers (Administration on Aging, 2006). These gender differences have important social and economic implications, especially for older women. For example, more older wives are caring for their husbands than vice versa. Many older women no longer have a spouse with whom to share living expenses. There are also intergenerational impacts; for example, family members are more likely to be caring for an aged mother or grandmother.

Most widows and widowers make a successful transition to living without their spouse. When they do not, social workers may become involved. The challenges posed by bereavement may be most problematic for those who have outlived most of their close friends and family members. Social workers have long been involved in organizing and conducting bereavement and support programs with demonstrated effectiveness in helping older people following the death of their spouse (Lee & Bakk, 2001). Traditional gender role differentiation, especially among current cohorts of older people, may also mean that men and women need to learn new skills following a spouse's incapacitation or death. Part of the resilience of older people is their ability to take on new roles later in life, which social workers can facilitate. Social workers must also consider the needs of women and men who have never married and do not have children or other immediate family members to assist them in old age. Those who are gay, lesbian, bisexual, or transgender may have particular needs and may want to make special provisions about whom they want involved in decision making about their care as they age and about final arrangements after their death.

HELPING OLDER PEOPLE OF COLOR

In 2004, about 82 percent of the elderly population (age sixty-five and over) were non-Hispanic whites, while the remaining 18 percent were people of color. People of color are projected to comprise 25 percent of the total older population by the year 2030. Currently, African Americans are the largest group, making up 8 percent of the elderly population of color, followed by Hispanics (6%), Asians and Pacific Islanders (3%), and American Indians and Native Alaskans (less than 1%) (Administration on Aging, 2006). Elders of color vary in health and socioeconomic status and in their use of formal and informal supports. They may suffer economic and health deprivations in old age due to inequities they experienced throughout their lives. Despite these adversities, they generally continue to use unique cultural capacities and personal, family, and community strengths and resources to successfully cope with stressful life events in their later years (Hooyman & Kiyak, 2005).

Researchers have consistently found that people of color have low utilization rates of mainstream health care and social services. When making referrals, social workers need to ensure that elder care and other services are culturally relevant (see chapter 4). Social workers must develop relationships with ethnic social and religious organizations that can assist in coordinating and linking elders of color with services. Depending on level of acculturation, successful social service provision to older immigrants may hinge on the availability of bicultural and bilingual staff or community members who can reach out and identify those who need services, publicize their availability, and promote their use.

ADDRESSING LOW INCOME, POVERTY, AND HOMELESSNESS

In 2004, among older Americans who reported income, 38 percent had yearly incomes of less than $10,000, and only 27 percent had incomes of $25,000 or more (Administration on Aging, 2006). The median income for older men was $21,102, as opposed to only $12,080 for older women. Social Security, the federal government's social insurance program for retired workers and their spouses and younger disabled workers, is the major income source for 90 percent of older Americans. Workers contribute to Social Security during their working years and are guaranteed payments after they retire. Fifty-six percent of older people also reported income from assets, while 44 percent had income from public and private pensions. Only 23 percent of older people reported earnings from employment as a major income source, though older people are needed in the workforce because of their expertise. The Social Security tax contributions they made while working also help support the growing number of retirees.

Many women and people of color in today's older generation worked full-time throughout their adult lives but earned low wages, often due to gender and racial discrimination, which results in inadequate retirement income. Other women were stay-at-home wives and mothers whose primary social role was to manage the household and raise their children, which may also leave them with economic difficulties in old age. A couple's Social Security retirement income is reduced when a spouse dies, and private pensions may be significantly reduced or terminated.

Many Americans are concerned about the long-range solvency of the Social Security program. Though retirees paid into the Social Security program while they were working and are entitled to benefits, payments have increased and there are more retirees to support. Payments to retirees are actually financed by the contributions of today's workers. The growth of the older population means that the program is supporting more and more people, but compared to previous generations, there are fewer workers to help support each retiree. Suggestions to ensure the financial stability of Social Security in the years ahead include reducing future benefits, raising the retirement age, and reducing the annual cost-of-living adjustments. All these approaches could be particularly harmful to low-income beneficiaries, whom social workers often serve.

Current debate centers on partially or fully privatizing Social Security. This would allow workers to invest their Social Security taxes in private financial market investments (e.g., annuities, stocks, bonds). The volatility of the investment market and investors' lack of knowledge could put retirees at risk of not having adequate income to meet their retirement needs (DiNitto, 2007). Hard data are lacking, but social workers are likely to oppose privatizing Social Security because the goals of this social insurance program are collective and differ from those of private insurance focused only on individual contributors. Social Security has worked well since it was enacted in 1935. It is the nation's most effective antipoverty program. Though program adjustments will need to be made, one view is that major changes like privatization are not warranted. Along with groups like the American Association of Retired Persons and the Gray Panthers, social workers are using their political action skills to see that Social Security remains solvent and true to its social insurance mission to protect older people in retirement.

The poverty rate for older Americans has reached historic lows of about 10 percent, but another 7 percent with incomes up to 25 percent above the poverty level are classified as "near-poor" (Administration on Aging, 2006). Most older people have incomes adequate to meet their basic economic needs and are, as a whole, better off economically than were their parents and grandparents. However, many subgroups of older people, such as older women, elders of color, the oldest-old, and older people living alone, face substantial poverty rates. In 2004, the poverty rate was higher for older women (12%) than for older men (7%) (Administration on Aging, 2006). Older African Americans (24%), Hispanics (19%), and Asians (14%) were far more likely to be poor than older whites (8%). The most economically vulnerable are older women of color living alone. For example, about 40 percent of older African American and Hispanic women living alone have poverty-level incomes. Ironically, near-poor older people may be less financially secure than those living below the poverty line. Low-income elders may not qualify for government programs that those living in poverty may be able to access, which makes it difficult for them to obtain adequate health care, afford safe and secure housing, and maintain good nutrition.

The primary safety net for older Americans with little or no income from employment, savings, investments, or Social Security is the Supplemental Security Income (SSI) program. SSI provides cash benefits to those sixty-five and older, as well as to younger individuals who are blind or permanently and totally disabled. This federally established public assistance program is financed primarily by the income taxes citizens pay to the federal government. In 2006, the monthly federal SSI payment was $603 for an individual and $904 for a couple, but payments vary across the country because most states add to the federal SSI payment. Some states and communities help poor elderly people through programs that are often called general assistance or general relief. These benefits are generally available only to people who do not qualify for other programs such as Social Security and SSI. Chapter 13 describes public assistance programs at greater length.

Social workers assisting low-income elders must first see that their health-care needs and nutritional status and the adequacy and safety of their housing are thoroughly assessed. They must also be sensitive to potential situations of abuse or neglect, especially self-neglect among elders who experience extreme economic deprivation. Social work intervention with this population often centers on assessing eligibility for programs that provide concrete services and economic resources, and helping clients identify and access social service and health-care programs that can help them meet basic needs. Social workers assisting older clients with low incomes master the eligibility requirements and other rules of programs like SSI and general assistance in order to help clients secure all the benefits to which they are entitled. They also take other steps to help them get services. For instance, it is well known that many older people who would qualify for food stamp benefits do not know about the program or, if they do, assume that they do not meet its eligibility requirements or feel stigmatized about participating in a welfare program. Social workers provide education about public assistance and other programs, assist with the application process, and address physical barriers like the need for transportation to program offices and attitudinal barriers like stigma.

Homeless older people are a special concern of social workers. Living on the streets and in shelters, they are highly vulnerable to physical assault, sexual abuse, and other crimes. These individuals generally have histories of imprisonment, substance abuse, marital disruption and family violence, living alone with no kin support, cognitive or physical impairments, or mental illness (Cohen, Sokolovsky, & Crane, 2001). The scholarly literature generally labels homeless individuals as young as fifty years old part of the older homeless population because these men and women often physically resemble people in the general population who are ten to twenty years older than they are. A major national study found that about 9 percent of single homeless clients are fifty-five or older (Burt, Aron, Douglas, Valente, Lee, & Iwen, 1999). It may take a substantial period of befriending long-term homeless individuals before they will allow social workers to help them secure medical care, temporary or permanent shelter, economic or legal aid, jobs, or other assistance. Social workers who engage in this work perform a tremendous service for very vulnerable clients.

MEETING HEALTH-CARE NEEDS

About a third of older Americans have a severe disability, and the risk rises sharply with age (Administration on Aging, 2006). Disability and illness can cause declines in functioning and can limit a person's ability to engage in basic activities (e.g., ambulating, bathing, toileting) or independent activities of daily living (e.g., shopping, meal preparation, housework, money management). In 2002, about half of all older men and almost one-third of older women reported having trouble hearing, and almost 20 percent of older people had vision problems (Federal Interagency Forum on Aging-Related Statistics, 2004).

Falls are the leading cause of injury and disability among older Americans, and each year, many older people die of fall-related injuries. Gerontological social workers in settings like senior centers and outpatient health programs educate older people and their families about the dangers associated with falls and precautions that can be taken to prevent them, such as the use of grab bars and better lighting in homes.

Among American elders, cancer, diabetes, and heart disease are the major causes of death, and arthritis is the leading cause of disability and functional impairment. Early detection and prompt treatment of such illnesses, along with healthy habits such as proper nutrition, regular physical activity and exercise, and smoking cessation, help older people achieve and maintain good health (National Center for Chronic Disease Prevention and Health Promotion, 2005). This underscores the need for gerontological social workers to be involved in health promotion and to make health-screening services available to their clients.

An important role of social workers is helping older people communicate with their physicians and other health-care providers about preventive care, medical conditions, symptom management, and medications they are taking, including side effects. Many people, young and old, are often overwhelmed by the information they are given at medical appointments and need help remembering it. Though medical personnel are doing a better job of communicating with older people, some fail to talk directly to the older person or do not speak loudly enough for patients with hearing loss (social workers may also fail to do these things). They may also not take the time to write instructions clearly, concisely, and legibly. In this era of managed care, they often schedule appointments so close together that they do not have sufficient time to hear a patient's concerns or to think about the patient holistically. They may be too quick to provide medication when the problem could be addressed differently. Social workers act as advocates to ensure that all of the patient's needs are addressed appropriately. Social workers also often help coordinate and arrange transportation to medical appointments.

To meet older persons' medical needs, social workers need extensive knowledge of the Medicare and Medicaid programs. Medicare pays many of the health-care costs of Americans sixty-five and over and of younger individuals receiving Social Security disability benefits. The oldest parts of Medicare are hospital insurance (Part A) and supplemental medical insurance (Part B). Part A benefits cover costs associated with hospital care, physician-ordered home health care, and end-of-life hospice care. Eligible individuals who want Part B coverage pay a monthly fee that is modest enough that most participate. Benefits paid under Part B cover the greater portion of payments for outpatient medical services provided by physicians and many other medical providers. Medicare Part C is a newer addition; it provides alternatives to parts A and B for obtaining insurance coverage, like health maintenance organizations for older people, which are available in some communities.

Medicare generally does not pay for preventive health care, custodial nursing home care, or eyeglasses and hearing aids. Because of these costs, coverage gaps, and exclusions, many Medicare enrollees who can afford it purchase medigap insurance policies to supplement their Medicare benefits, and some purchase long-term care insurance. A pressing concern of older people today is the rising cost of prescription drugs. In 2006, Medicare Part D was added to provide prescription drug insurance. Part D is helping many older people with their prescription drug costs, but it is complicated because Congress decided to allow private insurers to offer plans that vary in cost and coverage. Social workers have been busy assisting many older clients in deciding which prescription drug insurance plan to purchase to get the best value, and how to apply.

Established along with Medicare in 1965, Medicaid is a public assistance program that can help poor and low-income elderly individuals pay the portion of health-care expenses that Medicare does not cover. Both the federal and state governments finance Medicaid, so the benefits provided can vary from state to state. Medicare and Medicaid rules change often and can be daunting to master, and participants, especially those in immediate need, often need social workers' help in navigating them. A fast-growing area of practice is home health-care social work. Home health social workers make home visits to help clients get the services they need to remain at home.

At any moment in time, only 5 percent of the older population resides in a nursing home, but a substantial amount of Medicaid funding goes toward paying for this long-term (custodial) care for older persons. Of the Medicaid funds expended for long-term care, 75 percent goes to nursing home care; only 25 percent is used for community-based home health services. This institutional bias in long-term care funding means that older people with limited financial resources who require formal long-term care services are often forced to enter a nursing home (Hooyman & Kiyak, 2005). Social workers are dedicated to helping elders live in the settings of their choice and look for ways to help elders exercise self-determination through Medicare, Medicaid, and other resources and through advocacy to alter existing policies and programs that limit choice.

Nursing homes are generally required to have social workers on staff or employed as consultants. These social workers play many important roles in the lives of patients. They are part of multidisciplinary teams of service providers that have a role in establishing policies that directly affect residents' lives. The social worker conducts a comprehensive psychosocial assessment of each client to identify needs and ensure that the resident maintains the highest quality of life possible. Social workers have continuous contact with residents and are the experts on community resources that can improve residents' lives and assist those who can return home or to other community residences. Social workers also maintain contact with family members about patients' needs and well-being. Social workers advocate for individual nursing home residents and for residents as a group. They also work to prevent abuse and intervene should it occur.

NUTRITION AND SOCIAL SERVICES

The Older Americans Act (OAA), originally passed in 1965, supports a number of services for older people. To qualify for services under the OAA, a person must generally be sixty or older. There are special provisions for grants to tribes for services to older American Indians living on reservations.

This eighty-year-old woman visits a drop-in center that offers seniors lunch and a variety of activities, ensuring that clients lead healthy and active lives.
© Mary Whelens

A volunteer for Meals on Wheels delivers meals to the elderly in Boise, Idaho.
© David R. Frazier Photolibrary/Alamy

Social workers who work with older people are very familiar with OAA-funded programs in their area and can quickly direct clients to the services they need.

Title III of the OAA provides funding for community-based aging programs and services such as outreach, case management, transportation, provision of information and referrals, services for family caregivers, housing services, legal assistance, crime prevention, and in-home services for the frail elderly. Perhaps the best-known services are meals served at congregate sites like senior centers and home-delivered meals (often called Meals on Wheels). The importance of helping older clients meet nutritional needs must be underscored since proper nutrition is essential to good health. Older people who live alone may no longer be able to prepare meals or may lack motivation to eat adequately. Depression can also lead to lack of appetite. Social workers and other staff and volunteers involved with programs that provide congregate and home-delivered meals are able to identify those who may need additional services.

A service sorely lacking for older people in many communities is transportation. Public transportation services geared to older people and individuals who are disabled increase mobility, allow for participation in many activities, and enhance the quality of life. They may also encourage older people to stop driving when they can no longer do so safely.

The federal government also provides Social Services Block Grants to states. In recent years, block grant funding has been severely reduced. Since these funds are not earmarked for people of a specific age, the social service needs of older people often compete with the needs of younger groups for block grant funding. Historically, states have allocated most of these funds for services to families with dependent children. When states have used block grant funding for older adults, it has primarily been for adult protective services, adult day care, and meal programs (Atchley & Barusch, 2004; Hooyman & Kiyak, 2005). Social workers generally take an intergenerational approach to advocacy by emphasizing that we must work to meet the needs of people of all ages.

ADDRESSING MENTAL HEALTH PROBLEMS

Normal aging is not characterized by cognitive problems or mental disorders, but increased age does increase the risk of these problems. Delirium and dementia are cognitive disorders that can affect people at any age but more commonly occur in older people. They share some common symptoms such as memory loss, confusion, disorientation, and loss of intellectual functioning. Delirium, however, is characterized by a sudden acute onset of symptoms, while the onset of dementia is usually slow and insidious. When its causes are identified and properly treated, delirium is reversible. The symptoms and cognitive changes associated with dementia, although sometimes treatable, are generally irreversible. Delirium can be associated with a variety of conditions such as viral or bacterial infections, malnutrition, substance abuse, and medication interactions.

The most prevalent form of dementia is associated with Alzheimer's disease, a serious mental health condition that affects mainly older people. As the older population grows, Alzheimer's disease poses an increasing threat, especially to the oldest-old. The disease is estimated to affect half of individuals age eighty-five and older, as it did former president Ronald Reagan (Evans, Funkenstein, Albert, Scherr, Cook, Chown, et al., 1989). Dementia can also occur with conditions such as cardiovascular disease, Parkinson's disease, and Down syndrome (Baptist Memorial Health Care, 2005). Social workers are often employed in nursing homes and community day programs designed to meet the psychosocial and environmental needs of people with advanced Alzheimer's disease and other dementias, such as reducing agitation and preventing residents from wandering off the property.

Depression is the most common mental health problem affecting older people. An estimated 8–20 percent of older people living in the general community suffer from depression (U.S. Department of Health and Human Services, 1999). Among the symptoms of depression are depressed mood, loss of interest in daily activities, significant weight loss or weight gain, difficulty sleeping or excessive sleeping, restlessness, fatigue or loss of energy, feelings of worthlessness or guilt, difficulty concentrating, indecisiveness, and recurrent thoughts of death or suicide. Depression has been linked to the many losses elders may experience, such as loss of loved ones and friends and a job or income, and changes that often accompany illness, physical decline, and loneliness. Depression has also been associated with medical problems such as stroke, Alzheimer's disease and other dementias, and nutritional deficits.

Older people with severe depression are at increased risk of suicide, and suicide rates increase with age (National Center for Injury Prevention and Control, 2004). Non-Hispanic white men over the age of eighty have the highest suicide rate in the United States. Older people tend to use highly lethal methods that are likely to result in a completed suicide. Because of lowered recuperative capacity, they are less likely to recover from a suicide attempt than younger people. It is suspected that suicide attempts and completions among older people are underreported.

Older people may not report feelings of depression to family members or physicians because they are ashamed of these feelings or do not believe in disclosing such personal problems to others. Some fear that others will think they are crazy and place them in a nursing home or psychiatric hospital. Many older people also allow dementia and depression to go untreated because family, friends, and professionals believe such declines are inevitable and irreversible. Primary-care physicians may lack the expertise to diagnose depression. Social workers are frequently the first to identify their older clients' depressive symptoms and must remain alert for symptoms of depression in older clients. Social workers screen for mental health problems and help older individuals and family members understand that with prompt diagnosis and treatment, these problems can often be controlled or reversed (Hooyman & Kiyak, 2005). A number of tools, such as the Geriatric Depression Scale (Yesavage & Brink, 1983), can help social workers assess clients for depression. Treatment may include medication, psychotherapy, or a combination of both. Some social workers specialize in treating depression and related problems in older clients.

ADDRESSING ALCOHOL AND DRUG PROBLEMS

Older people are much less likely than younger people to use illicit drugs, but a significant number (17%) of older individuals are estimated to abuse alcohol or prescription medications (National Substance Abuse and Mental Health Services Association, 2005). This can pose serious health risks. For instance, alcohol abuse has been linked to medical problems like hypertension, heart disease, stroke, liver problems, and dementia (Vinton & Wambach, 2005). Older people are more likely than younger people to take medications and to misuse or abuse prescription or over-the-counter drugs. Those who use alcohol and prescription or over-the-counter drugs together risk drug-alcohol interactions that can have life-threatening or other serious medical consequences. Older adults may have multiple medical conditions and may be treated by more than one physician. Those who do not provide physicians with information about all their medications run the risk of experiencing dangerous drug interactions. Their failure to fully disclose is often unintentional. Older patients should be reminded to take a list of their medications to all doctors' appointments.

Alcohol and drug abuse are often hidden behaviors among older people. People often don't think of a silver-haired grandmother drinking alone and excessively. Gerontological social workers should be able to identify signs of misuse or abuse of such substances, such as slurred speech and falls that may be incorrectly attributed to other causes. Comprehensive psychosocial assessments should seek client information about medication and alcohol use. Research indicates that addiction treatment approaches such as counseling and occupational and recreational therapy can be successful with older individuals. There is also evidence that preventive educational programs can help older people (and family caregivers) avoid alcohol and medication interactions and learn about other problems related to alcohol and drug use and abuse (Vinton & Wambach, 2005).

HELPING CAREGIVERS

Family members and friends provide most elder care. Family caregiving often enables elders to live in the community by delaying the need or making it unnecessary for them to enter long-term care institutions such as nursing homes and assisted living facilities. The National Alliance for Caregiving and the American Association of Retired Persons (2004) report that an estimated 34 million caregivers in this country provide unpaid care to people over the age of fifty. Older adults are most likely to be cared for by their spouses, usually wives, followed by adult children, usually daughters or daughters-in-law (Spillman & Pezzin, 2000).

Research shows that caring for an elder can be a meaningful and rewarding experience for family members (Yamamoto-Mitani, Ishigaki, Kawahara-Maekawa, Kuniyoshi, Hayashi, Hasagawa, et al., 2003). Through caregiving, family members are able to express love and affection, and many report increased self-esteem and life satisfaction from caregiving activities (Kramer, 1997; Noonan & Tennstedt, 1997). Caregiving can also have negative consequences, such as stress; feelings of anger, depression, guilt, anxiety, loneliness, and isolation; and physical health problems (Pinquart & Sorenson, 2003). Gerontological social workers help family caregivers manage their responsibilities. To cope with the physical demands of caregiving, they may help caregivers obtain housekeeping services or personal care attendants for their older family members or respite care so caregivers can have some time for themselves. To help with the psychological and emotional demands of caregiving, they may conduct caregiver support groups and provide psychotherapeutic counseling. A number of assessment tools, such as the Cost of Care Index (Kosberg & Cairl, 1986) and the Zarit Burden Interview (Zarit, Reever, & Bach-Peterson, 1980), can help social workers determine the types and severity of problems that family caregivers are experiencing. Social workers help family caregivers manage the stresses and burdens that could overwhelm them and force them to abandon their caregiving role.

Social workers can also help family members resolve differences of opinion about meeting an older person's needs and can help family members grapple with difficult decisions about nursing homes or other placements and end-of-life issues. Social work services can result in positive outcomes for caregivers as well as for older people.

UTILIZING RELIGIOUS RESOURCES

Almost 60 percent of older people characterize themselves as strongly religious (Benjamins, 2004). For example, over 80 percent of African American elders are church members, and churches are often vital sources of support in their daily lives (Logan, 1996). Leaders of churches, synagogues, mosques, and other religious institutions are often older people who play important roles in these organizations (Hooyman & Kiyak, 2005). Through participation in religious organizations, older people develop friendships and receive emotional support and instrumental help from other church members (Cutler & Hendricks, 2000). Social workers recognize the importance of religion in the lives of older people and assess whether their clients' spiritual needs are being met. Older people also often engage in non-organizational religious behaviors such as praying privately, reading religious material, listening to religious music, or watching religious programming on television (McFadden, 1995). Social workers ensure that older people who are homebound due to illness, disability, or lack of transportation have access to these resources (Benjamins, 2004).

Religious organizations emphasize the virtue of helping others. Many provide social services specifically for older people, such as educational and recreational programs, support groups, visitations, counseling, transportation, meal provision, home repair assistance, financial assistance, and health care (McFadden, 1995; Nathanson & Tirrito, 1998). Some religious organizations operate assisted living facilities and nursing homes that are open to people of any denomination. Social workers link elders to these services and help religious organizations to assess community needs, develop and implement educational and service activities, provide information about community resources, and refer members who need services to appropriate resources.

ENCOURAGING COMMUNITY INVOLVEMENT

Social workers encourage older people to participate in community organizations like churches, political parties, volunteer service agencies, hobby and sports groups, professional associations, and fraternal organizations. These activities combat isolation and help older people maintain or enhance their social and psychological well-being through meaningful activities and interaction with others. Many local, state, and national organizations such as the League of Women Voters and the American Association of Retired Persons provide opportunities for political participation and advocacy work. The kinds of organizations in which older people participate often vary according to education, socioeconomic status, and race and ethnicity. Social service agencies and senior organizations such as the Retired Senior Volunteer Program, the Service Corps of Retired Executives, and the Senior Companion Program offer older people opportunities to provide volunteer services. Older people engage in volunteer work in many settings, such as senior centers, schools, hospitals, libraries, child-care centers, and nursing homes (Hooyman & Kiyak, 2005). Many of these older people have engaged in volunteer activities throughout their lives. Others are taking advantage of their retirement from full-time employment to share their talents and skills. Using one's time and talents to help others may provide continued meaning and purpose in life.

ADULT PROTECTIVE SERVICES

This section comes last in this chapter, but adult protective service programs meet critical needs. Some older adults are physically or emotionally abused or financially exploited by family, caretakers, or others. Self-neglect occurs when an older person cannot care for him- or herself or is unwilling to receive assistance from others. State adult protective service programs often employ social workers to investigate cases brought to their attention and, when warranted, take action by securing needed services. This may mean removing an older person from his or her current living environment to a nursing home or other facility or to the home of an individual, couple, or family who provides care for a fee. If the older person is mentally incapacitated, the court may appoint a guardian to help the person with decision making and finances. Guardians may also require oversight provided by social workers to ensure that they are carrying out their roles appropriately.

Social workers may also serve as ombudsmen who help residents of nursing homes or other facilities with care concerns, including neglect and abuse. In all cases, the social worker's focus is on protecting the rights of the older person and following the client's wishes to the extent possible.

SUMMARY

This chapter has provided information about the aging population and gerontological social work practice. The authors of this chapter have been social work practitioners with older people and their families and can attest to how professionally rewarding this work is. There is great satisfaction in contributing to older people's quality of life. Given the shortage of social workers prepared to practice with older people, social work students should be encouraged to learn more about educational and practice opportunities in this exciting and challenging area. The nation's older population needs social workers' direct practice, advocacy, administration, and policy skills.

SUGGESTED READING

Berkman, B., & Hartootyan, L. (Eds.). (2003). *Social work and health care in an aging society: Education, policy, practice, and research.* New York: Springer. This book highlights research on improving the physical and mental health and well-being of older people and their caregivers. There are excellent reviews of research on such topics as late-life depression, dementia, special challenges faced by African American elders, case management, elder abuse, aging individuals with developmental disabilities, grandparents raising grandchildren, and geriatric assessment in social work practice.

Binstock, R. H., & George, L. K. (Eds.). (2006). *Handbook of aging and the social sciences* (6th ed.). Burlington, MA: Academic Press. This book summarizes and evaluates recent research on the social aspects of aging from the perspectives of such disciplines and professions as anthropology, demography, epidemiology, psychology, bioethics, economics, law, political science, and sociology.

Birren, J. E., & Schaie, K. W. (Eds.). (2006). *Handbook of the psychology of aging* (6th ed.). Burlington, MA: Academic Press. This book summarizes and evaluates an extensive array of recent research on topics that focus on psychological functioning and psychological processes related to aging and old age.

Hooyman, N. R., & Kiyak, H. A. (2005). *Social gerontology: A multidisciplinary perspective* (7th ed.). Boston: Allyn and Bacon. This book provides an excellent multidisciplinary overview of aging and how the older population affects and is affected by society. Among the many topics covered are the social consequences of physical aging, psychological changes and aging, well-being and chronic disease in later life, cognitive functioning and aging, and informal caregiving.

McInnis-Dittrich, K. (2005). *Social work with elders: A biopsychosocial approach to assessment and intervention* (2nd ed.). Boston: Allyn and Bacon. This book focuses on subjects that are important to gerontological social workers. It provides material on assessment and intervention for a variety of gerontological practice topics, such as cognitive and emotional functioning, alcohol and drug abuse, elder abuse and neglect, working with caregivers of frail elders, and people dealing with end-of-life issues.

THE WORLD WIDE WEB OF SOCIAL WORK

Administration on Aging http://www.aoa.gov
The AoA is a federal government agency. Sections of its Web site entitled "Elders and Families" and "Professionals" provide an extensive array of useful information and listings of resources on age-related topics of interest to older people, their caregivers, and professionals who work with elders.

American Association of Retired Persons http://www.aarp.org/internetresources
The AARP's Web site offers links to many sites with information important to older individuals and their families, as well as researchers, students, and professionals. Most of the links are to government agencies and nonprofit organizations. Commercial sites are included only if they contain a great deal of free information useful for older adults.

Association for Gerontology Education in Social Work
http://www.agesocialwork.org
This association provides leadership and assistance to social work education programs and educators interested in the field of aging with a primary goal of integrating gerontological content into social work education curricula.

Geriatric Social Work Initiative http://www.gswi.org
The Geriatric Social Work Initiative, supported by the John A. Hartford Foundation, collaborates with social work education programs to help prepare future social workers for work in the field of aging. Its Web site provides information about the organization's programs and funding opportunities, current aging issues, social work careers in aging, and aging-related educational and consumer resources.

Gerontological Society of America http://www.geron.org
The GSA is a multidisciplinary organization with more than 5,000 members involved in the field of aging. The organization provides information about aging targeted toward researchers, educators, practitioners, and policy makers.

National Council on Aging http://www.ncoa.org
The NCOA is a 3,800-member nonprofit organization dedicated to promoting the dignity, self-determination, health, independence, and contributions of older adults. It provides education, leadership, service, and advocacy to advance the field of aging.

National Institute on Aging http://www.nia.nih.gov
The National Institute on Aging is one of the institutes that make up the federal agency called the National Institutes of Health. The Web site provides health information related to human aging, as well as information regarding funding for career training programs in aging and funding opportunities for biomedical and psychosocial research in aging.

13 Poverty in the United States: History, Explanations, and Opportunities for Social Work

**Annelies K. Hagemeister and
Paul Force-Emery Mackie**

This chapter discusses poverty and its connections to social work in the United States. You will learn that poverty and society's attempts to address it have a long and complex history, and that public and private responses have vacillated widely and have met with varying degrees of success. Understanding the complexities of poverty requires knowledge about theoretical positions that guide how we explain and address poverty. You will learn about several of these theories as well as the extent of poverty in the United States. Social workers are particularly concerned about poverty because of its negative consequences, and because many of our clients are living in or close to poverty. Those who live without an adequate income are more likely to live in substandard housing and unsafe neighborhoods. They are less likely to have health insurance, and more likely to suffer higher rates of physical and mental health problems and disabilities and to die earlier (Syme, 1998). Persistent poverty also takes a toll on the human spirit, leading to despair and hopelessness. This chapter concludes by discussing some of the many ways social workers are working to end poverty and help those living in poverty.

HISTORICAL PERSPECTIVES ON POVERTY

There have always been people who have some difficulty meeting their basic human needs due to a lack of economic resources. Generally, we refer to this as the condition of *poverty*. While poverty exists across nations, this chapter focuses on poverty in the United States. We begin with a look at the history of aid to the poor.

The Elizabethan Poor Law

Though this discussion could begin in several places, we start with the most widely recognized roots of U.S. programs and policies that help those in poverty. This takes us back to seventeenth-century England. Queen Elizabeth was in power, and cities such as London were beginning to grow into large urban centers of commerce, trade, and industry. Many people left their connections to the land and an agrarian feudal way of life and migrated to cities to live and work. In the process, many experienced the ravages of poverty as changes in the economy and society continued to occur at a rapid rate. Prior to this time, it had been the responsibility of relatives and local churches or communities to care for those unable to meet their own needs. This type of help is called *mutual aid*. As people moved far from their home communities, a new response to poverty was needed.

In this context, the Elizabethan poor law of 1601 emerged (Trattner, 1999). The Poor Law Act was the first well-documented, structured plan to give public officials guidelines on how to address poverty (Trattner, 1999). It directed officials to categorize the poor in order to determine their worthiness for aid. This led to the concept of the worthy or deserving poor versus the unworthy or undeserving poor and a process still used today known as *means testing*. Means testing is establishing criteria and a process to verify a person's or family's need and eligibility for aid. Work tests were also used to determine if a person was able bodied (capable of work) or not. Relatives were required to help the needy whenever possible. If one had no relatives, the parish or town was supposed to help. Thus, this period saw the first public financing of poverty programs that were required by the central government, financed by taxes, and administered locally by the parish or town.

Colonial Response to Economic Dependency

The Elizabethan poor law was implemented at approximately the same time that the Puritan settlers and others began colonizing the eastern seaboard of what would become the United States of America. These new immigrants drew on many aspects of their Protestant English traditions; the so-called Protestant work ethic, the belief that hard work is the key to moral and economic prosperity, continued to influence these immigrants' views and responses to helping the poor, even though most of the early colonists themselves faced poverty in a challenging and often unforgiving new context (Trattner, 1999). Adapting to a new land involved hardships for all, but the new settlers continued to view poverty as the result of individual and moral defects. Resources to aid those who encountered tragedies like accidents or illnesses were scarce. A dual welfare system began to develop in which both public (local and state government) and private (religious) sectors—as well as the family—bore some responsibility for assisting the poor. There was also a strong feeling that providing charitable assistance to those in need created dependency—a sentiment that resonates even today.

Poverty from the Nineteenth Century through the Progressive Era

During the nineteenth century, there was a growth of *indoor relief,* which took the form of institutions—poorhouses, asylums, and workhouses—where the poor lived and often worked, usually under wretched conditions (Trattner, 1999). At the same time, there was limited *outdoor relief*—assistance given to people in their homes. By the mid-1800s, the federal government had begun to provide economic help for some people, mostly military veterans. In addition, citizen reformers such as Dorothea Dix worked to obtain federal funds for those who were poor, especially those with mental illnesses (Trattner, 1999). However, the provision of economic support for impoverished citizens was not perceived as being part of the federal government's responsibility to its citizens.

After the Civil War ended in 1865, and as a huge wave of European immigrants arrived in the Unites States around the turn of the century, the population increased tremendously and the profession of social work began to develop in a formal sense. In addition, industrialization spread rapidly to many parts of the country, especially the East and upper Midwest. Many people from rural areas, including large numbers of freed slaves, made the trek to the industrial centers in the North. The areas that felt the greatest impact of industrialization, immigration, and migration were large cities like New York, Boston, Philadelphia, St. Louis, and Chicago. This surge in the growth of urban centers brought about many new challenges for city dwellers, including the growth of urban slums that bred poverty and disease (see, e.g., Riis, 1890/1997). Increased discontent with social problems became the catalyst for change (McGeer, 2003). This was the beginning of the Progressive Era, the period between about 1870 and 1915, when many new ideas about social welfare emerged and organizations working to address poverty began creating programs based on these ideas.

Programs and services to help the poor came in the form of the Charity Organization Societies and settlement houses. Though these approaches developed around the same time, they used different strategies to assist those in poverty. Charity Organization Society workers visited people in their homes in order to determine their needs. In settlement houses in many large northeastern and midwestern cities, such as Jane Addams's Hull House in Chicago, women and men from wealthy college-educated families lived in poor urban communities and helped those in need, especially recent immigrants. By 1900 there were hundreds of such establishments whose purpose was to "remake the working class" (McGeer, 2003). Organized labor and other reform movements, which were often spearheaded by early social workers and labor reformers, resulted in the passage of child labor laws, insurance for workers, and public aid for mothers and the elderly and the blind.

The profession of social work blossomed at the turn of the twentieth century due to efforts aimed directly at helping poor clients and their families and also broader social advocacy efforts such as developing kindergartens, improving maternal and child health, ending child labor, and addressing delinquency. Another important social work role was documenting social conditions. In many cases this meant collecting and reporting census data about the living and working conditions of those living in the urban slums in order to provide evidence of the need for social change.

The Great Depression: An Opportunity for Federal Government Reforms

After World War I ended, many Americans felt uplifted and optimistic. But this period would not last long. In 1929 the Great Depression hit the United States very hard. Prosperity and hopes for economic growth were dashed when the U.S. stock market crashed. In its wake, many people—upper, middle, and working class—lost their jobs, their homes, and any savings they had.

President Herbert Hoover did not take the initiative to help those in poverty and subsequently lost the next presidential election to Franklin Delano Roosevelt. Roosevelt's administration included social reformers who had developed significant social programs in New York while he was governor. These reformers guided the federal government's response to poverty in Roosevelt's New Deal administration. With the help of the socially minded individuals in his cabinet such as Harry Hopkins and Frances Perkins, Roosevelt developed and carried out several important poverty reduction efforts such as the Federal Emergency Relief Act (1933) and the Social Security Act of 1935. The Social Security Act remains the cornerstone of social welfare legislation over seven decades later.

The establishment of these large federal programs ushered in a new era in the provision of direct aid to citizens. To this day, professional social workers administer many of these social welfare programs. Understanding these federal and state antipoverty programs, both *social insurance* and *public assistance,* and how clients can gain access to them is a central part of the social work knowledge and skill base. Table 13.1 shows the differences between public assistance (commonly referred to as welfare) and social insurance, and table 13.2 describes the major programs available today.

Table 13.1 Antipoverty programs

Social insurance approach	Public assistance approach
■ Attached to paid employment ■ Contributions must be made before benefits can be claimed ■ No income or wealth limitations ■ Income maintenance programs: worker's compensation; unemployment compensation; Old Age, Survivors, and Disability Insurance (often called Social Security) ■ Health insurance: Medicare (Part A: Hospital Insurance; Parts B and C: Supplemental Medical Insurance; Part D: Prescription Drug Benefit)	■ Financed from general tax revenue ■ No required contribution for benefits ■ Means tested (based on income and assets) ■ Income maintenance programs: Temporary Assistance for Needy Families, General Assistance, Supplemental Security Income ■ Health insurance: Medicaid, Children's Health Insurance Program ■ In-kind programs: food stamps; Special Supplemental Nutrition for Women, Infants and Children; energy assistance; school meals

Compiled by Nancy M. Fitzsimons, Department of Social Work, Minnesota State University, Mankato.

Table 13.2 Current income maintenance benefit programs

Program Name	Who benefits?	What type of benefit is it?	How is it delivered?	How is it financed?
Old Age, Survivors, and Disability Insurance (Social Security)	Workers upon retirement or disability; spouses and dependents (children) of deceased, disabled, or retired workers	Cash; universal benefit (available to all who contributed)	Federal program administered by the Social Security Administration	Federal Insurance Contributions Act (FICA) tax paid by worker and employer on specified amount of wages
Unemployment insurance	Laid-off workers	Cash; universal benefit	Overseen by the U.S. Department of Labor; amount of benefits, eligibility, and length of benefits determined by states	Employers contribute to a trust fund; states pay for first twenty-six weeks (typical maximum benefit); federal-state extended benefits of thirteen weeks (50/50 financing) during periods of high unemployment
Worker's compensation	Workers injured as the result of a work-related accident or illness; families of workers who are killed as the result of a work-related accident or illness	May include cash benefit, medical assistance, rehabilitation services, disability and death benefit; universal benefit	State program; great variability from state to state	Varies by state; most businesses purchase insurance from private companies; some self-insure

Table 13.2 *Continued*

Supplemental Security Income	Poor elderly, disabled children and adults; available to U.S. citizens and some legal immigrants	Cash; means tested	Federal program; administered by the Social Security Administration	Federal general revenue taxes; federal benefits supplemented by most states
General Assistance	Varies by jurisdiction; usually low-income individuals or families ineligible or waiting for TANF or Supplemental Security Income	Usually cash; means tested	State, county, or local government; thirty-five states have General Assistance programs; twenty-four have a statewide program	State, county, and/or local tax revenue
Special Supplemental Nutrition Program for Women, Infants and Children	Low-income women who are pregnant, breast-feeding, or postpartum and their children up to age five who are judged to be at nutritional risk	Voucher to purchase certain types of food, nutrition education; means tested at 185% of federal poverty level	Administered by the U.S. Department of Agriculture's Food and Nutrition Service through state departments of health or human services; implemented by local, county, or state offices	Federal general tax revenue, categorical grant to states
Food stamps	Low-income individuals and families	Debit card (electronic benefits transfer); means tested generally at 130% of federal poverty level	Administered by the U.S. Department of Agricultura; federal government determines eligibility criteria; state and local health and human service agencies process applications and provide benefits	Federal general tax revenue; federal, state, and local governments share administrative costs
Temporary Assistance to Needy Families	Low-income families with children, children living with foster families or other caretakers	Means tested; work requirements for parents unless exempt; sixty-month lifetime limit on benefits; usually cash benefits and employment services; participants may be eligible for other subsidized programs	Administered by each state-designated TANF program (each state has a different name); states also contract with other agencies for services like job search and preparation	Funded by a combination of TANF block grants and state funds

Compiled by Nancy M. Fitzsimons, Department of Social Work, Minnesota State University, Mankato.

The War on Poverty

Many social scientists and economists believe that the economic activity generated as a result of World War II was the main reason the United States returned to prosperity after the Great Depression. After World War II ended in 1945, surviving soldiers returned home, working women returned to the household from the factory, the birthrate soared, the number of single-family homes sky-rocketed, and Americans adjusted to a new social reality. Like the 1920s, the 1950s were generally viewed as a positive, upbeat time during which the national economy thrived. Despite this economic prosperity, many people were still living in poverty, particularly those in the lower rungs of the working class and African Americans. As the civil rights movement developed momentum, Americans again wondered how it was that so many were left impoverished in a land of plenty (see, e.g., Harrington, 1962).

President John F. Kennedy, a man born of privilege, was moved by this situation and saw the problem of an impoverished underclass as inexcusable in the United States. He and others began work to change this situa-

Many people in the United States and around the world do not have the financial resources to afford food. Social workers reach out to people like this woman, who rummages through trash in the street in search of food.
© Steve Liss

tion, though his life was cut short by his assassination. His successor, Lyndon B. Johnson, took up the reins and continued developing a set of policies and programs to help those in poverty. The predominant view at this time was that monetary government assistance should not be given directly to those in poverty; rather it was felt that training, education, and economic opportunity should be focused on. Thus, the 1960s saw significant amendments and new programmatic initiatives aimed at preventing poverty, commonly known as the war on poverty. Between 1962 and 1972, the federal government established or significantly revised no fewer than a dozen social welfare programs. These programs, often implemented and staffed by social workers, included Aid to Families with Dependent Children (AFDC); Head Start; food stamps; the Special Supplemental Nutrition Program for Women, Infants and Children; Medicare; and Medicaid.

Programs for Economic Assistance in the 1980s and 1990s

During the 1980s and 1990s, many people became disillusioned with the welfare programs that had been developed in the 1960s and early 1970s, in particular AFDC. As the number of single mothers and program participants continued to grow, concern about welfare dependency also grew. Though only a small part of aid to those in poverty, AFDC became the target of discontent and the focus of welfare reform efforts. There was a movement to ensure that adults receiving assistance worked for their benefits. Under the administration of Republican President Ronald Reagan, a more conservative approach developed, which included deregulation and devolution (allowing the states greater freedom to design and administer welfare programs) and reductions in federal spending for public assistance. Eligibility requirements for public assistance were tightened, and a call was issued for private organizations, faith communities, and the volunteer and nonprofit sectors to resume caring for those in poverty.

The Family Support Act (1988) was only the first step in these changes. It placed more emphasis on collecting child support from noncustodial parents and increasing work requirements for AFDC recipients. During the 1992 presidential campaign, welfare reform was a major issue of debate. In 1992, the nation's new president, Democrat Bill Clinton, vowed to "end welfare as we know it." The Republican-controlled Congress made the biggest change to public assistance since 1935, and Clinton signed the bill. The reform legislation was called the Personal Responsibility and Work Opportunity Reconciliation Act of 1996 (PRWORA). This act eliminated AFDC and replaced it with the current program, Temporary Assistance for Needy Families (TANF).

Whereas AFDC was an entitlement program (families who qualified could participate until their youngest child turned eighteen), TANF gave states direct control over the program, set a five-year time limit on participation for many families, and increased work requirements. Many social workers feel that although AFDC needed revamping, PRWORA was too draconian and that in adopting the act, the country moved from fighting a war on poverty to fighting a war on the poor.

State and county social service offices and the social workers they employ are the frontline administrators of TANF. At the state level, administrators must understand the complex details of the program, since they are the fiscal liaisons between service agencies and the federal government. State-level TANF work also includes the evaluation of the program in each state, a process in which social workers are often involved. At the county or agency level, social workers may determine applicants' eligibility for the program or, more often, help parents plan their employment strategies, comply with program rules, and become self-sufficient before their sixty-month eligibility for assistance runs out. Social workers are also involved as advocates and activists, informing and lobbying state policy makers about the needs of service recipients, problems with the program, and how TANF can be improved. Social workers are involved in similar ways with the many other programs described in table 13.2.

PERSPECTIVES ON POVERTY IN THE UNITED STATES

Attempting to explain poverty is a complicated and arduous process. Over time, several theories of poverty have emerged; these have had varying degrees of success in explaining poverty's root causes and what it will take to end poverty. In this section, we discuss three main theoretical explanations.

Individual Explanations

Individual explanations for poverty include the argument that people are unable to succeed due to "personal failings," such as genetic inferiority. Though some individuals have severe disabilities or illnesses that prevent them from earning a living, social workers do not believe that there is evidence that any group of people is genetically inferior to another or that genetics is a credible explanation for the large numbers of individuals and families who fall into poverty. Some scholars continue to promote that explanation (see, e.g., Herrnstein & Murray, 1994) in spite of the overwhelming evidence against it.

Another individual explanation is that some people fail to function effectively for psychological reasons (Zucker & Weiner, 1993). These individuals are seen as being unwilling to succeed in our market-driven economic system and are labeled unmotivated, lazy, indolent, or irresponsible (Rank, Hong, & Hirschl, 2003). In this context, some people describe poverty as a conscious choice.

In the post–World War II era leading up to President Lyndon Johnson's war on poverty, another psychological factor used to explain poverty was mental illness (Curran, 2002). For example, social service professionals largely viewed white single mothers receiving welfare assistance as neurotic, while they saw African American females receiving the same assistance as having character or personality disorders. Psychoanalysis and similar therapeutic interventions were viewed as appropriate treatment to correct these neurotic behaviors and character disorders (Curran, 2002). The field of social work became complicit by embracing individual therapy as an appropriate approach to reducing poverty (Herman, 1995). While intended to empower and enlighten clients, therapeutic interventions ultimately laid blame on victims and promoted sexism, racism, and classism (Curran, 2002).

Do psychological explanations for poverty hold water? Research comparing the motivation and attitudes of the poor and nonpoor have found little difference between the two groups (Rank, 1994). In other words, most people want to work and to succeed. Given this knowledge, if we are to understand the reasons for poverty, we must search elsewhere for more sufficient explanations.

Cultural Explanations

Oscar Lewis (1959) studied poverty from an anthropological or cultural perspective and in so doing set off a hailstorm of debate. Lewis introduced the idea of a "culture of poverty" defined in terms of a set of values, beliefs, and behaviors among the poor that differ from those of the nonpoor. He contended that these beliefs and behaviors are handed down from one generation to the next. Lewis used seventy distinct elements divided into four categories to describe the culture of poverty. His first category focused on people who do not belong to social, professional, or community organizations; labor unions; or political groups, in which most members of society typically engage, or so he contended. Because they are not immersed in the larger culture or society and are thus less likely to enjoy the benefits of social supports and networks, community resources, or other mechanisms, known as *social capital*, that lead to productive economy activity, he viewed these individuals as distrustful of social institutions (e.g., police departments, schools, and social services). Lewis's second category focused on communities comprised largely of those in dire economic straits, communities he saw as lacking organization or activities beyond the family unit. His theory was that because residents do not engage in activities that support the betterment of the community, these communities suffer from lower-quality public services, social services, and schools and a lack of safety. All these factors perpetuate poverty among residents.

Lewis's third element was the family unit. He argued that families sometimes fail to socialize children to become healthy, empowered, active adults. Youths in these families, he maintained, are more likely to give birth at an early age, thus engendering large numbers of single-parent (and typically female-headed) households that lack resources for raising children. Dropping out of school and unemployment are also more common in these families. Lewis's fourth category focused on individual conduct. He contended that people living in poverty typically suffer from weak egos, have poor impulse control, find delaying gratification difficult, and have a sense of doom and fatalism.

Lewis argued that by the age of about seven, children enveloped in the culture of poverty have absorbed its values and are likely to remain in and perpetuate poverty in the next generation. Lewis distinguished cultural explanations for poverty from individual explanations, noting that those living in a culture of poverty do so because they were socialized at a young age to live in this state, not necessarily because of individual personal failings.

A decade later, Edward Banfield (1970) took the culture-of-poverty explanation one step further by describing a permanent state or culture of poverty. He divided the poor into two groups. The first group included those temporarily out of work, people with disabilities, divorced women with children, and others who can benefit from occasional government social support. This group was thought to maintain middle-class values and would likely recover from poverty because of these values. He attributed the poverty of the second group, the "permanent lower-class," to a lack of motivation or desire to improve their place in society. Banfield (1970) believed that "the lower-class individual lives from moment to moment. If he has any awareness of a future, it is of something fixed, faded, beyond his control: things happen *to* him, he does not *make* them happen. . . . Whatever he cannot consume immediately he considers valueless" (p. 53).

As a group, social workers do not support explanations for poverty that place overwhelming blame on impoverished individuals or communities for their state of affairs. According to Leacock (1971), the culture of poverty explanation does not in fact explain poverty but rather perpetuates it through discrimination and bias against those in poverty. If a true culture of poverty existed, poverty rates would not rise and fall as the U.S. economy expands and contracts. In periods of low unemployment, more people go to work; in periods of high unemployment, more people have no job to go to and may need government assistance. Recently, the theory of a culture of poverty has seen a resurgence among some educators and social services professionals.

Structural Explanations

Structural explanations describe poverty as directly related to factors and failings in larger social and economic systems, including the capitalist marketplace and the social welfare safety net. According to this perspective, in order to address poverty, changes in the structure of society, the economy, and the mechanisms that reduce opportunities for all citizens to succeed economically must take place. Proponents of this perspective do not assume that people fail due to their own lack of effort or shortcomings. Instead, they seek to understand the political, social, and economic contributors to poverty. In this context, we visit the works of scholars such as Leonard Beeghley and Jonathan Kozol.

According to Beeghley (1983, 1989), poverty in the United States is a trap that is difficult to escape. For example, children whose families lack basic economic resources are less likely to continue their education beyond high school and escape poverty themselves. Subsequent generations also find it difficult to escape the trap of poverty—not because they lack motivation but because they are more likely to live in a poor community with deficient schools and services and a lack of opportunity. Without positive and effective interventions, this environment will only decline further over time, making it increasingly difficult for residents to escape poverty. Box 13.1 illustrates how class structure creates barriers to the pursuit of higher education. Jeffrey and Susan, the young people depicted in this vignette, face different futures, not because their parents have different aspirations for them, but because Jeffrey's parents do not have the education and resources that Susan's parents have.

Table 13.3 demonstrates the powerful effect that education has on income. The table shows that the median annual earnings of a person with a master's degree ($46,679) are nearly four times those of a person who did not complete high school ($12,269). One of the important roles of social workers is helping families to help their children remain in school and assisting adults to increase their education and training. But we must dig deeper to determine why it is so difficult for some Americans to escape poverty. Among the most prominent structural explanations is institutional discrimination in the forms of sexism and racism.

Table 13.3 also shows the effects of sexism on income. Even at the same educational level, women's median annual income is 61–73 percent that of men's income. Though this table does not control for all factors, it does sug-

Box 13.1   Trapped by Class in America

Jeffrey, a high school senior, wants to go to college. His grades and class rank are high enough for acceptance at a state university, but not good enough for him to be awarded a scholarship, which he needs, as his parents do not have the financial resources to help him pay tuition. Jeffrey's father has a high school education. He works on the assembly line at a local factory. His mother has an associate's degree from a community college. She is employed as a certified nurse's aide. Both parents work full-time, with a combined income of about $63,000 per year. Jeffrey's two younger siblings also live at home. Jeffrey's parents support his desire to attend college but do not know how to access financial aid to help him pay for it. As his senior year nears its end, Jeffrey has been accepted at a local state university and has received his financial aid package. In light of his parent's income, there is an expectation that they pay a certain portion of the costs, which they are not able to do. Due to the lack of funds, Jeffrey does not attend college and instead joins his father at the factory. Although he maintains his goal of attending college and takes some classes, Jeffrey never earns a college degree. Two years after he begins working at the factory, Jeffrey receives notice that the company has decided to close.

Susan, a classmate of Jeffrey's, has a very different experience, though they have much in common. Susan has about the same grade point average as Jeffrey and, like him, does not receive an academic scholarship, which means she and her parents must pay what financial aid doesn't cover. Unlike Jeffrey's parents, both of Susan's parents have college degrees. Her father has a bachelor's degree in business and is a financial analyst. Her mother has a master's degree in social work and is a county child protection worker. While Susan's parents have never considered themselves rich, they have set aside a small amount of money each month since Susan was born for her college education. Throughout the years, they have felt comfortable that they will be able to help Susan and her younger sister attend a state college. When Susan receives her acceptance letter, her parents make plans to cover the difference between financial aid and the cost of tuition, books, and living expenses. Susan leaves home in the fall to attend college and graduates four years later.

gest that women may have difficulty earning what men earn due to the family responsibilities that women often shoulder or problems that befall women more than men, such as domestic violence. Even among full-time workers, there is a substantial earning gap between men and women. The table shows that across all ethnic groups, men have a higher median income than women.

Table 13.3 also shows the effect of racial discrimination. With few exceptions, at all levels of education, white men have higher earnings than all other groups. Most of us are aware of overt racism—hatred of one person by another based on external characteristics or features—which is usually fairly easy to identify. Being able to identify a problem is the first step necessary to develop ways to address the problem. As a nation, the United

Table 13.3   Median annual income (for the population eighteen years and older), 2003

	No high school diploma	High school diploma	Bachelor's degree	Master's degree
Total population	$12,267	$19,523	$36,217	$46,679
All males	$15,194	$23,502	$42,009	$53,978
All females	$ 9,340	$15,545	$30,426	$39,381
Asian females	$ 9,640	$15,815	$27,138	$33,537
Asian males	$15,009	$24,545	$41,373	$62,356
Black females	$ 8,922	$15,386	$35,357	$41,237
Black males	$12,178	$21,082	$39,443	$42,239
Hispanic females	$ 9,455	$15,441	$29,533	$41,831
Hispanic males	$16,940	$21,864	$36,757	$50,255
White females	$ 9,342	$15,460	$29,676	$40,920
White males	$16,650	$26,518	$50,463	$61,064

Source: U.S. Census Bureau. (2003). *Education attainment in the United States: 2003, Detailed tables for current population report, P20-550.* Retrieved March 31, 2007, from http://www.census.gov/population/www/socdemo/education/cps2003.html

States has worked to address overt racism and discrimination through civil rights laws and other laws and policies that forbid and attach punishments to discriminatory practices. For example, if someone is fired from a job and, when asked, the manager states, "Well, we just want younger employees," this is overt age discrimination. The manager did not have a legally viable argument for the firing. As a nation, Americans have determined that we do not want a society that discriminates against people because of their race, age, or gender—or have we?

Institutional racism differs from overt racism (also see chapter 4). Institutional racism and discrimination are deeply embedded in the fabric of society. They occur when the hatred, dislike, or negative attitudes of one group toward another group become so commonplace that they go virtually unnoticed, at least by the majority. Deeply entrenched racism and discrimination in American society are closely connected to poverty.

Jonathan Kozol has written several books that address institutional racism and discrimination and poverty, with a special emphasis on their negative effects on children. Kozol's books (1991, 1995, 2001) provide disturbing illustrations of the lives of people living in some of the most impoverished inner-city neighborhoods of New York; East Saint Louis, Illinois; and other poverty-stricken communities in America. Kozol focuses on poverty in inner-city neighborhoods inhabited largely by people of color; he argues that this does not occur by accident. It is grounded in institutional and societal racism that encourages placing dumps, landfills, sewage plants, prisons,

Police officers offer leadership and companionship to minority youths in an inner-city neighborhood. Social workers promote programs such as these.
©Victor de Schwanberg/Alamy

and other undesirable facilities in poor neighborhoods as opposed to wealthier communities. He describes how many inner-city poor have essentially given up and have resigned themselves to the fact that the only place they can afford to live is the dilapidated buildings and rundown neighborhoods in which public housing is available. Subsidized housing arguably could be built nearly anywhere; however, it is typically built in troubled communities that have had difficulty maintaining businesses, homes, and safe environments for people to live and work. For example, there are forty garbage dump facilities and a city sewage treatment center in the impoverished areas of Hunts Point and Mott Haven in New York City. In Mott Haven, an incinerator facility receives medical waste from New York City hospitals. Originally, this facility was to be built on the East Side of Manhattan, but due to local concerns about the negative effects it would have on the health of children, it went to Mott Haven. These facilities in Hunts Point and Mott Haven give off an odor "bad enough so that children throw up on their way to school" (Kozol, 2001, p. 88).

Children victimized by institutional racism and discrimination are more likely to grow up in a world that is impoverished, attend schools that are inadequate, traverse streets that are unsafe, and live in communities that have fewer opportunities for optimal development. These children are less likely to achieve their full potential than those who live in a different environment or were born of a different ethnicity. Maria, a sixteen-year-old living in the impoverished community of the South Bronx, a mostly Hispanic and African American community, describes how she feels people perceive her and her community: "If people in New York woke up one day and learned that we were gone, that we had simply died or left for somewhere else . . . I think they would be relieved. . . . I think they look at us as obstacles to moving forward" (in Kozol, 1995, p. 39). Sadly, Maria's story is not unique. Jason DeParle's (2004) book, written a decade after Kozol spoke with Maria, describes nearly the same conditions of poverty, race issues, and discrimination as those discussed by Kozol. More than a decade after the implementation of major welfare reforms, we should ask whether or not much has changed for the better in the lives of those living in poverty. Like DeParle (2004), as social workers we are concerned that poverty has once again disappeared from the domestic policy agenda. When major hurricanes struck the states along the Gulf Coast in 2005, there was a brief moment of recognition of poverty and its relationship to institutional racism, but attention to this problem seems to have subsided once again.

Other structural factors have contributed to poverty in the United States. For example, industrialization and technological development have bypassed large segments of Appalachia, one of the poorest areas in the United States, as well as other areas. In addition, the exodus of business and economic development activity has plagued already-deteriorating inner cities. As steel mills close in the northeastern United States, auto plants lay off workers in the Midwest, and textile mills in the South move operations overseas, workers suffer. While the rapid growth of technology and globalization, interrelated structural forces, have had many positive effects, they have not occurred without negative consequences. Globalization refers to the ever-increasing integration of nation-states and people around the world. The growth of technology and globalization has also resulted in a restructuring of a paid labor force that has not always been kind to U.S. workers (Van Wormer, 2004). Americans have long worn clothes and shoes made by laborers in other countries who work for a pittance of what workers in this country earn. Today, skilled workers are being displaced by workers in other countries—a call for technical support or a catalog purchase may result in a conversation with an employee on another continent. Computer programming and other jobs requiring advanced education are also being outsourced to other countries. Other forces such as government deregulation of business, free trade agreements that eliminate tariffs on imported produce and merchandise, and reduced labor union participation have affected U.S. workers' income, job security, and access to affordable health care (Van Wormer, 2004). These changes in the structure of the labor force have occurred at the same time that many government programs intended to help people in poverty have been scaled back, leaving more Americans in precarious economic circumstances.

ABSOLUTE VERSUS RELATIVE CONCEPTIONS OF POVERTY

Poverty can be defined in absolute terms and in relative terms. Absolute definitions take into account income and sometimes other sources of wealth (e.g., savings, investments). In the United States, the official government measure of poverty is the *poverty threshold* (also referred to as the poverty level or poverty line, though these are not official government terms). The poverty threshold is an absolute measure of poverty because individuals either fall above or below it (DiNitto, 2007). In 2005, an individual under age sixty-five in the United States was considered poor if his or her annual income was less than $10,160, and a family of four (two adults and two children) was considered poor if its annual income was less than $19,806. Before Congress raised the federally established minimum wage in 2007, it had been $5.15 an hour since 1997. Someone who worked forty hours per week for fifty weeks earned $10,300, and two parents who worked full-time earned $20,600. Perhaps conveniently, both the individual and the family would have been above the poverty line in 2005. However, at $5.15 an hour, the minimum wage was at a fifty-year low in terms of purchasing power, and the formula for calculating poverty thresholds has not been updated since the 1960s.

Though the formula is adjusted for inflation each year, it has not been revised to account for the escalation in housing costs (rent and mortgage, which absorb a far larger percentage of household income than they used to). There are many other problems with the current federal definition of poverty. For example, it does not take into account the drastic differences in the cost of living in different communities across the United States, nor does it account for the astronomical costs of child care and health insurance. Think about what it costs to live in your community. Would $10,000 allow most individuals—or would $20,000 allow most families—to cover their necessities?

Relative definitions of income or poverty consider how an individual's or family's income or wealth compares with others' income or wealth. Relative definitions can be illustrated nationally and cross-nationally. Within the United States there is a very large gap between the incomes of households. In 2005, the top one-fifth of all households garnered 50 percent of the nation's income; the lowest one-fifth of households had just over 3 percent (DeNavas-Walt, Proctor, & Lee, 2006). The U.S. population has become increasingly polarized economically. However, if you contrast this with the average income in many developing nations where the definition of extreme poverty is measured in incomes of pennies per day, virtually all Americans are wealthy.

Another important aspect of relative definitions of poverty is how people think of themselves financially (DiNitto, 2007). Some people who fall below the federal poverty threshold may not consider themselves poor. Their home may be paid for, or they live frugally but don't think of themselves as deprived. On the other hand, many people whom we consider to be middle class may see themselves as poor or in need. They may have high housing costs, several children, or large medical bills that drain their income. They may not live as well as many others in the United States. From their perspective, they live in poverty.

WHO WILL EXPERIENCE POVERTY?

Each year the federal government uses census data to take a "statistical snapshot" of poverty in the United States. In 2005, 37 million Americans, nearly 13 percent of the U.S. population, lived below the federally established poverty threshold (DeNauas-Walt et al., 2006). The poverty rate for whites was 8 percent, compared to 11 percent for Asians, 22 percent for Hispanics, and 25 percent for blacks and American Indians. The poverty rate for children was 18 percent (8% lived in extreme poverty). For those ages eighteen to sixty-four, the poverty rate was 11 percent, and for those age sixty-five and older, it was 10 percent (3% lived in extreme poverty). The poverty rates for households headed by single women, especially single women of color, were much higher. For example, 39 percent of black and Hispanic households headed by single women were in poverty. Many more Americans are teetering precariously at the brink of poverty though they are not officially living below the federal poverty line. For example, 5 percent of those under age eighteen, and 7 percent of those age sixty-five and older, are at between 100 percent and 125 percent of the poverty threshold. Poverty is lowest in the Northeast and Midwest (where 11% of residents live in poverty) and highest in the West (13%) and the South (14%). What may be a surprise to many is that poverty is somewhat higher in rural areas than in urban areas (chapter 15 discusses poverty in rural America), a fact that challenges commonly held stereotypes. In 2002, just over 14 percent of people living in rural areas were affected by poverty, compared to nearly 12 percent in urban areas (Economic Research Service, 2004).

What is the likelihood that any of us will live below the poverty threshold as adults? Many college students reading this book may be living on what the federal government defines as a poverty-level income. Furthermore, what is the likelihood that we will receive public assistance to pay for food, housing, child care, or other necessities? In One Nation, Underprivileged: Why American Poverty Affects Us All, Rank (2004) discusses these questions and explores structural aspects of poverty in the United States. What he says might surprise you.

Rank found that at age twenty, 11 percent of Americans are poor. By age forty, 36 percent have lived in poverty for at least one year, and by the generally accepted age of retirement (sixty-five), 51 percent have spent at least one year in poverty. By age seventy-five, the figure rises to 59 percent. Simply put, by age sixty-five, one out of every two Americans will have lived in poverty for at least one year. For males, the poverty rate at age twenty is 10 percent, compared to 11 percent for females. By age forty, 34 percent of males and 36 percent of females have lived in poverty for at least a year. By age sixty-five, the rate for males is 48 percent, compared to 52 percent for females. People of color experience even higher rates of poverty. At age twenty, 30 percent of African Americans have been poor. By age forty, 66 percent of all African Americans have experienced at least one year of poverty, and by age sixty-five, the number has increased to 84 percent. When you consider this data, it becomes clear that poverty is a much more common experience than most of us think.

If poverty is this common, what about public assistance? There is a stigma attached to receiving public assistance and a general belief that many of those who receive it do not deserve the "free lunch." Rank (2004) also studied the rate at which Americans participate in a cash or in-kind public assistance program. As noted in table 13.2, cash assistance programs include TANF, Supplemental Security Income, and general assistance. In-kind programs provide specific goods or services, such as food, housing, and medical care (e.g., Medicaid). Rank found that at age twenty, 14 percent of Americans have participated in at least one public assistance program, but that by age forty, this number has increased to 44 percent. By age sixty-five, 65 percent of Americans have at some point received some form of public aid.

This information, as well as the effects of catastrophic events such as Hurricanes Katrina and Rita, should raise alarm about poverty in the United States. According to Rank and Hirschl's (1999, 2001) work, half of all Americans will experience a period of poverty by age sixty-five, and 65 percent will receive public assistance. Unless we are willing to say that every other person is lazy, or six out of ten are unmotivated, we must seriously consider the possibility that most poverty is not grounded in personal attitudes or culture, but rather in circumstances often out of the control of those affected.

POVERTY AND SOCIAL WORK TODAY

Today, few social workers are employed directly as eligibility workers who determine whether applicants qualify for TANF, food stamps, or other public assistance programs. These jobs have become much more routine than they once were and are now often done by technicians. Since many clients are in crisis when they apply for aid (e.g., their spouse has left them, they are facing eviction, they cannot work because their child is seriously ill), many would argue that social workers should be assisting clients from the moment they walk in the door of the public assistance office. Social workers are more likely to be employed by workforce commissions or similar agencies, helping adults receiving public assistance plan strategies for self-sufficiency, including finding a job, acquiring skill training, locating child care, and arranging transportation. The exodus of social workers from public welfare offices may have fueled accusations that social work has abandoned its historic mission to serve the poor. On the other hand, our observation is that social workers remain at the front lines of the battle against poverty.

Because social work's main aim is to help people achieve optimal functioning, almost everything social workers do can be thought of as an antipoverty effort. Whether it is assisting an individual recently released from prison to reenter the community, using crisis intervention to help a person with serious mental illness avoid a long hospital stay, or teaching eighteen-year-olds leaving foster care the life skills they will need to make a successful transition to independent living, social workers are helping people avoid or escape poverty. Social workers also take every opportunity they can to provide accurate information and to correct misconceptions about poverty. Recognizing that accumulating wealth through home ownership and savings is a key to avoiding poverty, social workers are involved not only in programs that help people budget and get out of debt but also in programs that help low-income individuals save through individual development accounts. Individual development accounts match a portion of the savings that individuals accumulate themselves for purposes such as attending school or achieving the American dream by purchasing a home.

Additionally, many social workers address childhood poverty. Early intervention is considered key. The Head Start preschool program, a core program of the 1960s war on poverty, is still used across the country. Head Start social workers serve as family outreach advocates and work closely with low-income families to enrich the lives of children so they are ready for elementary school. Research indicates that high-quality Head Start programs can increase employment and other positive life outcomes, including reduced poverty (see DiNitto, 2007). Social workers who serve in schools and in afterschool programs like Communities in Schools or Achievement Plus in St. Paul, Minnesota, also help children succeed academically and avoid delinquency. Social workers in the Women's, Infants and Children program help to ensure that low-income women give birth to healthy children and keep their children healthy with nutritious diets. Social workers also help to see that eligible children are enrolled in Medicaid; the State Children's Health Insurance Program, referred to as CHIP, which accepts many children whose family income is up to 200 percent of the poverty threshold; and other state and local health programs. Social workers also work in programs like the Jobs Corps to help young people learn skills and work habits that will lead to stable employment. Social workers also serve as staff or volunteers with the Volunteers in Service to America, often referred to as the domestic Peace Corps, and with the many similar efforts that provide service in low-income areas, such as the Retired and Senior Volunteer Program.

Since social workers take a systematic view of the world and see most poverty as structurally caused, they are not satisfied with simply putting a Band-Aid on the poverty-induced problems faced by individuals and families. They want to root out poverty and inequality. That is why social workers are working in community action and community development agencies to revitalize communities. In these agencies, social workers may seek grant and foundation funding to rehabilitate or build affordable housing, attract businesses and create jobs, or improve neighborhood safety and community infrastructure (e.g., libraries, parks, and community centers where youths can engage in productive activities). Social workers may also organize community residents to fight city hall or, more often, to work with city hall or the county board to improve conditions by cleaning up toxic waste sites, ameliorate relationships with law enforcement, and ensure that police patrol neighborhoods and curtail drug trafficking. Empowering individuals and communities to advocate for themselves is among the most important work social workers do.

Social workers interested in tackling poverty through public policy do so by working to reduce gender and race discrimination and increase social and economic justice. They are employed by organizations like the Food Research and Action Center, which is based in Washington, D.C., and works on policy and partnerships to end hunger, and the Center on Budget and Policy Priorities, which conducts research and analyzes issues like social insurance, public assistance, and tax policies that affect low- and moderate-income Americans. Many similar programs operate in states across the country. For example, the Affirmative Options Coalition in Minnesota works with over fifty member agencies and organizations to advocate public policy change affecting welfare and work. Through grassroots organizing and activism, Affirmative Options promotes social policies that eliminate barriers to work and provide opportunities for low-income families to achieve economic security. Many social workers are involved in the coalition's work; in fact, its director is a social worker! The coalition has successfully advocated policies related to the Minnesota Family Investment Program (the state's TANF/welfare-to-work program), including increased access to education and training and expansion of the Working Family Credit (a tax credit for low-income working families).

As part of their own civic engagement, social workers are involved in grassroots community programs (see box 13.2) and organizations such as the Poor People's Economic Human Rights Campaign, which unites poor

Box 13.2 Capital IDEA

Maria had been employed as a custodian at her church for almost as many years as she had been married. The pay was not good and she received no benefits, but she loved working for Father Joe. Lately, however, Maria had been feeling desperate to find a new job. She felt custodial work would be too physically demanding for her now, but her larger concern was her daughter. Her daughter had recently been diagnosed with leukemia, and with no health insurance, Maria was worried about how she would pay the medical bills with such a low income. "I can't keep this job any longer. But what else can I do? I have no other job skills."

Maria's story was one of many I heard as an Austin Interfaith leader. Austin Interfaith, an Industrial Areas Foundation affiliate, was assessing the need for a job training program that would help underemployed and unemployed individuals obtain living-wage employment. As part of this assessment, leaders like me were doing individual and group meetings to determine the need. The more stories I heard, the more my "cold anger" (Rogers, 1990) burned. From my own parish, I learned about Theresa, who had left her abusive husband and was participating in a job training program that was offering little in the way of skills that would enable her to land a decent job, leading her to consider marrying again just to support herself. Patricia had been an employee for thirty years at a company that offered no retirement plan. People were working long hours in difficult jobs without fair compensation.

Austin Interfaith had been hearing stories like this in our communities for years. But our assessment did not formally begin until the business community approached us. For several years Austin Interfaith operated a summer youth employment program. The business community was impressed with our program and with the youths. "Can you help us find dependable adults to work for us? How about the parents of those kids? We are always in need!" they told us.

After scores of meetings with prospective trainees and businesses, Capital IDEA, in Austin, Texas, was born. We tailored it to meet the needs of both groups by offering free tuition, books, day care, transportation, and counseling to people willing to invest their time and energy to pursue an associate's degree. Capital IDEA is dramatically different from most job training programs, especially because it offers training for jobs with a career ladder that pay a living wage. Hundreds of people have completed the program and now have wonderful new careers. Some of the graduates who have pursued medical careers make more money than I do!

Austin Interfaith knew that in order to make sure that the program stayed true to its goals, it would be important to retain control over Capital IDEA, so the bylaws we wrote specified that the board majority must be Austin Interfaith leaders. Today Austin Interfaith continues to assist Capital IDEA recruit participants and secure funding.

The three years I devoted to developing Capital IDEA and serving as one of the first board members were incredibly rewarding even though I did not get paid one cent. I met the most amazing people! Austin Interfaith and other Industrial Areas Foundation affiliates offer social workers an opportunity to use our skills and passion in the fight for social justice. I highly recommend it!

Karen A. Gray
Assistant Professor
University of South Carolina,
College of Social Work

people across color lines to see that everyone has good health care, housing, living-wage jobs, and quality education. They also work in their own faith communities to achieve these ends. Social workers are also working to end world hunger and poverty, as chapter 15 discusses.

SUMMARY

In this chapter you learned that poverty is a major problem in the United States. For more than one hundred years, social workers have been at the forefront of programs, services, advocacy, and activism for those affected by poverty. Many Americans will live below the poverty line at some point in their lives. It is the social worker's job to understand the causes and consequences of poverty and to take action to bring about changes with and for clients and communities. Whether this change takes place at the individual, community, state, or national level, whether it involves helping a person find a job or making major changes to state or federal legislation, social workers are there to lead the charge. Social workers have many opportunities to end poverty. We hope that you take up the call.

SUGGESTED READING

DeParle, J. (2004). *American dream: Three women, ten kids, and a nation's drive to end welfare.* New York: Viking/Penguin. DeParle examines welfare reform's impact on three sisters and their children in Milwaukee, Wisconsin. He takes what happens at the political level in Washington, D.C., and brings it to the street level in this well-written and moving journalistic account of how these women and their children fared after the implementation of TANF.

Hage, D. (2004). *Reforming welfare by rewarding work: One state's successful experiment.* Minneapolis: University of Minnesota Press. In the late 1980s, then-governor of Minnesota Rudy Perpich brought together citizen experts to redesign welfare. What resulted was a groundbreaking antipoverty program—the Minnesota Family Investment Program. This book intertwines the story of the Minnesota Family Investment Program's development with three families' experiences on welfare.

Hays, S. (2004). *Flat broke with children: Women in the age of welfare reform.* New York: Oxford University Press. This book is based on firsthand accounts of how welfare reform has affected America's poor. It provides an interesting analysis of the cultural and political assumptions behind American welfare laws and many contradictory welfare provisions.

Iceland, J. (2003). *Poverty in America: A handbook.* Berkeley and Los Angeles: University of California Press. While poverty has been with us a long time, the way we think about it has changed a lot over time. This book offers an in-depth discussion of trends, patterns, and causes of poverty in the United States and includes statistical information, historical data, and social scientific theory. Iceland considers questions such as, Why does poverty remain so pervasive? Is it unavoidable? What can we expect over the next few years? What are the limits of public policy? The book is concise, easy to read, and very useful for students studying social welfare.

Mittelstadt, J. (2005). *From welfare to workfare: The unintended consequences of liberal reform.* Chapel Hill: University of North Carolina Press. In 1996, President Clinton and the Republican-controlled Congress vowed to "end welfare as we know it." Mittelstadt argues that "workfare" was not a new idea and explores how women, work, and welfare all became concerns of the liberal welfare state beginning just after World War II. She examines family welfare reform from 1940 through the 1960s, a period that is generally poorly understood, and discusses the unintended and far-reaching consequences of public debates and disagreements over welfare reform.

Rank, M. R. (2004). *One nation, underprivileged: Why American poverty affects us all.* New York: Oxford University Press. Rank reveals a shocking reality: more than half of adult Americans will spend at least a year of their lives in poverty, and 65 percent will receive public assistance. Rank uses the game of musical chairs, in which there are ten players but only eight chairs, to help the reader understand how we are all at risk. While scholars and politicians focus on the two players still standing when the music stops, Rank asks us to consider why the game has to produce losers. Rank deconstructs myths about poverty and helps us to understand that it is something experienced by the majority of Americans and that we all share responsibility for making sure that there are enough resources to go around so that no one is left out in the end.

THE WORLD WIDE WEB OF SOCIAL WORK

Center on Hunger and Poverty http://www.centeronhunger.org

This research center at the Heller School of Social Policy and Management of Brandeis University is an outgrowth of the Harvard-based Physician Task Force on Hunger in America, which studied the extent and causes of hunger during the 1980s. The center also addresses hunger's root causes—poverty and income inequality.

Center on Urban Poverty and Social Change http://povertycenter.cwru.edu

Housed at Case Western Reserve University, the center addresses the problems of persistent and concentrated urban poverty and is dedicated to understanding how social and economic changes affect low-income communities, and how living in these communities affects residents' well-being.

Institute for Research on Poverty http://www.irp.wisc.edu

The IRP is an interdisciplinary research center that investigates the causes and consequences of poverty and social inequality in the United States. It is one of three area poverty research centers sponsored by the U.S. Department of Health and Human Services. Housed at the University of Wisconsin–Madison, it focuses on poverty and family welfare in the Midwest.

Institute on Race and Poverty http://irpumn.org

The institute, which is housed at the University of Minnesota–Twin Cities, investigates ways that policies and practices affect people of color and other disadvantaged groups. It works to ensure that individuals have access to opportunity and that communities develop in ways that promote opportunity and maintain regional stability.

National Center for Children in Poverty http://www.nccp.org/

NCCP is a nonpartisan research organization at the Mailman School of Public Health at Columbia University. It promotes the economic security, health, and well-being of America's low-income families and children through the strategic use of national and state resources.

National Poverty Center http://www.npc.umich.edu/

The NPC was established in 2002 as a nonpartisan research center at the University of Michigan's Gerald R. Ford School of Public Policy. It conducts and promotes multidisciplinary policy-relevant research on the causes and consequences of poverty and provides mentoring and training to young scholars.

Rural Policy Research Institute http://www.rupri.org

Located at the University of Missouri–Columbia, RUPRI focuses on reducing poverty across the rural-urban continuum. The site's animated time-series mapping feature allows visitors to view changes in poverty rates across the United States from 1960 to 2000.

**U.S. Department of Health and Human Services
http://aspe.hhs.gov/poverty/index.shtml**

This federal government Web site provides information and data about U.S. federal poverty guidelines and how poverty is measured.

14 Social Work Practice in the Justice System

Diane S. Young

The criminal justice field holds many possibilities for meaningful social work. Although only a small proportion of social workers practice in criminal justice settings, many who do so find the work challenging and rewarding. This chapter provides an overview of several components of the justice system (law enforcement, courts, corrections, and juvenile justice). Within each of these areas, it describes social work roles and explores contemporary issues. There are many opportunities to make a positive professional impact in the justice system. As discussed in this chapter, the challenges may seem formidable at times, but there are promising approaches to build upon.

RELEVANCE OF SOCIAL WORK TO CRIMINAL JUSTICE

The social work profession's involvement in the justice system began in the area of corrections (Brownell & Roberts, 2002). In the late nineteenth and early twentieth centuries, much social work activity was directed toward institutionalized adults and juveniles, as well as individuals on probation. Social workers advocated juvenile justice reform and better conditions of confinement for adults. The first director of the federal Office of Juvenile Justice and Delinquency Prevention was social worker Ira Schwartz, and this office was instrumental in allocating federal funds to states for the removal of many juveniles from adult jails and for the development of youth programs (Brownell & Roberts, 2002). Social workers were actively involved with the National Conference of Charities and Corrections, which was formed in 1879 and later became the National Conference of Social Work (Miller, 1995; Roberts & Brownell, 1999). Indeed, prior to the 1970s, during the years when rehabilitation was a more accepted correctional philosophy, social workers were visible in probation, parole, and correctional facilities (Treger & Allen, 1997). Social workers' influence also extended to other aspects of the justice system. They were instrumental in the creation of the first juvenile court in Chicago in 1899 (Gumz, 2004). They were even employed in police departments, and as early as 1924, there were recommendations for social workers to enter police departments to work with juveniles and plan delinquency prevention programs (Van Winkle, 1924).

As social work continued to evolve, however, it largely abandoned the field of corrections and other justice settings (Gibelman, 1995). Several reasons have been offered for the profession's move away from this field. Predominant among these is the coercive nature of corrections, which is contrary to the social work profession's emphasis on client self-determination (Fox, 1983; Miller, 1995). Similarly, in direct social work practice (practice with individuals, families, and groups), the emphasis is on providing care and treatment to clients in a nonjudgmental way. In criminal justice, the approach to offenders is primarily one of control and punishment from an authoritative position, rather than one of rehabilitation. As corrections has embraced retribution as a correctional philosophy, it has pulled farther away from the value stance of most social workers. These basic philosophical differences between the fields have discouraged social workers from active involvement in many criminal justice settings. In addition, the profession's shift in focus from community involvement and work with the disenfranchised to a greater interest in psychotherapy and individual treatment may have contributed to a declining presence in corrections (Gumz, 2004). Even though social work as a profession is not as active in criminal justice settings as it once was, there is substantial evidence that the need for the profession's involvement is greater than ever.

The number of individuals caught up in the justice system in the United States is increasing. Between 1995 and 2004, the increase in state, federal, and jail prisoners averaged 3.5 percent annually (Harrison & Beck, 2005). At the end of 2003, just over 3 percent of the U.S. adult population, or about one in every thirty-two adults, was either incarcerated, on probation, or on parole (Glaze & Palla, 2004). About 70 percent of the adults under correctional control, over 4.8 million individuals, are supervised in the community (Glaze & Palla, 2004). These individuals and their family members often need services provided by social workers in a wide variety of agency settings, as do the large number of individuals who cycle in and out of jails and prisons.

People of color are disproportionately represented behind bars and make up 65 percent of the prison population (Harrison & Beck, 2004). The lifetime likelihood of going to prison is 28 percent for black men, 16 percent for Hispanic men, and just over 4 percent for white men (Bonczar & Beck, 1997). As social workers strive to address societal practices and policies that adversely affect certain groups, the tremendous racial and ethnic disparities among correctional populations deserve attention.

There is a great deal of overlap between offending populations and the individuals and families with whom social workers come into contact in other settings. For example, about 16 percent of male and 23 percent of female jail inmates have been identified as mentally ill (Ditton, 1999). Many incarcerated individuals need treatment for co-occurring disorders. Almost

65 percent of mentally ill jail inmates have reported being under the influence of drugs or alcohol at the time of their offense (Ditton, 1999). The rate of confirmed AIDS cases among the U.S. prison population is over three times the rate in the general U.S. population (Maruschak, 2004). Almost 60 percent of female state prisoners report having experienced prior physical or sexual abuse (Greenfeld & Snell, 1999). In addition, almost 70 percent of state prisoners report histories of regular drug use (Mumola, 1999).

The annual rate of growth in the number of incarcerated women has increased faster than that for men over the past ten years (Harrison & Beck, 2005), with much of this increase due to changes in drug laws and harsher sentencing for drug offenses. Indeed, the proportions of women convicted of violent crimes and property crimes have decreased, while the proportion of drug offenders has grown (Greenfeld & Snell, 1999). Many of these women would benefit from substance abuse treatment that takes into consideration their life histories and circumstances. Social workers employed in treatment programs, as well as within correctional settings, are well positioned to address these needs.

When women go to prison, over 70 percent of them leave behind children under age eighteen. These children and the children's caregivers often need social supports and come to the attention of social workers in public assistance and child welfare settings (Young & Smith, 2000). In addition, about 6 percent of female state prisoners are pregnant upon entering prison (Snell, 1994), and it is the rare correctional facility that allows mothers to keep their infants with them after birth. It is important to assist these families at the earliest opportunity, as there is a strong correlation between maternal incarceration and future criminal behavior and imprisonment (Bloom & Steinhart, 1993; Jose-Kampfner, 1991). Also, a significant proportion of incarcerated parents were homeless and poor prior to entering jail or prison. Eighteen percent of mothers in state prison and 8 percent of fathers reported being homelessness for a period of time in the year prior to incarceration (Mumola, 2000). These social problems profoundly affect families, and social workers come into contact with individuals and families experiencing multiple problems, including justice system involvement.

THE CRIMINAL JUSTICE SYSTEM

Because of its highly decentralized nature, it really is not accurate to speak or think about the justice system in the United States as one system. Rather, the criminal and juvenile justice organizations and entities that make up the totality of the U.S. justice system are more accurately described as many systems with different funding sources and administrative structures. Thus, when the justice system is referred to in this chapter, the totality of these multiple systems is the referent. The justice system has three major components: law enforcement, the courts, and corrections. If these components are seen on a continuum, law enforcement encompasses the beginning of the continuum, courts the middle, and corrections the end.

LAW ENFORCEMENT

Law enforcement is the largest of the three components. The various organizations that constitute law enforcement include state and local law enforcement agencies, such as city and municipal police departments, county sheriffs' offices, and state police agencies. Several federal agencies also employ law enforcement agents, such as the Federal Bureau of Investigation; the Internal Revenue Service Criminal Investigation Division; the Bureau of Alcohol, Tobacco, and Firearms; U.S. Citizenship and Immigration Services (formerly the Immigration and Naturalization Service); the United States Marshals Service; the United States Customs Service; the United States Secret Service; the Drug Enforcement Administration; and the Central Intelligence Agency. In 2004, there were over 14,000 state and local law enforcement agencies with over one million full-time employees (Federal Bureau of Investigations, 2005). Local agencies range in size from one full-time sworn officer with general arrest powers to over 35,500 sworn officers in 2004 at the New York City Police Department, the nation's largest law enforcement agency (Federal Bureau of Investigations, 2005). Law enforcement is the most costly component of the justice system, with over $72 billion spent on police protection in 2001, just under $57 billion on corrections, and almost $38 billion on judicial and legal services (Bauer & Owens, 2004). Between 1982 and 2001, the average annual expenditure increase for police protection was 7 percent at state and local levels, and 10 percent at the federal level (Bauer & Owens, 2004).

Law enforcement officers investigate crimes, make arrests, and are the gatekeepers to the justice system for most people. Most of the time, however, local and state law enforcement officers are maintaining order and fulfilling service responsibilities, such as traffic control, giving information, settling disputes, assisting stranded motorists or the injured, and providing what are often thought of as social service functions (Barlow, 2000). Indeed, a 1999 survey on contacts between police and the public found that 21 percent of U.S. residents (almost 44 million people) had had at least one face-to-face contact with police within the year, and only 3 percent of these contacts occurred because the police suspected involvement in a crime (Langan, Greenfeld, Smith, Durose, & Levin, 2001).

Although there has been some social work involvement in police agencies historically, the two professions have largely worked independently of each other, and their relationship has often been adversarial (Dean, Lumb, Proctor, Klopovic, Hyatt, & Hamby, 2000). It may be that the contemporary focus on community policing provides an opportunity for social workers to become more engaged in this aspect of the justice system. Community policing emphasizes problem solving, partnerships, prevention, and organizational change with efforts directed toward improving the relationship between police and the public (Dean et al., 2000). Dean and colleagues suggest that developing partnerships between human service agencies and the police is one possible extension of the focus on problem solving in community policing. There is good reason for this. Police officers are often ill equipped to handle many social problems that come to their attention, such as domestic violence, mental health problems, and substance abuse, which are often complex and long-standing problems that result in repeated calls to the police for assistance. The police are available for immediate response but are not able to provide the social and therapeutic services required for preventing and ending these repetitive cycles. It is here that social work and police partnerships are sorely needed.

The North Carolina Governor's Crime Commission and the North Carolina Department of Crime Control and Public Safety sponsored a study to examine social work and police partnerships and to identify effective practices of existing partnerships (Dean et al., 2000). A key goal of the study was to determine the impact of the partnerships. The authors concluded that there were clear indications in the five sites studied that the partnerships were effective in improving responses to the needs of individuals with serious problems. Initial resistance to the partnership by some law enforcement officers faded quickly. Social work roles and responsibilities involve going with the police on initial calls, or on their own the following day, and providing case management services that might include assessment, referrals for interim services, monitoring of client progress, advocacy, emotional support to victims, coordination of services to clients, follow-up visits to the home, counseling, and development of service plans. Social workers and police in these partnerships are involved in cross-training, and the social workers serve as police department liaisons to other community agencies. Box 14.1 describes two of the unique social work and police partnerships identified in the study.

Box 14.1   Social Work–Police Partnerships

The Orange County Office of the Sheriff Crisis Intervention Unit is a social work and police partnership that operates in a rural area, where human services are often more limited than they are in urban centers. Two full-time social workers and one attorney form this unit. They respond to phone calls and walk-ins and accept referrals from deputies. Each day, they review all calls for service and call or send a letter if any needs are indicated. In addition, if a crime was committed, they contact the victim to offer services. Each month, an interagency meeting addresses mutual concerns and discusses cases that need

---

Box 14.1 *Continued*

resolution. The structure and format are also useful for identifying gaps and overlap in services. The collaboration has become an integral part of the local service network, and due to its success, the county funds all positions.

Located in a community policing substation, the Juvenile Gang Intervention Task Force consists of four juvenile detectives and one social worker. The task force's primary purpose is to reduce youth involvement in gang activity. The social worker carries a caseload of twelve juvenile gang members and meets with them twice a month at first. The social worker accompanies the detectives on gang-related calls, meets with the parents of identified gang members, makes referrals for services, and provides input to the court. The task force also keeps an intelligence database on gang members in the area and benefits from participating in a monthly meeting where over one hundred organizations come together to address local issues. The result has been a reduction in gang-related activity and the development of a regional approach to community problem solving.

Source: Dean, C. W., Lumb, R., Proctor, K., Klopovic, J., Hyatt, A., & Hamby, R. (2000, October). *Social work and law enforcement partnerships: A summons to the village. Strategies and effective practices.* Raleigh, NC: Governor's Crime Commission.

COURTS

The many courts at local, state, and federal levels have differing jurisdictions and levels of authority to hear and resolve certain kinds of cases. Criminal courts are in the middle of the justice continuum between law enforcement and corrections. They become involved around the time criminal charges are filed and remain engaged all the way through to sentencing, other disposition of the case, or the appeals process. Thus, they encompass prosecution and pretrial services, adjudication, and sanctions. The federal government, and each state government, determines what constitutes a crime and creates laws, and criminal courts hear matters regarding legal violations. Misdemeanors are crimes typically punishable by a maximum of one year of incarceration. Felonies are more serious offenses, typically punishable by more than one year of incarceration. At the state level, most felony matters are handled in courts of general jurisdiction, often called circuit or superior courts, and misdemeanors are dealt with in courts of limited jurisdiction, often called lower courts (Barlow, 2000). Most judicial and legal spending occurs at state and local levels; only about $8 billion of the almost $38 billion spent in 2001 on judicial and legal services was expended at the federal level (Bauer & Owens, 2004).

Courts see a tremendous amount of activity. In 2002, state and federal courts convicted over 1,114,000 adults on felony charges, with state courts accounting for 94 percent of this total (Durose & Langan, 2004). In state courts, about 78 percent of felony convictions occurred within one year of arrest (Durose & Langan, 2004). Certainly not all felony arrests result in felony convictions. For example, for every one hundred arrests for murder in 2002, seventy resulted in felony convictions, and for every one hundred arrests for burglary, fifty resulted in felony convictions (Durose & Langan, 2004). The number of state court convictions in 2002 was 20 percent greater than in 1994, but a lower proportion of felony convictions resulted from trials (5% in 2002 and 11% in 1994). The vast majority of felony convictions result from guilty pleas, many through plea bargaining, where the defense and prosecution negotiate over charges and sentences and the defendant enters a guilty plea in exchange for leniency in sentencing.

Pretrial Services

Social work employment related to judicial and legal work may be most common in pretrial diversion services, the preparation of pre-sentence investigations, and victim and witness assistance programs. Pretrial diversion services seek to temporarily remove defendants from the criminal justice system to community-based services and treatment. The hope is that, with the right supports, defendants will become productive and law-abiding citizens and avoid the often-negative consequences of formal prosecution. These programs are housed in probation departments, courthouses, jails, and independent agencies and have greatly increased in number since 1990 (Clark & Henry, 2003). According to a large survey of pretrial diversion programs conducted in 2001, from 1997 to 2001, many programs increased their work with individuals with mental illnesses or those charged with domestic violence offenses (Clark & Henry, 2003). Social workers find their assessment, case management, and counseling skills; their knowledge of special populations; and an ecological perspective particularly useful in this work.

When there is a felony conviction, pre-sentence investigations are conducted to help the judge decide on the most appropriate sentence for the defendant. Probation officers (some probation officers are social workers) typically prepare these written reports based on an investigation of factors such as the circumstances surrounding the crime; the offender's criminal history, educational and employment background, and social history; and treatment resources available in the community. The report includes a recommendation from the probation officer. Though judges are certainly not bound to the recommendation and often have limitations imposed on their sentencing discretion because of legislative mandates, the pre-sentence investigations can provide helpful background information that may influence the resulting sentence.

Victim and Witness Assistance

Victim and witness assistance services are located primarily in prosecutors' offices and courthouses and were developed over the past thirty years to respond to the concern that the criminal justice system largely ignored the needs of victims and witnesses (Roberts & Fisher, 1997). Victim services might also be located within police departments, hospitals, and not-for-profit social service agencies. Social workers, either volunteers or employees, who work at victim and witness assistance programs provide a range of services including crisis counseling; trauma assessment; referrals to address immediate needs related to safety, shelter, and transportation; assistance with compensation forms; orientation to the judicial process; follow-up visits; assistance developing victim impact statements; notification regarding hearings; and referrals to social service agencies for long-term needs (National Association of Social Workers, n.d.; Roberts & Fisher, 1997).

Specialized Courts

A relatively new and developing area for social work employment is in the specialized problem-solving courts that are being created to respond to defendants with persistent problems that contribute to their involvement in the criminal justice system. Service providers, including social workers, are often part of the treatment or case management team that provides services to specialized court defendants and progress reports to the court.

Drug courts, the first of these specialized courts, were introduced in 1989 in Florida (National Criminal Justice Reference Service, n.d.). Drug courts provide selected individuals (such as nonviolent first-time offenders) with alcohol- and drug-related charges with access to comprehensive treatment and entice them to stay in treatment through the use of incentives (such as deferred adjudication) and sanctions (which may include revocation or jail time). More recently, communities are creating mental health courts and domestic violence courts. Mental health courts seek to engage criminally involved individuals with mental illnesses in treatment in order to stop the cycle of worsening mental health and criminal behavior (Bernstein & Seltzer, 2004). Successful program completion typically results in dismissed or lessened charges or sanctions. In some locations, partnerships between human service agencies and police departments have resulted in a better response to clients with severe mental illnesses or emotional difficulties (Dean et al., 2000). They can also mean better relationships between local courts and community mental health and social service agencies, which result in fewer individuals falling through the cracks.

About 17,000 individuals graduate annually from drug court (Roman, Townsend, & Bhati, 2003). A national study of recidivism rates for drug court graduates found that about 16 percent were arrested for a serious offense within the first year of graduation, and nearly 28 percent within the second year (Roman et al., 2003), still a significant improvement over most other treatment models. Outcome studies are needed to assess the long-term effectiveness of specialized courts in achieving their intended goals, particularly as the development of these courts seems to be a continuing trend.

One additional but often-overlooked area related to social work involvement with the courts deserves comment. Box 14.2 describes the social worker's role in death penalty mitigation cases.

Box 14.2   Social Work in Death Penalty Mitigation Investigations

Julie Schroeder (2003), writing about the role of the social worker in death penalty mitigation, states that the "goal of capital mitigation is to provide the jury with information about a client's life circumstances so that they might consider the punishment of life in prison without the benefit of parole rather than the death penalty" (p. 424). In this work, the social worker is an integral part of a multidisciplinary defense team and performs a number of essential tasks. The social worker conducts a multidimensional assessment using an ecological approach to understand the offender and the offender's family. Information is gathered, ideally going back three generations, and extensive interviewing is part of this process. Any available documents generated about the client are reviewed, requiring that contact be made with schools, churches, hospitals, treatment centers, social service agencies, public assistance offices, and any other settings the client has had contact with throughout his or her life. It can be difficult to engage the client and family members in this intensive process, and the social worker must assist families as they manage their feelings and prepare for trial and sentencing. At times the social worker facilitates communication between attorneys and client. Social workers use crisis intervention skills with families who must be quickly prepared for the penalty phase, which comes very soon after a guilty verdict is announced. They write a report that is available to the prosecution. It draws on all gathered life history information and ties in what is empirically known about criminal behavior. The social worker might also engage in advocacy so that the client receives appropriate mental health services throughout the judicial process.

Source: Schroeder, J. (2003). Forging a new practice area: Social work's role in death penalty mitigation investigations. *Families in Society: The Journal of Contemporary Human Services, 84*(3), 423–432.

CORRECTIONS

The corrections component of the adult justice system is primarily concerned with the control of individuals accused or convicted of criminal offenses. Like law enforcement agencies and courts, corrections organizations are administered at local, state, and federal levels. A primary function of the corrections component is to ensure that offenders complete the sentences that the respective judicial system orders. Sentences range from options where personal freedom is extremely limited (e.g., incarceration) to sentences where one has more freedom while still under correctional control (e.g., diversion into treatment, probation, electronic surveillance in one's home). This section on corrections discusses incarceration and alternatives to it.

Incarceration

The United States currently incarcerates more of its residents per capita than any other nation in the world, at 726 per 100,000 residents, up from 601 in 1995 (Harrison & Beck, 2005). At midyear 2004, over 2 million individuals were incarcerated in U.S. prisons and jails, about 1.2 million were housed in state prisons, about 170,000 were held in federal prisons, and about 700,000 were held in local jails. Private prisons held 98,792 inmates (Harrison & Beck, 2005). The number of correctional facilities has increased greatly in the past few decades to house the expanding number of prisoners. State and federal prisons typically house individuals convicted of felonies and serving sentences of more than one year. Jail populations are much more diverse and hold pretrial detainees, individuals serving sentences of less than one year, persons convicted of felonies and awaiting sentencing or transportation to prison, probation and parole violators awaiting hearings, and in some jurisdictions, juveniles and individuals with mental illnesses while they are waiting to be transported elsewhere. In addition, some local jails hold state or federal prisoners because of overcrowding in state and federal facilities.

There is debate over whether the government should allow private contractors to construct and operate correctional facilities. At midyear 2004, about 7 percent of all prison inmates were held in privately operated facilities (Harrison & Beck, 2005). States such as Florida, where 89 percent of incarcerated juveniles and a third of incarcerated adults are housed in private facilities, have moved much faster toward privatization. Arguments for privatization include the view that private contractors may be able to build and operate facilities at less cost than government can and that legal liability may be reduced if private contractors adhere to accreditation standards. (These standards are optional, but accredited facilities are more often successful when faced with legal action against them.) Arguments against privatization include the view that the private sector has no business performing a government function (the incarceration of its citizens), and that because private contractors are given a per diem charge per inmate, there is no incentive to expend resources on quality care and treatment (Mays & Winfree, 2005). Corrections Corporation of America is the largest manager of private correctional facilities in the United States and the fifth-largest corrections system, smaller only than the federal government's and those of three states (Corrections Corporation of America, n.d.). Founded in 1983, its goal is to offer quality corrections at a cost to taxpayers that is cheaper than what the government could do. Whether Corrections Corporation of

America and other private corrections industries are successful in achieving this goal deserves close scrutiny. There are indications that private prisons have saved very little money while contributing to large profits for shareholders. In addition, some private correctional facilities are characterized by severe staff shortages, higher rates of violent incidents than government-run facilities, and lack of inmate programs (Bates, 2006). If public dollars are used to maximize private profits through the implementation of practices that jeopardize prisoner and community safety, such as not hiring a sufficient number of trained staff or shortchanging rehabilitative programs for prisoners, this is not wise public policy. These issues deserve empirical exploration and further discussion, as the number of privately operated facilities and those held there has greatly increased over the last decade (Stephan & Karberg, 2003).

Social workers take on a number of roles within correctional facilities. Social workers with an undergraduate degree may be employed as corrections counselors. In this multifaceted role, they conduct assessments, provide information about adjusting to the facility, engage in crisis intervention, participate in mediation and assist with problem resolution, provide short-term counseling and group work, advocate adequate services and treatment (e.g., educational and vocational services, appropriate health and mental health services), and promote safety and security by helping minimize tension and participating in inmate housing placement decisions. Social workers might also provide education and treatment in a specific area, such as drug and alcohol abuse counseling or violence prevention. Box 14.3 describes one prison social worker's perspective about helping

---

Box 14.3 A Prison Social Worker's Perspective: Examining Effects of Victimization

An important component of the rehabilitative process is a serious examination of the crimes an offender has committed. Emphasis should be placed on helping offenders understand the consequences of crime for victims. Through the use of discussion, activities, and presentations by previously victimized individuals, the offender is encouraged to personalize his or her crimes by considering not just the physical consequences of crime, but the emotional and financial consequences as well. Using the domino effect, all victims are considered, beginning with primary victims, and then branching out to examine the consequences for secondary victims, such as the victim's family members, friends, and neighbors. In treatment, the offender is also encouraged to examine the consequences for his or her own loved ones, who are victimized by the offender's absence while he or she is in prison. Prison social workers who help offenders focus on their victimizing behaviors in essence become a voice for all victims.

George Service, CSW
Corrections Counselor
Mohawk Correctional Facility
Rome, NY

offenders understand how their crimes are experienced by victims. This work takes place within the context of a violence prevention program in a men's prison. More recently, there has been a greater recognition of the importance of release planning and assisting prisoners with their reentry to the community, especially for specific populations such as individuals with mental illnesses. This provides a relatively new avenue for social work involvement.

About a third of jails nationwide employ social workers to provide mental health services to inmates (Goldstrom, Henderson, Male, & Manderscheid, 1998). Facilities typically prefer practitioners working with this specialized population to have a graduate degree, but not always. Many jails and prisons have units designated to hold individuals with mental illnesses who have trouble functioning in general housing due to symptoms of their mental disorders. Indeed, the demand on correctional systems to house and manage severely mentally ill individuals has greatly increased as community resources for mental health care have decreased. Many of these individuals also have alcohol or drug problems and require treatment for both. In most facilities, treatment needs far exceed availability of services, and the primary focus is on stabilization. For example, the most common mental health services in jails are intake screening and evaluation, crisis intervention and suicide prevention, and prescription of psychotropic medications (Young, 2002). As long as individuals with mental illnesses are held in correctional facilities, quality care should be provided, and social workers can advocate and work toward this goal.

Alternatives to Incarceration

The recidivism rate for previously incarcerated individuals is high. Within three years of release from prison, almost 52 percent were back in prison; 67 percent had been rearrested for a new offense (Langan & Levin, 2002). The fiscal cost of incarceration, particularly in light of its seemingly limited effectiveness, has necessitated the consideration and extensive use of alternative methods of correctional control. Alternatives to incarceration include fines, community service, diversion into treatment, probation, parole, house arrest or electronic monitoring, and sentencing to a halfway house or work-release facility. These are considered community-based alternatives, because the offender spends at least part of the time in the community, although still under correctional control.

The most common form of correctional supervision in the United States is probation. At midyear 2003, over 4 million adults were on probation (Glaze & Palla, 2004). Probation conditionally allows an individual to remain in the community instead of serving time in jail or prison. This practice was developed in the United States during the nineteenth century as an outgrowth of the concern of a Boston cobbler, John Augustus. He visited the Boston jails as a volunteer and asked local judges to release their younger, less serious offenders into his custody pending final disposition of their cases (National Association of Social Workers, 1987). The practice was soon adopted for adult offenders. In 2003, about 25 percent of probationers were convicted of a drug-law violation, and about 17 percent for driving while intoxicated (Glaze & Palla, 2004). Parole is also a common alternative to incarceration. With parole, part of an offender's sentence is served outside prison, after a time in prison. In 2003, about 775,000 individuals were on parole (Glaze & Palla, 2004), although discretionary release by a parole board is becoming increasingly less common as many states and the federal system have changed from indeterminate to determinate sentencing structures. Under determinate sentencing, a fixed sentence is given, rather than a range of time, and automatic release to post-release supervision when the sentence has been served is becoming more common (Mays & Winfree, 2005).

Probation or community supervision officers and parole officers (some are social workers) supervise individuals on probation and parole or post-release supervision, doing their best to ensure that their charges comply with both standard and special conditions of probation or parole. Standard conditions typically apply to all probationers and parolees and include requirements such as reporting regularly to the officer and committing no new crimes. Special conditions are tailored to the offender and might involve requirements such as participation in drug treatment or community service. Officers' duties include visiting probationers' and parolees' homes or employment sites, developing service plans, reviewing requirements with clients, monitoring compliance with all conditions, assisting with drug testing, providing referrals to treatment or other social services as appropriate, making arrests when violations occur, preparing progress reports or recommendations for the court, and encouraging clients to make positive life changes. Box 14.4 illustrates a probation officer's work with a client.

Many probation and parole officers find this line of work rewarding; at the same time, some aspects of the job are especially challenging. One challenge is that the job involves both therapeutic and punitive roles. For example, probation officers advocate for and encourage clients to participate in treatment opportunities. Officers may develop one-to-one relationships with clients and provide brief counseling. On the other hand, they also at times recommend to the court that a client return to jail or prison for noncompliance. Many officers carry firearms for their own protection and for when they make arrests. In addition to these conflicting roles, another challenge is that caseload sizes can be so large that it is extremely difficult to be thorough and effective. Caseload size varies greatly by jurisdiction and by the nature of the clientele, but some stretch to more than one hun-

---

Box 14.4 Probation Case Illustration

Janine was a twenty-one-year-old female arrested for selling cocaine to an undercover police officer. She associated with several gang members and had a criminal record of shoplifting and possessing marijuana. Janine reported a daily habit of smoking marijuana and admitted to using cocaine, Ecstasy, and alcohol on a weekly basis. After completing a drug and alcohol assessment, Janine's probation officer, a social worker, recommended that she participate in a thirty-day inpatient program at the local jail. During that time, the probation officer met with Janine to assess her current needs. After consulting with her counselor, the probation officer recommended that Janine go straight from jail into an inpatient treatment program. The court agreed.

Janine entered the inpatient treatment program on a Thursday and was terminated from treatment the following Monday due to her poor attitude. The probation officer immediately met with her and her mother to discuss the situation. Janine had many excuses as to why she was terminated from treatment. Due to the violation, Janine had to appear before the judge to address the situation. The judge admonished Janine for her actions, and the course of action was left to the probation officer's discretion. The probation officer arranged for Janine to enter a halfway house, but she was not at all agreeable to doing so. Her mother wanted her to live at home. The probation officer did not believe her mother's residence was a healthy environment for her, as all of Janine's siblings had criminal records and used marijuana. Janine then suggested she stay with a cousin who was employed as a teacher and did not have

a criminal record. Although the probation officer really believed that Janine would benefit from the structure of a halfway house, she also knew that if Janine was not agreeable to the treatment, she would sabotage it. The probation officer wanted Janine to take responsibility for her recovery from drugs and from the criminal lifestyle that she was gravitating toward. The probation officer agreed to allow her to stay with her cousin, with the understanding that if it did not work out, Janine would go to the halfway house.

Janine stayed with her cousin for several months, remained drug free, and made all her counseling and probation appointments. Unfortunately, Janine had an argument with her cousin, and her cousin told her to leave. Janine went to stay with a friend on a temporary basis until the probation officer could secure a place for her at the halfway house. While staying with her friend, Janine was arrested for shoplifting. Although it may seem that Janine failed since she was arrested while on supervision, she was actually doing well; she remained abstinent from drugs, as evidenced by her drug tests. She was sanctioned for being rearrested by being placed on a curfew. She also had to face the charges in a local court. Janine secured a place in the halfway house and did very well there. At her sentencing, Janine received a sentence of time served and a brief period of supervision to follow.

Ellen Phillips, MSW
Senior U.S. Probation Officer
U.S. Probation Office, Northern District of New York
Syracuse, NY

---

dred clients (Mays & Winfree, 2005). Social workers must find ways to manage conflicting roles and time demands if they are to be effective in their work.

JUVENILE JUSTICE

The juvenile justice system in the United States, like the adult justice system, is composed of many different organizations and entities with different funding sources and administrative structures. There are three primary components: prevention and diversion, juvenile courts, and juvenile corrections (Champion, 1998). For about the past hundred years, juveniles and adults accused of crimes have been treated differently (Barlow, 2000). A primary reason for this is the belief that children's behavior is more malleable than that of adults, and that given the proper guidance and opportunities for habilitation or rehabilitation, children will be deterred from future criminal activity. In addition, children have not had time to mature and are considered less responsible for their actions. In an attempt to match the system's response to each child's needs, juvenile justice system authorities are permitted to exercise a great deal of discretion at the stage of arrest and throughout the judicial process. This has not always worked in the best interest of the child, however, and in recent decades the Supreme Court has mandated increased due process protections for juveniles, such as the right to counsel, to receive written notification of the charges against them, and to cross-examine witnesses (Champion, 1998).

Juvenile courts typically hear petitions alleging that a juvenile fits in one of three categories: dependent or neglected, a status offender, or delinquent. Status offenses, such as running away, missing school, or being out of a parent's control, would not be crimes if committed by an adult. Delinquent acts, such as robbery, assault, or theft, are crimes if committed by an adult. After a hearing, the juvenile court judge adjudicates, or takes action on, the petition. Outcomes range from dismissal of the case to long-term confinement in a secure facility, with many options in between. In addition, some youths are prosecuted in the adult criminal court system, even though they are younger than eighteen years of age. Box 14.5 discusses this controversial issue.

In 2002, the juvenile arrest rate for violent crimes was the lowest it had been since 1980; in fact, between 1995 to 2002, it decreased (Snyder, 2004). Even so, juvenile crime makes up 17 percent of all arrests (Snyder, 2004). Almost 2.3 million juveniles were arrested in 2002, and just over 92,000 of these arrests were for violent crimes (Snyder, 2004). Twenty-nine percent of all juvenile arrestees were females (Snyder, 2004). The female offender population, both juvenile and adult, is growing at a faster rate than the male offender population (Harrison & Beck, 2005).

The most common outcome for juveniles adjudicated as delinquent or status offenders is probation (Champion, 1998), yet a significant proportion are placed in public or private residential settings. Secure residential settings include detention centers and training schools. Nonsecure residential settings include group homes, camps, and ranches (Dwyer, 1997). Just over 96,600 charged or adjudicated youths were being held in 2,852 public and

Box 14.5   Juveniles Prosecuted in Adult Court

At midyear 2004, 2,477 people under age eighteen—108 females and 2,369 males—were in state prisons in the United States (Harrison & Beck, 2005). This number has declined since 1995, when there were 5,309 youths in state prisons (Harrison & Beck, 2005). A profile of juveniles in corrections in 1999 indicated that a "person" offense (e.g., homicide, sexual assault, robbery) was the most serious conviction of 62 percent of youths held in state prisons, and a property crime (e.g., burglary, motor vehicle theft) was the most serious offense of 22 percent (Sickmund, 2004). In some states, juveniles who are a certain minimum age and/or charged with specified crimes are referred directly to criminal court; 7 percent of all juvenile arrests in 2002 were referred directly (Snyder, 2004). In other situations, the juvenile court gives its authority over the juvenile to the adult system. Cases waived to criminal court often involve serious charges that, if committed by an adult, would result in lengthy incarceration or the death penalty, and situations where the treatment and security available in the juvenile system are not believed to be sufficient to meet the needs of the juvenile or the public (Barlow, 2000).

Most juveniles in the adult court system, however, are not there because a judge has determined that the young offender is beyond the help of the juvenile justice system. In the last decade or so, many states have enacted laws that give prosecutors the discretion to send youths directly to the adult court system. In addition, state laws may automatically require a youth's case to be tried in adult court based on his or her age, type of alleged crime, or both. This means that judges made the decision to try juveniles as adults in only 15 percent of all such cases (Building Blocks for Youth, 2005). There is little agreement across the states about the minimum age at which a youth should be transferred to the adult system or for which crimes. The practice of sending juveniles directly to adult court is especially severe for racial and ethnic minorities. Currently, about 82 percent of juveniles prosecuted in adult courts are minority youths (Building Blocks for Youth, 2005). Proponents of prosecuting juveniles in adult court believe that a sentence in the juvenile system is not "just desserts" for the serious crimes that some juveniles commit, particularly for violent offenses, and that public safety is not adequately protected by a juvenile sentence. Opponents of this practice suggest that sending juveniles to adult court is tantamount to throwing them away at an age when individuals are not fully cognizant of the consequences of their behavior and are still malleable. What is your opinion?

private residential facilities on October 22, 2003 (Snyder & Sickmund, 2006). About 28 percent of all juvenile residential placements were in private facilities (Snyder & Sickmund, 2006). Between 1995 and 2003, the number of status offenders in residential placements declined (Snyder & Sickmund, 2006), although the goal of the Juvenile Justice and Delinquency Prevention Act of 1974 to deinstitutionalize status offenders has not been realized (McNeece & Jackson, 2004). Like incarcerated adults, a dispro-

Juvenile inmates at a detention center outside Laredo, Texas, begin the day with an hour of physical activity. Juveniles in these facilities often suffering mental illness and drug addiction and can be helped by social workers.
© Steve Liss

Residents of this home for juvenile offenders practice the photography skills they have learned in a program set up by a social worker and a photographer. The skills they learn here will enable them to make a successful return to the community.
© Mary Whelens

portionate number of youths of color are in residential placements compared to white youths. In 2003, about 61 percent of juveniles in custody were of ethnic and racial minority background (Snyder & Sickmund, 2006).

The social work profession has had a long history of involvement with juvenile justice in prevention and diversion, juvenile courts, and juvenile corrections (Alexander, 1997), but currently, the profession's presence is minimal. Just over 5 percent of certified and licensed social workers work in criminal justice settings where at least half of the caseload comprises adolescents (Center for Health Workforce Studies, 2005). This figure is not reflective of the many meaningful roles that social workers can fill in these settings at micro and macro levels.

Much juvenile justice work occurs at the stage of prevention and diversion and in probation. Social workers are employed in community-based agencies, such as diversion programs, treatment agencies, or group homes, where they provide services such as assessment, case management, and individual and group counseling for youths. They also are employed in detention facilities, providing mental health and other counseling or treatment services for youths who are detained or serving sentences. An important role in justice settings is that of the advocate, who works to ensure that youths receive appropriate and needed services. Social workers' knowledge and training are assets in settings that address systems, child and adolescent development, and the importance of thinking holistically about the problems and challenges young people face when interventions targeted toward behavioral change are being planned.

Although individuals with graduate degrees fill many of the mezzo and macro roles in juvenile justice settings, this is not always the case, especially if one has several years of experience working in the justice system. Direct practice experience with justice system clients is especially helpful when work responsibilities call for program planning and evaluation, resource development, needs assessment, and grant writing. A deeper understanding of the issues often comes with this practice experience.

CHALLENGES FOR SOCIAL WORKERS

Social workers face some particular challenges working in the justice system. Although not exclusive to justice settings and clientele, these challenges are ever present in the justice system.

Working in a Host Setting

Host settings are "organizations whose mission and decision making are defined and dominated by people who are not social workers" (Dane & Simon, 1991, p. 208). To maintain employment in these settings, social workers must prove themselves valuable to the mission or overall welfare of the host. This can be especially difficult in criminal justice settings, where the primary focuses are public safety and facility security, in contrast to the social worker's primary concern with client well-being. Social workers must find ways to support the organization's work while addressing legitimate client needs. For example, with incarcerated individuals, social workers must respect and take seriously the policies and practices imposed by the facility unless it would be unethical to do so. Corrections personnel are entrusted with the safety and security of inmates, staff, and the community. Social workers who attempt to subvert institutional rules do little to help anyone. This caution is appropriate for work on behalf of people under community supervision as well, for they live under court-imposed conditions. On the other hand, recognizing the influence of the environment underscores the need for advocacy. Many aspects of correctional policy need changing, and social workers should advocate changes that would enhance individual well-being and promote rehabilitation.

Working with Mandated Clients

Mandated clients are individuals ordered to treatment or coerced there, typically by the offer of alternatives to treatment that are very unpleasant, such as incarceration. These clients might not acknowledge the problems they have, and even if they do, they might not want help. Social workers face significant challenges engaging and working with mandated clients in criminal justice settings. The difficulty lies in the need to develop a therapeutic or helping relationship with the client in order to help the client develop and work toward meaningful and realistic goals. At the same time, the social worker may be required to report to judicial or correctional authorities on client progress, motivation, and compliance.

The National Association of Social Workers (1999) Code of Ethics acknowledges that social workers are likely to have mandated clients, and that it is essential to inform these clients about "the nature and extent of services and about the extent of clients' right to refuse service" (1.03d). In addition, social workers should clearly discuss with clients "circumstances where confidential information may be requested and where disclosure of confidential information may be legally required" (1.07e) and the potential consequences of such disclosure (1.07d). Social workers have dual responsibility to their clients and to society. This is particularly true in criminal justice settings. Thus, social workers also encourage clients' *socially responsible* self-determination (National Association of Social Workers, 1999). In doing so, social workers should be careful not to disregard the wishes of mandated clients but rather seek to engage clients "as partners in the helping process" (National Association of Social Workers, 1999).

RESTORATIVE JUSTICE: A LOOK TOWARD THE FUTURE

A promising approach frequently referred to as restorative justice requires a new way of thinking about and responding to criminal behavior. Restorative processes fit well with the values and orientation of social work and provide another avenue for social workers to become actively involved in justice issues. Restorative justice views crime as harm done to people and communities, and the emphasis in responding to crime is on repairing the harm (Zehr, 2002). Partly because victims' needs and perspectives have been largely overlooked in the adversarial justice system, restorative approaches have gained interest in certain areas of the country. There are currently different models in operation throughout the United States and in several different countries, with names such as victim-offender mediation, family group conferencing, community reparative boards, and healing circles (Bazemore & Umbreit, 2001; Van Wormer, 2002). In the various approaches, offenders, victims, and community members are involved in the criminal justice process. Offenders are asked for real accountability, typically through genuine dialogue with victims or community members, restitution, and community service. Offenders are also provided the opportunity to regain their dignity and to become connected or reconnected to the community. Restorative justice is most commonly applied with juvenile offenders and with adults who have committed minor crimes, although restorative processes are also used with more serious offenses and may be concurrent with an offender's incarceration. Restorative justice provides a balanced response to the needs of victims, offenders, and communities, and many social workers appreciate its focus on healing and repairing relationships and its strength-based approach. Social workers' roles often include preparing victims and offenders for their meetings with each other and facilitating victim-offender mediation sessions.

SUMMARY

The problems of criminally involved juveniles and adults touch not only their own lives but also the lives of their families and communities. Social workers can contribute at multiple levels and in many settings to help offenders make positive changes and to bring about positive changes in the justice system. When such change occurs, society also benefits. At the macro level, social workers are needed to shape policies and develop and administer programs that are just and responsive to complex human needs. Reformers working outside specific criminal justice facilities, perhaps in legal organizations or as lobbyists, can promote laws and policies that advance rehabilitation. At the micro level, social workers are needed inside law enforcement agencies, court systems, and correctional facilities, where they work to make these places more humane and effective, and with individuals to bring about constructive changes, one client at a time. There is even a role for social workers who do not really want to be involved with the justice system or its clients. Social workers are needed in communities, schools, and agencies and organizations to assist families with the problems they face and to work to change systems that contribute to social ills. Prevention work is vital if individuals are to be diverted from justice system involvement in the first place. There is mounting evidence that the public wants more from the justice system than retribution or punishment. Much of the public values rehabilitation and restoration as well. Social workers have an important role to play in working toward a greater balance between these priorities.

SUGGESTED READING

Conover, T. (2000). *Newjack: Guarding Sing Sing.* New York: Random House. This book describes the experiences of Ted Conover, a prison guard who took the job for the purpose of learning and writing about prison and what it is like for those who work there. The people he worked with did not know that he was writing a book.

O'Brien, P. (2001). *Making it in the "free world": Women in transition from prison.* Albany: State University of New York Press. This is a discussion of the results of a qualitative study that explores the challenges facing a sample of women as they reenter their communities after serving prison time.

Santos, M. G. (2004). *About prison.* Belmont, CA: Wadsworth/Thomson. Santos, a federal prisoner serving a long sentence for drug-related charges, provides an insider's perspective on life in prison.

Sommers, E. K. (1995). *Voices from within: Women who have broken the law.* Toronto: University of Toronto Press. This book discusses the results of a qualitative study that explored how a sample of women in prison came to be involved in criminal behavior leading to incarceration.

THE WORLD WIDE WEB OF SOCIAL WORK

American Probation and Parole Association http://www.appa-net.org
This is an international association that is actively involved with probation, parole, and community corrections in adult and juvenile justice. The site explores issues relevant to community-based corrections and offers a list of publications, links, and training information.

Criminal Justice System Processing Flowchart
http://www.fsu.edu/~crimdo/cj-flowchart.html
Maintained by the Department of Criminology and Criminal Justice at Florida State University, this Web site describes the sequence of events in the criminal justice system.

Human Rights Watch Prison Project http://www.hrw.org/advocacy/prisons

This is an independent nongovernmental organization committed to protecting human rights around the world. The Web site offers a wealth of information on prison conditions around the world, international human rights standards applicable to prisoners, and prison-related activities of the United Nations and other organizations.

National Criminal Justice Reference Service http://www.ncjrs.org

This reference service is a federally funded resource that supports research, policy, and program development. The Web site provides information and statistics about crime, victims, offenders, and the juvenile and adult justice systems in the United States, including law enforcement, courts, and corrections.

Office for Victims of Crime http://www.ovc.gov

This office was established in 1988 to provide leadership and funding for crime victims. Sponsored by the U.S. Department of Justice Publications, this site provides links and information on programs that benefit crime victims.

The Sentencing Project http://www.sentencingproject.org

This national organization advocates sentencing reform and alternatives to incarceration. The Web site provides information about crime, courts, sentencing, criminal justice policy analysis, punishment, alternatives to incarceration, jails, prisons, race, economic class, and reform and focuses on the development of alternative sentencing programs.

Sourcebook of Criminal Justice Statistics http://www.albany.edu/sourcebook

Operated by the University of Albany, New York, and funded by the U.S. Department of Justice, Bureau of Justice Statistics, this indexed and fully searchable site presents data tables on criminal justice topics from over one hundred sources.

Victim-Offender Reconciliation Program Information and Resource Center http://www.vorp.com

This program promotes restorative justice approaches to crime as a more effective and humane response than incarceration. The Web site offers articles, training, and consulting on restorative justice and victim-offender mediation.

Rural Social Work Practice

Suzie T. Cashwell and Mary Margaret Just

Rural social work offers opportunities to practice with a variety of people and to address a variety of social concerns. The nature of rural communities provides many challenges. This chapter describes rural communities in the United States and provides a glimpse into rural social work practice.

Hundreds of works of American literature are set in rural America. From the steamy, seamy environs of William Faulkner's Yoknapatawpha County, Mississippi, to the rural Western setting of E. Annie Proulx's cowboy love story "Brokeback Mountain," each of these works gives particular impressions of life in rural areas. Popular culture reinforces the many inaccurate ideas that people have about rural America. One myth is that these rural communities are pastoral Edens where people live a purer, simpler life than they do in cities. Rural areas are, however, far from uniform, simple, or uncomplicated. One of the most exciting parts of rural social work practice is the diversity that thrives in rural America. Cars share the roads with Amish horse-drawn buggies in rural Ohio. A Mexican grocery store on Main Street in Morehead, Kentucky, sells to a growing Spanish-speaking population in Appalachia. Vietnamese refugees from a former French colony in Asia survive hurricanes on the shores of the Gulf of Mexico along with the French-speaking descendants of refugees from Acadia. Social workers who practice in rural areas often find themselves in the thick of these complex communities.

While there are similarities between rural social work and urban social work, rural practice is unique in many ways. For example, the area a rural social worker covers may require her to drive many miles to see clients. When driving is impossible in areas like Alaska, and clients are many miles away, social workers may travel by airplane or boat. Rural social work also offers many opportunities for creativity, since the policies and procedures written in Washington, D.C., and state capitals are often based on assumptions that do not apply to rural realities. For example, regulations that require clients to come to offices to renew their applications for Temporary Assistance for Needy Families, Medicaid, or food stamps may be an undue burden for people who have no car and no access to public transportation and live far from welfare offices. Complying with job search and work requirements may be nearly impossible.

Social workers may be the only social service professionals in rural areas. Because they possess skills and knowledge that no one else in the community may have, rural social workers often command special respect from doctors, lawyers, clergy, and other community professionals. Clients are not always aware of social workers' qualifications, but they respect social workers, who help them meet basic needs or provide services like affordable mental health care. In rural areas, the people social workers know, to whom they are related, and who want to know them can also be very important. Above all, social workers in rural and urban communities fare best when they are genuine and professional, no matter what the situation.

DEFINING RURAL AMERICA

Most of us are positive that New York City is not rural, but we have a more difficult time deciding if Paris, Kentucky (population 9,183), or Bowling Green, Kentucky (population 49,296), is rural. Both Paris and Bowling Green are certainly much more rural than New York City, but not as rural as Betsy Lane, Kentucky (population 450), or South Union, Kentucky (population 75). Rural describes a continuum.

The U.S. Census Bureau (2005) defines *rural* simply as not urban. An urban area is defined as "a large central place and adjacent densely settled census blocks that together have a total population of at least 2,500 for urban clusters, or 50,000, for urbanized areas." According to the Economic Research Service (2004), rural America comprises 80 percent of the nation's land, and only 20 percent of the nation's total population. Some see *rural* as describing areas with fewer jobs, a lack of cultural amenities, and inadequate health and human services. These perceptions create a negative image and obscure what rural residents are doing to preserve economic and social opportunities in their communities and attract new ones.

Many rural areas are rich in natural and human-made resources, which allows residents to be creative and innovative. Historically, the natural resources have been extracted to profit a few people in other areas, but in a number of rural areas, natural resources are being preserved for local benefit and ecotourism. Cultural artifacts can be found in public schools and regional universities (music, art, and drama productions), church music programs, and libraries. In the end, determining if the area where one works is rural may be more about a feeling or sense of community than about Census Bureau definitions.

PERSPECTIVES ON RURAL LIFE

Who are the approximately 20 percent (over 59 million people) of the nation's population who live in rural areas? What are their ways of life?

What unique challenges do they face? What are the opportunities for social workers in these communities? Before we can explore those questions, we need to examine some of the characteristics of rural life. To do so, we look at media portrayals, culture and diversity, economics, and social trends that affect rural life and contribute to social work practice opportunities.

The Media

Close your eyes and reflect one moment on the word *rural*. What comes to mind? A small, tidy white house down a long dirt road? An open pasture with cows? Abandoned one-room schoolhouses? From Horace Greeley's "Go West, young man, go West!" which encouraged nineteenth-century white Americans to fill what had been American Indian lands, to TV shows like *The Beverly Hillbillies* and Paris Hilton's *The Simple Life*, the media presents models of rural life that promote political agendas or commercial interests. Rural social workers are concerned with how to use the media to better serve clients. The Internet, twenty-four-hour news via satellites, and cell towers are shrinking the electronic divide between urban and rural America (Ginsberg, 2005), but this brings with it the risk of simply importing urban perceptions and reinforcing the oversimplification of rural reality.

After Hurricanes Katrina and Rita in the fall of 2005, the national media failed to focus on the plight of the rural communities in Louisiana, Mississippi, and Texas that were hit and destroyed. The impact on large cities such as New Orleans and Houston overshadowed the impact on Waverly, Mississippi, and Vidor, Texas. Rural social workers often find themselves functioning in the role of public relations representatives so their clients can get needed resources. The Rural Social Work Caucus, a group of professional social workers and educators dedicated to rural social work practice, have identified a need for improved media communication for matters concerning rural areas. This group used the Internet to identify gaps in information about disaster relief and relay the concerns of the non-metropolitan areas devastated by the storms. Caucus members used Listservs and e-mail to provide the online addresses of radio stations in the affected areas to social work educators, students, and practitioners, which enabled them to obtain information that was not provided by the national news.

Culture and Diversity

Social workers must recognize rural commonalities and show respect for accepted community norms and standards. Though particular cultural groups and their values may dominate in certain regions, rural areas are seldom populated by individuals who are all of the same race, ethnicity, religion, political allegiance, or socioeconomic status. For centuries, people of color have lived in the economically disadvantaged rural communities of the Deep South and the Southwest, and on American Indian reservations in the North. However, in Appalachia, the economically disadvantaged population is primarily white and of European descent. In the past two decades, rural areas have seen an influx of political refugees from Eastern European countries such as Bosnia-Herzegovina.

Rural residents are also diverse with respect to language. Since immigrants first came to what is now the United States, there have been rural residents whose first language was not English. Norwegians, Swedes, and Danes came to the Midwest, and people from German-speaking areas settled in Pennsylvania and the Hill Country of Texas. Spanish-speaking people remained in California and the Southwest even after the United States claimed that land. Due to recent trends in immigration, social workers in rural communities frequently work with families from other countries who have little or no command of English. Social workers who are fluent in Spanish or other languages are as highly valued in rural areas as they are in urban areas, and culturally competent services are a must no matter where one practices.

Parochialism and Patriotism

Parochialism and patriotism, a strong loyalty to one's community and country, are core components of rural culture. Respondents in a Kellogg Foundation (2001) study described rural Americans as hardworking and having a strong sense of family and commitment to community. The standing of an individual's family in the community often strongly influences his or her access to opportunity and power. For example, if a social worker comes from a family that has resided in the community for multiple generations and the community views that family in a positive light, then it is more likely the worker will be able to be effective. Politics in rural communities tends to be personal. Candidates are often elected due to whom they are or are not related to rather than party affiliation or political platform.

Rural Americans are often veterans of the armed services, and their family names appear on the memorials on courthouse lawns. There is a strong sense that one does one's duty for "God and Country." Rural areas tend to be conservative, and residents have a strong allegiance to constitutional values such as the right to hold property and bear arms. However, some rural communities, from enclaves of aging hippies to armed camps of survivalists, are known for liberal, laissez-faire, or extremist attitudes.

Given that rural communities tend to be wary of outsiders due to repeated incidents of newcomers exploiting rural residents, social work practitioners who are not from rural areas may have to prove themselves before they can deliver services effectively. Even natives may need to prove themselves when they become professional social workers, due to the fear that these newly credentialed individuals may have sold out to city ways. There are some types of social work, particularly child welfare, in which ignorance of local culture and standards can lead to tragic errors in judgment. On the other hand, objectivity may be extremely difficult for the worker to maintain, and even more difficult to convince the community of, if the worker is kin to people who are being investigated or to law enforcement and court personnel. Therefore, rural social workers need to integrate themselves into the community in order to be seen as fair, objective, and part of the community.

Fundamentalism and Fatalism

Residents of rural areas tend to be fundamentalist. Sticking to fundamentalist biological, social, economic, psychological, philosophical, and religious beliefs may be necessary for survival in remote, sparsely populated areas. A fatalist perspective is not uncommon among those who depend upon the land for survival. Droughts, flooding, some illnesses, and many injuries are beyond farmers' control and are viewed as acts of God and God's will.

Across much of the southern United States, Baptists outnumber other religious groups, while in other regions the majority may be Catholic, as in rural Louisiana, or Amish, as in parts of Pennsylvania. Although the community may have one dominant faith, other faiths are also frequently represented (Ginsberg, 2005). The majority faith tends to have considerable influence on community culture, but rural America brings together people who espouse a variety of religions and conflicting religious views. Although Moravians and Czech Catholics both came to Texas from what is now the Czech Republic, lingering resentments dating back to the Protestant Reformation can make placing a Moravian woman and a Czech Catholic woman in the same room at a nursing home problematic. The social worker often takes responsibility for helping agencies, staff, and community residents understand and appreciate diversity.

In many rural communities, clergy have significant influence. Watkins (2004) writes that "In communities with few highly educated persons, ministers hold high status, and their influence increases by the fact that they often reinforce messages handed down by tradition, rather than introducing new ideas as mental health professionals or other well educated newcomers are likely to do" (p. 6). However, today many members of the clergy are educated in contemporary theories of mental health and are glad to refer people to social workers with expertise in mental health, alcohol and drug problems, or other areas. For example, in rural Michigan, the pastor of a small church might call a social worker to ask where he can send a woman whose husband is abusing her. Social workers see the clergy as resources as well as referral sources who can communicate important messages about the prevention of social problems and intervention to congregants.

Rural and urban religious institutions face many similar challenges, such as declining memberships over the past thirty years. Rural congregations are also suffering from a lack of younger people due to out-migration, which further restricts the services and programs they can offer (Kimbrough-Melton, 2001). Cashwell and McNeece (2000) found that women in rural communities who are leaving welfare do not seek assistance from churches. This may be explained by diminished church resources caused by shrinking memberships, depressed economies, and increases in the percentage of members who are extremely poor. Furthermore, rural churches have difficulty attracting clergy. Rural ministers may be laypeople who have to work full-time in addition to their responsibility for a church. Rural social workers too often find that the informal and formal church resources they once used to help their clients are disappearing.

DEMOGRAPHIC, ECONOMIC, AND SOCIAL CONCERNS

Social workers work to understand the rapidly changing socioeconomic and demographic trends that rural communities are facing and help communities respond.

Population Shifts

Though the population of rural areas declined as urban centers boomed, between 2000 and 2003, rural populations grew by .4 percent, compared to 1.3 percent in urban areas (Economic Research Service, 2004). While out-migration has slowed, it remains a problem in rural areas, especially among the young. Most rural-area growth is associated with the increase in bedroom communities adjacent to urban centers. Bedroom communities offer rural scenery and a quieter way of life while allowing residents to earn urban-area incomes (Economic Research Service, 2004). The bulk of this in-migration occurred in the rural South and West (Kimbrough-Melton, 2001). In the upper Midwest and New England, tourism and recreation have led to some growth, and an increase in the Hispanic population accounts for some growth in rural counties in the South, West, and Midwest (Economic Research Service, 2004).

Rural areas have seen a larger increase in the percentage of the elderly in the population. The aging of rural America will increase health and human services caseloads and at the same time provide opportunities for social workers to encourage change. For example, older people vote more than younger people, which gives social workers leverage with local politicians to help create needed services. The growing number of voting seniors may have influenced the nation's funding sources, such as the National Institute of Health, which has recently begun to focus on rural areas, and will hopefully lead to more federal funding for services.

Education

Social workers in public education have many opportunities to have an impact on young people's lives. Eighty percent of the counties with the lowest educational achievement in the United States are located in rural communities, and over 70 percent are in the rural South (Gibbs, 2005). As chapter 13 noted, low levels of education and persistent poverty are closely related. For example, 24 percent of rural residents over the age of eighteen lack a high school education, compared to 17 percent of urban residents (Kimbrough-Melton, 2001). Rural residents are less likely than urban residents to attend college, and those who do enroll are less likely to graduate. The problem is even more pervasive on reservations. American Indians have the lowest level of education of any major ethnic group. Improving children's chances of academic achievement is a critical role of social workers.

The one-room schoolhouse once met much of rural America's educational needs. Over the past few decades, many small communities lost their schools as school districts consolidated to save money (Kimbrough-Melton, 2001). In consolidated school districts, some children catch the bus before the sun comes up and spend two hours or more each day traveling to and from school. Consolidation also altered relationships between parents and teachers. Teachers are no longer neighbors with whom parents attend church and shop in the local grocery store. Even if parents and teachers recognize one another at the Super Wal-Mart in a neighboring town, they may not take the time or feel it is the appropriate place to talk about a child. Likewise, school social workers in larger districts may not have natural connections with families. The social worker can be seen as a stranger, unfamiliar and perhaps even hostile to the family. Rural school social workers need to establish a reputation for being genuinely helpful despite barriers posed by distance and suspicion.

Employment and Economic Activity

Several factors have shaped the employment and unemployment picture in rural areas. Although farming was once the primary rural occupation, rural communities everywhere are in transition. The family farm is gone, and agribusiness corporations have become America's main food producers.

Rural areas have also been disproportionately affected by the loss of textile and apparel jobs over the last few years, especially in the Southeast, where plants were concentrated (Economic Research Service, 2004). Lost jobs are like falling dominos, affecting individuals' and families' abilities to meet basic needs for food, shelter, health care, and healthy recreation. Unemployment creates tensions within marriages, breaks up families, and damages self-esteem and the ability to achieve personal goals and live up to personal and societal expectations. Young people who wish to remain in rural communities may be forced to move to suburban and rural areas for decent jobs (McLaughlin, 2002).

Shifting economies have forced many rural communities to redefine their economic and social institutions. Some now rely on tourism. Main streets that were once home to grocery stores, hardware stores, restaurants, movie theaters, and locally owned banks now feature a succession of antique stores and craft boutiques. Some rural communities now host casinos at least nominally owned by American Indian tribes. Some areas have successfully attracted new industries because of lower operating costs and low-cost housing and attractive living environments for employees. The availability of qualified employees, access to training, and a transportation infrastructure can also make rural areas desirable locations for industry (Gale, McGranahan, Teixeira, & Greenberg, 1999). Rural areas that lack these characteristics and have been negatively affected by federal policies such as the North American Free Trade Agreement (which eliminates tariffs on many imported goods) have suffered.

Military installation closures have affected rural areas as well. Rural areas, which depended on military dollars for their schools as well as private employment, have been forced to find creative economic markets for this land. For example, the site of Wurtsmith Air Force Base in Michigan was used to increase the number of factories and availability of affordable housing, and the closure of Kincheloe Air Force Base led to the creation of two correctional facilities. The establishment of so many prisons in rural areas has increased employment opportunities and also raised questions about whether this type of industry is best for rural communities or for the many individuals from urban areas who are incarcerated there (Huling, 2002).

Housing

Although 76 percent of U.S. families in nonmetropolitan areas own their own homes, as opposed to 70 percent in metropolitan areas (U.S. Census Bureau, 2007), rural families are three times more likely to live in mobile homes (Kimbrough-Melton, 2001). Since the value of mobile homes depreciates rapidly, they do not provide the financial equity of houses. Mobile homes also present greater safety risks in tornadoes, hurricanes, and other natural disasters. Furthermore, 15 percent of rural counties are housing stressed, meaning that at least 30 percent of homes are considered too costly relative to family income or too crowded, or they lack some basic facility like a kitchen or bathroom (Economic Research Service, 2004). Affordable housing is in critically short supply all across the United States.

In rural areas, temporary housing facilities, such as homeless shelters and domestic violence shelters, are likely to serve a ten-county area with as few as ten to twenty beds. Social workers in child protective services agencies may remove children from families living in unsafe or substandard housing and find it difficult to return them when no adequate housing is available for them.

Transportation

Thirteen of every fourteen rural households own an automobile, but 57 percent of low-income rural residents do not own a car, and 40 percent live in areas with no form of public transportation (Kimbrough-Melton, 2001). Less than 10 percent of welfare recipients have a car (Stommes & Brown, 2002). Individuals and families without a car or truck who live miles from the near-

It is often difficult for clients in rural areas to access transportation to get to necessary appointments. Here a social worker in rural West Virginia provides an elderly client with transportation to a clinic.
© Mary Whelens

est town may have to rely on family members or friends to get to stores, doctors, clinics, hospitals, public assistance offices, and other necessary appointments. Getting a ride may involve paying for fuel or much more exorbitant costs. It may also mean hitchhiking, which can be dangerous.

Where it does exist, public transportation may not be flexible or reliable (Marson & Powell, 2000). What serves as public transportation may vary widely from location to location. One estimate is that approximately 50 percent of rural counties nationwide have some form of public transit system, but it is usually available only in the more populated rural areas (Stommes & Brown, 2002). Railroads have been eliminating stops for over fifty years, so small town and rural residents have lost access to an affordable means of travel for both short and long trips. Bus services that once linked communities have vanished. County-based, grant-dependent programs often get start-up funds, not ongoing funds; transportation generally stops at the county line today and is gone tomorrow (Stommes & Brown, 2002). A program can document the need for fifty vehicles and get funds for one (Stommes & Brown, 2002). The situation becomes particularly problematic if the public vehicle breaks down or the driver becomes incapacitated. The lack of low-cost public transportation may prohibit travel to nearby counties for work, medical appointments, and other needs. Even if taxis are available, they may be too costly for many to use.

Rural social workers often advocate the development and better utilization of transportation resources. They are involved in finding grant opportunities; writing grants; collaborating with community action programs, area agencies on aging, and county and municipal governments; negotiating with nonprofit groups; and sorting out issues of liability and insurance, which are always factors whether transportation is provided free or for a fee.

Poverty and Homelessness

In 2005, the rural median annual income hovered around $37,600 and averaged about $11,000 less than the urban median income (DeNavas-Walt, Proctor, & Lee, 2006). Nearly 12 percent of rural households are food insecure, which means that all household members consistently lack food sufficient for an active, healthy life (Economic Research Service, 2004). In the aggregate, rural areas have somewhat less poverty than inner cities, but both have substantially more poverty than the suburbs. Poverty is the major challenge facing rural communities. Fourteen percent of rural households are poor, compared to 12 percent of urban households (DeNavas-Walt et al., 2006). Ninety-five percent of the counties with a poverty rate of over 20 percent in every census since 1960 are rural (Miller & Weber, 2004). Only 2 percent of urban counties suffer from persistent poverty, but 16 percent of rural counties qualify as persistent-poverty counties. In the South, over 25 percent of the population lives in counties with persistent poverty

(Economic Research Service, 2004). Like their urban counterparts, people of color in nonmetropolitan areas face much higher poverty rates than whites; for American Indians and African Americans, rates are three times higher, and for Hispanics they are two-and-a-half times higher (Economic Research Service, 2004).

Child poverty rates in the United States are higher than in most industrialized nations, and this is only worse in rural areas of the United States. Children in rural areas are more likely to be poor, to receive food assistance, and to have no health insurance than children in urban areas (see table 15.1) (Economic Research Service, 2004; Harris & Zimmerman, 2003). Only in the Midwest does poverty in metropolitan areas exceed poverty in nonmetropolitan areas. American Indian children in northern Plains states and children living in central Appalachia, the Deep South, and states bordering Mexico are the most likely to be poor (Rogers, 2005). Poverty rates for older Americans in rural areas also exceed rates for older Americans in urban areas. Rural social workers learn to help individuals and families use the limited resources available, encourage communities to support services for low-income individuals, and advocate state and national policies and funding to alleviate poverty.

Table 15.1   Poverty rates of children (eighteen years old and younger) by region and residence, 2001

Area	Total child poverty rate	Nonmetro child poverty rate	Metro child poverty rate
South	18.9%	24.9%	17.3%
Northeast	14.7%	20.1%	14.1%
Midwest	13.3%	13.0%	13.4%
West	16.0%	20.9%	15.3%
United States	16.3%	20.3%	15.4%

Source: U.S. Census Bureau. (2002). *Current population survey*. Retrieved February 25, 2007, from http://www.census.gov/hhes/www/poverty/poverty.html

The urban homeless seem to gather in public spaces. In rural areas, homeless individuals tend to live with family or friends in the community and move often. The rural homeless person is most likely to be white and female. She is probably employed, married, and homeless due to domestic violence rather than substance abuse, characteristics that differ from those of most urban homeless individuals (Kimbrough-Melton, 2001).

Among the newer groups of homeless people are the thousands of rural residents in the states bordering the Gulf of Mexico who were displaced by Hurricanes Katrina and Rita. People across the South, particularly in rural areas, lost their homes, possessions, families, and friends, and much of the social infrastructure and the social services safety net evaporated with the storm. The National Association of Social Workers sent out a call for help,

In the United States, children in rural areas—especially children of color—are at increased risk of living in poverty. This child lives in a migrant labor camp in rural Michigan.
© Mary Whelens

and social workers will be helping people deal with the aftermath of the hurricanes for years to come. Social workers working for agencies such as the American Red Cross are experts in disaster preparedness and response. Social workers must be able to communicate effectively with the have-nots who need help, as well as the haves who can support social welfare efforts. Social workers give a voice to the voiceless. They use their crisis intervention and communication skills and their creativity to help people find stable and affordable housing and reestablish their lives.

Crime

Despite visions of rural areas as crime-free Meccas where people leave their doors unlocked, in 1998, there were over 848,000 arrests in rural counties. Urban crimes tend to occur in public places; rural crimes occur more often in homes, and the offender is more likely to be someone the victim knows (National Center on Rural Justice and Crime, 2004). Deviant behavior may be less tolerated in rural areas than in urban areas. Alcohol and drug abuse are seen as having a higher correlation with violent crimes in rural areas than in urban areas (Jobes, 1999).

Methamphetamines, also known as meth, speed, and ice, have been produced since the late 1800s. Over the last decade, isolated rural areas have become meth production havens. According to National Public Radio (2004), 949 meth labs in rural areas nationwide were reported in 1998, and 9,385 in 2003. Social workers specializing in drug and alcohol treatment are not the only ones concerned. Those in health care and child welfare have been forced to develop new resources and ways of intervening. As box 15.1 demonstrates, meth labs are a tremendous concern of child welfare workers in rural areas.

Box 15.1 Picking up Kids from a Meth Lab

Sherri is a social worker at the local child welfare office in the community in which she was born and raised. She receives a crisis call at seven o'clock on Saturday night. The local law enforcement officers inform her that they are at a house out on the far side of the county. They need her to place three children in foster care. The parents, Lee and Louise, are being arrested for manufacturing and distributing drugs.

Sherri knows a little about this family. She and Louise were friendly in high school. Louise's family was very vocal about their belief that all alcohol should be banned in the community. In the 1950s, her grandparents led crusades to maintain Prohibition in Oklahoma. When that war was lost, they continued to fight to restrict the locations and times at which alcohol could be sold. She remembers Lee vaguely. He moved to the area his senior year of high school. His father had been arrested several times for marijuana possession.

Sherri drives the thirty miles from her home to the far side of the county. She is thinking about where to place the three children. According to the officer, they are all under five years old. She turns off the main paved road. The road is full of ruts, potholes, and rocks. She hopes her car will make it.

Upon arriving at the home, Sherri notices that there is trash all over the yard and the windows of the mobile home are covered in tinfoil. In addition to beer cans, she sees sinus pill boxes, drain cleaner jugs, and camp fuel containers scattered all over. As she begins to walk into the house, the officer stops her and tells her she can't go inside because it is dangerous. She smells a strong odor as she steps back. The deputy directs her to the sheriff's car, where the three children are sitting in the backseat in oversized T-shirts advertising the softball team of the local sheriff's office. She informs the officer that she needs to go in and get their stuff. He replies, "I am sorry. They can't take anything with them. This is a meth house. Everything is toxic. Once we are through here, everything will be destroyed."

Sherri must now try to minimize the children's trauma at being separated from their parents without so much as their own clothes and toys. She will need to find a foster home willing to take three children under the age of five. She will begin making calls once she is back in mobile phone range. For now, Sherri puts the three children in car seats and begins back down the dirt road. She will interview the parents at the county jail the next morning.

Mutual-Aid and Natural Helping Networks

Rural areas often lack readily available and affordable child care, health care, housing, and transportation (Kimbrough-Melton, 2001). Despite the effects of out-migration on the social network required for mutual aid, friends and neighbors in rural areas traditionally provide services that private and not-for-profit associations provide in urban areas, such as child care. Private insurance and government payments for health services have disrupted the barter system for services that rural residents once employed. For example, one wonders how the state Medicaid program calculates "usual charges" for a country doctor in rural south Georgia known for treating individuals in exchange for fresh garden vegetables.

COMMUNITY-BASED SOCIAL WORK PRACTICE

Both urban and rural social workers work in public agencies; nonprofit agencies, including faith-based service organizations; and for-profit organizations, including private practice. They also work with similar populations—children, families, older adults, and individuals with physical and mental disabilities—and have the same skills, knowledge, values, and ethics. The difference between their work lies in the context and environment.

Allocating Scarce Resources

If allocating scarce public resources is a rational process, it can be argued that urban workers provide more units of service than rural workers. If allocation of resources is political and dependent on campaign donations or the number of votes an area can deliver, cities likely win. However, if allocations depend on lobbying efforts, then administrators, workers, support staff, and service recipients can inform policy makers about the needs in rural areas, making the most of personal contacts and well-publicized visits to county seats, state capitals, and Washington, D.C. Legislative advocacy is a critical part of the work social workers do in rural areas, and some rural areas benefit because many of their representatives and senators have long tenure in Congress or state legislatures.

Becoming Part of Rural Communities

Despite repeated cautions, there are always those who come to rural areas determined to bring enlightenment to rural residents. New workers need skill and patience to make their education and experience useful to the communities and people they serve. Establishing commonalities, becoming a part of the community to the extent possible, and understanding an area's history and power structure take time. Nobody likes the carpetbaggers who rush in saying that they are there to help but instead intend to do well for themselves and then proceed to the next opportunity.

On the other hand, being from an area does not necessarily mean that one truly understands all segments of the community or knows the local history as various groups and individuals remember it. Furthermore, one can never be certain that family prestige or notoriety will translate into power or community disrespect. Whether you are a traditional student returning to a rural community as an educated young adult or a nontraditional student making the transition from your former status in the community, as a newly minted responsible professional, you should always be cautious and circumspect in this situation.

Rural social workers have many opportunities to learn from the community. In fact, social workers in rural areas are often forced to learn faster and learn more skills due to the scarcity of professionals. Ginsberg (2005) suggests that social workers in rural areas can have more independence, more chances to see results from their efforts, and a greater likelihood of prestige and promotion. Although the roles, skills, and knowledge required for rural social work are similar to those needed by social workers in urban areas, the ways in which those roles, skills, and knowledge are used can be different. Sitting next to the county judge or county commissioner most mornings at the local café before the workday begins can make for a relationship that most urban social workers would find difficult to cultivate.

Education for Rural Social Work Practice

In rural areas, a BSW may be the only degree you need. However, it should not be the only education you want. Many regional universities offer a BSW and an MSW tailored to the needs of the service area, in this case, rural social work. Child welfare agencies across the country fund BSW and MSW education. Some provide paid work-release time and cover the costs of tuition, books, and fees, but programs vary from state to state and usually require some form of work repayment. Two federal programs—the National Health Service Corps Loan Repayment Program and the Perkins Loan Forgiveness Program—forgive at least part of educational loans in exchange for work in underserved areas.

To be lifelong learners, social workers in rural areas need access to university libraries with databases that offer full-text versions of articles from hundreds of professional journals. Since most rural public libraries do not collect journals for any profession, a good Internet connection is a necessity for accessing resources that are available online. Continuing education workshops and conferences also help social workers continue to gain competency in a wide variety of areas. Workshops are not often held in rural areas, so social workers must travel to cities to attend them. Workshops and conferences offer professional revitalization and put rural practitioners, who may have few colleagues in their areas, in touch with other social workers and related professionals. Rural workers are grateful when workshop presenters come to them. More workshops and conferences are being held online, and in addition, some universities offer social work degree programs via the Internet. This is a controversial practice for a profession where face-to-face contact is highly valued, but it is expanding educational opportunities, especially in remote areas and for those who cannot relocate to earn a degree.

Usually rural social workers do not specialize in one practice arena or one practice level. The rural social worker is often a jack-of-all-trades; he or she must master some areas, know who is master of others, and juggle many responsibilities. BSW education is predicated on the generalist practice model discussed in chapters 1 and 2. Generalists learn the problem-solving model of social work practice, which can be applied to virtually any area of practice. Any social worker using the generalist practice model works at micro, mezzo, and macro levels. In rural areas, social workers must transcend the traditional generalist model to develop an integrated model so they can practice at all levels simultaneously (Parsons, Jorgensen, & Hernandez, 1994). For example, family preservation social workers in rural areas probably work with children, their parents or other caretakers, the family as a group, the children's schools, and the courts. They also work on community development so that families get the resources they need, provide education, and advocate policy changes in their agencies and at the county, state, and federal levels so their rural clientele will be better served.

Strengths-Based Social Work Practice

Given the nature and culture of rural communities, social workers need to embrace a model that assumes that people already have ways to meet their needs. Individuals, families, groups, organizations, and communities have skills that work, even if these skills don't work the way other models prescribe (Parsons et al., 1994). Problem-focused models can define clients as dysfunctional, and communities as lacking resources, strengths, and links to sources of power. These definitions are themselves not particularly functional. A strengths-based model operates on the premise that individuals and families who function at any level are functional. Discerning how individuals, families, groups, organizations, and communities do function, and the sources of power they have, provides the strengths perspective that facilitates positive outcomes for each of these social systems (Saleebey, 1996).

In addition to individual and family strengths, rural communities benefit from natural helping networks of friends, religious groups, civic organizations, agricultural extension services, and other organizations. Perhaps the classic example of a natural helping network is the barn raising. When someone needs a barn, family and friends gather to help erect one. Today there is less need for barns, but the concept remains the same. Rural families and neighbors are known for helping, but as in other communities, ties may be weakening. Social workers not only utilize existing networks to assist clients, but they also help to strengthen networks that are financially strapped or face more problems than they can address.

Practice Challenges

A number of social work practice challenges are unique to rural communities.

The Goldfish Bowl   The smaller the rural community is, the greater is the likelihood that everyone knows just about everyone else. Living in this kind of goldfish bowl is one of the greatest challenges rural social workers face (see box 15.2). Social workers, especially those whose contacts are initially unwelcome (e.g., child abuse and neglect investigations, probation and parole cases, and mental health commitments), may feel that they are being closely scrutinized. Social workers can find it difficult to have a drink

---

Box 15.2   Living in a Goldfish Bowl

Betty, a child protection and permanency worker, is also a wife and mother in a rural town of about 1,000 people. Her latest assignment is assessing the situation at the Jones home. Mrs. Jones has recently become the caretaker of her grandchildren because her daughter, who lived in a nearby city, abandoned them. As usual, when Mrs. Jones comes to the front door, Betty thinks, "She looks familiar. Where have I seen her?"

After leaving the Jones house, Betty stops at a convenience store for gas and coffee. While she is checking out, the clerk asks, "How are things at the Jones place?" Betty responds with her standard quizzical look that says, "Would you want me to tell if it were you?" The clerk relates the story later to a friend, saying, "That social worker isn't real friendly, just sticks up her nose and goes on."

Betty and her husband drive to the local café for dinner. Mrs. Jones is there working behind the cash register. While Betty and her husband are eating, Mrs. Jones sits down at their table and begins to discuss how much getting promoted from the kitchen to the cash register will help her income. Mrs. Jones is very excited about this development in her life. Betty's husband and everyone else in the café can't help hearing everything Mrs. Jones says. Betty quietly tells Ms. Jones she'll see her tomorrow and they can talk then.

Betty is sure that if she loses her temper with her children in the grocery store, the news will be all over town in a nanosecond. Since she grew up in a small town, living in a goldfish bowl is not a new experience, and she maintains her awareness of the potential consequences of her actions, and her sense of humor.

at the local watering hole or do anything else that might compromise their reputations. Social workers' own families may encounter problems that draw the community's attention. In cities, neighbors may not think or care about what people do in their own homes, where they shop or what they buy, where they attend church, or what their problems are, but in rural areas, chances are that the neighbors know and care for one reason or another. Thus, rural social workers must establish their own comfort zones in the communities in which they both live and work.

Dual Relationships   A dual relationship exists when a social worker and current or former client have a relationship in addition to that of worker and client. A dual relationship can also involve a client's family members. Most people recognize that having a sexual relationship with a client is forbidden, but there are many other situations where social workers must avoid dual relationships. For example, when the emergency plumber who arrives at a social worker's home happens to be the father of a young man the social worker helped enter chemical dependency treatment in lieu of going to jail, the plumber may insist on doing the work for free. Though the social worker expresses appreciation for the plumber's offer, he also explains why he cannot accept the offer and promptly writes a check for the service. In rural communities, social workers often must conduct their day-to-day business in establishments where clients or their family members work.

Many other dual relationship situations present themselves in rural communities. For example, there might be only one social worker at the only good nursing home in the county. The mother of the local Rotary Club president is a resident, and the social worker is the Rotary Club secretary. Another resident is the father of the social worker's minister. Though you may not think of it this way, these cases present the perils of dual relationships. The social worker must take care not to give preferential treatment to these residents because of her relationship with their family members. If a fellow member of the church congregation approaches an urban social worker for help finding refuge from domestic violence, she may be able to refer the person to one of several shelters in the area. In rural areas, one shelter may serve several counties, and since the shelter is probably full, the rural county social worker may have to help the church member find another safe place to stay. In order to maintain professional boundaries and avoid a dual relationship, that place generally would not be the social worker's own home.

In rural areas, dealing with child protective services can be particularly personal and political, especially if the worker is from the area. For example, an on-call worker cannot answer a call to investigate her first cousin for child abuse, and she may prefer not to be assigned the call if the person being investigated is her minister, doctor, former teacher, or someone she knows well. Relationships do affect the assignment of investigations and ongoing service responsibilities, and sensitivity and creativity are often necessary when the number of staff is limited and relationships must be considered.

The NASW (1999) Code of Ethics cautions social workers to avoid dual relationships and, when they are unavoidable, demands frequent evaluation of "risk of exploitation and potential harm to the client" (section 1.06). This standard places considerable responsibility on rural social workers, who are highly likely to have other relationships with clients. Bosien and Bosch (2005) provide guidance for the rural practitioner who must handle dual relationships: social workers must maintain a heightened awareness of dual relationships. Developing any personal relationships with clients or former clients must be done cautiously and evaluated based on the client; the nature, intensity, and length of the social work intervention; and the likelihood of a future professional relationship. Since the social worker is always responsible for maintaining appropriate boundaries, he or she must have an advance plan for handling situations that may arise. In addition, training on handling dual relationships must be part of formal social work education and continuing education.

Confidentiality   In rural communities, client confidentiality can be difficult to maintain, and anonymity is nearly impossible, no matter how social workers try to uphold this obligation. When making home visits, a social worker may try to protect client confidentiality by parking where neighbors will not spot her car. Nevertheless, social workers often drive their own vehicles (which almost everyone recognizes) or a state car with the state emblem on the door (which everyone recognizes). The neighbors are very likely to speculate on what is happening, often because they already know that something is going on.

To protect confidentiality, the social worker must discuss with the client the possibility of encountering each other in public and role play how to handle encounters. Social workers must ask their own family members and friends not to ask questions about cases and, if they do, must handle questions efficiently and effectively without breaching confidentiality.

Situations that test social workers' skills in maintaining client confidentially often arise. Imagine that a child welfare worker comes to school to talk with a child about a report of abuse or neglect. Suppose the student aide on duty in the principal's office at the time the worker arrives is one of the agency's foster children and therefore knows the social worker. If no one thinks to send the aide on an errand or otherwise divert her attention, the aide will know that something is wrong. The social worker cannot foresee every possibility, but even when secrecy is not an option, discretion is.

Serving a Large Area Serving a large geographic area is a common challenge for rural social workers. Since workers may drive over two hundred miles a day, a reliable personal or agency vehicle is a necessity. Workers often get crisis calls regarding clients who live one or more counties away. In these cases, social workers learn to ask questions that will help them obtain an accurate description of the client's condition. Sometimes crises can or must be handled with phone calls to the appropriate authorities, such as law enforcement officers, in the immediate area. Often the situation can only be resolved or will be best resolved if the social worker goes to the client. In these situations, social workers give what instructions they can to control the situation until they arrive, provide an honest estimate of their arrival time, and drive cautiously, sometimes in unpredictable weather. Before the use of mobile phones became widespread, serving large areas was even more problematic, and workers still deal with areas in which mobile phones do not work well or at all. On many days, travel time may exceed the time spent with clients.

Practice Opportunities Though eligibility workers in public assistance programs may not be social workers, high poverty rates in some rural communities mean that social workers are likely to help clients get help from income assistance programs. Social workers who encounter less-than-respectful treatment of public assistance program applicants and participants from other professionals or the public have opportunities to show by example or more direct instruction the way individuals in need should be addressed and treated. Changes in public assistance (welfare) laws that require individuals to work for benefits can provide challenges for public assistance recipients and the social workers who assist them. In areas where unemployment is high, recipients may be exempt from this requirement.

In rural areas, health-care services may be even less adequate than in urban areas, especially for those without money or insurance. Health-care social work often involves working with physicians, nurses, and allied health professionals in the area. While differences of opinion may arise and turf wars sometimes ensue, there are also opportunities for building alliances that to some extent compensate for limited resources. Since some rural communities do not even have a doctor, social workers may be part of community efforts to attract physicians and other health-care providers to the area as well as expand insurance coverage and other routes to health care for rural residents.

Finding competent and full-time in-home caregivers for adults who are disabled is challenging in urban areas, often difficult in small towns, virtually impossible in rural areas, and very expensive everywhere. For better or for worse, nursing homes are an essential part of the health and social safety net in rural areas. Since federal law requires that all nursing homes employ a social worker—part time if the home has fewer than 110 beds, and full time if the nursing home is larger—nursing home social work is another employment opportunity in rural areas.

As chapter 7 discussed, the deinstitutionalization of individuals with severe mental illness is a notorious problem for both urban and rural areas because community-based mental health services are seriously underfunded and particularly sparse in rural areas. Individuals with severe mental illness and those with intellectual disabilities generally do not have a driver's license and are often unemployed. In remote areas they can become particularly isolated. Social work offers opportunities for developing long-term relationships with clients who need continuous or intermittent services, helping them live independently in the community, and building support systems that meet individual and community needs. For those who have entrepreneurial gifts and have developed the skills needed to obtain reimbursement from multiple funding sources, private practice in a small town can be ideal.

Child welfare agencies are begging for more social workers, especially in rural areas. Departments of child welfare and child protective services have benefited from federal funding for undergraduate and graduate study focused on child protection and permanency services (see chapter 11). In some states, child welfare certification programs move social work graduates directly from practicum to working with the agency without the months-long training period usually required before a new employee is ready to carry a caseload. In rural areas, these social workers often have added responsibilities of supervision, but turnover among child welfare workers is high. Many who move from urban to rural areas to fill these jobs do not stay long. Younger workers may prefer the lifestyles or the greater potential for meeting a life partner that more populous areas offer.

Some social workers are also employed in residential facilities that serve dependent or delinquent youths. Although residential children's homes (once called orphanages) are no longer as common as they once were, there are still young people who need this care. Residential facilities that specialize in meeting these children's needs and enhancing their ability to live in society as adults are often found in rural areas. Some are church-based programs that have long served children in need, and some are newer private programs that teach youths survival and independence skills. Social workers often hold positions in state agencies responsible for regulating these programs to ensure that children are being well cared for.

Domestic violence and elder abuse occur in rural as well as urban areas and at all socioeconomic levels. As chapter 12 discusses, adults may also neglect themselves due to mental or physical disabilities (see box 15.3). Adults can easily fall through holes in the social safety net, which tend to be larger in rural areas. Social workers' abilities to intervene effectively at every level from the individual to greater society and to evaluate the effectiveness of the intervention are an important aspect of adult pro-

---

Box 15.3 **Meeting a Disabled Woman's Needs in a Rural Community**

Sally is sixty years old. She has arthritis, fibromyalgia, multiple allergies, and type 2 diabetes. Her parents have long been deceased. Her only sibling, a brother, lives a day's drive away. She wants nothing to do with him since he sexually abused her when they were children. She says her faith has enabled her to let go of her fear and anger, but she has found that keeping her distance from him is better for her peace of mind. He remains very self-centered and has been in legal trouble for his involvement with minor females.

Sally lives in the house where she grew up, a few miles out of the county seat in the town where she went to school and worked as long as she was able. She never married. She is reluctant to ask anyone for help. She doesn't invite people to visit any more because she doesn't want anyone to see what her mother's immaculate house has become. Until she was no longer able to work, Sally was the secretary for a lawyer who was a close friend of her parents. He helped with her application for Social Security Disability Insurance. It was a long process involving a great deal of paperwork and an appeals process.

When a church member recently dropped by unexpectedly for the annual stewardship campaign, Sally's untenable situation was apparent. When the visitor went to get Sally a drink, she found the refrigerator full of moldy leftovers and badly in need of defrosting. She saw mouse droppings and could tell that Sally's dogs had not been let out of the house for some time.

Sally was embarrassed but sensible enough to accept any help available. Her visitor called adult protective services. Although the worker did not open a case, she assisted Sally in talking with her doctor so that he could certify that she needed home health-care services, including housekeeping and nursing. The social worker called Meals on Wheels and More, a federally assisted program that provides food to home-bound individuals age sixty and older. Sally has begun receiving one hot meal a day, and volunteers are coming to make repairs to her home and clean the yard. The social worker has also assisted Sally in obtaining Medicaid benefits (health-care insurance available to some low-income individuals, including those who are disabled) in addition to her Medicare benefits. Medicaid will help cover her Medicare deductibles and other out-of-pocket health-care expenses. The social worker also helped her obtain Supplemental Security Income benefits (public assistance benefits for low-income individuals with disabilities) to supplement her meager Social Security Disability Insurance check. At least for now, Sally can stay in her home rather than go to a nursing home.

---

tective services, which can be just as personal and political as child protective services.

SUMMARY

Millions of Americans live in rural areas, which are characterized by low population density. These rural communities are more diverse in race, language, loyalties, and beliefs than is usually reflected by the media. Compared to urban areas, rural areas tend to have a higher proportion of older people, less adequate education systems, and fewer employment opportunities for residents. Rural social workers deal with the common array of contemporary social concerns, including lack of affordable housing and transportation; dwindling job opportunities, especially for those who are not well educated; poverty; crime; drug abuse; homelessness; and the aftermath of natural disasters.

Rural social work practice offers many challenges and opportunities, including finding creative ways to use resources that are often scattered and scarce. Some of the challenges the rural social worker faces are lack of privacy, concerns about dual relationships with neighbors and others who may be clients, difficulties maintaining client confidentiality, and caseloads spread over large areas. To address these challenges, rural social workers need to become part of the community, be lifelong learners, and master the ability to work with individuals, groups, and communities simultaneously. With few other human service professionals in the immediate area, rural social workers often operate with a great deal of autonomy, learn many skills, and have opportunities to meet the range of human needs.

SUGGESTED READING

Allison, D. (1993). *Bastard out of Carolina*. New York: Plume Books. This book offers a searing look at unwed motherhood, domestic tragedy, and child abuse in mid-twentieth-century South Carolina.

Daley, M. R., & Doughty, M. O. (2006). Ethics complaints in social work practice: A rural-urban comparison. *Journal of Social Work Values and Ethics, 3*(2). Retrieved April 30, 2007, from http://www.socialworker.com/jswve/content/view/28/44. This study challenges stereotypes related to ethical issues in rural social work practice. Rural practitioners cannot escape ethical dilemmas. The key is recognizing situations that will lead to complaints. This article provides an overview of the ethical complaint typology in rural areas that is useful to rural practitioners.

Gillespie, P. E. (Ed.). (1982). *Foxfire 7*. Garden City, NY: Anchor Books. This Appalachian history of Christian religious denominations and practices illuminates the history of beliefs and worship in a part of the rural South.

Ginsberg, L. H. (Ed.). (2005). *Social work in rural communities* (4th ed.). Alexandria, VA: Council on Social Work Education. This leading rural practice book, a collection of essays by twenty-six scholars, addresses the extensive opportunities for rural social work. The editor, Leon Ginsberg, is one of the leading rural social work academicians in the United States.

Martinez-Brawley, E. E. (2000). *Close to home: Human services and the small community.* Washington DC: NASW Press. The author shares her understanding, acquired through decades of study, of the background of and possibilities offered by small-town social work practice.

Parsons, R. J., Jorgensen, J. D., & Hernandez, S. H. (1994). *The integration of social work practice.* Pacific Grove, CA: Brooks/Cole. The authors use an empowerment framework to organize interventions that are appropriate for social work practice in rural areas. This book focuses on a habilitation approach to social work rather than a rehabilitation approach. The book will help readers understand social work practice from a holistic systems approach.

Scales, T., & Streeter, C. L. (2004). *Rural social work: Building and sustaining community assets.* Pacific Grove, CA: Brooks/Cole. This text provides perspectives for macropractice in rural areas. This rural practice book will help the reader to gain an understanding of the relationship between micropractice and marcopractice in rural areas. It also provides a theoretical framework for understanding rural communities.

THE WORLD WIDE WEB OF SOCIAL WORK

Economic Research Service http://www.ers.usda.gov
ERS is part of the United States Department of Agriculture. It offers a comprehensive examination of rural issues and publishes two Web-based journals.

Library at the School of Social Work, University of Wisconsin–Madison http://www.library.wisc.edu/libraries/SocialWork/ruralsw.html
The Web site of the School of Social Work at the University of Wisconsin–Madison posts an updated list of Web sites relevant to rural social work.

Rural Social Work Caucus http://www.marson-and-associates.com/rural
We recommend membership in the Rural Social Work Caucus for students and professionals interested in rural practice. The caucus's Web site provides links to many resources and demonstrates how dependent rural social work is upon individuals who are willing to volunteer their time and skills.

Select Rural Social Welfare Websites https://portfolio.du.edu/portfolio/getportfoliofile?uid=20100
Paul Mackie, a graduate of the Graduate School of Social Work at the University of Denver, has prepared a useful list of Web sites with information about different rural social welfare issues.

Southern Rural Development Center http://srdc.msstate.edu
This center provides grants for rural social services and offers numerous publications for both scholarly and lay audiences.

16 International Social Work: Challenges and Opportunities in a Global Society

James Midgley

The profession of social work has spread around the globe. It is no longer an American or Western European phenomenon. Although there are no reliable estimates of the total number of professionally qualified social workers in the world today, the International Federation of Social Workers reports that its eighty national member associations together represent about a half-million social workers. In 1997, Garber reported that the International Association of Schools of Social Work had about 1,700 member schools in more than one hundred countries.

Social workers have been engaged in international activities for many years, and these activities have been intensifying in recent years. In the United States, many more social workers have engaged in forms of professional practice that involve collaboration with colleagues in other countries. Many more American social workers now attend international meetings and conferences, and many take study tours to learn about social work abroad. More international content is now being included in the social work curricula of American schools of social work, and many schools have established collaborative partnerships with schools of social work in other countries. It is now common for American schools to have international agreements for collaborative research and training activities. Florida State University, for example, offers student field placements in South Africa under the supervision of University of KwaZulu Natal. Many social work educators from other countries come to the United States to study the country's social services and social work practice approaches, and many American social workers go abroad to learn about the problems they face and the services and approaches they use.

The term *international social work* is widely used today to refer to these and other activities. However, the term is not well defined, and different writers use it to mean different things. While this can be frustrating, most social workers understand the term to refer to social work practice with people in different countries or to the professional exchanges that take place among social workers in different countries. Originally, the term was used to refer to social work practice in international agencies such as the

United Nations or the Red Cross, but today it describes all forms of social work practice involving international clients. Additionally, it reflects a growing awareness among social workers of the impact of international forces on professional practice everywhere. In its broadest sense, international social work includes everything from public social work services provided in the American Southwest to undocumented immigrants to private adoption services for American citizens adopting Romanian children, as well as services provided through international relief organizations to internally displaced people in Ethiopia.

This chapter provides an overview of the field that will be helpful to those of you who want to know more about international social work. It begins with an overview of the international linkages that have characterized social work's evolution, beginning when the profession was developed in the early twentieth century, and of the features of social work in different parts of the world today. Next, the chapter focuses on international social work practice, including opportunities for social workers to practice in other countries and in international social service and development agencies. However, special emphasis is given to the fact that all social workers in the United States now routinely encounter clients from other countries. In view of the increasing exposure of social workers to international realities, the chapter argues that international social work practice should be viewed not only as taking place abroad but as an integral part of everyday practice here in the United States. The chapter concludes with a discussion of the opportunities for and challenges of international social work today and by showing that a greater awareness and engagement with international realities can enrich the profession.

But first, the chapter provides a brief account of the historical development of the social work profession and an overview of the nature of social work practice in different countries. To understand international social work, one must be familiar with the way the profession evolved and appreciate how social workers in different parts of the world seek to foster social work's goals. Both will facilitate a better understanding of international social work.

HISTORY OF INTERNATIONAL SOCIAL WORK

Modern-day social work began to emerge in Europe and North America in the late nineteenth century. Although means of communication were not as well developed as they are today, the founders of social work in different countries communicated and shared experiences with each other. This resulted in the diffusion of new ideas to different parts of the world. One well-documented example of how an innovation in one country influenced social work's development in another country is the visit of Jane Addams and her friend Ellen Gates Starr to Toynbee Hall in London. Toynbee Hall was the first settlement house in the world. Addams and Starr were impressed with the settlement house idea. After returning to Chicago, in 1889, they established the Hull House settlement (Kendall, 2000). The first school of social work established in South America—and, indeed, outside Europe and North America—was opened in Santiago, Chile, in 1925 as a result of a collaboration between René Sand, a Belgian physician and secretary of the International Red Cross, and Alejandro Del Rio, a physician and Chilean government official. With Sand's help, Del Rio studied developments in Europe and, on his return to Chile, persuaded the Chilean government to establish a professional training school. The school subsequently merged with the Catholic University in Santiago. Sand also helped recruit a Belgian colleague, Jenny Bernier, to be the school's first director (Kendall, 2000).

Western Influences and the Spread of Social Work

Developments in professional social work in the United States were also adopted by Europeans and spread to Asia, Africa, the Caribbean, and the Pacific and Australasia. In some cases, missionaries played a key role. For example, in India, the Reverend Clifford Manshardt, a missionary employed by the American Board of Missions in Western India, established the country's first settlement house in 1926. It was located in a shantytown community in Bombay called Nagpada. Rev. Manshardt subsequently met Sir Dorabji Tata, the wealthy Indian industrialist, and as a result of their collaboration, the world-renowned Tata Institute of the Social Sciences was created in 1936. The institute was the first professional social work school in India, and Rev. Manshardt became its first director (Kendall, 2000). It continues to be one of India's most prestigious schools of social work and an internationally recognized leader in social work education.

The British imperial government in London also encouraged the introduction of social service programs in its colonial territories (Midgley, 1981). Usually this involved creating programs for young criminal offenders. Social workers from Britain were often recruited to establish these programs, and in time, they were augmented to respond to other pressing social needs such as child neglect, begging, and destitution. In many cases, a separate department of social welfare was established. For example, in 1943 the position of secretary of social services in the office of the colonial governor in Ghana was created. This development resulted in the creation in 1946 of a full-fledged department of social welfare and housing, which subsequently became known as the Department of Social Welfare and Community Development. The department assumed responsibility for a vocational training center for people with disabilities, several youth clubs, a juvenile court, and the probation service. It later expanded into rural areas by providing literacy education for farmers, village community centers, and assistance with small-scale agriculture and community road construction. In 1950, the department created its own social work training school, and in 1956, it entered into an agreement with the University of Ghana to establish a university-level social work program (Blavo & Apt, 1997).

The First International Professional Associations

An important event in the history of international social work was the creation of the first international professional associations. Healy (2001) reports that these associations evolved out of a major international social work conference held in Paris in July 1928 with representatives from forty-two countries. By the time a second international conference was held in Frankfurt, Germany, in 1932, three additional countries, including the United States, had joined. However, progress was severely impeded by the Second World War, and it was only in 1950 that a plan for reorganizing the group was discussed. The result of these efforts was the creation of the International Federation of Social Workers, established in 1956. Today, the federation represents national professional social work associations from eighty countries.

In 1929, forty-six schools from ten countries came together to found the International Committee of Schools of Social Work. The committee subsequently became known as the International Association of Schools of Social Work (Kendall, 2000). Today, the association represents schools of social work in more than one hundred countries.

Developments After World War II

In the years following World War II, the rise of Communist governments in Eastern Europe, China, and elsewhere impeded the international expansion of social work. Generally, these governments did not approve of social work. Although social work had been established in several countries that subsequently came under Communist rule, the profession was not well developed in these countries, and in many cases, the few social work schools that had been established disappeared. For example, schools of social work in China, which were among the oldest in Asia, were closed down after the Communist government came to power. On the other hand, in Poland, where the country's first school of social work was founded in 1925, professionally educated social workers continued to find employment in the government's social and health services (Healy, 2001).

While Communist governments in some parts of the world hampered the profession's development, social work expanded rapidly in the newly independent developing countries of the Global South in the 1950s and 1960s. In some cases, the foundations for social work's development had been laid by the colonial governments that had introduced public social service programs and supported the creation of social work schools. In the 1950s, the United Nations, which actively supported the international spread of social work, augmented the colonial governments' contributions.

United Nations advisors who traveled to the developing countries to assist governments to expand their welfare programs frequently proposed that professional social work schools be established. For example, in the early 1950s, a United Nations team advised the Pakistani government that professional training programs in social work were urgently needed to meet the staffing needs of the country's social welfare services. As a result, Pakistan's first professional school of social work was established in Lahore in 1954 (Midgley, 1981).

Recent Trends

Despite the retrenchment of government social service programs in many parts of the world in the 1970s and 1980s, social work programs continued to expand, particularly in Western industrial countries. In developing countries, on the other hand, serious debt problems and the imposition of structural adjustment programs by international agencies such as the World Bank have severely curtailed opportunities for professional practice in the public social services. However, the continued flow of international aid to the developing world has resulted in the expansion of nonprofit community-based organizations, many of which employ social workers.

Social work has also expanded in the former Soviet Union, the former Communist countries in Eastern Europe, and China. The first social work educational program in the Soviet Union was established at the Moscow Academy of Pedagogical Sciences during the Gorbachev administration in the mid-1980s, and by the early 1990s, about thirty social work programs had been created in the country (Guzetta, 1995). Social work schools have also been established in Eastern European countries such as Albania, Bulgaria, Lithuania, and Romania. There were similar developments in China in the late 1980s, when the government began to permit universities to establish social work courses. A unique feature of the development of social work in China has been a close collaboration between schools of social work in China and in Hong Kong and a determination on the part of Chinese social work educators to develop a curriculum that is uniquely suited to the country's needs (Yuen-Tsang & Sibin, 2002).

SOCIAL WORK ACROSS THE GLOBE: COMMONALITIES AND DIVERSITY

Although social workers have shared information and learned from each other for many years, it is only quite recently that detailed case studies describing social work practice in different parts of the world have become available (Hokenstad, Khinduka, & Midgley, 1992; Mayadas, Watts, & Elliott, 1997). However, these studies lack accurate statistical information about the number of social workers in different countries, and about their deployment in different fields of practice and agency settings. But they do show that social work around the world is characterized by similar as well as unique features and that, internationally, the profession exhibits both diversity and commonalities.

Because social work began in Europe and North America and then spread around the world, it is not surprising that social workers share common values, skills, and professional knowledge. Throughout the world, social work is characterized by its commitment to addressing social problems, meeting human needs, restoring social functioning, promoting social justice, and advocating progressive social change. Social workers are also identified by their involvement with particular fields of practice such as child welfare, mental health, medical social work, school social work, youth services, income maintenance and support programs, services to people with disabilities, probation and correctional social work, community organizing and development, and services to older adults. However, their involvement is largely problem focused, and they are primarily concerned with remediation. In most countries, social workers are responsible for addressing social problems such as child neglect and abuse (see box 16.1), mental illness, drug and alcohol dependence, family disintegration, juvenile delinquency, homelessness, and destitution.

Box 16.1   An American Social Work Student's Experience in International Social Work

My interest in social work took me a long way from my suburban Los Angeles upbringing to working with abandoned children in Romania. While only a teenager myself, I witnessed a younger cousin's unfortunate involvement with the child welfare system. This experience made me acutely aware of the vulnerability of children and their need for protection. I resolved then to make the reform of the child welfare system my life's work.

In college, I designed my own major in child development and public policy and developed a particular interest in orphanages and other forms of out-of-home care. From a description of emotional dwarfism in my freshman developmental psychology textbook, I learned about long-term institutionalization and its potentially severe consequences. I found it hard to accept that

Box 16.1 *Continued*

children could be so neglected, and I believed that I could help such children by providing my love and attention. That year, I established contact with Romanian Children's Relief, a non-governmental organization serving institutionalized children in Romania. Two years later, the opportunity to intern with this organization arose.

When I first entered an orphanage in Bucharest, some forty toddlers reacted to my presence by calling out, "Mama," and putting out their arms to be held or frantically clawing at me for attention. I felt utterly overwhelmed, fiercely protective and maternal, frightened of what their future held, amazed by their resilience, and moved by their attempts to reach out for love. When my internship ended, I pictured the faces of the children and made the decision to continue with Romanian Children's Relief after graduation. I prepared for the job by studying Romanian with a tutor and writing an honors thesis on Romania's child welfare system.

The original plan for my position with Romanian Children's Relief was that I would manage a new foster care support program in Bistrita, a small city in northern Transylvania. Ten days after I arrived, however, my role underwent a drastic change. The director of Romanian Children's Relief suddenly resigned. No one else in the organization was in a position to assume leadership, so I was asked to step into the job. It seemed impossible to say yes, given my complete lack of training for

the job, but impossible to say no, because the situation was so desperate. I plunged in. I worked eighteen-hour days for several months, struggling to learn how to manage a staff and three programs in a language I had begun to speak only six months earlier. In collaboration with an amazing staff and dedicated government and community partners, we created a support program for foster families that was recognized by the Romanian government as a model for replication and was the subject of a study by Case Western Reserve University. My proudest achievement of all was to hire and train staff members to succeed me so that I was able to leave the program in the hands of Romanian supervisors for the first time since the organization was founded ten years earlier.

Upon my return to the United States, I enrolled at the University of California, Berkeley, in the combined master's and PhD program in social welfare. My goal is to become a specialist in out-of-home care for children so that I can design programs, consult for nonprofit organizations and governments, and conduct research in this area. I envision a career in which I can support many national and international child welfare efforts through the sharing of knowledge.

Amy Conley, MSW
PhD Student
University of California, Berkeley

Another common feature of social work is the profession's link with public social services. Although social work was initially associated with the nonprofit sector, and particularly with charities and settlement houses, the profession's growth owed much to the new employment opportunities that were created when government social services expanded around the world during the twentieth century. As governments created new social service programs, the demand for professionally qualified social workers to staff these services increased. However, this situation is changing. In industrial countries, governments are increasingly contracting with non-profit and commercial providers, and thus reducing the number of professionally qualified social workers directly employed in the public sector. Budgetary difficulties and structural adjustment programs have resulted in a decline in the number of social workers in government service in many developing countries. Private practice has also become more common in some parts of the world. Nevertheless, governments continue to be a major employer of professional social workers in many countries. Even in the United States, where the number of social workers in the public services has fallen steadily, about a third of the members of the National Association of Social Workers are employed in the public sector (Leighninger & Midgley, 1997).

Although social work throughout the world shares common features, social work scholars and leaders in some countries often strongly advocate one practice approach or field of practice, which, they contend, should be given preference. As Hokenstad and Midgley (1997) note, social workers in India and South Africa have been encouraged to pay particular attention to economic development and to engage in forms of practice that promote development. In Latin America, emphasis has been placed on political activism, and social workers have been urged to mobilize poor people to campaign for social justice. In several African countries, social workers have been called on to help stem the AIDS pandemic, which has claimed so many lives and decimated so many families and communities.

In addition, social work in some countries has acquired unique features. For example, in European countries such as Denmark, Germany, and the Netherlands, social pedagogy has emerged as a distinctive branch of social work practice. Although social pedagogy is similar to community social work practice, it has a strong educational component and seeks to use educational techniques to promote community involvement. However, it is not limited to community settings, and it is also applied in residential care and youth work (Midgley, 1997). Another example comes from India, where social workers have historically been involved in personnel management, or labor welfare, as it is known. In many African countries, social workers have long been involved in rural community development work, using traditional community organizing techniques to mobilize local people to build feeder roads and bridges; engage in agricultural projects; construct community centers, schools, and health clinics; and promote village industries (Midgley, 1997).

These innovations and diverse forms of social work practice reveal the extent to which the social work profession in different countries has adapted to different economic and cultural contexts as well as challenges. However, the social work profession in most countries is relatively small and does not have great prestige or much national influence. Accordingly, the fact that social work has sought to address pressing social problems around the world does not mean that these problems have been solved. Today, problems such as poverty, family disintegration, malnutrition, alcohol and drug abuse, inequality, AIDS, child abuse and neglect, homelessness, mental illness, and social injustice persist on a huge scale. Nevertheless, social workers have made a difference, and their contribution has been recognized. Social workers around the world are known for their commitment to addressing these problems, promoting people's well-being, and advocating social justice. Increasingly, efforts are being made to address these problems at the international level. In addition to more frequent exchanges among social workers from different countries, the emergence of social work as a global profession has been accompanied by greater collaboration and engagement with international issues by social workers everywhere (Midgley, 1990).

INTERNATIONAL SOCIAL WORK PRACTICE

Historically, international social work has been viewed as a specialist field of practice undertaken by a small group of social workers with specialist skills (often including the ability to speak more than one language) or interests that equip them to work abroad. Some of the first publications about international social work defined the field in this way. When the first entry on the subject was published in the *Social Work Yearbook* in the United States in 1937, the author, George Warren, explained that international social work involved disaster relief, assistance to war victims and refugees, international public health measures, and involvement with international organizations such as the League of Nations and the International Labour Organization (Healy, 2001).

Walter Friedlander stressed this last aspect in his best-selling 1955 textbook, *Introduction to Social Welfare*, one of the first to contain a separate chapter on international social work. Friedlander noted that international social work was the youngest branch of the profession at the time, and that its goal was to promote the welfare of the world's people through the employment of social workers in international organizations such as the United Nations, the World Health Organization, the Red Cross, the YMCA and YWCA, and the International Child Welfare Union. At the time, many social workers still viewed international social work as a specialist field of practice that takes place in international agencies. The term has been broadened to describe a specialized field of practice involving social workers who practice abroad. However, many scholars who write about international social work today believe that this approach is too narrow. They point out that international social work practice does not only take place in international agencies, and that international social work should not be viewed only as taking place in other countries. They point out that today, many social workers in the United States encounter international realities in their daily practice. They routinely serve immigrants and refugees, and many deal with divorce and child custody cases involving a parent who comes from another country. These activities offer challenging opportunities for social workers in the United States to engage in international social work without actually living or working abroad. Clearly, international social work has become more complex than it once was. Accounts of the field must pay attention to the many different ways that social workers engage with international realities both here and abroad.

Social Work Practice and International Agencies

Social workers have long been involved with the major international social welfare agencies. They have found employment in international govern-

A social worker from Save the Children, a nongovernmental international agency that employs social workers, helps a young Rwandan refugee fill out paperwork.
© Mike Goldwater/Alamy

ment agencies such as the United Nations, including the United Nations High Commission for Refugees and UNICEF, and in nongovernmental agencies such as the Red Cross and Save the Children. In the early decades of the twentieth century, administrators of these international agencies and the founders of social work established close links. The Red Cross was one of the first international agencies to employ social workers.

Social workers also contributed to the creation of new international agencies such as Save the Children, which was established at the end of World War I by the British social worker Eglantyne Jebb (Healy, 2001). Today, the fund makes a major contribution to child welfare around the world. Like the Red Cross, the fund became a major employer of professionally qualified social workers.

Social workers were also actively involved in the League of Nations, the precursor to the United Nations. Although the League did not operate its own programs, it produced studies and reports that were used to publicize social problems such as drug abuse, prostitution, child labor, and the trafficking of women. The League also encouraged its member states to take steps to address these problems. Social workers played an important role as experts and advisers, and they helped draft these documents and disseminate the League's recommendations (Friedlander, 1955).

When the United Nations was established in 1945, social work had secured widespread international recognition, and, as noted earlier, the United Nations actively promoted the profession's international development during the 1950s and 1960s. The United Nations also employed social workers, particularly in its specialized agencies, such as the United Nations Relief and Rehabilitation Agency and UNICEF (Friedlander, 1975). The United Nations Relief and Rehabilitation Agency was established by the Allied powers in 1943 to provide emergency relief to the millions of people whose lives had been devastated by World War II. It became a major employer of social workers, who played a particularly important role in meeting the needs of refugees, orphans, and separated families (Friedlander, 1975).

Although these organizations hired social workers, the vast majority of their staff were not social workers. Over time, social work's influence within these organizations waned. In addition, the profession did not maintain the links that had been established with the administrators of these organizations. Any ambitions to staff these organizations with professionally qualified social workers gradually faded. By the 1980s, there was little evidence that social workers were playing a major role in these agencies. In addition, social workers were sometimes criticized for adhering to outdated practice approaches. For example, UNICEF became increasingly disenchanted with traditional child welfare casework practice and residential services, and social workers were seen as lacking involvement in prevention and developmental activities that could address the most pressing needs facing children in the developing world.

It appears that social workers have been more successful in finding employment in international nongovernmental agencies. Although accurate employment data are not available, social workers are reportedly employed in nongovernmental international organizations, where they work with poor communities, street children, women's groups, and people with disabilities in many parts of the world. Some use conventional casework approaches; others are engaged in a variety of developmental projects involving microenterprises, the development of community infrastructure, maternal and child health, and village crafts. Social workers employed in international agencies such as CARE, World Vision, Christian Aid, Save the Children, OXFAM, Caritas Internationalis, and Catholic Relief Services are deeply engaged in development work.

Social workers also practice in smaller international organizations involved in social service and development projects in the Global South. These include both secular and religious agencies. Many churches and missionary organizations manage programs of this kind. In addition to their traditional emphasis on establishing schools and hospitals, they are creating community development and social service projects. Often social work graduates with a spiritual vocation find employment in these agencies. Many secular organizations that provide services to needy children, the elderly, people with disabilities, and poor communities in other countries also provide opportunities for social workers to practice internationally.

Social Work Practice Abroad

In addition to working in well-established international social service and development organizations, social workers from the United States often find opportunities to work in other countries. While some are employed by American organizations that operate in these countries, others have found employment in local social welfare agencies. In either case, there is an expectation that these social workers will have a specialized knowledge of international affairs and the skills to work in other cultures.

Some American social workers are employed in other countries on a long-term basis, fulfilling their career aspirations to practice in international settings. Others do so for short periods of time. This is particularly true of newer graduates who wish to spend a year or two abroad. Often they have prior experience living and traveling abroad. It is not unusual for graduates who served as Peace Corps volunteers to want to return to the country in which they were placed or gain experience practicing in another country.

American social workers generally find it relatively easy to obtain employment abroad. Because of its high level of professionalization, organization, and standardization, social work in the United States is respected internationally. Since relatively few other countries provide social work education at the graduate level, American social workers who hold an MSW are particularly well regarded. Some social service agencies in other countries actively recruit American social workers. As a result of severe retrenchments in the social services and widespread disdain for the social work profession during the Thatcher years, Britain now has a severe shortage of professionally qualified social workers. Many British social services agencies are eager to employ American graduates. Several placement agencies in the United Kingdom have recruited social work graduates from American schools of social work. These agencies usually make the necessary arrangements for those who are hired.

Social workers who seek employment opportunities in other countries without the assistance of a placement agency are often challenged by such formalities as acquiring visas and other requirements for entry. This is particularly true in developing countries, where work permit and visa regulations can be quite restrictive. Although there is increasing interest in international economic and social development work among American social work graduates, few are able to make their own arrangements to work in development programs. Thus most are employed by organizations in the United States that operate such programs in the Global South.

Healy (2001) reports that efforts to persuade the U.S. government to provide employment opportunities for social workers in government agencies involved in international activities have been unsuccessful. A few social workers were placed in diplomatic missions in other countries as social welfare attachés in the 1960s, but this practice was discontinued. When the Peace Corps was established by President John F. Kennedy in 1961, social workers campaigned to persuade the Corps to give high priority to creating social service programs in developing countries, and to ensure that social workers played key roles in these programs. Although the Corps is involved in health-care and community development work, it has not given high priority to programs associated with professional social work. Although there is evidence that a significant number of social work students in the United States have served in the Peace Corps, it does not seem that many serve after they graduate.

Cultural competence is a vitally important aspect of social work practice in other countries. However, the importance of understanding cultural differences and practicing in a way that is sensitive to other cultures was not always emphasized. Nor was much attention paid to properly preparing social workers to practice in other countries. Often, no special preparation was thought to be necessary. In the past, many social workers who went abroad were counseled that all that was needed was a spirit of adventure, a friendly disposition, and a readiness to meet the challenges of living in another country. In addition, it was often naively assumed that the developing countries wanted to become economically and culturally similar to the industrial nations. Social workers from the United States and other industrial countries who went to work in developing countries were often regarded as agents of modernization who served to further strengthen the influence of Western culture in these societies (Midgley, 1981).

Today, the situation has changed, and there is a strong expectation that social workers who practice in other countries will be adequately prepared for the task. Great emphasis is now placed on cultural competence and on the need for social workers to be sensitive and respectful of cultural differences, as emphasized in chapter 4 and elsewhere in this text. This has placed new demands on schools of social work to provide specialized courses in international social work. It is also expected that conventional courses on cultural diversity will be broadened to include international content. The importance of language skills is also being stressed, and social workers seeking employment abroad are now encouraged to be fully acquainted with the economic, political, social, and cultural realities of the countries in which they intend to work.

International Social Work Practice in the Domestic Context

As a result of increased migration, travel, and globalization, social workers in many fields of practice in the United States now encounter international realities on a daily basis. Many more social workers routinely serve immigrant and refugee clients who come from other countries and have special needs. Many migrants are undocumented, work in low-paying jobs, are separated from their families, and face daunting challenges. For these reasons, immigrant families are likely to come into contact with social workers. However, the schools, health clinics, and family service agencies that employ social workers are seldom equipped to meet immigrants' unique needs. Although many immigrants are middle class and have well-paid jobs, they too may face challenges that come to the attention of professional social workers. Teenagers from immigrant families often face the challenges of cultural adjustment and of negotiating the demands of their parents, which may conflict with those of their peers. It is also more common today for Americans to have spouses or partners from other countries. Many meet their partners while traveling or studying abroad. Although the majority of these marriages are successful, problems may arise, and social workers who counsel these families need to understand their needs and circumstances. In dealing with these and other cases, social workers in the United States need to know how to manage the challenges presented by clients whose lives have been affected by international and multicultural experiences.

Of course, there are specialized agencies in the United States that are equipped to respond to the needs of immigrants and refugees. They often employ bilingual social workers who have a special knowledge of the clients' cultures. Many of these agencies work with immigrants from particular countries or regions. In addition, agencies that specialize in particular forms of social work practice such as international adoption and international child custody have also become more common. These agencies represent what Healy (2001) describes as the "international/domestic interface," and they offer opportunities for social workers in the United States to engage in international social work without actually living and working abroad.

Healy (2001) estimates that Americans adopted 15,000 children from other countries in 1998. Although all adoption work requires specialist skills, international adoptions are particularly challenging and are undertaken by specialized agencies with highly trained staff. International adoption is often time consuming and expensive. Adopting parents are often required to travel abroad and meet the legal requirements of the child's country of origin and of U.S. immigration, as well as other requirements. Sometimes these visits fail, and the disappointed family may require special counseling. Although most international adoptions are successful, families nevertheless need support and advice on raising their children to meet the challenges of cultural adjustment. International adoption experts such as Victor Groza (1997) are strongly in favor of families assisting their adopted children to develop an awareness and sensitivity to their cultural heritage. Of course, they also need to be helped to understand the demands placed on them by American culture. Clearly, specialized social work skills are needed for this task.

International adoption is only one example of how specialist skills and knowledge in international social work are being applied in the United States today. Similar skills are needed by social workers in family agencies dealing with child custody cases involving a parent from another country, and in child abduction cases, when one parent takes a child abroad without the other's consent. Since these cases comprise only a small part of the growing number of international cases that social workers in the United States encounter, it no longer makes sense to view international social work practice as a highly specialized field that takes place when social workers go abroad to practice or when they find employment in international agencies. Today, the international is infused in the domestic to a far greater extent than ever before, and there is an urgent need for all social workers to be aware of how their daily practice is affected by international encounters. The need for social workers to be adequately prepared to deal with these encounters poses a challenge for schools of social work to incorporate international and cross-cultural content into their curricula.

Challenges and Opportunities of International Social Work

As a result of improvements in communications, increased international migration, enhanced global trade, and the other forces of globalization that are fostering greater integration and interdependence among the world's nations, people are now more directly affected by international events. Compared to the situation a century ago, people today are better informed about developments in other countries, and many more people travel internationally and meet people from other cultures. This is affecting the way they experience and interpret the world. Although people's identities have historically been shaped by the immediate localities in which they live, growing numbers of people today have a greater appreciation for how their lives are affected by global change.

Like the members of other professions, social workers have been affected by the forces of globalization. As noted earlier, many American social workers are regularly required to address the needs of clients from other countries. Fortunately, social workers are recognizing the need to prepare themselves for these international realities. Some have made special efforts to enhance their knowledge of international events, and some have benefited from being better informed about social work in other parts of the world.

Many social workers find that greater engagement with international social work helps them appreciate the extent to which the problems they address are linked to global realities. This fosters a better understanding of human needs and social problems. Others recognize that international contacts enhance their professional skills. Some have adapted social work practice innovations from other countries and find that they are now better able to serve their clients. Although Hokenstad and Midgley (2004) suggest that it is increasingly common for social workers in the United States to apply innovations from other countries in their domestic work, the results are often improved when these innovations are applied with the appropriate modifications. Similarly, social workers usually find that learning about other cultures improves their knowledge of cultural diversity and their ability to practice competently.

Many social workers see their professional lives enriched as a result of engaging with their colleagues in other parts of the world. International exchanges in social work have clearly helped to promote the growth of social work as a profession, and they help individual practitioners enhance their knowledge and skills. By attending international conferences, reading international journals, and traveling to meet colleagues in other countries, social workers share information and experiences and enhance their under-standing of professional practice in other countries. All these factors con-tribute to social work's professional development and the improvement of professional practice.

Despite increased internationalization of the profession, many chal-lenges remain (Midgley, 2001). Social workers need to be better informed about global developments and better prepared to meet the challenges posed by a rapidly changing world. Social workers in the United States are not always well informed about international events. Many are also ill informed about social work in other countries. For example, many social workers do not understand the nuances of globalization and how its multi-faceted forces are affecting people's lives. There is a tendency in the acad-emic literature to oversimplify the issues and to reduce globalization to rhetorical condemnations (Midgley, 2004). Unfortunately, the literature has not helped practitioners understand the dynamics of globalization and the intricate ways it affects social work practice.

The academic community has a special responsibility to promote inter-national awareness among social work students. Of course, schools of social work have offered specialized courses in international social work and social welfare for many years. These courses became popular in the 1960s and 1970s, when Americans were exposed to events such as the Vietnam War and protests against it through television, cinema, and other media. It was also a time when knowledge about world poverty increased, and when many young people were inspired by the introduction of inter-national aid programs in the developing countries. With the creation of the Peace Corps in the 1960s, and the growth of university student exchanges and summer abroad programs, many spent time abroad and wished to return to work abroad. Accordingly, demand for specialized courses on international social work increased, and many more students expressed an interest in doing their field placements in other countries.

Some schools of social work in the United States responded to this demand by creating specialized courses on international social work or international social welfare. Some created concentrations in international social work in graduate programs. For example, the School of Social Work at the University of Pennsylvania developed a concentration in internation-al social development to provide specialized professional preparation for students interested in both international social work and the field of social development. Several other universities followed suit by establishing simi-lar concentrations, and this was accompanied by the creation of field place-ments in other countries (see box 16.2). Specialized centers concerned with international social work, such as the Center for International Social Work Studies at the University of Connecticut School of Social Work, were also established.

Box 16.2 An MSW Field Placement in South Africa

Waking up every day in rural Mtubatuba, South Africa, had the unmistakable effect of making me feel like a child who is behind the scenes of her favorite television show. I never felt that I had enough time to observe or learn the countless components of the Zulu culture and social work practice in which I found myself immersed. I was engaged in numerous activities on any given day at the Africa Center, my internship site, especially since my supervisor was the only social worker in the agency. On my journey to the center each day along with other students and staff from countries around the world, I rode through Mtubatuba Town, which had awakened hours earlier. Upon my eight o'clock arrival, one or two clients were already seated, waiting to meet with me and my supervisor.

I did almost everything with my supervisor because she needed to translate for me until I learned to speak conversational Zulu. Another reason I needed to be with my supervisor is that my agency, an HIV/AIDS research institute, only supplied manual vehicles, which I didn't know how to drive. Because of this, I had a unique supervisory relationship. Rather than spending a few hours per week with my supervisor, we had an all-day, every-day relationship. My supervisor and I set aside the first hour of the day for interviewing clients who did not have access to a telephone for scheduling appointments. If my supervisor had prior notice about a client, she would brief me, and we would then conduct the interview. I saw women, men, children, adolescents, orphans, families, elders, and sick clients. I made action plans for client problems ranging from non-delivery of government grant money or spousal work benefits to children's behavior problems, orphan care, learn-ing disabilities, and major crises due to health problems, disasters, and violence. After finishing the morning session, we traveled to homesteads within the very large service area of the Africa Center. These visits resulted from referrals given to my supervisor by staff conducting research within the community. Our objective for most visits was to conduct initial interviews or follow-up counseling sessions. We allotted most of our time each day to these visits, since at times the condition of the roads and the distance of the homes from the center delayed our travel. In the absence of street names or addresses, I became acutely aware of the value of neighbors, on whom we often had to rely for directions to a client's home.

In addition to making home visits, we met with community groups interested in becoming nonprofit organizations that would provide resources and care for their communities. We trained two of these groups to become child-care forums, groups responsible for identifying orphans and vulnerable children and marshalling resources for them. We met with the groups and conducted sessions on mapping, proposal and constitution writing, and application protocol. On occasion these training sessions would run from nine o'clock in the morning until three or four o'clock in the afternoon. Some of our sessions also involved project planning or completing a project with the group. One child-care forum, for example, applied for and received funding from my agency's charitable fund in order to buy groceries for twenty needy families it had identified in its area. We assisted in receiving the funds, opening a bank account, and delivering the food parcels to the community. Within the course of my day, I might also attend interdisciplinary staff meetings at the

---

Box 16.2 *Continued*

office, since my agency employed people in several different professions. At
times staff conducted these meetings in
Zulu, and I attempted to listen actively
and participate with my limited Zulu
proficiency. Although I often worked
through teatime and lunchtime, I did
enjoy these breaks because I gained

more experience with Zulu speakers
who were willing to help me sharpen
my language skills and teach me about
their culture.

Jandel Webb, MSW
PhD Student
Florida State University

This was an impressive initial commitment to international activities at
schools of social work. However, much more needs to be done if social
work is to prepare practitioners to meet the challenges posed by global
social change. Schools of social work, and the profession generally, need to
devote much more time and energy to international challenges. Many complex problems still need to be solved. For example, the problem of cultural
conflicts that arise when indigenous practices contradict Western humanitarian ideals still needs to be fully debated. The situation in Iraq is a prime
example. The incorporation of international human rights thinking and
practice into social work also needs more attention. The profession's commitment to social justice needs be broadened to more vigorously respond
to the flagrant abuses of human rights that occur in all parts of the world,
including the United States and other industrial countries. A controversial
example is the United Nations' call for the United States to shut down its
prison at the U.S. Naval Air Base in Guantanamo Bay, Cuba, and either
bring to trial or release the approximately five hundred detainees there,
most of whom were captured during the war in Afghanistan.

At a time when several American schools of social work are providing
technical assistance to schools of social work in other countries, or offering
professional education in other countries, avoiding professional imperialism (Midgley, 1981) and developing mutually reciprocal exchanges that
promote the sharing of experiences between equal partners are critical.
Social work also needs to grapple with the issue of whether cultural and
national identity is compatible with the ideals of global citizenship.
Although many social workers support efforts to promote international
cooperation, they may question the need to promote an ideology of inter-
nationalism within the profession. Current approaches to international
social work need broadening. The view that international social work is a
highly specialized field should be challenged, and efforts to mainstream
international social work should be redoubled. As social workers everywhere become more aware of the importance of international events in
their daily professional lives, international social work will hopefully

become a commonplace reality. The profession will then be better prepared to respond to the increasingly interdependent and integrated world in which we live, and better able to serve those who seek our help.

SUMMARY

International social work has become more prominent in social work education and practice. The growing immigrant population in the United States means that international social work practice is no longer confined to work abroad or international agencies with offices in the United States. The Council on Social Work Education has placed more emphasis on preparing students for practice in a world in which globalization is progressing at a rapid pace. Social work students are encouraged to take courses that will broaden their knowledge of other countries and other cultures in order to become politically and culturally astute. Proficiency in languages in addition to English is highly valuable. Social work has important roles to play, not only in delivering traditional social welfare services in an international context, but in helping to promote understanding across the borders of all countries.

SUGGESTED READING

Banerjee, D. (2000). *So you want to join the Peace Corps: What to know before you go.* Berkeley, CA: Ten Speed Press. A former Peace Corps volunteer addresses the concerns you might have about this important decision, from packing tips and living among the locals to medical services and staying in touch with friends and family at home. The book tells the stories of the experiences of volunteers, and statements of Peace Corps policy are provided for guidance.

Ferguson, I., Lavelette, M., & Whitmore, E. (Eds.). (2005). *Globalisation, global justice and social work.* London: Routledge. This book explores the global effects of neoliberal policies on welfare services in different countries, with contributions from social work academics, practitioners, and welfare activists around the world.

Hokenstad, M. C., & Midgley, J. (Eds.). (2004). *Lessons from abroad: Adapting international social welfare innovations.* Washington, DC: NASW Press. The contributors to this volume examine how domestic policies and practice can be enhanced through the documentation, analysis, and judicious adaptation of innovative approaches emanating from other countries in aging, child welfare, social security, mental health, and other areas.

International Social Work. This journal on issues relevant to international social work and social development is sponsored by the International Federation of Social Workers, the International Council on Social Work Education, and the International Association of Schools of Social Work. Published by Sage, it can be accessed at http://isw.sagepub.com.

McMichael, P. (2004). *Development and social change: A global perspective* (3rd ed.). Thousand Oaks, CA: Pine Forge Press. This volume discusses social change and development from a sociological perspective and examines the distribution of the world's material wealth and how noncommercial cultures view wealth.

THE WORLD WIDE WEB OF SOCIAL WORK

American Friends Service Committee http://www.afsc.org
This organization carries out service, development, social justice, and peace programs throughout the world. AFSC's work attracts the support and partnership of people of many races, religions, and cultures.

Global Social Work http://hometown.aol.com/egeratylsw/globalsw.html
This is an Internet-based international social work community for social workers, human services workers, humanitarian aid workers, and human rights organizations.

Global Social Work Network http://www.gswn.com
This organization provides information about licensing, education, and career opportunities. Networking is facilitated through a message board.

Peace Corps http://www.peacecorps.gov
This organization was established in 1961 to promote world peace and friendship. Its goals are to help other nations by supplying trained men and women and promoting an understanding of America and Americans, and a better understanding within America of other countries.

UNESCO http://portal.unesco.org/en/ev.php-URL_ID=29008&URL_DO=DO_TOPIC&URL_SECTION=201.html
The United Nations Educational, Scientific and Cultural Organization was founded in 1945. UNESCO promotes international cooperation among its 191 member states and six associate members in the fields of education, science, culture, and communication.

UNHCR http://www.unhcr.org/cgi-bin/texis/vtx/home
The Office of the United Nations High Commissioner for Refugees was established in 1950 by the United Nations General Assembly. The agency is mandated to lead and coordinate international action to protect refugees and resolve refugee problems worldwide.

17 The Future of Social Work: Preparing for the Next Century

C. Aaron McNeece and Diana M. DiNitto

If you are thinking about a career in social work, you may be wondering about the long-term implications of that decision. How stable will the profession be? Will it provide for a satisfying career twenty, thirty, or even forty years from now? What kind of work can you expect to do as a social worker in the years ahead? This chapter takes a look at what the profession of social work might look like in the future.

Making predictions about the future is, however, risky business, and the further away the future that one is attempting to predict, the greater the degree of uncertainty. Jim Dator (1999), director of the Future Studies Program at the University of Hawai'i, has declared that "Any useful idea about the future should appear to be ridiculous." There are no facts about the future, only speculation. Nevertheless, governments, business organizations, universities, religious institutions, and almost all other social groups make predictions about the future. The Social Security Administration must have a relatively good estimate of the number of workers who will retire in five, ten, and twenty years. Public schools must make plans regarding new school construction, teacher recruitment and hiring, and bus routes on the basis of projected population growth. To make a profit, General Motors needs to predict with a fair degree of accuracy how many people will decide to buy SUVs next year. When gas prices surge unexpectedly, GM's predictions may be well off the mark, and its profits decline.

Social work education programs and social service organizations are no different. State child welfare agencies try to project both future caseloads and future staffing needs. Universities make plans for hiring faculty and recruiting social work students. As this chapter is being written, the social work faculty at several universities, as well as the officers of the Council on Social Work Education, are engaged in long-term strategic planning processes with the belief that collecting data and making projections will allow them to plan for future developments in the field, which will in turn give them a greater degree of control over the future of social work education.

This chapter considers what some scholars have said about the impact of technology on the future of the social work profession and the expansion of knowledge for practice, future social work education, growth in specific areas of practice, trends affecting social work practice, and the roles and functions of social workers in the years ahead.

TECHNOLOGY

Computers have become a staple in the work of most agencies that employ social workers. Today, many caseworkers carry their laptops to the field, enter their reports before leaving the family's home, and send them back to the home office via their cell phone or a broadband connection. Instead of going into manila folder inside a filing cabinet, where it once went, the report resides on a silicon chip inside a computer—in a binary language that Jane Addams and Mary Richmond would have thought as foreign as Sanskrit or hieroglyphics.

Students studying social work today take technology for granted. They expect agencies to post job announcements on electronic bulletin boards, electronically deposit employees' paychecks directly into their bank accounts, and use e-mail as the primary mechanism for communication. Technologically, we have advanced so far in recent decades that it is difficult to imagine how much more change we will experience in the future, but more change is definitely on the way.

Voice recognition technology is being refined to the point that social workers of the future will more than likely simply dictate their field notes into a handheld device that will transform that information into pluses and minuses (or zeroes and ones), transmit it to the office, and store it in a readable file. Similarly, while in the field, the caseworker will be able to access a client's record via a handheld device by simply speaking a command. Vernon (2006) has predicted that a merger of case management systems and geographic information systems will result in more effective planning and delivery of social services.

Practice techniques will themselves benefit from technological advances. Biofeedback techniques used to help clients reduce stress or pain or address other problems will become more effective. Pharmacological advances are being made in the treatment of mental illness and substance abuse. These developments can help stabilize clients and enable them to make better use of the psychosocial treatments and services that social workers offer.

KNOWLEDGE DEVELOPMENT AND DISSEMINATION

Technology that can advance knowledge development is also progressing rapidly. Computer technology now allows social workers and other social scientists to collect vast amounts of data and conduct statistical analyses in a fraction of the time that it would have taken a few years ago. Most scholars agree that knowledge is growing at an exponential rate. Knowledge is developing so quickly that it has outpaced our ability to communicate it to the professionals who could use it to help their clients. During the past few decades, it generally took an agonizingly slow two or three years from the time a researcher made a discovery until news of that discovery was communicated to other scholars in a professional journal. It still takes a number of months and often a year or more from the time an author submits a manuscript until you can read it in a journal. In the meantime, it may already have been superseded by even newer discoveries.

The Internet holds the potential for the immediate dissemination of new scientific knowledge. The problem is that mechanisms for verifying and legitimizing new knowledge in a timely manner have not been implemented. Since the traditional method of conducting peer reviews of a scholar's research prior to publication takes so much time regardless of whether the information is disseminated on the printed page or on a Web site, some scholars have begun to post their research on independent Web sites without going through the process of peer review. However, most scholars are reluctant to use such information. How do we know it is legitimate and not the product of shoddy research, someone's idea of a practical joke, or worse? How will scholars and practitioners of the future be able to sift through the vast amounts of information available on the World Wide Web and distill those elements that are both legitimate and helpful (Sandell & Hayes, 2002)? This is a problem that you yourself may encounter as you decide which resources to use when writing papers for the classes you are taking.

Organizations such as the Campbell Collaboration and the Cochrane Collaboration are expending a great deal of effort to validate and communicate new knowledge. Campbell and Cochrane systematic reviews are published electronically so that they can be updated promptly as additional evidence becomes available. The process is faster than traditional peer reviews for printed journals, but it still takes time. Social workers can also access current information from sources such as the National Institute on Drug Abuse Clinical Trials Network and the Substance Abuse and Mental Health Services Administration–funded Addiction Technology Transfer Centers, which speed the dissemination from researchers to practitioners of new knowledge in the field of addictions.

Social workers and other human service professionals have a vested interest in ensuring that new knowledge is not disseminated before its validity has been verified. False information about new practice methods spread via the Internet could prove to be extremely harmful—both to clients and to the reputation of the profession. Refining our techniques for communicating new knowledge electronically should be a high-priority objective for social work researchers.

PREPARING SOCIAL WORKERS OF THE FUTURE

Technology has altered the very nature of the educational process as well. Twenty years ago the most common format for university courses was lecture and discussion. Instructors assigned one or two required textbooks and a list of readings from professional and scientific journals. They summarized the readings, asked students questions, tried to generate interesting discussions, and occasionally showed a film or videotape related to the lecture.

Times have changed. The traditional format is still used, of course, but most professors have brought the Internet into the classroom. Courses may offer chat rooms and discussion groups on a variety of topics. Term papers can be delivered through a digital drop box and returned electronically once the instructor has graded them. Most universities offer students the option of taking entire courses via the Internet. Some of these courses are taught in real time. In other cases, students may view lectures and related content via the Internet at their convenience. Many universities now offer complete degree programs online. The Council on Social Work Education (2002) allows the advanced-standing MSW program, except for field instruction classes, to be offered online. Field placements consisting entirely of "teletherapy" or electronic advocacy may be next.

The availability of online programs has eliminated place as a barrier to education. Courses can be taught in Tallahassee, Austin, Prague, or Kabul, and students anywhere in the world can enroll as long as they have a computer and Internet access. Approximately 40 percent of the graduate enrollment in social work education programs consists of part-time students, many of whom take one or two courses per semester online (Karger & Stoesz, 2003).

If you are considering a graduate program in social work, and you are serious about online options, you would do well to find out exactly what a program offers and whether it is legitimate. A recent Google search of "master of social work distance learning" brought up twenty-nine institutions purporting to offer an MSW degree. Closer inspection, however, revealed that most were actually called something like the master of human services or the master of human sciences, and none were accredited by the Council on Social Work Education. None of the graduates of those twenty-nine programs would be able to meet the state licensing requirements for social work without completing an additional degree from an accredited program.

PROFESSIONAL EDUCATION

Although there is a strong indication that the number of social work positions and the need for more social workers will continue to grow (Bureau of Labor Statistics, 2005), not everyone agrees. Karger and Stoesz (2003) believe that we actually have a surplus of social workers in the United

States, and that this surplus has kept the salaries of social workers relatively low and has lowered the quality of social work education programs and the competence of social work graduates. As the number of social work programs has expanded at both the undergraduate and graduate levels, they have been forced to compete for an applicant pool that is growing at a much slower rate. According to Karger and Stoesz (2003), one result of this increased competition has been an erosion of admissions standards. They recommend a moratorium on the development of new educational programs until a thorough study of labor market conditions, needs, and salaries has been conducted. Current policy requires a university proposing a new social work graduate or undergraduate program to demonstrate the need for that program; however, subsequent reviews for accreditation purposes do not require such a demonstration of need.

A factor that may be contributing to the contradiction between the Bureau of Labor Statistics' projection of a growing need for social workers and Karger and Stoesz's conclusion that we have an oversupply is the fact that many large human services agencies have deprofessionalized social work positions. In many states, the great majority of individuals holding positions that most people would describe as social work jobs do not hold a social work degree. They may have earned a degree in history, music, or English but completed a minimal number of credit hours in the social sciences and no course work in social work. It is possible that the reprofessionalization of social work could be achieved through the implementation of rigorous licensing laws and a licensing process that is not directed solely toward the practice of clinical social work. Society needs social workers who are well prepared in all areas of practice, including administration, community organization, and policy development and analysis, as well as clinical practice.

AREAS OF PRACTICE

Demographic changes in the population will likely determine which social work positions experience the greatest growth. According to the Bureau of Labor Statistics (2005), "The rapidly growing elderly population and the aging baby boom generation will create greater demand for health and social services, resulting in particularly rapid job growth among gerontology social workers." Some of this growth will be more pronounced in specific geographic areas. For example, the sun-belt states tend to attract retirees from other states and thus have a much greater need for social workers in gerontology. Other areas of above-average employment growth include home health-care services, substance abuse services, school social work, employee assistance programs, and private practice. However, the Bureau of Labor Statistics also predicts that agencies will increasingly restructure services and hire more lower-paid social and human service assistants instead of those who hold social work degrees—a phenomenon similar to what has occurred in other professions, such as nursing. The growth in employee assistance social work will occur through contracting—that is, public and private employers will purchase these services from private practitioners, an arrangement that will facilitate the reduction of such services during recessions. Other organizations like hospitals are also using contract social workers, who may be on call or who may work at particular times such as evenings, weekends, and holidays. Some social workers might prefer the flexibility of working *pro re nata* (as needed), also referred to as PRN. Others do it to supplement their income. Often, however, PRN work does not offer health-care, retirement, or other benefits that agency-based social workers are likely to receive.

PRIVATIZATION

Privatization will continue to occur in almost all human services as public welfare, child protection, and family service agencies and correctional programs increasingly contract with private organizations and individual practitioners to offer what used to be strictly public-sector services. Republican presidents since Ronald Reagan have placed a strong emphasis on privatization (DiNitto, 2007), and privatization has in recent years become an ideological principle of the Republican Party. Whether privatized services are more effective or save the government money is a question that is still being debated; these debates may, however, be irrelevant given the popularity of privatization among politicians. For example, in Florida, Governor Jeb Bush succeeded in completely privatizing the child welfare system by 2005, and the state is well on the way to privatizing corrections, mental health, and other social services.

Privatization of social services was intended to promote competition, an accepted economic concept. According to many who have studied the issue, however, competition frequently undermines the provision of services to the poor because agencies that provide services on a low- or no-fee basis cannot afford to employ lobbyists and often cannot compete with more financially secure agencies to get contracts (see, e.g., Day, 2006). The results have been a step backward in the public and social responsibility to aid those with limited economic resources and the promotion of a polarized or two-tier social service delivery system. For example, well-off individuals who have alcohol and drug problems can gain immediate admission to fancy rehabilitation centers, while poor individuals with the same problems often must wait a long time to be admitted to treatment programs that are likely underfunded and struggle to meet all the requests for services. People with health insurance are more likely to have a primary physician and get immediate treatment for medical problems than those without health insurance, who may have to seek care in emergency rooms at exorbitant costs. These situations present challenges to the social work profession's commitment to serve those who lack economic resources.

Privatization represents a sea change in social service delivery. Unless another sea change occurs in the political orientation of this country, future social workers can expect to find employment more frequently in private agencies or as independent contractors and less often in public organizations.

If current trends prevail, faith-based organizations will continue to gain significance as a source of publicly financed social services. Religious beliefs may motivate many individuals to choose a career of service, but there used to be a clear demarcation between publicly financed social services provided by government agencies or contracted out to secular agencies and privately funded social services provided by religious organizations. Churches played a dominant role in early American social welfare, but they were prohibited from receiving most governmental subsidies for the services they provided. One of George W. Bush's first actions as president was to establish the Office of Faith-Based and Community Initiatives and make it easier for religious organizations to compete for federal social welfare service funding.

Many conservatives favor religious social services, which they regard as rooted in "morality, private charity, and direct compassion" (Gilbert & Terrell, 2005, p. 165); they assert that such services are preferable to bureaucratic and inefficient public programs. Liberals note that there is no compelling evidence to suggest that such services are any cheaper or more effective than public programs and, perhaps more importantly, that such funding of services offered by religious organizations violates the separation between church and state. Time will tell if future presidential administrations will hold similar philosophies regarding the provision of public funds to religious organizations. If they do, this too may lead to more changes in the nature of social work employment. Some MSW programs have teamed up with master's of divinity programs to offer joint degree programs similar to those they already offer with other professions such as law and public administration.

EVIDENCE-BASED PRACTICE

Whatever the auspices of the delivery system, social services of the future are more likely than ever before to be designed on the basis of empirical research and delivered by social workers who have been trained in models and methods of evidence-based practice (McNeece & Thyer, 2004). Third-party payers are increasingly demanding that professionals show evidence of the benefits of the services they render. What distinguishes evidence-based practice from other models of social work intervention is that "the practitioner is seen as having an ethical and professional *obligation* to seek out the best available evidence (if any), weigh its scientific credibility and applicability in terms of the client's circumstances, values, and preferences, and apply it if appropriate as a first choice treatment option" (McNeece & Thyer, 2004, p. 10).

The days of social workers passing down the practice wisdom of one generation to the next are numbered. In addition to the logic of using the best available research to inform practice decisions, legal factors also contribute to the recent emphasis on evidence-based practice. In April 2000, the Colorado Court of Appeals unanimously upheld the conviction and sentence of psychotherapist Connell Watkins in the death of a client, ten-year-old Candace Newmaker (Pankratz, 2003). The child suffocated during a seventy-minute "rebirthing" session, during which she was wrapped in a sheet and pillows were placed on top of her. There was no research evidence to support the use of this technique, which was supposed to help the child bond with her adoptive mother. Watkins is currently serving a sixteen-year prison sentence. Cases such as this call attention to the importance of using evidence-based practice and should serve as a warning to any social worker thinking about using an unproven therapeutic technique with a client, especially a juvenile client.

To make intelligent judgments about which micro, mezzo, and macro intervention techniques are appropriate, social workers will need to keep abreast of the research literature. To adequately interpret the research literature, they will need more education in research methods and statistics than most BSW and MSW programs currently offer. Though it has become common to shorten the length of MSW programs for students who have a BSW, it is possible that the length of all MSW programs will increase. There have been several proposals over the past decade to convert the standard MSW program to a three-year doctor of social work (DSW) program. The additional time would allow students to acquire more education in evidence-based practice and more supervised micro, mezzo, or macro practicum opportunities. It is possible that those with a DSW will be perceived more favorably in comparison with those who hold practice doctorates in fields like psychology or master's degrees in business administration or public administration. The DSW would focus on practice, while the PhD in social work would retain its focus on preparing students to conduct independent research and become faculty members.

MACROPRACTICE AND MICROPRACTICE

Ginsberg (2006) predicts that almost all social workers will be employed in direct services work in the future. Many individuals are drawn to social work because they want to work directly with individuals and families, but social workers might want to ask themselves if they would be content to see Ginsberg's prediction come true. If social workers do not increase their involvement in community organization (helping people learn to advocate for themselves), agency administration (setting the tone and direction for the work agencies do), and the political process (which influences almost everything social workers do at the micro, mezzo, and macro levels), they and the clients they serve will be at a great disadvantage. Whether it is in a full-time position or part of one's civic engagement, social workers can play many roles in the political process. Some work with advocacy groups and organizations dedicated to lobbying or research organizations and think tanks devoted to devising solutions to biopsychosocial problems. Others do policy analysis and development for local, state, and federal agencies. Some are staff members for legislators and legislative committees or become elected officials (e.g., school board members, city or county commissioners, and state or U.S. representatives and senators). Many volunteer for political campaigns. Social workers aren't really social workers if they stand on the sidelines, simply hoping things will improve.

SOCIAL WORK AND YOUR FUTURE

We hope that this book has given you an understanding of the social work profession in general and an indication of whether a career in social work may be right for you. Volunteer work and field placements can also help you make this important decision. You might remember from chapter 1 that social workers are more likely than Americans in general to describe their lives as exciting. A degree in social work offers so many career options that the sky is the limit!

Many students who earn a BSW enroll immediately in an MSW program because the master's degree not only expands career opportunities, but it can also increase one's salary. Others decide to gain work experience before pursuing the MSW. A small group of individuals with the MSW decides to pursue a PhD in social work, usually because they wish to become faculty members in social work education programs, researchers in universities or other organizations, or policy analysts or administrators in large human service organizations. Some students use a bachelor's degree in social work as a springboard to a career in law, medicine, or public administration, among other fields. The principles of social work practice can be valuable in many professions. Whatever path you take, we wish you the best in your educational endeavors and a rewarding career in your chosen field.

■ References

1 Social Work: A Challenging Profession

Addams, J. (1897). Social settlements. *Proceedings,* National Conference of Catholic Charities.

Allen, H., Eskridge, C., Latessa, E., & Vito, G. (1985). *Probation and parole in America.* New York: Free Press.

American Nurses Association. (2007). *ANA's definition of nursing.* Retrieved March 16, 2007, from http://nursingworld.org/nursecareer

Association of Social Work Boards. (2005). *Licensing requirements.* Retrieved July 15, 2005, from http://www.aswb.org/lic_req.shtml

Axinn, J., & Stern, M. (2005). *Social welfare: A history of the American response to need* (6th ed.). Boston: Allyn and Bacon.

Barkow, J. (1978). Social norms, the self, and sociobiology: Building on the ideas of A. I. Hallowell. *Current Anthropologist, 19*(1), 99–112.

Bartlett, H. (1970). *The common base of social work practice.* New York: NASW Press.

Council on Social Work Education. (2003). *Handbook of accreditation standards and procedures* (5th ed.). Arlington, VA: Author.

Davenport, J., & Davenport, J. (1997, Winter). Social workers: Fad-chasing jackasses or still on the side of the angels? *The New Social Worker, 4*(1). Retrieved August 8, 2005, from http://www.socialworker.com/home/Feature_Articles/General/Social_Workers:_Fad-Chasing_Jackasses_or_Still_on_the_Side_of_the_Angels?

Freeman, M., & Valentine, D. (2004). Through the eyes of Hollywood: Images of social workers in film. *Social Work, 49,* 151–161.

Frumkin, M., & O'Connor, G. (1985). Where has the profession gone? Where is it going? Social work's search for identity. *Urban and Social Change Review, 18*(1), 13–19.

Gambrill, E. (2003). Evidence-based practice: Sea change or the emperor's new clothes? *Journal of Social Work Education, 39* (1), 3–24.

Gibelman, M., & Schervish, P. (1997). *Who we are: A second look.* Washington, DC: NASW Press.

Gibelman, M., & Sweifach, J. (2004). *Acting on our values: Do human service professionals volunteer?* Paper presented at the sixth International Conference of the International Society for Third-Sector Research, Toronto, Ontario.

Greenwood, E. (1957). Attributes of a profession. *Social Work, 3,* 44–55.

Hiersteiner, C., & Peterson, K. (1999). Crafting a usable past: The care-centered practice narrative in social work. *Affilia: Journal of Women and Social Work, 14*(2), 144–162.

Hodge, D. (2004). Who we are, where we come from, and some of our perceptions: Comparison of social workers and the general population. *Social Work, 49,* 261–268.

Karger, H., & Stoesz, D. (2003). The growth of social work education programs, 1985–1999: Its impact on economic and educational factors related to the profession of social work. *Journal of Social Work Education, 39*(2), 279–295.

Kinderknecht, C. (1995). *Social work ethical violations: The experience of one state regulatory board.* Doctoral dissertation, University of Kansas.

Kristeller, J. L., & Johnson, T. (2005). Cultivating loving kindness: A two-stage model of the effects of meditation on empathy, compassion, and altruism. *Zygon: Journal of Religion and Science, 40*(2), 391–407.

Kropotkin, P. (1925). *Mutual aid: A factor of evolution.* New York: Knopf.

Krugman, P. (2003, September 14). The tax-cut con. *New York Times*, section 6, p. 54.

LeCroy, C., & Stinson, E. L. (2004). The public's perception of social work: Is it what we think it is? *Social Work, 49*, 164–174.

Lennon, T. (2005). *Statistics on social work education in the United States: 2003.* Alexandria, VA: Council on Social Work Education.

National Association of Social Workers. (2003). *Practice research network.* Demographics, PRN 2:2. Retrieved June 10, 2007, from http://www.nasw/org/naswprn/surveyTwo/Datagram2.pdf

National Association of Social Workers. (2006). *Assuring the sufficiency of a frontline workforce: A national study of licensed social workers.* Washington, DC: Author.

National Association of Social Workers. (2007). *Professional development.* Retrieved January 28, 2007, from http://www.naswdc.org/pdev/default.asp

Popple, P., & Leighninger, L. (2005). *Social work, social welfare, and American society* (6th ed.). Boston: Allyn and Bacon.

Powell, A. C. (1923). The church in social work. *Opportunity,* 15.

O'Connell, P. (1993). Who cares for the poor? *Commonweal, 120*(19), 35–37.

Rainford, W. (2004). Paternalistic regulation of women: Exploring punitive sanctions in the TANF program. *Affilia: Journal of Women and Social Work, 19*(3) 289–304.

Richmond, M. (1917). *Social diagnosis.* New York: Russell Sage Foundation.

Richmond, M., & Hall, F. (1974). *A study of nine hundred and eighty-five widows.* New York: Arno Press.

Sanchez, A., & Cuesta, J. (2005). Altruism may arise from individual selection. *Journal of Theoretical Biology, 235*(2), 233–241.

Sanders, D. (1973). *The impact of reform movements on social policy change: The case of social insurance.* Fair Lawn, NJ: R. E. Burdick.

Seligman, M. (1995). The effectiveness of psychotherapy: The *Consumer Reports* study. *American Psychologist, 50*, 965–974.

Social Work History Station. (n.d.). *A poor people's history.* Retrieved March 7, 2007, from http://www.boisestate.edu/socwork/dhuff/us

Specht, H. (1972). The deprofessionalization of social work. *Social Work, 17*(2), 3–15.

Specht, H., & Courtney, M. (1994). *Unfaithful angels: How social work has abandoned its mission.* New York: Free Press.

Timms, N., & Timms, R. (1982). *Dictionary of social welfare.* London: Routledge.

Trattner, W. I. (1999). *From poor law to welfare state: A history of social welfare in America* (6th ed.). New York: Free Press.

U.S. Bureau of Labor Statistics. (2001). *Employment and earnings, 48(11). Table 11. Employed persons by detailed occupation, sex, race, and Hispanic origin.* Washington, DC: United States Government Printing Office.

U.S. Bureau of Labor Statistics. (2005). *Social workers.* Retrieved July 13, 2005, from http://stats.bls.gov/oco/pdf/ocos060.pdf

Wuenschel, P. (2005). *Who's managing our agencies and what do they think they're doing? A challenge for the social work profession.* Doctoral dissertation, University of Houston.

2 Theory and Practice of Social Work with Individuals, Families, and Groups

Allen-Meares, P. (2006). Where do we go from here? Mental health workers and the implementation of an evidence-based practice. In C. Franklin, M. B. Harris, & P. Allen-Meares (Eds.), *The school services sourcebook: A guide for school-based professionals* (pp. 1189–1194). New York: Oxford University Press.

Barker, R. L. (1995). *The social work dictionary* (3rd ed.). Washington, DC: NASW Press.

Beck, A. (1982). *Cognitive therapy for depression.* New York: Guilford Press.

Beckett, J. O., & Johnson, H. C. (1995). Human development. In R. L. Edwards (Ed.), *The encyclopedia of social work* (19th ed., pp. 1385–1405). Washington, DC: NASW Press.

Berger, R., Federico, R., & McBreen, J. (1991). *Human behavior: A perspective for the helping professions* (3rd ed.). White Plains, NY: Longman.

Council on Social Work Education. (2002, November). *Educational policy and accreditation standards.* Retrieved June 21, 2005, from http://www.cswe.org/NR/rdonlyres/111833A0-C4F5-475C-8FEB-EA740FF4D9F1/0/EPAS.pdf

Craighead, W. E., Hart, A. B., Craighead, L. W., & Ilardi, S. S. (2002). Psychosocial treatments for major depressive disorder. In P. E. Nathan & J. M. Gorman (Eds.), *Treatments that work* (pp. 261–286). New York: Oxford University Press.

Epstein, L. (1995). Brief task-centered practice. In R. L. Edwards (Ed.), *The encyclopedia of social work* (19th ed., pp. 313–323). Washington, DC: NASW Press.

Fanger, M. T. (1995). Brief therapies. In R. L. Edwards (Ed.), *The encyclopedia of social work* (19th ed., pp. 323–334). Washington, DC: NASW Press.

Franklin, C., Kim, J., & Tripodi, S. (2006). Solution-focused, brief therapy interventions for students at-risk to dropout. In C. Franklin, M. B. Harris, & P. Allen-Meares (Eds.), *The school services sourcebook: A guide for school-based professionals* (pp. 1132–1147). New York: Oxford University Press.

Franklin, C., & Moore, K. (1999). Solution-focused, brief family therapy. In C. Franklin & C. Jordan (Eds.), *Family practice: Brief systems methods for social work* (pp. 224–256). Pacific Grove, CA: Brooks/Cole.

Germain, C. B. (1991). *Human behavior and the social environment: An ecological view.* New York: Columbia University Press.

Gibbs, L. E. (2003). *Evidence-based practice for the helping professions: A practical guide with integrated multimedia.* Pacific Grove, CA: Brooks/Cole–Thomson Learning.

Gingerich, W., & Eisengart, S. (2000). Solution-focused, brief therapy: A review of the outcome research. *Family Process, 39*(4) 477–496.

Granvold, D. K. (1994). Concepts and methods of cognitive treatment. In D. K. Granvold (Ed.), *Cognitive and behavioral treatment: Methods and applications* (pp. 3–31). Belmont, CA: Brooks/Cole.

Granvold, D. K. (1995). Cognitive treatment. In R. L. Edwards (Ed.), *The encyclopedia of social work* (19th ed., Vol. 1, pp. 525–538). Washington, DC: NASW Press.

Harris, M., & Franklin, C. (2004). Evidence-based life skills interventions for pregnant and parenting adolescents in school settings. In A. R. Roberts & K. R. Yeager (Eds.), *Evidence-based practice manual: Research and outcomes measure in human services* (pp. 312–323). New York: Oxford University Press.

Helton, M., & Jackson, L. (1997). *Social work practice with families.* Needham Heights, MA: Allyn and Bacon.

Henggeler, S.W., Schoenwald, S., Borduin, C., Rowland, M., & Cunningham, P. (1998). *Multisystemic treatment of antisocial behavior in children and adolescents.* New York: Guilford Press.

Hepworth, D. H., Rooney, R., & Larsen, J. (2002). *Direct social work practice: Theory and skills* (6th ed.). Belmont, CA: Wadsworth.

Jantzen, C., Harris, O., Jordan, C., & Franklin, C. (2006). *Family treatment: Evidence-based practice with populations at risk.* Pacific Grove, CA: Brooks/Cole.

Lazarus, R. S., & Launier, R. (1978). Stress-related transactions between person and environment. In L. A. Pervin & M. Lewis (Eds.), *Perspectives in interactional psychology* (pp. 287–327). New York: Plenum.

Lee, J. (1996). The empowerment approach to social work practice. In F. J. Turner (Ed.), *Social work treatment: Interlocking theoretical approaches* (4th ed., pp. 218–249). New York: Free Press.

National Association of Social Workers. (1999). *Code of ethics of the National Association of Social Workers.* Washington, DC: Author.

Perlman, H. H. (1986). The problem-solving theory. In F. J. Turner (Ed.), *Social work treatment: Interlocking theoretical perspectives* (3rd ed., pp. 245–266). New York: Free Press.

Reid, W. J. (1996). Task-centered social work. In F. J. Turner (Ed.), *Social work treatment: Interlocking theoretical approaches* (4th ed., pp. 617–640). New York: Free Press.

Saleebey, D. (1997). *The strengths perspective in social work practice.* White Plains, NY: Longman.

Schriver, J. (2004). *Human behavior and the social environment: Shifting paradigms in essential knowledge for social work practice* (4th ed.). Boston: Allyn and Bacon.

Turner, F. J. (1995). Social work practice: Theoretical base. In R. L. Edwards (Ed.), *The encyclopedia of social work* (18th ed., pp. 2258–2265). Washington, DC: NASW Press.

Turner, F. J. (1996). *Social work treatment: Interlocking theoretical approaches* (4th ed.). New York: Free Press.

Turner, J., & Jaco, R. M. (1996). Problem-solving theory and social work treatment. In F. J. Turner (Ed.), *Social work treatment: Interlocking theoretical approaches* (4th ed., pp. 503–522). New York: Free Press.

Werner, E. E. (1989). High-risk children in young adulthood: A longitudinal study from birth to 32 years. *Journal of Orthopsychiatry, 59*(2), 72–81.

Zastrow, C., & Kirst-Ashman, K. (2004). *Understanding human behavior and the social environment* (6th ed.). Belmont, CA: Brooks/Cole–Thomson Learning.

3 Social Work with Organizations, Communities, and Larger Systems

American Association of Social Workers. (1929). *Social casework: Generic and specific concepts.* New York: Author.

Backman, E., & Smith, S. (2000). Healthy organizations, unhealthy communities. *Nonprofit Management and Leadership, 10*(4), 355–373.

Brown, J. C. (1940). *Public relief: 1929–1939.* New York: Henry Holt.

Burghardt, S., & Fabricant, M. (1987). Radical social work. In A. Minahan (Ed.), *The encyclopedia of social work* (18th ed., Vol. 2, pp. 455–462). Silver Spring, MD: NASW Press.

Burns, E. (1961). Social policy: Step-child of the curriculum. In *Education for social work: Proceedings of the annual program meeting.* New York: Council on Social Work Education.

Chaskin, R. (1997). Perspectives on neighborhood and community: A review of the literature. *Social Service Review, 71*(4), 522–547.

Chaskin, R., Brown, P., Venkatesh, S., & Vidal, A. (2001). *Building community capacity.* New York: Aldine de Gruyter.

DiNitto, D. M. (2007). *Social welfare: Politics and public policy. With research navigator* (6th ed.). Boston: Allyn and Bacon.

Eikenberry, A., & Kluver, J. (2004). The marketization of the nonprofit sector: Civil society at risk? *Public Administration Review, 64*(2), 132–139.

Fisher, J. (1980). *The response of social work to the Depression.* Cambridge, MA: Schenkman.

Fisher, R. (2005). History, context, and emerging issues for community practice. In M. Weil (Ed.), *The handbook of community practice* (pp. 34–58). Thousand Oaks, CA: Sage.

Garvin, C. S., & Cox, F. M. (1995). A history of community organizing since the Civil War with special reference to oppressed communities. In J. Rothman, J. L. Erlich, & J. Tropman (Eds.), *Strategies of community intervention* (pp. 64–99). Itasca, IL: F. E. Peacock.

Gilchrist, A. (2000). The well-connected community: Networking to the "edge of chaos." *Community Development Journal, 35*(3), 264–275.

Hasenfeld, Y. (2000). Social welfare administration and organizational theory. In R. Patti (Ed.), *The handbook of social welfare management* (pp. 89–112). Thousand Oaks, CA: Sage.

Hoefer, R. (2003). Administrative skills and degrees: The "best place" debate rages on. *Administration in Social Work, 27*(1), 25–46.

Hollis, E., & Taylor, A. (1951). *Social work education in the United States: The report of a study made for the National Council on Social Work Education.* New York: Columbia University Press.

Jacobs, R. (2003). Toward a political sociology of civil society. In B. Dobratz, L. Waldner, & T. Buzzell (Eds.), *Political sociology for the 21st century* (pp. 19–47). New York: JAI.

Jones, C. O. (1984). *An introduction to the study of public policy* (3rd ed.). Belmont, CA: Brooks/Cole.

Kobrin, S. (1959). The Chicago Area Project: A 25-year assessment. *Annals of the American Academy of Political and Social Science, 233,* 19–29.

Longres, J. (1996). Radical social work: Is there a future? In P. Raffoul & C. McNeece (Eds.), *Future issues in social work practice* (pp. 229–239). Boston: Allyn and Bacon.

Lynn, L. (2002). Social services and the state: The public appropriation of private charity. *Social Service Review, 76*(1), 58–82.

McNutt, J. (2000). Organizing cyberspace: Strategies for teaching about community practice and technology. *Journal of Community Practice, 7*(1), 95–109.

Midgley, J. (2000). The definition of social policy. In J. Midgley, M. Tracy, & M. Livermore (Eds.), *The handbook of social policy* (pp. 3–10). Thousand Oaks, CA: Sage.

Midgley, J., Tracy, M., & Livermore, M. (2000). Introduction. In J. Midgley, M. Tracy, & M. Livermore (Eds.), *The handbook of social policy* (pp. xi–xv). Thousand Oaks, CA: Sage.

Mizrahi, T., & Rosenthal, B. (1993). Managing dynamic tensions in social change coalitions. In T. Mizrahi & J. Morrison (Eds.), *Community organization and social administration: Advances, trends and emerging principles* (pp. 11–40). New York: Haworth Press.

Palloff, R., & Pratt, K. (1999). *Building learning communities in cyberspace: Effective strategies for the online classroom.* San Francisco: Jossey-Bass.

Patti, R. (1983). *Social welfare administration: Managing social programs in a developmental context.* Englewood Cliffs, NJ: Prentice Hall.

Patti, R. (2000). The landscape of social welfare management. In R. Patti (Ed.), *The handbook of social welfare management* (pp. 3–26). Thousand Oaks, CA: Sage.

Putnam, R. (1995). Bowling alone: America's declining social capital. *Journal of Democracy, 6,* 65–78.

Smith, D. H. (1992). A neglected type of voluntary nonprofit organization: Exploration of the semiformal, fluid-membership organization. *Nonprofit and Voluntary Sector Quarterly, 21*(3), 251–269.

Smith, D. H. (1997). Grassroots associations are important: Some theory and a review of the impact literature. *Nonprofit and Voluntary Sector Quarterly, 26*(3), 269–306.

Thompson, J. D. (1961). Common elements in administration. In E. Reed (Ed.), *Social welfare administration* (pp. 16–29). New York: Columbia University Press.

Trecker, H. B. (1977). *Social work administration: Principles and practice* (Rev. ed.). New York: Association Press.

Valocchi, S. (n.d.). *A way of thinking about the history of community organizing.* Retrieved May 23, 2005, from http://www.trincoll.edu/depts/tcn/valocchi.htm

Weil, M. (2005). Introduction: Contexts and challenges for 21st century communities. In M. Weil (Ed.), *The handbook of community practice* (pp. 3–33). Thousand Oaks, CA: Sage.

Weil, M., & Gamble, D. (2005). Evolution, models, and the changing context of community practice. In M. Weil (Ed.), *The handbook of community practice* (pp. 117–149). Thousand Oaks, CA: Sage.

Wernet, S. (1994). A case study of adaptation in a nonprofit human service organization. *Journal of Community Practice, 1*(3), 93–113.

Wernet, S. (2002). The role of the Internet in educating social work practitioners as online advocates. In S. F. Hick & J. G. McNutt (Eds.), *Advocacy, activism and the Internet: Community organization and social policy* (pp. 59–70). Chicago: Lyceum Books.

Wernet, S. (2004). *Community practice in the 21st century.* Seoul, South Korea: Korea National Council of University Social Welfare Agencies.

Wildavsky, A. (1979). *Speaking truth to power: The art and craft of policy analysis.* Boston: Little, Brown.

Wimpfheimer, S. (2004). Leadership and management competencies defined by practicing social work managers: An overview of standards developed by the National Network for Social Work Managers. *Administration in Social Work, 28*(1), 45–56.

4 Culturally Competent Social Work Practice

Brave Heart, M. (2001). Culturally and historically congruent clinical social work assessment with native clients. In R. Fong & S. Furuto (Eds.), *Culturally competent practice: Skills, interventions, and evaluations* (pp. 163–177). Boston: Allyn and Bacon.

D'Avanzo, C. E., Frye, B., & Froman, R. (1994). Culture, stress and substance use in Cambodian refugee women. *Journal of Studies on Alcohol, 55,* 420–426.

Devore, W., & Schlesinger, E. (1999). *Ethnic-sensitive social work practice* (5th ed.). Boston: Allyn and Bacon.

Dhooper, S., & Moore, S. (2001). *Social work practice with culturally diverse people.* Thousand Oaks, CA: Sage.

Doctors Without Borders. (2000). *A refugee camp in the heart of the city: Curriculum for teachers.* New York: Author. Retrieved May 19, 2006, from http://refugeecamp.org/curriculum

Falicov, C. (1998). *Latino families in therapy: A guide to multicultural practice.* New York: Guilford Press.

Fong, R. (Ed.). (2004). *Culturally competent practice with immigrant and refugee children and families.* New York: Guilford Press.

Fong, R. (2005). Social work practice with multiracial/multiethnic clients. In D. Lum (Ed.), *Cultural competence: Practice stages, and client systems* (pp. 146–172). Belmont, CA: Brooks/Cole.

Fong, R., Boyd, T., & Browne, C. (1999). The Gandhi technique: A biculturalization approach for empowering Asian and Pacific Islander families. *Journal of Multicultural Social Work, 7,* 95–110.

Fong, R., & Furuto, S. (Eds.). (2001). *Culturally competent practice: Skills, interventions, and evaluations.* Boston: Allyn and Bacon.

Fong, R., McRoy, R., & Hendricks, C. (Eds.). (2006). *Intersecting child welfare, substance abuse, and family violence: Culturally competent approaches.* Alexandria, VA: Council on Social Work Education.

Fong, R., & Mokuau, N. (1994). Not simply "Asian Americans": A periodical literature review on Asians and Pacific Islanders. *Social Work, 39,* 298–305.

Galan, F. (2001). Intervention with Mexican American families. In R. Fong & S. Furuto (Eds.), *Culturally competent practice: Skills, interventions, and evaluations* (pp. 255–268). Boston: Allyn and Bacon.

Gordon, M. (1978). *Human nature, class, and ethnicity.* New York: Oxford University Press.

Green, D., Rodriguez, C., & Fong, R. (2005). *Collaborative responses in addressing disproportionality: A look at dynamic community responses.* Paper presented at the Baccalaureate Social Work Educators Conference, Austin, TX.

Green, J. (1999). *Cultural awareness in the human services: A multi-ethnic approach* (3rd ed.). Boston: Allyn and Bacon.

Guadalupe, K., & Lum, D. (2005). *Multicultural contextual practice: Diversity and transcendence.* Belmont, CA: Brooks/Cole.

Harvey, A. (2001). Individual and family intervention skills with African Americans: An Afrocentric approach. In R. Fong & S. Furuto (Eds.), *Culturally competent practice: Skills, interventions, and evaluations* (pp. 225–240). Boston: Allyn and Bacon.

Hernandez, M., & Isaacs, M. (1998). *Promoting cultural competence in children's mental health services.* Baltimore: Paul A. Brookes.

Jung, M. (1998). *Chinese American family therapy: A new model for clinicians.* San Francisco: Jossey-Bass.

Lecca, P., Quervalu, I., Nunes, J., & Gonzales, H. (1998). *Cultural competency in health, social, and human services.* New York: Garland.

Lum, D. (2000). *Social work practice and people of color: A process-stage approach.* Belmont, CA: Brooks/Cole.

Lum, D. (Ed.). (2003). *Culturally competent practice: A framework for understanding diverse groups and justice issues* (2nd ed.). Belmont, CA: Brooks/Cole.

Marsiglia, F., & Menjivar, C. (2004). Nicaraguan and Salvadoran children and families. In R. Fong (Ed.), *Culturally competent practice with immigrant and refugee children and families* (pp. 253–273). New York: Guilford Press.

Mokuau, N. (1990). A family-centered approach in Native Hawaiian culture. *Families in Society: The Journal of Contemporary Human Services, 71*(10), 607–613.

Mokuau, N. (Ed.). (1991). *Handbook of social services for Asian and Pacific Islanders.* New York: Greenwood Press.

Norton, D. (1978). *The dual perspective: The inclusion of ethnic minority content in the social work curriculum.* New York: Council on Social Work Education.

O'Melia, M., & Miley, K. (Eds.). (2002). *Pathways to power: Readings in contextual social work practice.* Boston: Allyn and Bacon.

Pukui, M., Haertig, E., & Lee, C. (1971). *Ho'oponopono: Nana I Ke Kuma* (Vol. 1). Honolulu, HI: Queen Liliuokalani Children's Center.

Ross-Sheriff, F., & Husain, A. (2004). South Asian Muslim children and families. In R. Fong (Ed.), *Culturally competent practice with immigrant and refugee children and families* (pp. 163–182). New York: Guilford Press.

U.S. Census Bureau. (2000). *Census briefs and special reports: Overview of race and Hispanic origin.* Retrieved September 8, 2006, from http://www.census.gov/prod/2001pubs/c2kbro1-1.pdf

U.S. Census Bureau. (2003, June). *The foreign-born population: 2000.* Retrieved June 11, 2007, from http://www.census.gov/prod/2003pubs/c2kbr-34.pdf

Weaver, H. (2005). *Exploration in cultural competence: Journeys to the four directions.* Belmont, CA: Brooks/Cole.

Webb, N. (Ed.). (2001). *Culturally diverse parent-child and family relationships: A guide for social workers and other practitioners.* New York: Columbia University Press.

Winters, L., & DeBose, H. (Eds.). (2003). *New faces in a changing America: Multi-racial identity in the 21st century.* Thousand Oaks, CA: Sage.

Yellow Bird, M. (2001). Critical values and First Nations people. In R. Fong & S. Furuto (Eds.), *Culturally competent practice: Skills, interventions, and evaluations* (pp. 61–74). Boston: Allyn and Bacon.

Zuniga, M. (2004). Latino children and families. In R. Fong (Ed.), *Culturally competent practice with immigrant and refugee children and families* (pp. 183–201). New York: Guilford Press.

5 Gender and Social Work Practice

Abbey, A., & McAuslan, P. (2004). A longitudinal examination of male college students' perpetration of sexual assault. *Journal of Consulting and Clinical Psychology, 72*(5), 747–756.

American Psychiatric Association. (2000). *Diagnostic and statistical manual of mental disorders* (4th ed., text rev.). Washington, DC: Author.

Artz, N., Munger, J., & Purdy, W. (1999). Gender issues in advertising language. *Women and Language, 22*(2), 20–26.

Banister, E., & Schreiber, R. (2001). Young women's health concerns: Revealing paradox. *Health Care for Women International, 22*(7), 633–648.

Beisie, L. (2000, October 24). Step aside yuppies, here come "dewks." *Christian Science Monitor, 92*(233). Retrieved August 6, 2005, from the Gale Group RDS database.

Bent-Goodley, T. B. (2005). Culture and domestic violence. *Journal of Interpersonal Violence, 20*(2), 195–203.

Bertakis, K. D., Helms, L. J., Callahan, E. J., Azari, R., Leigh, P., & Robbins, J. A. (2001). Patient gender differences in the diagnosis of depression in primary care. *Journal of Women's Health and Gender-Based Medicine, 10*(7), 689–698.

Besthorn, F. H., & McMillen, D. P. (2002). The oppression of women and nature: Ecofeminism as a framework for an expanded ecological social work. *Families in Society: The Journal of Contemporary Human Services, 83*(3), 221–233.

Black, B., & Weisz, A. (2003). Dating violence: Help-seeking behaviors of African American middle schoolers. *Violence Against Women, 9*(2), 187–206.

Bowie, S., & Hancock, H. (2001). African Americans and graduate school education: A study of career choice influences and strategies to reverse enrollment decline. *Journal of Social Work Education, 36*(3), 429–448.

Callahan, M. R., Tolman, R. M., & Saunders, D. G. (2003). Adolescent dating violence victimization and psychological well-being. *Journal of Adolescent Research, 18*(6), 664–681.

Center for Disease Control. (2006). *Abortion surveillance: United States, 2003.* Retrieved January 25, 2007, from http://www.cdc.gov/mmwr/preview/mmwrhtml/ss5511a1.htm

Chernesky, R. H. (1995). Feminist administration style, structure, purpose. In N. Van Den Bergh (Ed.), *Feminist practice in the 21st century* (pp. 70–88). Washington, DC: NASW Press.

Cho, M. (1996). Immigrant women are more often victims of family violence. In D. L. Bender, B. Leone, S. Barbour, B. Stalcup, & A. E. Sadler (Eds.), *Family violence* (pp. 132–138). San Diego, CA: Greenhaven Press.

Clark, E. J. (2006, May). Closing the gender pay gap. *NASW News,* p. 3.

Courtois, C. (1993). Vicarious traumatization of the therapist. *National Center for PTSD Clinical Newsletter, 3*(2), 1.

Davis, D. R., & DiNitto, D. M. (2005). Gender and the use of drugs and alcohol: Fact, fiction, and unanswered questions. In C. A. McNeece & D. M. DiNitto (Eds.), *Chemical dependency: A systems approach* (pp. 503–545). Boston: Allyn and Bacon.

DiPalma, S., & Topper, B. (2001). Social work academia: Is the glass ceiling beginning to crack? *Affilia: Journal of Women and Social Work, 16*(1), 31–45.

Fineran, S., & Bennett, L. (1999). Gender and power issues of peer sexual harassment among teenagers. *Journal of Interpersonal Violence, 14*(6), 626–641.

Fisher, B. S., & Cullen, F. T. (2000). Measuring the sexual victimization of college women: Evolution, current controversies, and future research. *Criminal Justice, 4,* 317–390.

Fisher, B. S., Cullen, F. T., & Turner, M. G. (2002). Being pursued: Stalking victimization in a national study of college women. *Criminology and Public Policy, 1*(2), 257–609.

Gibelman, M., & Schervish, P. H. (1995). Pay equity in social work: Not! *Social Work, 40*(5), 622–629.

Green, H. (1999, March 15). Web wisdom [Review of the book *Shaping markets when customers make the rules*]. *Business Week.* Retrieved July 25, 2005, from http://www.businessweek.com/1999/99_11/b3620046.htm

Hansen, F. J., & Osborne, D. (1995). Portrayal of women and elderly patients in psychotropic drug advertisements. *Women and Therapy, 16*(1), 129–141.

hooks, b. (2000). Feminism: A movement to end sexist oppression. In M. Adams, W. J. Blumenfeld, R. Castaneda, H. W. Hackman, M. L. Peters, & X. Zuniga (Eds.), *Readings for diversity and social justice* (pp. 238–240). New York: Routledge.

Hyde, C., & Deal, K. (2003). Does gender matter? Male and female participation in social work classrooms. *Affilia: Journal of Women and Social Work, 18*(2), 192–209.

Iliffe, G., & Steed, L. G. (2000). Exploring the counselor's experience of working with perpetrators and survivors of domestic violence. *Journal of Interpersonal Violence, 15*(4), 393-412.

Institute of Management and Administration. (2003). *Survey reveals trends in the U.S. workforce: Women have lower salaries.* Retrieved August 5, 2005, from the Gale Group RDS database.

Kasle, S., Wilhelm, M. S., & Reed, K. L. (2002). Optimal health and well-being for women: Definitions and strategies derived from focus groups of women. *Women's Health Issues, 12*(4), 178–190.

Katz, J. (2000). Pornography and men's consciousness. In M. Adams, W. J. Blumenfeld, R. Castaneda, H. W. Hackman, M. L. Peters, & X. Zuniga (Eds.), *Readings for diversity and social justice* (pp. 247–251). New York: Routledge.

Kernsmith, R., & Kernsmith, P. (2005, July). *Female pornography use and sexual coercion perpetration*. Poster presented at the eighth International Family Violence Research Conference, Portsmouth, NH.

Kimmel, M. S. (2000). Masculinity as homophobia: Fear, shame and silence in the construction of gender identity. In M. Adams, W. J. Blumenfeld, R. Castaneda, H. W. Hackman, M. L. Peters, & X. Zuniga (Eds.), *Readings for diversity and social justice* (pp. 213–219). New York: Routledge.

Kravetz, D. (1976). Sexism in a woman's profession. *Social Work, 21*(6), 421–426.

Landrine, H., & Klonoff, E. A. (1997). *Discrimination against women: Prevalence, consequences, remedies*. Thousand Oaks, CA: Sage.

Letellier, P. (1996). Gays are often victims of domestic violence. In D. L. Bender, B. Leone, S. Barbour, B. Stalcup, & A. E. Sadler (Eds.), *Family violence* (pp. 149–152). San Diego, CA: Greenhaven Press.

Lie, S. S., & O'Leary, V. (1990). *Storming the tower*. East Brunswick, NJ: Nichols Publishing.

Lorber, J. (2000). "Night to his day": The social construction of gender. In M. Adams, W. J. Blumenfeld, R. Castaneda, H. W. Hackman, M. L. Peters, & X. Zuniga (Eds.), *Readings for diversity and social justice* (pp. 203–213). New York: Routledge.

Mansfield, A. K., Addis, M. E., & Courtenay, W. (2005). Measurement of men's help seeking: Development and evaluation of the barriers to help seeking scale. *Psychology of Men and Masculinity, 6*(2), 95–108.

McFarlane, J. M. (1999). Stalking and intimate partner femicide. *Homicide Studies, 3*(4), 300–316.

Molidor, C., & Tolman, R. M. (1998). Gender and contextual factors in adolescent dating violence. *Violence Against Women, 4*(2), 180–194.

National Abortion Federation. (2003). *Teenage women, abortion, and the law*. Retrieved July 17, 2005, from http://www.prochoice.org/about_abortion/facts/teenage_women.html

National Association of Social Workers. (2003). *Social work speaks* (6th ed.). Washington DC: National Association of Social Workers.

National Association of Social Workers. (2005). *Code of ethics of the National Association of Social Workers*. Retrieved November 16, 2005, from http://www.socialworkers.org/pubs/code/code.asp

National Institute of Mental Health. (2000). *Depression: What every woman should know*. Retrieved July 18, 2005, from http://www.nimh.nih.gov/publicat/depwomen knows.cfm

Nes, J. A., & Iadicola, P. (1989). Toward a definition of feminist social work: A comparison of liberal, radical, and socialist models. *Social Work, 34*(1), 12–21.

Newman, B. M., & Newman, P. R. (1999). *Developing through life: A psychosocial approach* (7th ed.). Belmont, CA: Brook/Cole Wadsworth.

Ramirez, O. (1998). Mexican American children and adolescents. In J. T. Gibbs & L. N. Huang (Eds.), *Children of color: Psychological interventions with culturally diverse youth* (pp. 215–239). San Francisco: Jossey-Bass.

Rape, Abuse and Incest National Network. (n.d.). *Statistics*. Retrieved January 16, 2007, from http://www.rainn.org/statistics/index.html

Stamps, L. E. (2002). Maternal preference in child custody decision. *Journal of Divorce and Remarriage, 37*(1/2), 1–11.

Steinem, G. (2000). Revving up for the next twenty-five years. In M. Adams, W. J. Blumenfeld, R. Castaneda, H. W. Hackman, M. L. Peters, & X. Zuniga (Eds.), *Readings for diversity and social justice* (pp. 256–260). New York: Routledge.

Swim, J. K., & Cohen, L. L. (1997). Overt, covert, and subtle sexism: A comparison between attitudes toward women and modern sexism scales. *Psychology of Women Quarterly, 21*, 103–118.

Tjaden, P., & Thoennes, N. (1998, April). *Stalking in America: Findings from the National Violence Against Women Survey.* Retrieved October 5, 2005, from http://www.ncjrs.org/txtfiles/169592.txt

Tjaden, P., & Thoennes, N. (2000). *Full report of the prevalence, incidence, and consequences of violence against women: Findings from the National Violence Against Women Survey.* Washington, DC: U.S. Department of Justice.

Upadhyay, S. (1999, November). Rights-gulf: Women's rights defined by equality and economics. *Interpress Service.* Retrieved August 6, 2005, from Gale Group RDS database.

U.S. Census Bureau. (2004). *Poverty status in the past 12 months.* Retrieved October 5, 2005, from http://factfinder.census.gov/servlet/STTable?_bm=y&-geo_id=01000US&-qr_name=ACS_2005_EST_G00_S1702&-ds_name=ACS_2005_EST_G00_

U.S. Census Bureau. (2005). *Employment status by sex: 2000.* Retrieved October 22, 2005, from http://factfinder.census.gov/servlet/STTable?_bm=y&-geo_id=01000US&-qr_name=ACS_2005_EST_G00_S2301&-Tables=('ACS_2005_EST_G00_S2301')&-ds_name=ACS_2005_EST_G00_&-_lang=en&-redoLog=false&-st=st

U.S. Census Bureau. (2006). *Custodial mothers and fathers and their child support: 2003.* Retrieved January 27, 2007, from http://www.census.gov/prod/2006pubs/p60-230.pdf

Van Den Bergh, N. (Ed.). (1995). *Feminist practice in the 21st century.* Washington, DC: NASW Press.

Weisz, A., & Black, B. (in press). *Relationships should not hurt: Programs to reduce dating violence and sexual assault.* New York: Columbia University Press.

Women's Research and Education Institute. (n.d.). *Women in the military.* Retrieved July 18, 2005, from http://www.wrei.org/MilitaryWomen.htm

World Health Organization. (2005). *The World Health report 2005: Make every mother and child count.* Geneva, Switzerland: Author.

Zawacki, T., Abbey, A., Buck, P., McAuslan, P., & Clinton-Sherrod, A. M. (2003). Perpetrators of alcohol-involved sexual assaults: How do they differ from other sexual assault perpetrators and nonperpetrators? *Aggressive Behavior, 29*, 366–380.

6 Social Work Practice with Gay, Lesbian, Bisexual, and Transgender People

Arnup, K. (1999). Out in this world: The social and legal context of gay and lesbian families. *Journal of Gay and Lesbian Social Services, 10*, 1–26.

Bailey, J. M. (1996). Gender identity. In R. C. Savin-Williams & K. M. Cohen (Eds.), *The lives of lesbians, gays, and bisexuals: Children to adults* (pp. 71–93). Fort Worth, TX: Harcourt Brace.

Boxer, A. M. (2007). Gay, lesbian, and bisexual aging into the twenty-first century: An overview and introduction. *International Journal of Sexuality and Gender Studies, 2*(3/4), 187–197.

Brown, L. (1995). Lesbian identities: Concepts and issues. In A. R. D'Augelli & C. J. Patterson (Eds.), *Lesbian, gay, and bisexual identities over the lifespan: Psychological perspectives* (pp. 3–23). New York: Oxford University Press.

Cass, V. C. (1984). Homosexual identity formation: Testing a theoretical model. *Journal of Sex Research, 20*(2), 143–167.

Centers for Disease Control and Prevention. (2007, January). *A glance at the HIV/AIDS epidemic.* Retrieved March 10, 2007, from http://www.cdc.gov/hiv/resources/factsheets/At-A-Glance.htm

Chan, C. S. (1992). Cultural considerations in counseling Asian American lesbians and gay men. In S. Dworkin & F. Gutierrez (Eds.), *Counseling gay men and lesbians: Journey to the end of the rainbow* (pp. 115–124). Alexandria, VA: American Association for Counseling and Development.

Children of Lesbians and Gays Everywhere. (n.d.). *About COLAGE.* Retrieved May 15, 2007, from http://www.colage.org/about

Coleman, E. (1982). Developmental stages of the coming out process. *Journal of Homosexuality, 7*(2/3), 31–43.

Council on Social Work Education. (2004). *Educational policy and accreditation standards.* Alexandria, VA: Author.

Crisp, C. L., & DiNitto, D. M. (2005). Substance abuse treatment with sexual minorities. In C. A. McNeece & D. M. DiNitto, *Chemical dependency: A systems approach* (3rd ed., pp. 401–422). Boston: Allyn and Bacon.

Crisp, D., Priest, B., & Torgerson, A. (1998). African American gay men: Developmental issues, choices and self-concept. *Family Therapy, 25*, 161–168.

Currah, P., & Minter, S. (2000). *Transgender equality: A handbook for activists and policymakers.* Washington, DC: Policy Institute of the National Gay and Lesbian Task Force.

Davies, D. (1996). Toward a model of gay affirmative therapy. In D. Davies & C. Neal (Eds.), *Pink therapy: A guide for counselors and therapists working with gay, lesbian and bisexual clients* (pp. 24–40). Philadelphia: Open University Press.

Fisher-Borne, M. (2006). Making the link: Domestic violence in the GLBT community. In L. Messinger & D. F. Morrow, *Case studies on sexual orientation and gender expression in social work practice* (pp. 96–98). New York: Columbia University Press.

Fox, R. C. (1995). Bisexual identities. In A. R. D'Augelli & C. J. Patterson (Eds.), *Lesbian, gay, and bisexual identities over the lifespan: Psychological perspectives* (pp. 48–86). New York: Oxford University Press.

Gay, Lesbian and Straight Education Network. (2003, January 23). *Coming out: A guide for youth and their allies.* Retrieved May 18, 2007, from http://www.glsen.org/cgi-bin/iowa/all/library/record/1290.html

Gay, Lesbian and Straight Education Network. (2005, October 17). *FAQs: About student organizing.* Retrieved April 29, 2007, from http://www.glsen.org/cgi-bin/iowa/all/news/record/1876.html

Gilman, S. E., Cochran, S. S., Mays, V. M., Hughes, M., Ostrow, D., & Kessler, R. C. (2001). Risk of psychiatric disorders among individuals reporting same-sex sexual partners in the National Comorbidity Survey. *American Journal of Public Health, 91*(6), 933–939.

Gonsiorek, J. C. (1995). Gay male identities: Concepts and issues. In A. R. D'Augelli & C. J. Patterson (Eds.), *Lesbian, gay, and bisexual identities over the lifespan: Psychological perspectives* (pp. 24–47). New York: Oxford University Press.

Greene, B. (1996). Lesbians and gay men of color: The legacy of ethnosexual mythologies in heterosexism. In E. D. Rothblum & L. A. Bonds (Eds.), *Preventing heterosexism and homophobia* (pp. 59–70). Thousand Oaks, CA: Sage.

Hartman, A. (1999). The long road to equality: Lesbians and social policy. In J. Laird (Ed.), *Lesbians and lesbian families* (pp. 91–120). New York: Columbia University Press.

Howard, R. (2006, November 8). *Four legal documents every LGBT person needs.* Paper presented at the Creating Change Conference, Kansas City, Missouri.

Human Rights Campaign Foundation. (2002). *State of the family: Laws and legislation affecting gay, lesbian, bisexual, and transgender families.* Washington, DC: Author. Retrieved March 11, 2007, from http://www.hrc.org/Template.cfm?Section=Home&ContentID=31608&TEMPLATE=/ContentManagement/ContentDisplay.cfm

Human Rights Campaign Foundation. (2007a). *Domestic partner benefits.* Retrieved March 11, 2007, from http://www.hrc.org/Template.cfm?Section=The_Issues&Template=/TaggedPage/TaggedPageDisplay.cfm&TPLID=26&ContentID=31366

Human Rights Campaign Foundation. (2007b). *Marriage/relationship recognition.* Retrieved March 13, 2007, from http://www.hrc.org/Template.cfm?Section=Center&Template=/TaggedPage/TaggedPageDisplay.cfm&TPLID=63&ContentID=15110

Hunter, J., & Schaecher, R. (1995). Gay and lesbian adolescents. In R. L. Edwards (Ed.), *The encyclopedia of social work* (19th ed., pp. 1055–1063). Washington, DC: NASW Press.

Hunter, S., & Hickerson, J. C. (2003). *Affirmative practice: Understanding and working with lesbian, gay, bisexual, and transgender persons.* Washington, DC: NASW Press.

Kinsey, A. C., Pomeroy, W. B., & Martin, C. E. (1948). *Sexual behavior in the human male.* Philadelphia: W. B. Saunders.

LAMBDA GLBT Community Services. (1997–2005). *LAMBDA gay and lesbian antiviolence project.* Retrieved March 13, 2007, from http://www.lambda.org/hatecr1.htm

Lee, J. A. (1994). *The empowerment approach to social work practice.* New York: Columbia University Press.

Leslie, D. R., Perina, B. A., & Maqueda, M. C. (2001). Clinical issues with transgender individuals. In Substance Abuse and Mental Health Services Administration (Ed.), *A provider's introduction to substance abuse treatment for lesbian, gay, bisexual, and transgender individuals* (pp. 91–97). (DHHS Publication No. SMA 01-3498). Rockville, MD: U.S. Department of Health and Human Services.

Lombardi, E. (2007). Public health and trans-people: Barriers to care and strategies to improve treatment. In I. H. Meyer & M. E. Northridge (Eds.), *The health of sexual minorities: Public health perspectives on lesbian, gay, bisexual and transgender populations* (pp. 638–652). New York: Springer.

McVinney, D. (2001). Clinical issues with bisexual clients. In Substance Abuse and Mental Health Services Administration (Ed.), *A provider's introduction to sub-*

stance abuse treatment for lesbian, gay, bisexual, and transgender individuals (pp. 87–90). (DHHS Publication No. SMA 01-3498). Rockville, MD: U.S. Department of Health and Human Services.

Morales, E. S. (1996). Gender roles among Latino gay and bisexual men: Implications for family and couple therapy. In J. Laird & R. J. Green (Eds.), *Lesbians and gays in families and couples: A handbook for therapists* (pp. 272–297). San Francisco: Jossey-Bass.

Morrow. D. F. (2006). Coming out as gay, lesbian, bisexual, and transgender. In D. F. Morrow & L. Messinger (Eds.), *Sexual orientation and gender expression in social work practice* (pp. 129–149). New York: Columbia University Press.

National Association of Social Workers. (1999). *Code of ethics of the National Association of Social Workers*. Washington, DC: Author. Retrieved March 13, 2007, from http://www.naswdc.org/pubs/code/code.asp

National Association of Social Workers. (2007). *Social workers and legal developments in gay rights*. Retrieved May 18, 2007, from http://www.socialworkers.org/ldf/legal_issue/200311.asp?back=yes

National Coalition of Anti-Violence Programs. (2006). *Anti-lesbian, gay, bisexual and transgender violence in 2005*. New York: Author. Retrieved March 10, 2007, from http://www.ncavp.org/common/document_files/Reports/2005%20National%20HV%20Report%20(Release%20Draft).pdf

National Committee on Lesbian, Gay, and Bisexual Issues, National Association of Social Workers. (2000, January 21). *Position statement: "Reparative" and "conversion" therapies for lesbians and gay men*. Washington, DC: Author. Retrieved March 31, 2007, from http://www.socialworkers.org/diversity/lgb/reparative.asp

Onken, S. J. (1999, June). *GLBT, disabled and rural: Intersections of identity and issues*. Paper presented at Out on the Prairie: A National Conference on Gay, Lesbian, Bisexual and Transgender Issues and Human Service Related Practice in Rural Areas, Grand Forks, ND.

Parents and Friends of Lesbians and Gays. (2002). *Be yourself: Questions and answers for gay, lesbian, bisexual and transgender youth*. Washington, DC: Author.

Patton, C. (2005). *Anti-lesbian, gay, bisexual and transgender violence in 2005*. New York: National Coalition of Anti-Violence Programs.

Ramos, J. (1994). *Companeras: Latina lesbians*. New York: Routledge.

Saltzburg, S. (2004). Learning that an adolescent child is gay or lesbian: The parent experience. *Social Work, 49*(1), 109–118.

Savin-Williams, R. (1998). *". . . And then I became gay": Young men's stories*. New York: Routledge.

Savin-Williams, R. (2005). *The new gay teenager*. Cambridge, MA: Harvard University Press.

Sears, R. B., Gates, G., & Rubenstein, W. B. (2005, September). *Same-sex couples and same-sex couples raising children in the United States: Data from census 2000*. Los Angeles, CA: Williams Project on Sexual Orientation Law and Public Policy, UCLA School of Law. Retrieved March 11, 2007, from http://www.law.ucla.edu/williamsinstitute/publications/Policy-Census-index.html

Sloan, L. M. (1992). *Lesbian battering*. Paper presented at the Southwest Regional Social Sciences Conference, Austin, TX.

Stokes, J. P., & Peterson, J. L. (1998). Homophobia, self-esteem, and risk for HIV among African American men who have sex with men. *AIDS Education and Prevention, 10*(3), 278–292.

Troiden, R. R. (1993). The formation of homosexual identities. In L. D. Garnets & D. C. Kimmel (Eds.), *Psychological perspectives on lesbian and gay male experiences* (pp. 191–217). New York: Columbia University Press.

Tuerk, C. (1998, July). Stages parents go through when a child comes out. *In the Family*, p. 16.

Van Den Bergh, N., & Crisp, C. (2004). Defining culturally competent practice with sexual minorities: Implications for social work education and practice. *Journal of Social Work Education, 40*(2), 221–238.

Wishik, H., & Pierce, C. (1995). *Sexual orientation and identity: Heterosexual, lesbian, gay, and bisexual journeys.* Laconia, NH: New Dynamics.

Zimmerman, B. (1992). What has never been: An overview of lesbian feminist literary criticism. In W. R. Dynes & S. Donaldson (Eds.), *Lesbianism* (pp. 341–365). New York: Garland.

7 Mental Illness and Social Work Practice

American Psychiatric Association. (2000). *Diagnostic and statistical manual of mental disorders* (4th ed., text rev.). Washington, DC: Author.

Anderson, C. M., Reiss, D. M., & Hogarty, G. (1986). *Schizophrenia and the family: A practitioner's guide to psychoeducation and management.* New York: Guilford Press.

Austin, D. M. (1986). *A history of social work education.* Austin: School of Social Work, University of Texas at Austin.

Black, W. G. (1993). Military-induced family separation: Stress reduction interventions. *Social Work, 38*, 273–280.

Center for Substance Abuse Treatment. (2005). *Substance abuse treatment for persons with co-occurring disorders.* Treatment Improvement Protocol Series 42 (DHHS Publication No. SMA 05-3992). Rockville, MD: Substance Abuse and Mental Health Services Administration.

Corcoran, J., & Walsh, J. (Eds.). (2006). *Clinical assessment and diagnosis in social work practice.* New York: Oxford University Press.

Goldman, H. H., & Morrissey, J. P. (1985). The alchemy of mental health policy: Homelessness and the fourth cycle of reform. *American Journal of Public Health, 75*, 727–731.

Grob, G. N. (1994). *The mad among us: A history of the care of America's mentally ill.* New York: Free Press.

Hicks-Coolick, A., Burnside-Eaton, P., & Peters, A. (2003). Homeless children: Needs and services. *Child and Youth Care Forum, 32*(40), 197–210.

Hoffman, D., & Rosenheck, R. (2001). Homeless mothers with severe mental illness and their children: Predictors of family reunification. *Psychiatric Rehabilitation Journal, 25*(2), 163–169.

International Center on Clubhouse Development. (2002). *What is a clubhouse?* Retrieved February 4, 2007, from http://www.iccd.org/base.asp?SectionID=2

Janzen, C., Harris, O., Jordan, C., & Franklin, C. (2006). *Family treatment: Evidence-based practice with populations at risk* (4th ed.). Belmont, CA: Thompson Brooks-Cole.

Jayaratne, S., Davis-Sacks, M. L., & Chess, W. A. (1991). Private practice may be good for your health and well-being. *Social Work, 36*(3), 224–229.

Jordan, C., Lewellen, A., & Vandiver, V. (1995). Psychoeducation for minority families: A social work perspective. *International Journal of Mental Health, 23*(4), 27–43.

Kessler, R. C., Berglund, P., Demler, O., Jin, R., Merikangas, K. R., & Walters, E. E. (2005). Lifetime prevalence and age-of-onset distributions of *DSM-IV* disorders in the National Comorbidity Survey Replication. *Archives of General Psychiatry, 62*, 593–602.

Kessler, R. C., Nelson, C. B., McGonagle, K. A., Edlund, M. J., Frank, R. G., & Leaf, P. J. (1996). The epidemiology of co-occurring addictive and mental disorders: Implications for prevention and service utilization. *American Journal of Orthopsychiatry, 66*, 17–31.

Lambert, M. (Ed.). (2004). *Bergin and Garfield's handbook of psychotherapy and behavior change* (5th ed.). New York: Wiley.

Marshall, M., & Lockwood, A. (2007). Assertive community treatment of people with severe mental disorders [Abstract]. *Cochrane Database of Systematic Reviews, 1*. Retrieved February 4, 2007, from http://www.cochrane.org/reviews/en/ab001089.html

McHugo, G. J., Drake, R. E., Burton, H. L., & Ackerson, T. H. (1995). A scale for assessing the stage of substance abuse treatment in persons with severe mental illness. *Journal of Nervous and Mental Disease, 183*, 762–767.

Mental Health America. (2007a). *Children's mental health statistics*. Retrieved February 4, 2007, from http://www1.nmha.org/children/prevent/stats.cfm

Mental Health America. (2007b). *Young people and suicide: Teen suicide*. Retrieved February 8, 2007, from http://www.nmha.org/index.cfm?objectid=C7DF98D7-1372-4D20-C8A64BC67FFA74CD

Mental Health Systems Act of 1980, 42 U.S.C. § 9501 (2000).

Miller, W. R., & Rollnick, S. (2002). *Motivational interviewing: Preparing people for change* (2nd ed.). New York: Guilford Press.

Morrissey, J. P., & Goldman, H. H. (1984). Cycles of reform in the care of the chronically mentally ill. *Hospital and Community Psychiatry, 35*, 785–793.

Mueser, K. T., Drake, R. E., & Wallach, M. A. (1998). Dual diagnosis: A review of etiological theories. *Addictive Behaviors, 23*, 717–734.

National Association of Social Workers. (2006). *Assuring the sufficiency of a frontline workforce: A national study of licensed social workers*. Washington, DC: Author.

National Center for Injury Prevention and Control. (2004). *Welcome to WISQARS*. Retrieved February 4, 2007, from http://www.cdc.gov/ncipc/wisqars

National Institute of Mental Health. (2003). *In harm's way: Suicide in America* (NIH Publication No. 03-4594). Bethesda, MD: Author.

Poulin, J. (2005). *Strengths-based generalist practice: A collaborative approach* (2nd ed.). Belmont, CA: Brooks/Cole.

President's New Freedom Commission on Mental Health. (2003, July 22). *Achieving the promise: Transforming mental health care in America.* Retrieved January 3, 2006, from http://www.mentalhealthcommission.gov/reports/reports.htm

Protection and Advocacy for Mentally Ill Individuals Act of 1986, 42 U.S.C. § 10841 (2000).

Richards, P. S., & Bergin, A. E. (2002). *A spiritual strategy for counseling and psychotherapy.* Washington, DC: American Psychological Association.

Shern, D. L., Tsemberis, S., Anthony, W., Lovell, A., Richmond, L. Felton, C., et al. (2000). Serving street-dwelling individuals with psychiatric disabilities: Outcomes of a psychiatric rehabilitation clinical trial. *American Journal of Public Health, 90*(12), 1872–1878.

Smith, E. J. (1990). Ethnic identify development: Toward the development of a theory within the context of majority/minority status. *Journal of Counseling and Development, 70*(1), 181–188.

Stein, L. I., & Test, M. A. (1980). Alternative to mental hospital treatment: I. Conceptual model, treatment program, and clinical evaluation. *Archives of General Psychiatry, 37,* 392–397.

Substance Abuse and Mental Health Services Administration. (2006). *Results from the 2005 National Survey on Drug Use and Health: National findings.* Office of Applied Studies, NSDUH Series H-30 (DHHS Publication No. SMA 06-4194). Rockville, MD: Author.

Sullivan, G., Burnam, A., & Koegel, P. (2002). Pathways to homelessness among the mentally ill. *Social Psychiatry and Psychiatric Epidemiology, 35,* 444–450.

Tarvis, C. (1991). The measure of women: Paradoxes and perspectives in the study of gender. In J. D. Goodchilds (Ed.), *Psychological perspectives on human diversity in America* (pp. 91–136). Washington, DC: American Psychological Association.

U.S. Department of Health and Human Services. (1999). *Mental health: A report of the Surgeon General—executive summary.* Rockville, MD: U.S. Department of Health and Human Services, Substance Abuse and Mental Health Services Administration, National Institutes of Health, National Institute of Mental Health.

Wallace, M. E. (1982). Private practice: A nationwide study. *Social Work, 27*(3), 262–267.

Walthrap, C. M., Petras, H., Mandell, D. S., Stephens, R. L., Holden, E. W., & Leaf, P. J. (2004). Gender differences in patterns of risk factors among children receiving mental health services. *Journal of Behavioral Health Services and Research, 31*(3), 297–311.

Wang, P. S., Lane, M., Olfson, M., Pincus, H. A., Wells, K. B., & Kessler, R. C. (2005). Twelve-month use of mental health services in the United States: Results from the National Comorbidity Survey Replication. *Archives of General Psychiatry, 62*(6), 629–640.

Webb. D. K. (2004). *Good chemistry: Co-leader's manual.* Austin, TX: Author.

Wetzel, J. W. (1994). Women of the world: The wonder class—a global perspective on women and mental health. In L. V. Davis (Ed.), *Building on women's strengths: A social work agenda for the twenty-first century* (pp. 229–243). New York: Haworth Press.

8 Addictions and Social Work Practice

American Psychiatric Association. (2000). *Diagnostic and statistical manual of mental disorders* (4th ed., text rev.). Washington, DC: Author.

Amodeo, M., Robb, N., Peou, S., & Tran, H. (1996). Adapting mainstream substance-abuse interventions for Southeast Asian clients. *Families in Society: The Journal of Contemporary Human Services, 77*, 403–413.

Azrin, N. H., Donohue, B., Besalel, V. A., Kogan, E. S., & Acierno, R. (1994). Youth drug abuse treatment: A controlled study. *Journal of Child and Adolescent Substance Abuse, 3*(3), 1–16.

Babor, T. F., Higgins-Biddle, J. C., Saunders, J. B., & Monteiro, M. G. (2001). *AUDIT: The Alcohol Use Disorders Identification Test: Guidelines for use in primary care* (2nd ed.). Geneva, Switzerland: World Health Organization. Retrieved October 30, 2005, from http://www.who.int/substance_abuse/en

Center for Substance Abuse Treatment. (n.d.). *Buprenorphine.* Retrieved March 6, 2007, from http://www.buprenorphine.samhsa.gov/index.html

Center for Substance Abuse Treatment. (2005). *Substance abuse treatment for persons with co-occurring disorders.* Treatment Improvement Protocol Series 42 (DHHS Publication No. SMA 05-3992). Rockville, MD: Substance Abuse and Mental Health Services Administration.

Centers for Disease Control and Prevention. (2007, February 26). *Targeting tobacco use: The nation's leading cause of death.* Retrieved March 6, 2007, from http://www.cdc.gov/nccdphp/publications/aag/osh.htm

Crisp, C. L., & DiNitto, D. M. (2005). Substance abuse treatment with sexual minorities. In C. A. McNeece & D. M. DiNitto, *Chemical dependency: A systems approach* (3rd ed., pp. 401–422). Boston: Allyn and Bacon.

DiNitto, D. M. (2002). War and peace: Social work and the state of chemical dependency treatment in the United States. *Journal of Social Work Practice in the Addictions, 2*(3/4), 7–29.

DiNitto, D. M. (2005a). The future of social work practice in addictions. *Advances in Social Work, 6*(1), 202–209.

DiNitto, D. M. (2005b). *Social welfare: Politics and public policy. With research navigator* (6th ed.). Boston: Allyn and Bacon.

Engs, R. (2004). *How can I manage compulsive shopping and spending (shopoholism).* Bloomington: Trustees of Indiana University & Ruth C. Engs. Retrieved November 19, 2006, from http://www.indiana.edu/~engs/hints/shop.html

Ewing, J. A. (1984). Detecting alcoholism: The CAGE questionnaire. *Journal of the American Medical Association, 252*(14), 1905–1907.

Fahls-Stewart, W., O'Farrell, T. J., Feehan, M., Birchler, G. R., Tiller, S., & McFarlin, S. K. (2000). Behavioral couples therapy versus individual-based treatment for male substance-abusing patients: An evaluation of significant individual change and comparison of improvement rates. *Journal of Substance Abuse Treatment, 18*, 249–254.

Galanter, M. (1997). Network therapy. In J. H. Lowinson, P. Ruiz, R. B. Millman, & J. G. Langrod (Eds.), *Substance abuse: A comprehensive textbook* (pp. 478–484). Baltimore: Williams and Wilkins.

Hay Group. (2001, February 15). *Employer health care dollars spent on addiction treatment.* Chevy Chase, MD: American Society of Addiction Medicine. Retrieved November 13, 2005, from http://www.asam.org/pressrel/hay.htm

Lesieur, H. R., & Blume, S. B. (1987). The South Oaks Gambling Screen (SOGS): A new instrument for the identification of pathological gamblers. *American Journal of Psychiatry, 144,* 1184–1188.

Levin, J. D. (1989). *Alcoholism: A bio-psychosocial approach.* New York: Hemisphere.

Marlatt, G. A., & Gordon, J. R. (Eds.). (1985). *Relapse prevention: Maintenance strategies in the treatment of addictive behaviors.* New York: Guilford Press.

McLellan, A. T., Lewis, D. C., O'Brien, C. P., & Kleber, H. D. (2000). Drug dependence, a chronic medical illness: Implications for treatment, insurance, and outcomes evaluation. *Journal of the American Medical Association, 284*(13), 1689–1695.

McNeece, C. A. (2003). After the war on drugs is over: Implications for social work education. *Journal of Social Work Education, 39*(2), 1–20.

McNeece, C. A., & DiNitto, D. M. (2005). *Chemical dependency: A systems approach* (3rd ed.). Boston: Allyn and Bacon.

Meyers, R. J., & Miller, W. R. (Eds.). (2001). *A community reinforcement approach to addiction treatment.* Cambridge: Cambridge University Press.

Miller, W. R., & Rollnick, S. (2002). *Motivational interviewing: Preparing people for change* (2nd ed.). New York: Guilford Press.

Miller, W. R., & Sanchez, V. C. (1994). Motivating young adults for treatment and lifestyle change. In G. S. Howard & P. E. Nathan (Eds.), *Issues in alcohol use and misuse by young adults* (pp. 55–81). Notre Dame, IN: University of Notre Dame Press.

Miller, W. R., & Weisner, C. M. (Eds.). (2002). *Changing substance abuse through health and social systems.* New York: Kluwer Academic/Plenum.

Najavits, L. M., & Weiss, R. D. (1994). Variations in therapist effectiveness in treatment. *Addiction, 89,* 679–688.

National Association of Social Workers. (2006). *Assuring the sufficiency of a frontline workforce: A study of licensed social workers.* Washington, DC: Author.

National Institute of Diabetes and Digestive and Kidney Diseases. (2004). *Gastrointestinal surgery for obesity.* Bethesda, MD: National Institutes of Health. Retrieved May 27, 2006, from http://win.niddk.nih.gov/publications/gastric.htm

National Institute on Alcohol Abuse and Alcoholism. (2000). *Tenth special report to the U.S. Congress on alcohol and health.* Bethesda, MD: U.S. Department of Health and Human Services.

National Institute on Drug Abuse. (2000). *Principles of drug addiction treatment: A research-based guide.* Bethesda, MD: U.S. Department of Health and Human Services.

National Research Council. (1999). *Pathological gambling: A critical review.* Washington, DC: National Academy Press.

Oakley-Browne, M. A., Adams, P., & Mobberley, P. M. (2004, October). *Interventions for pathological gambling: A systematic review* [Abstract]. Cape Town, South Africa: Cochrane Collaboration. Retrieved November 13, 2005, from http://www.cochrane.org/colloquia/abstracts/capetown/capetownPB27.html

Office of Applied Studies. (2005, September 8). *Overview of findings from the 2004 National Survey on Drug Use and Health.* Rockville, MD: Substance Abuse and Mental Health Services Administration. Retrieved October 8, 2005, from http://www.oas.samhsa.gov/nsduh/2k4nsduh/2k4overview/2k4overview.htm#toc

O'Neill, J. V. (2001, January). Expertise in addictions said crucial. *NASW News,* 10.

Prochaska, J. O., DiClemente, C. C., & Norcross, J. C. (1992). In search of how people change: Applications to addictive behaviors. *American Psychologist, 47*(9), 1102–1114.

Schmidt, S. E., Liddle, H. A., & Dakof, G. A. (1996). Effects of multidimensional family therapy: Relationship of changes in parenting practices to symptom reduction in adolescent substance abuse. *Journal of Family Psychology, 10*(1), 1–16.

Sexual Compulsives Anonymous. (n.d.). *Are you sexually compulsive?* Retrieved March 6, 2007, from http://www.sca-recovery.org/compulsive.htm

Society for the Advancement of Sexual Health. (2007). *Am I a sex addict?* Retrieved March 6, 2007, from http://sash.net/content/view/46/53

Steinbeck, K. (2005). Childhood obesity: Treatment options. *Best Practice and Research: Clinical Endocrinology and Metabolism, 19*(3), 455–469.

Straussner, S. L. A., & Senreich, E. (2002). Educating social workers to work with individuals affected by substance use disorders. *Substance Abuse, 23*(3 Suppl.), 319–340.

Substance Abuse and Mental Health Services Administration. (2006). *Treatment episode data set (TEDS). Highlights—2004. National admissions to substance abuse treatment services.* DASIS Series S-31 (DHHS Publication No. SMA 0604140). Rockville, MD: U.S. Department of Health and Human Services.

U.S. Department of Health and Human Services. (1998, April 20). *Research shows needle exchange programs reduce HIV infections without increasing drug use* [Press release]. Retrieved November 13, 2005, from http://www.hhs.gov/news/press/1998pres/980420a.html

U.S. Department of Health and Human Services. (2001). *The Surgeon General's call to action to prevent and decrease overweight and obesity.* Rockville, MD: Public Health Service, Office of the Surgeon General. Retrieved March 6, 2007, from http://www.surgeongeneral.gov/topics/obesity/calltoaction/CalltoAction.pdf

U.S. Sentencing Commission. (2002, May). *Report to the Congress: Cocaine and federal sentencing policy.* Washington, DC: Author. Retrieved November 13, 2005, from http://www.ussc.gov/r_congress/02crack/2002crackrpt.htm

Winters, K. (1999). *Screening and assessing adolescents for substance use disorders.* Treatment Improvement Protocol Series 31 (DHHS Publication No. SMA 99-3282). Rockville, MD: Substance Abuse and Mental Health Services Administration.

9 Social Work Practice in Health-Care Settings

Badger, L, Ackerson, B., Buttell, F., & Rand, E. (1997). The case for integration of social work psychosocial services into rural primary care practices. *Health and Social Work, 22*(1), 20–29.

Burns, J. (1993). Subacute care feeds need to diversify. *Modern Healthcare, 38,* 34–36.

Cabot, R. (1955). Hospital and dispensary social work. In D. Goldstein (Ed.), *Expanding horizons in medical social work* (pp. 255–270). Chicago: University of Chicago Press. (Originally published in 1928)

Cannon, I. (1913). *Social work in hospitals.* New York: Russell Sage Foundation.

Centers for Medicare and Medicaid Services. (2006, February 28). *National health expenditure data: Historical.* Retrieved March 27, 2006, from http://www.cms.hhs.gov/NationalHealthExpendData/02_NationalHealthAccountsHistorical.asp#TopOfPage

Center to Advance Palliative Care. (2002). *Evolution in the United States.* Retrieved July 12, 2005, from http://64.85.16.230/educate/content/rationale/evolutioninus.html

Cook, C., Freedman, J., Freedman, L., Arick, R., & Miller, M. (1996). Screening for social and environmental problems in a VA primary care setting. *Health and Social Work, 21*(1), 41–47.

Cowles, L. (2003). *Social work in the health field* (2nd ed.). New York: Haworth Press.

DeNavas-Walt, C., Proctor, B. D., & Lee, C. H. (2006, August). *Income, poverty, and health insurance coverage in the United States: 2005* (U.S. Census Bureau, Current Population Reports, P60-231).Washington, DC: U.S. Government Printing Office. Retrieved April 13, 2007, from http://www.census.gov/prod/2006pubs/p60-231.pdf

Department of Veterans Affairs. (2004). *Veteran's health administration: Social work in the Department of Veterans Affairs.* Retrieved August 8, 2005, from http://www1.va.gov/socialwork/page.cfm?pg=2

Dodds, T. A. (1993). Richard Cabot: Medical reformer during the Progressive Era (1890–1920) [Electronic version]. *Annals of Internal Medicine, 119*(5), 417–422.

Geva, J., & Weinman, M. (1995). Social work perspective on organ procurement. *Health and Social Work, 20*(4), 287–294.

Gray, B. (1991). *The profit motive and patient care.* Cambridge, MA: Harvard University Press.

Harrington, C., Woolhandler, S., Mullan, J., & Himmelstein, D. (2002). Does investor-ownership of nursing homes compromise the quality of care? *International Journal of Health Services, 32*(2), 315–325.

Hayslip, B., & Leon, J. (1992). *Hospice care.* Newbury Park, CA: Sage.

Himmelstein, D. U., Warren, E., Thorne, D., & Woolhandler, S. (2005, February 2). MarketWatch: Illness and injury as contributors to bankruptcy. *Health Affairs.* Retrieved February 28, 2007, from http://content.healthaffairs.org/cgi/content/full/hlthaff.w5.63/DC1

Humphreys, M., & Falck, H. (1990). Maintaining social work standards in for-profit hospitals. *Health and Social Work, 15*(1), 75–77.

Ingersoll-Dayton, B., Schroepfer, T., Pryce, J., & Waarala, C. (2003). Enhancing relationships in nursing homes through empowerment. *Social Work, 48*(3), 420–424.

Johnson, L., & Yanca, S. (2001). *Social work practice: A generalist approach.* Needham Heights, MA: Allyn and Bacon.

Kadushin, G., (2004). Home health care utilization: A review of the research for social work. *Health and Social Work, 29*(3), 219–245

Kaiser Commission on Medicaid and the Uninsured. (2005). *Covering the uninsured: Growing need, strained resources.* Retrieved November 23, 2003, from http://www.kff.org/uninsured/7429.cfm

Kerr, D. (1993). Mother Mary Aikenhead, the Irish Sisters of Charity and Our Lady's Hospice for Dying. *American Journal of Hospice and Palliative Care, 10*(3), 13–20.

Leiby, J. (1978). *A history of social welfare and social work in the United States.* New York: Columbia University Press.

Mizrahi, T., & Abramson, J. (1985). Sources of strain between physicians and social workers: Implications for social workers in health care settings. *Social Work and Health Care, 10,* 33–51.

Nacman, M. (1977). Social work in health settings: A historical review. *Social Work in Health Care, 2*(4), 407–418.

National Association of Social Workers. (1994). *NASW clinical indicators for social work and psychosocial services in nephrology settings.* Retrieved August 5, 2005, from http://www.naswdc.org/practice/standards/nephrology_settings.asp

National Association of Social Workers. (2003). *Social work speaks: NASW policy statements.* Washington, DC: Author.

National Institutes of Health. (2000). *Healthy people 2010.* Retrieved August 20, 2005, from http://www.healthypeople.gov/document/HTML/Volume1/04CKD.html

Netting, E. E., & Williams, F. G. (1996). Case manager–physician collaboration: Implications for professional identity, roles, and relationships. *Health and Social Work, 21*(3), 216–225.

Robinson, J. (1999). *The corporate practice of medicine: Competition and innovation in health care.* Berkeley and Los Angeles: University of California Press.

Ross, J. (1993). Redefining hospital social work: An embattled professional domain. *Health and Social Work, 18*(4), 243.

Saleebey, D. (1997). *Strengths perspective in social work practice.* Needham Heights, MA: Allyn and Bacon.

Saunders, C. (1996). A personal therapeutic journey [Electronic version]. *British Medical Journal, 7072*(313), 1599–1601.

Schneider, A., Hyer, K., & Luptak, M. (2000). Suggestions to social workers for surviving in managed care. *Health and Social Work, 125*(4), 276–279.

Specht, R., & Craig, G. (1985). *Human development: A social work approach.* Englewood Cliffs, NJ: Prentice Hall.

Trattner, W. (1994). *From poor law to welfare state.* New York: Free Press.

U.S. Department of Health and Human Services. (2005). *Frequently asked questions.* Retrieved July 20, 2005, from www.organdonor.gov/faq.html

Vaghy, A. (1998). Report identifies health care issues affecting social work education. *Social Work Education Reporter, 46*(3), 8–36.

Wernet, S. (1999). *Managed care in human services.* Chicago: Lyceum Books.

Williams, B. (1994). Comparison of services among different types of home health agencies. *Medical Care, 32,* 1134–1152.

World Health Organization. (1947). Constitution of the World Health Organization, signed on July 22, 1946, in New York City. *International Organization, 1*(1), 225–239.

10 Disabilities: The Fight for Inclusion Continues

American Association on Mental Retardation. (2002). *Mental retardation: Definition, classification, and system of supports* (10th ed.). Washington, DC: Author.

Americans with Disabilities Act of 1990, Pub. L. No. 101-336, 104 Stat. 327 (1991).

Autism Speaks. (2007). *Facts about autism.* Retrieved May 6, 2007, from http://www.autismspeaks.com/whatisit/facts.php

Beaulaurier, R. L., & Taylor, S. H. (2001). Social work practice with people with disabilities in the era of disability rights. *Social Work in Health Care, 32*(4), 67–91.

Briggs, M. H. (1997). Team definition. In K. G. Butler (Ed.), *Building early interventions teams: Working together for children and families* (pp. 13–21). Gaithersburg, MD: Aspen.

DePoy, E., & Miller, M. (1996). Preparation of social workers for serving individuals with developmental disabilities: A brief report. *Mental Retardation, 34,* 54–57.

DeWeaver, K. L. (1995). Developmental disabilities: Definitions and policies. In R. L. Edwards (Ed.), *The encyclopedia of social work* (19th ed., pp. 712–720). Washington, DC: NASW Press.

DeWeaver, K. L., & Johnson, P. J. (1983). Case management in rural areas for the developmentally disabled. *Human Services in the Rural Environment, 8*(4), 23–31.

DeWeaver, K. L., & Kropf, N. P. (1992). Persons with mental retardation: A forgotten minority in education. *Journal of Social Work Education, 28*(1), 36–46.

Dickerson, M. U. (1981). *Social work practice with the mentally retarded.* New York: Free Press.

Drew, C. J., & Hardman, M. L. (2004). *Mental retardation: A lifespan approach to people with intellectual disabilities* (8th ed.). Upper Saddle River, NJ: Pearson Merrill Prentice Hall.

Fishley, P. (1992). I am John. *Health and Social Work, 17*(2), 151–157.

Freedman, R. I., & Boyer, N. C. (2000). The power to choose: Supports for families caring for individuals with developmental disabilities. *Health and Social Work, 25*(1), 59–68.

Galambos, C. (2004). Social work practice with people with disabilities: Are we doing enough? *Health and Social Work, 29*(3), 163–165.

Gilson, S. F., Bricout, J. C., & Baskind, F. R. (1998). Listening to the voices of individuals with disabilities. *Families in Society: The Journal of Contemporary Human Services, 79*(2), 188–196.

Graziano, A. M. (2002). *Developmental disabilities: Introduction to a diverse field.* Boston: Allyn and Bacon.

Hahn, J. E., & Marks, B. A. (Eds.). (2003). *The nursing clinics of North America: Intellectual and developmental disabilities.* Philadelphia: W. B. Saunders.

Han, L., Barrilleaux, C. B., & Quadagno, J. (1996). Race and gender differences in the distribution of home and community-based services in Florida. *Journal of Aging and Social Policy, 7*(3/4), 93–107.

Institute of Medicine. (1991). *A model of disability.* Washington, DC: National Academy Press.

Jones, G. C. (1999). *Predicting factors affecting health care access and service utilization for persons with disabilities.* Unpublished doctoral dissertation, University of Georgia.

Keigher, S. M. (2000). Emerging issues in mental retardation: Self-determination versus self-interest. *Health and Social Work, 25*(3), 163–168.

Liese, H., Clevenger, R., & Hanley, B. (1999). Joining university affiliated programs and schools of social work: A collaborative model for disabilities curriculum development and training. *Journal of Social Work Education, 35*(1), 63–69.

Mackelprang, R. W., & Salsgiver, R. O. (1996). People with disabilities and social work: Historical and contemporary issues. *Social Work, 41*(1), 7–14.

Mackelprang, R. W., & Salsgiver, R. O. (1999). *Disability: A diversity model approach in human service practice.* Pacific Grove, CA: Brooks/Cole.

Malone, D. M., McKinsey, P. D., Thyer, B. A., & Straka, E. (2000). Social work early intervention for young children with developmental disabilities. *Health and Social Work, 25*(3), 169–180.

May, G. E., & Raske, M. B. (Eds.). (2005). *Ending disability discrimination: Strategies for social workers.* Boston: Pearson, Allyn and Bacon.

Mudrick, N. R. (1991). An underdeveloped role for occupational social work: Facilitating the employment of people with disabilities. *Social Work, 36*(6), 490–495.

Palley, H. A., & Van Hollen, V. (2000). Long-term care for people with developmental disabilities: A critical analysis. *Health and Social Work, 25*(3), 181–189.

Rothman, J. R. (2003). *Social work practice across disability.* Boston: Allyn and Bacon.

Russo, R. J. (1999). Applying a strengths-based practice approach in working with people with developmental disabilities and their families. *Families in Society: The Journal of Contemporary Human Services, 80*(1), 25–33.

Thierry, J. M. (2000). Observations from the CDC: Increasing breast and cervical cancer screening among women with disabilities. *Journal of Women's Health and Gender-Based Medicine, 9*(1), 9–12.

Underwood, L., & Thyer, B. A. (1990). Social work practice with the mentally retarded: Reducing self-injurious behaviors using non-aversive methods. *Areté, 15*(1), 14–23.

Valentine, D. P., McDermott, S., & Anderson, D. (1998). Mothers of adults with mental retardation: Is race a factor in perceptions of burdens and gratifications? *Families in Society: The Journal of Contemporary Human Services, 79*(6), 577–584.

Wikler, L. (1981). Chronic stresses of families of mentally retarded children. *Family Relations, 30*(2), 281–288.

World Health Organization. (1980). *International classification of impairments, disabilities, and handicaps.* Geneva, Switzerland: Author.

World Health Organization. (1993). *International classification of impairments, disabilities, and handicaps* (2nd ed.). Geneva, Switzerland: Author.

11 Social Work with Children and Their Families

Administration for Children and Families. (1997). *National study of protective, preventive, and reunification services delivered to children and their families.* Retrieved July 13, 2005, from http://www.acf.hhs.gov/programs/cb/publications/97 natstudy/

Allen, M. L., & Nixon, R. (2000). The Foster Care Independence Act and John H. Chafee Foster Care Independence Program: New catalysts for reform for young people aging out of foster care. *Journal of Poverty Law and Policy, 7*(2), 197–216.

Allen-Meares, P., & Fraser, M. W. (2004). *Intervention with children and adolescents: An interdisciplinary perspective.* Boston: Pearson Allyn and Bacon.

American Humane Association. (2003, September). *Fathers and their families: The untapped resource for children involved in the child welfare system.* Retrieved July 30, 2005, from http://www.americanhumane.org/site/DocServer/cpl_aug_03.pdf?docID=1401

Annie E. Casey Foundation. (2003). *The unsolved challenge of system reform: The condition of the frontline human services workforce.* Retrieved January 1, 2006, from http://www.aecf.org/publications/data/report_rev.pdf

Badeau, S. (2005). *Child welfare and the courts: Pew Commission on Foster Care.* Retrieved August 8, 2005, from http://pewfostercare.org/docs/index

Barth, R. P., Gibbs, D. A., & Siebenaler, K. (2001). *Assessing the field of postadoption services: Family needs, program models, and evaluation issues.* Washington, DC: U.S. Department of Health and Human Services.

Children's Bureau. (2002). *The AFCARS Report: Interim FY 2000 estimates as of August 2002.* Washington, DC: U.S. Department of Health and Human Services.

Children's Defense Fund. (2000, June). *Domestic violence and its impact on children.* Retrieved February 1, 2005, from http://www.childrensdefense.org/site/PageServer?pagename=childwelfare_domesticviolence_factsheet

Children's Defense Fund. (2004, July). *Financial assistance for grandparents and other relatives raising children.* Retrieved May 13, 2005, from http://www.childrensdefense.org/site/Docserver/financialassistance.pdf?docID468

Children's Defense Fund. (2005, June). *13 million children face food insecurity.* Retrieved January 30, 2006, from http://www.childrensdefense.org/site/News2?page=NewsArticle&id=6642

Child Welfare League of America. (1998). *Minimum education required by state child welfare agencies, percent, by degree type.* Washington, DC: Author.

Child Welfare League of America. (2001). *Alcohol, other drugs and child welfare.* Washington, DC: Author.

Council on Accreditation. (2005, July 19). *Connecticut DCF to seek accreditation from leading national accrediting body for public child welfare systems.* Retrieved January 3, 2006, from http://www.coanet.org/front3/page.cfm?sect+18cont+3575

DeNavas-Walt, D., Proctor, B. D., & Lee, C. H. (2006). *Income, poverty, and health insurance coverage in the United States: 2005* (U.S. Census Bureau, Current Population Reports, P-60-231). Washington, DC: U.S. Government Printing Office.

DiNitto, D. M. (2007). *Social welfare: Politics and public policy. With research navigator* (6th ed.). Boston: Allyn and Bacon.

Downs, S. W., Moore, E., McFadden, E. J., & Costin, L. B. (2000). *Child welfare and family services: Policies and practices* (6th ed.). Boston: Allyn and Bacon.

Edin, K. (2003). Few good men: Why poor mothers stay single. In A. S. Skolnick & J. H. Skolnick (Eds.), *Families in transition* (12th ed., pp. 161–170). Boston: Allyn and Bacon.

Gibson, D. L., & Noble, D. N. (2002). Children and families who fly beneath the radar screen: One agency's mission. *Family Ministry, 16*(4), 47–59.

Glicken, M. D., & Sechrest, D. K. (2003). *The role of the helping professions in treating the victims and perpetrators of violence.* Boston: Allyn and Bacon.

Gracey, M. (2002). Child health in an urbanizing world. *Acta Paediatrica, 91,* 1–8.

Kids count data book. (2004). Baltimore: Annie E. Casey Foundation.

Moniz, C., & Gorin, S. (2003). *Health and health care policy: A social work perspective.* Boston: Allyn and Bacon.

Mosher, W. D., & Bachrach, C. A. (1996). Understanding U.S. fertility: Continuity and change in the National Survey of Family Growth. *Family Planning Perspectives, 28*(1), 4–12.

Nissly, J. A., Mor Barak, M. E., & Levin, A. (2004). Stress, social support, and workers' intentions to leave their jobs in public child welfare. *Administration in Social Work, 29*(1), 79–100.

Noble, D. N., & Gibson, D. L. (1994). Family values in action: Family connectedness for children in substitute care. *Child and Youth Care Forum, 23*(6), 315–328.

Noble, D. N., & Jones, S. H. (2006). Mental health issues affecting urban children. In N. K. Phillips & S. L. A. Straussner (Eds.), *Children in the urban environment: Linking social policy and clinical practice* (pp. 97–121). Springfield, IL: Charles C. Thomas.

Oswald, D. P., Coutinho, M. J., Best, A. M., & Singh, N. N. (1999). Ethnic representation in special education: The influence of school-related economic and demographic variables. *Journal of Special Education, 32*(4), 194–206.

Petr, C. G. (1998). *Social work with children and their families: Pragmatic foundations.* New York: Oxford University Press.

Pew Commission on Foster Care. (2005). *A child's journey through the child welfare system.* Retrieved August 8, 2005, from http://pewfostercare.org/research/docs/journey.pdf

Roussel, J. (2005, July 27). Infant legally abandoned outside hospital under Texas' "Baby Moses" law. *Texas State University–San Marcos University Star, 3.*

Steele, W. (2004). Helping traumatized children. In S. L. A. Straussner & N. K. Phillips (Eds.), *Understanding mass violence: A social work perspective* (pp. 41–56). Boston: Pearson Allyn and Bacon.

U.S. General Accounting Office. (2003). *Child welfare: HHS could play a greater role in helping child welfare agencies recruit and retain staff.* Washington, DC: Author.

U.S. Government Accountability Office. (2005, June). *Child welfare: Better data and evaluations could improve processes and programs for adopting children with special needs.* Retrieved January 27, 2007, from http://www.gao.gov/new.items/do5292.pdf

Winton, C. A. (2003). *Children as caregivers: Parental and parentified children.* Boston: Allyn and Bacon.

12 Gerontological Social Work

Administration on Aging. (2006). *A profile of older Americans: 2005.* Retrieved November 30, 2006, from http://www.aoa.gov/prof/Statistics/profile/2005/3.asp

Atchley, R. C., & Barusch, A. S. (2004). *Social forces and aging* (10th ed.). Belmont, CA: Wadsworth.

Baptist Memorial Health Care. (2005). *Dementia.* Retrieved August 17, 2005, from http://www.baptistonline.org/health/library/agin4121.asp

Benjamins, M. R. (2004). Religion and functional health among the elderly: Is there a relationship and is it constant? *Journal of Aging and Health, 16*(3), 355–374.

Burt, M. R., Aron, L. Y., Douglas, T., Valente, J., Lee, E., & Iwen, B. (1999). *Homelessness: Programs and the people they serve. Findings of the National Survey of Homeless Assistance Providers and Clients.* Washington, DC: Urban Institute. Retrieved December 4, 2006, from http://www.urban.org/url.cfm?ID=310291

Cohen, C. I., Sokolovsky, J., & Crane, M. (2001). Aging, homelessness, and the law. *International Journal of Law and Psychiatry, 24,* 167–181.

CSWE SAGE-SW. (2000). *National aging competencies survey report.* Retrieved August 17, 2005, from http://www.cswe.org/sage-sw/resrep/competenciesrep.htm

Cutler, S. J., & Hendricks, J. (2000). Age differences in voluntary association memberships: Fact or artifact. *Journal of Gerontology, 55B,* S98–S107.

DiNitto, D. M. (2007). *Social welfare: Politics and public policy. With research navigator* (6th ed.). Boston: Allyn and Bacon.

Evans, D. A., Funkenstein, H. H., Albert, M. S., Scherr, P. A., Cook, N. R., Chown, M. J., et al. (1989). Prevalence of Alzheimer's disease in a community population of older persons: Higher than previously reported. *Journal of the American Medical Association, 262*(18), 2551–2556.

Federal Interagency Forum on Aging-Related Statistics. (2004). *Older Americans 2004: Key indicators of well-being.* Retrieved August 17, 2005, from http://www.agingstats.gov/chartbook2004/pr2004.html

Greene, R. R. (2000). *Social work with the aged and their families.* Hawthorne, NY: Aldine de Gruyter.

He, W., Sengupta, M., Velkoff, V. A., & DeBarros, K. A. (2005). *65+ in the United States: 2005* (U.S. Census Bureau, Current Population Reports, P23-209). Washington, DC: U.S. Government Printing Office.

Hooyman, N. R., & Kiyak, H. A. (2005). *Social gerontology: A multidisciplinary perspective* (7th ed.). Boston: Allyn and Bacon.

Kosberg, J. I., & Cairl, R. (1986). The Cost of Care Index: A case management tool for screening informal caregivers. *The Gerontologist, 26,* 273–278.

Kosberg, J. I., & Kaufman, A. V. (2002). Gerontological social work: Issues and imperatives for education and practice. *Electronic Journal of Social Work, 1*(1), 1–15.

Kramer, B. J. (1997). Gain in the caregiver experience: Where are we? What next? *The Gerontologist, 37,* 218–232.

Lee, C. D., & Bakk, L. (2001). Later-life transition into widowhood. *Journal of Gerontological Social Work, 35*(3), 51–63.

Logan, S. L. (1996). *The black family.* Boulder, CO: Westview Press.

McFadden, S. H. (1995). Religion and well-being in aging persons in an aging society. *Journal of Social Issues, 51*(2), 161–175.

Nathanson, I. L., & Tirrito, T. T. (1998). *Gerontological social work: Theory into practice.* New York: Springer.

National Alliance for Caregiving & American Association of Retired Persons. (2004). *Caregiving in the U.S.* Retrieved May 11, 2004, from http://research.aarp.org/il/us_caregiving.pdf

National Center for Chronic Disease Prevention and Health Promotion. (2005). *Health information for older adults.* Retrieved August, 17, 2005, from http://www.cdc.gov/aging/health_issues.htm#5

National Center for Injury Prevention and Control. (2004). *Suicide: Fact sheet.* Retrieved August 17, 2005, from http://www.cdc.gov/ncipc/factsheets/suifacts.htm

National Substance Abuse and Mental Health Services Association. (2005). *Older adult substance abuse and mental health technical assistance center.* Retrieved July 17, 2005, from http://www.samhsa.gov/aging/age_05.aspx

Noonan, A., & Tennstedt, S. (1997). Meaning in caregiving and its contribution to caregiver well-being. *The Gerontologist, 37,* 785–794.

Pinquart, M., & Sorenson, S. (2003). Differences between caregivers and non-caregivers in psychological health and physical health: A meta-analysis. *Psychology and Aging, 18,* 250–267.

Spillman, P., & Pezzin, L. (2000). Potential and active family caregivers: Changing networks and the sandwich generation. *Milbank Quarterly, 78,* 347–374.

U.S. Department of Health and Human Services. (1999). *Mental health: A report of the Surgeon General—executive summary.* Rockville, MD: U.S. Department of Health and Human Services, Substance Abuse and Mental Health Services Administration, National Institutes of Health, National Institute of Mental Health.

Vinton, L., & Wambach, K. G. (2005). Alcohol and drug use among elderly people. In C. A. McNeece & D. M. DiNitto, *Chemical dependency: A systems approach* (3rd ed., pp. 484–502). Boston: Allyn and Bacon.

Yamamoto-Mitani, N., Ishigaki, K., Kawahara-Maekawa, N., Kuniyoshi, M., Hayashi, K., Hasagawa, K., et al. (2003). Factors of positive appraisal of care among Japanese family caregivers of older adults. *Research in Nursing and Health, 26,* 337–350.

Yesavage, J. A., & Brink, T. L. (1983). Development and validation of a geriatric depression screening scale: A preliminary report. *Journal of Psychiatric Research, 17*(1), 37–49.

Zarit, S. H., Reever, K. E., & Bach-Peterson, J. (1980). Relatives of the impaired elderly: Correlates of feelings of burden. *The Gerontologist, 20,* 649–655.

13 Poverty in the United States: History, Explanations, and Opportunities for Social Work

Banfield, E. C. (1970). *The unheavenly city: The nature and future of our urban crisis.* Boston: Little, Brown.

Beeghley, L. (1983). *Living poorly in America.* New York: Praeger.

Beeghley, L. (1989). Individual and structural explanations of poverty. *Population Research and Policy Review, 7*(3), 201–222.

Curran, L. (2002). The psychology of poverty: Professional social work and aid to dependent children in postwar America: 1946–1963. *Social Service Review, 76*(3), 365–386.

DeNavas-Walt, C., Proctor, B. D., & Lee, C. H. (2006, August). *Income, poverty, and health insurance coverage in the United States: 2005* (U.S. Census Bureau, Current Population Reports, P60-231).Washington, DC: U.S. Government Printing Office.

DeParle, J. (2004). *American dream: Three women, ten kids, and a nation's drive to end welfare.* New York: Viking.

DiNitto, D. M. (2007). *Social welfare: Politics and public policy. With research navigator* (6th ed.). Boston: Allyn and Bacon.

Economic Research Service. (2004). *Rural poverty at a glance* (Rural Development Research Report No. 100). Retrieved August 2, 2005, from http://www.ers.usda.gov/publications/rdrr100/rdrr100_lowres.pdf

Harrington, M. (1962). *The other America: Poverty in the United States.* New York: Macmillan.

Herman, E. (1995). *The romance of American psychology: Political culture in the age of experts.* Berkeley and Los Angeles: University of California Press.

Herrnstein, R. J., & Murray, C. (1994). *The bell curve: Intelligence and class structure in American life.* New York: Free Press.

Hirschl, T. A., & Rank, M. R. (1991). The effects of population density on welfare participation. *Social Forces, 70,* 225–235.

Kozol, J. (1991). *Savage inequalities: Children in America's schools.* New York: Crown.

Kozol, J. (1995). *Amazing grace: The lives of children and the conscience of a nation.* New York: Harper Perennial.

Kozol, J. (2001). *Ordinary resurrections: Children in the years of hope.* New York: Harper Perennial.

Leacock, E. B. (1971). *The culture of poverty: A critique.* New York: Simon & Schuster.

Lewis, O. (1959). *Five families: Mexican case studies in the culture of poverty.* New York: Basic Books.

Maynars, R. A. (1997). *Kids having kids: Economic costs and social consequences of teen pregnancy.* Washington, DC: Urban Institute Press.

McGeer, M. (2003). *A fierce discontent: The rise and fall of the progressive movement in America.* New York: Oxford University Press.

Rank, M. R. (1994). *Living on the edge: The realities of welfare in America.* New York: Columbia University Press.

Rank, M. R. (2004). *One nation, underprivileged: Why poverty in America affects us all.* New York: Columbia University Press.

Rank, M. R., & Hirschl, T. A. (1999). The likelihood of poverty across the American adult life span. *Social Work, 44,* 201–216.

Rank, M. R., & Hirschl, T. A. (2001). The occurrence of poverty across the life cycle: Evidence from the PSID. *Journal of Policy Analysis and Management, 20,* 737–755.

Rank, M. R., Hong, H.-S., & Hirschl, T. A. (2003). American poverty as a structural failing: Evidence and arguments. *Journal of Sociology and Social Welfare, 30*(4), 3–29.

Riis, J. A. (1997). *How the other half lives.* New York: Penguin. (Originally published in 1890)

Rogers, M. B. (1990). *Cold anger: A story of faith and power politics.* Denton: University of North Texas Press.

Syme, S. L. (1998). Social and economic disparities in health: Thoughts and interventions. *Milbank Quarterly, 76*(3), 493–505.

Trattner, W. I. (1999). *From poor law to welfare state: A history of social welfare in America*. New York: Free Press.

Van Wormer, K. (2004). Globalization, work and social work in the USA. In N.-T. Tan & A. Rowlands (Eds.), *Social work around the world III* (pp. 48–60). Berne, Switzerland: IFSW Press.

Zucker, G. S., & Weiner, B. (1993). Conservatism and perceptions of poverty: An attributional analysis. *Journal of Applied Social Psychology, 23*(12), 925–943.

14 Social Work Practice in the Justice System

Alexander, A., Jr. (1997). Juvenile delinquency and social work practice. In C. A. McNeece & A. R. Roberts (Eds.), *Policy and practice in the justice system* (pp. 181–197). Chicago: Nelson-Hall.

Barlow, H. D. (2000). *Criminal justice in America*. Upper Saddle River, NJ: Prentice Hall.

Bates, E. (2006). Prisons for profit. In K. C. Haas & G. P. Alpert (Eds.), *The dilemmas of corrections* (pp. 526–537). Long Grove, IL: Waveland Press.

Bauer, L., & Owens, S. D. (2004). *Justice expenditure and employment in the United States, 2001* (U.S. Department of Justice Publication No. NCJ 202792). Washington, DC: U.S. Government Printing Office.

Bazemore, G., & Umbreit, M. (2001). *A comparison of four restorative conferencing models* (U.S. Department of Justice Publication No. NCJ 184738). Washington, DC: U.S. Government Printing Office.

Bernstein, R., & Seltzer, T. (2004). *The role of mental health courts in system reform.* Retrieved April 1, 2005, from http://www.bazelon.org/issues/criminalization/publications/mentalhealthcourts

Bloom, B., & Steinhart, D. (1993). *Why punish the children? A reappraisal of the children of incarcerated mothers in America*. San Francisco: National Council on Crime and Delinquency.

Bonczar, T. P., & Beck, A. J. (1997). *Lifetime likelihood of going to state or federal prison* (U.S. Department of Justice Publication No. NCJ 160092). Washington, DC: U.S. Government Printing Office.

Brownell, P., & Roberts, A. R. (2002). A century of social work in criminal justice and correctional settings. *Journal of Offender Rehabilitation, 35*(2), 1–17.

Building Blocks for Youth. (2005). *Transfer to adult court/Trying kids as adults*. Retrieved November 11, 2005 from http://www.buildingblocksforyouth.org/issues/transfer/facts_transfer.html

Center for Health Workforce Studies. (2005). *Report to NASW congress*. Albany: State University of New York, School of Public Health.

Champion, D. J. (1998). *Criminal justice in the United States* (2nd ed.). Chicago: Nelson-Hall.

Clark, J., & Henry, D. A. (2003). *Pretrial services programming at the start of the 21st century: A survey of pretrial services programs* (U.S. Department of Justice Publication No. NCJ 199773). Washington, DC: U.S. Government Printing Office.

Corrections Corporation of America. (n.d.). *About CCA*. Retrieved November 2, 2006, from http://www.correctionscorp.com/aboutcca.html

Dane, B. O., & Simon, B. L. (1991). Resident guests: Social workers in host settings. *Social Work, 36*(3), 208–213.

Dean, C. W., Lumb, R., Proctor, K., Klopovic, J., Hyatt, A., & Hamby, R. (2000, October). *Social work and law enforcement partnerships: A summons to the village. Strategies and effective practices.* Raleigh, NC: Governor's Crime Commission.

Ditton, P. M. (1999). *Mental health and treatment of inmates and probationers* (U.S. Department of Justice Publication No. NCJ 174463). Washington, DC: U.S. Government Printing Office.

Durose, M. R., & Langan, P. A. (2004). *Felony sentences in state courts, 2002* (U.S. Department of Justice Publication No. NCJ 206916). Washington, DC: U.S. Government Printing Office.

Dwyer, D. C. (1997). Juvenile corrections: Its implications for social work practice. In C. A. McNeece & A. R. Roberts (Eds.), *Policy and practice in the justice system* (pp. xi–xiii). Chicago: Nelson-Hall.

Federal Bureau of Investigation. (2005). *Crime in the United States, 2004: Uniform crime reports.* Retrieved May 13, 2006, from http://www.fbi.gov/ucr/cius_04/law_enforcement_personnel?index.index.html

Fox, V. (1983). Forward. In A. R. Roberts (Ed.), *Social work in juvenile and criminal justice settings* (pp. ix–xv). Springfield, IL: Charles C. Thomas.

Gibelman, M. (1995). *What social workers do.* Washington, DC: NASW.

Glaze, L. E., & Palla, S. (2004). *Probation and parole in the United States, 2003* (U.S. Department of Justice Publication No. NCJ 205336). Washington, DC: U.S. Government Printing Office.

Goldstrom, I., Henderson, M., Male, A., & Manderscheid, R. W. (1998). Jail mental health services: A national survey. In Center for Mental Health Services (Ed.), *Mental health, United States, 1998* (pp. 176–187). Washington, DC: U.S. Government Printing Office.

Greenfeld, L. A., & Snell, T. L. (1999). *Women offenders* (U.S. Department of Justice Publication No. NCJ 175688). Washington, DC: U.S. Government Printing Office.

Gumz, E. J. (2004). American social work, corrections and restorative justice: An appraisal. *International Journal of Offender Therapy and Comparative Criminology, 48*(4), 449–460.

Harrison, P. M., & Beck, A. J. (2004). *Prisoners in 2003* (U.S. Department of Justice Publication No. NCJ 205335). Washington DC: U.S. Government Printing Office.

Harrison, P. M., & Beck, A. J. (2005). *Prison and jail inmates at midyear 2004* (U.S. Department of Justice Publication No. NCJ 208801). Washington DC: U.S. Government Printing Office.

Jose-Kampfner, C. (1991, August). Michigan program makes children's visits meaningful. *Corrections Today,* 130–134.

Langan, P. A., Greenfeld, L. A., Smith, S. K., Durose, M. R., & Levin, D. J. (2001). *Contacts between police and the public: Findings from the 1999 national survey* (U.S. Department of Justice Publication No. NCJ 184957). Washington DC: U.S. Government Printing Office.

Langan, P. A., & Levin, D. J. (2002). *Recidivism of prisoners released in 1994* (U.S. Department of Justice Publication No. NCJ 193427). Washington DC: U.S. Government Printing Office.

Maruschak, L. M. (2004). *HIV in prisons and jails, 2002* (U.S. Department of Justice Publication No. NCJ 205333). Washington, DC: U.S. Government Printing Office.

Mays, G. L., & Winfree, L. T. (2005). *Essentials of corrections* (3rd ed.). Belmont, CA: Thomson/Wadsworth.

McNeece, C. A., & Jackson, S. (2004). Juvenile justice policy: Current trends and 21st-century issues. In A. R. Roberts (Ed.), *Juvenile justice sourcebook: Past, present, and future* (pp. 41–68). New York: Oxford University Press.

McNeece, C. A., & Roberts, A. R. (1997). Preface. In C. A. McNeece & A. R. Roberts (Eds.), *Policy and practice in the justice system* (pp. xi–xiii). Chicago: Nelson-Hall.

Miller, J. G. (1995). Criminal justice: Social work roles. In R. L. Edwards (Ed.), *The encyclopedia of social work* (19th ed., pp. 653–659). Washington, DC: NASW Press.

Mumola, C. J. (1999). *Substance abuse and treatment, state and federal prisoners, 1997* (U.S. Department of Justice Publication No. NCJ 172871). Washington, DC: U.S. Government Printing Office.

Mumola, C. J. (2000). *Incarcerated parents and their children* (U.S. Department of Justice Publication No. NCJ 182335). Washington, DC: U.S. Government Printing Office.

National Association of Social Workers. (1987). *The encyclopedia of social work* (18th ed., Vol. 1). Silver Spring, MD: NASW Press.

National Association of Social Workers. (1999). *Code of ethics of the National Association of Social Workers.* Retrieved April 6, 2005, from http://www.social workers.org/pubs/code

National Association of Social Workers. (n.d.). *Victim assistance programs provide an array of services to crime victims.* Retrieved April 6, 2005, from http://www. naswnys.org/crime_victims/victim_assistance_programs_provi.htm

National Criminal Justice Reference Service. (n.d.). *In the spotlight—drug courts: Summary.* Retrieved April 1, 2005, from http://www.ncjrs.org/drug_courts/summary.html

Roberts, A. R., & Brownell, P. (1999). A century of forensic social work: Bridging the past to the present. *Social Work, 44*(4), 359–369.

Roberts, A. R., & Fisher, P. (1997). Policy, administration, and direct service roles in victim/witness assistance programs. In C. A. McNeece & A. R. Roberts (Eds.), *Policy and practice in the justice system* (pp. 127–142). Chicago: Nelson-Hall.

Roman, J., Townsend, W., & Bhati, A. S. (2003). *Recidivism rates for drug court graduates: Nationally based estimates, final report* (Document No. 201229). Washington, DC: Urban Institute.

Schroeder, J. (2003). Forging a new practice area: Social work's role in death penalty mitigation investigations. *Families in Society: The Journal of Contemporary Human Services, 84*(3), 423–432.

Sickmund, M. (2004). *Juveniles in corrections* (U.S. Department of Justice Publication No. NCJ 202885). Washington, DC: U.S. Government Printing Office.

Snell, T. L. (1994). *Women in prison* (U.S. Department of Justice Publication No. NCJ 145321). Washington, DC: U.S. Government Printing Office.

Snyder, H. N. (2004). *Juvenile arrests 2002* (U.S. Department of Justice Publication No. NCJ 204608). Washington, DC: U.S. Government Printing Office.

Snyder, H. N., & Sickmund, M. (2006). *Juvenile offenders and victims: 2006 national report*. Washington, DC: U.S. Department of Justice, Office of Justice Programs, Office of Juvenile Justice and Delinquency Prevention.

Stephan, J. J., & Karberg, J. C. (2003). *Census of state and federal correctional facilities, 2000* (U.S. Department of Justice Publication No. NCJ 198272). Washington, DC: U.S. Government Printing Office.

Treger, H., & Allen, G. F. (1997). Social work in the justice system: An overview. In A. R. Roberts (Ed.), *Social work in juvenile and criminal justice settings* (2nd ed., pp. 19–33). Springfield, IL: Charles C. Thomas.

Van Winkle, M. (1924). The policewomen. *Proceedings of the fifty-first annual session of the National Conference of Social Work*. Chicago: University of Chicago Press.

Van Wormer, K. (2002). Restorative justice and social work. *Social Work Today, 2*(1).

Young, D. S. (2002). Non-psychiatric services provided in a mental health unit in a county jail. *Journal of Offender Rehabilitation, 35*(2), 63–82.

Young, D. S., & Smith, C. J. (2000). When moms are incarcerated: The needs of children, mothers, and caregivers. *Families in Society: The Journal of Contemporary Human Services, 81*(2), 130–141.

Zehr, H. (2002). *The little book of restorative justice*. Intercourse, PA: Good Books.

15 Rural Social Work Practice

Bosien, L. S., & Bosch, L. A. (2005). Dual relationships and rural social work: Is there a rural code? In L. H. Ginsberg (Ed.), *Social work in rural communities* (4th ed., pp. 189–204). Alexandria, VA: Council on Social Work Education.

Cashwell, S. T., & McNeece, C. A. (2000). Smoke and mirrors: The shifting dependency of former rural welfare mothers. *Rural Social Work, 6*(1), 17–25.

DeNavas-Walt, C., Proctor, B. D., & Lee, C. H. (2006, August). *Income, poverty, and health insurance coverage in the United States: 2005* (U.S. Census Bureau, Current Population Reports, P60-231).Washington, DC: U.S. Government Printing Office.

Economic Research Service. (2004). *Rural poverty at a glance* (Rural Development Research Report No. 100). Retrieved July 3, 2005, from http://www.ers.usda.gov/publications/rdrr100/rdrr100.pdf

Gale, H. F., McGranahan, D. A., Teixeira, R., & Greenberg, E. (1999). *Rural competitiveness: Results of the 1997 rural manufacturing survey* (Agricultural Economics Report No. 776). Retrieved September 22, 2005, from http://www.ers.usda.gov/publications/aer776

Gibbs, R. (2005, June). Most low-education counties are in the nonmetro South. *Amber Waves*. Retrieved February 25, 2007, from http://www.ers.usda.gov/AmberWaves/June05/pdf/FindingsRAJune05.pdf

Ginsberg, L. (2005). *Social work in rural communities* (4th ed.). Alexandria, VA: Council on Social Work Education.

Harris, R. P., & Zimmerman, N. J. (2003). *Children and poverty in the rural South*. SRDC Policy Series No. 2. Mississippi State, MS: Southern Rural Development Center.

Huling, T. (2002). Building a prison economy in rural America. In M. Mauer & M. Chesney-Lind (Eds.), *Invisible punishment: The collateral consequences of mass imprisonment*. New York: New Press. Retrieved March 3, 2007, from http://www.prisonpolicy.org/scans/building.html

Jobes, C. P. (1999). Residential stability and crime in small rural agricultural and recreational towns. *Pacific Sociological Association, 42*, 501–524.

Kellogg Foundation. (2001). *Perceptions of rural America*. Retrieved February 25, 2007, from http://www.wkkf.org/Default.aspx?LanguageID=0

Kimbrough-Melton, R. (2001). *Institute of family and neighborhood life fact sheet: Rural life today*. Retrieved February 25, 2007, from http://virtual.clemson.edu/groups/ifnl/PDFs/rural_life_today_fact_sheet.pdf

Marson, S. M., & Powell, R. M. (2000). Resolving the transportation problem in a rural community: A case study of Robeson County's (USA) solution to TANF (Temporary Aid for Needy Families). *Rural Social Work, 6*(1), 26–32.

McLaughlin, K. D. (2002). Income inequality in America: Nonmetro income levels lower than metro, but income inequality did not increase as fast. *Rural America, 17*(2), 14–20.

Miller, K. K., & Weber, A. B. (2004). How do persistent poverty dynamics and demographics vary across the rural-urban continuum? *Measuring Rural Diversity, 1*, 1–7.

National Association of Social Workers. (1999). *Code of ethics of the National Association of Social Workers*. Washington, DC: Author.

National Center on Rural Justice and Crime. (2004). *Rural crime facts*. Retrieved July 19, 2005, from http://virtual.clemson.edu/groups/ncrj/rural_crime_facts.htm

National Public Radio. (2004, August 12). Meth a growing menace in rural America. *Morning Edition*. Retrieved February 25, 2007, from http://www.npr.org/templates/story/story.php?storyId=3805074

Parsons, R. J., Jorgensen, J. D., & Hernandez, S. H. (1994). *The integration of social work practice*. Pacific Grove, CA: Brooks/Cole.

Rogers, C. C. (2005). *Rural children at a glance*. Economic Information Bulletin No. 1. Retrieved July 3, 2005, from http://www.ers.usda.gov/publications/EIB1/

Saleebey, D. (1996). The strengths perspective in social work practice: Extensions and cautions. *Social Work, 41*, 296–306.

Stommes, E. S., & Brown, D. M. (2002). Transportation in rural America: Issues for the 21st century. *Rural America, 16*(4), 2–10.

U.S. Census Bureau. (2005). *Question and answer center: Rural*. Retrieved November 12, 2005, from http://ask.census.gov/cgi-bin/askcensus.cfg/php/enduser/std_alp.php?p_lva=&p_li=&p_page=1&p_new_search=1&p_search_text=rural

U.S. Census Bureau. (2007). *Housing vacancies and homeownership: Fourth quarter 2006*. Retrieved March 3, 2007, from http://www.census.gov/hhes/www/housing/hvs/qtr406/q406tab6.html

Watkins, T. R. (2004). Natural helping networks: Assets for rural communities. In T. L. Scales & C. L. Streeter (Eds.), *Rural social work: Building and sustaining community assets* (pp. 65–76). Belmont, CA: Brooks/Cole.

16 International Social Work: Challenges and Opportunities in a Global Society

Blavo, E. Q., & Apt, N. A. (1997). Ghana. In N. S. Mayadas, T. D. Watts, & D. Elliott (Eds.), *International handbook on social work theory and practice* (pp. 320–343). Westport, CT: Greenwood Press.

Friedlander, W. (1955). *Introduction to social welfare*. New York: Prentice Hall.

Friedlander, W. (1975). *International social welfare*. Englewood Cliffs, NJ: Prentice Hall.

Garber, R. (1997). Social work education in international context: Current trends and future directions. In M. C. Hokenstad & J. Midgley (Eds.), *Issues in international social work* (pp. 159–171). Washington, DC: NASW Press.

Groza, V. (1997). Adoptions. In R. L. Edwards (Ed.), *The encyclopedia of social work, 1997 supplement* (19th ed., pp. 1–14). Washington, DC: NASW Press.

Guzetta, C. (1995). Central and Eastern Europe. In T. D. Watts, D. Elliott, & N. S. Mayadas (Eds.), *International handbook on social work education* (pp. 191–210). Westport, CT: Greenwood Press.

Healy, L. M. (2001). *International social work: Professional action in an interdependent world*. New York: Oxford University Press.

Hokenstad, M. C., Khinduka, S. K., & Midgley, J. (Eds.). (1992). *Profiles in international social work*. Washington, DC: NASW Press.

Hokenstad, M. C., & Midgley, J. (Eds.). (1997). *Issues in international social work*. Washington, DC: NASW Press.

Hokenstad, M. C., & Midgley, J. (Eds.). (2004). *Lessons from abroad: Adapting international social welfare innovations*. Washington, DC: NASW Press.

Kendall, K. (1974). Foreword. In P. J. Stickney & R. J. Resnick (Eds.), *World guide to social work education* (pp. i–v). New York: International Association of Schools of Social Work.

Kendall, K. (2000). *Social work education: Its origins in Europe*. Alexandria, VA: Council on Social Work Education.

Landa Jocano, F. (1980). *Social work in the Philippines: A historical overview*. Manila, Philippines: New Day.

Leighninger, L., & Midgley, J. (1997). The United States of America. In N. S. Mayadas, T. D. Watts, & D. Elliott (Eds.), *International handbook on social work theory and practice* (pp. 9–28). Westport, CT: Greenwood Press.

Mayadas, N. S., Watts, T. D., & Elliott, D. (Eds.). (1997). *International handbook on social work theory and practice*. Westport, CT: Greenwood Press.

Midgley, J. (1981). *Professional imperialism: Social work in the third world*. London: Heinemann.

Midgley, J. (1990). International social work: Learning from the third world. *Social Work, 35*(3), 295–301.

Midgley, J. (1997). *Social welfare in global context*. Thousand Oaks, CA: Sage.

Midgley, J. (2001). Issues in international social work: Resolving critical debates in the profession. *Journal of Social Work, 1*(1), 21–35.

Midgley, J. (2004). The complexities of globalization: Challenges to social work. In N.-T. Tan & A. Rowlands (Eds.), *Social work around the world III* (pp. 13–29). Bern, Switzerland: IFSW Press.

Yuen-Tsang, A. W. K., & Sibin, W. (2002). Tensions confronting the development of social work education in China: Challenges and opportunities. *International Social Work, 45*(4), 375–388.

17 The Future of Social Work: Preparing for the Next Century

Bureau of Labor Statistics. (2005). *Social workers*. Retrieved October 25, 2005, from http://stats.bls.gov/oco/pdf/ocos060.pdf

Council on Social Work Education. (2002). *Summary information on master of social work programs: 2001–2002*. Alexandria, VA: Author.

Dator, J. (1999). *Y2K as a futurist's dream*. Retrieved May 29, 2006, from http://www.futures.hawaii.edu/dator/futures/Y2KDream.html

Day, P. J. (2006). *A new history of social welfare* (5th ed.). Boston: Allyn and Bacon.

DiNitto, D. M. (2007). *Social welfare: Politics and public policy. With research navigator* (6th ed.). Boston: Allyn and Bacon.

Gilbert, N., & Terrell, P. (2005). *Dimension of social welfare policy* (6th ed.). Boston: Allyn and Bacon.

Ginsberg, L. (2006). The future of social work as a profession. *Advances in Social Work, 6*(1), 7–16.

Karger, H. J., & Stoesz, D. (2003). The growth of social work education program, 1985–1999: Its impact on economic and educational factors related to the profession of social work. *Journal of Social Work Education, 39*(2), 279–295.

McNeece, C. A., & Thyer, B. A. (2004). Evidence-based practice and social work. *Journal of Evidence-Based Social Work, 1*(1), 7–25.

Pankratz, H. (August 29, 2003). *Court upholds conviction in "rebirthing" death*. Retrieved October 25, 2005, from http://www.rickross.com/reference/rebirthing/rebirthing25.html

Sandell, K. S., & Hayes, S. (2002). The Web's impact on social work education: Opportunities, challenges, and future directions. *Journal of Social Work Education, 38*(1), 85–99.

Vernon, R. (2006). Technology convergence and social work: When case management meets geographic information. *Advances in Social Work, 6*(1), 91–96.

■ Contributors

Angela Ausbrooks (MSSW, PhD, University of Texas at Austin) is assistant professor at the School of Social Work at Texas State University–San Marcos.

Gary Bailey (MSSW, Boston University) is associate professor at Simmons College School of Social Work.

Beverly Black (MSSW, University of Wisconsin–Madison; PhD, University of Texas at Austin) is professor in the School of Social Work at the University of Texas at Arlington.

Suzie T. Cashwell (MSW, PhD, Florida State University) is associate professor at Western Kentucky University's Department of Social Work.

Catherine Crisp (PhD, University of Texas at Austin) is assistant professor at the University of Kansas School of Social Welfare.

Kevin L. DeWeaver (MSW, West Virginia University; PhD, Florida State University) is professor and director of the doctoral program at the School of Social Work at the University of Georgia.

Rowena Fong (MSW, University of California at Berkeley; EdD, Harvard University) is Ruby Lee Piester Centennial Professor in Services to Children and Families and BSW program director at the University of Texas at Austin School of Social Work.

Cynthia Franklin (MSSW, PhD, University of Texas at Arlington) is Stiernberg/Spencer Family Professor in Mental Health and coordinator of the clinical social work concentration at the University of Texas at Austin School of Social Work.

Annelies K. Hagemeister (MA, MSW, PhD, University of Minnesota, Twin Cities) is assistant professor and graduate admissions coordinator in the Department of Social Work at Minnesota State University, Mankato.

Daniel Harkness (MSW, PhD, University of Kansas) is a licensed clinical social worker and professor at the School of Social Work at Boise State University in Idaho.

Janet M. Joiner (MSW, Western Michigan University; PhD, Wayne State University) is director of admissions and student services at the School of Social Work at Wayne State University.

Catheleen Jordan (MSSW, University of Texas at Arlington; PhD, University of California at Berkeley) is professor in the School of Social Work at the University of Texas at Arlington.

Mary Margaret Just (MSW, Oklahoma University; PhD, University of Texas at Austin) is associate professor of social work in the Department of Sociology, Social Work, and Criminology at Morehead State University.

Allan Kaufman (MSW, Adelphi University; PhD, Florida State University) is professor at the University of Alabama School of Social Work.

Robin Kennedy (MS, University of North Texas; MSSW, PhD, University of Texas at Austin) is associate professor in the Division of Social Work at California State University, Sacramento.

Ara Lewellen (MSSW, PhD, University of Texas at Arlington) is retired from the Department of Social Work at Texas A&M–Commerce.

Paul Force-Emery Mackie (MSW, Washington University in St. Louis; PhD, University of Denver) is assistant professor and Title IV-E child welfare co-facilitator in the Department of Social Work at Minnesota State University, Mankato.

James Midgley (MSc, London School of Economics; MSocSc, PhD, University of Cape Town) is Harry and Riva Specht Professor at the University of California at Berkeley School of Social Welfare.

Dorinda N. Noble (MSW, Tulane University; PhD, University of Texas at Austin) is professor and director of the School of Social Work at Texas State University–San Marcos.

Steve J. Onken (MSW, PhD, University of Texas at Austin) is a mental health research associate with the School of Social Work and Social Sciences Research Institute at the University of Hawai'i at Manoa.

Linda Openshaw (MSW, DSW, University of Utah) is associate professor in the Department of Social Work at Texas A&M–Commerce.

Will Rainford (MSW, Washington University in St. Louis; PhD, University of California at Berkeley) is associate professor of social work and chair of the MSW program at Boise State University.

Virginia Rondero Hernandez (MSW, California State University, Sacramento; PhD, Case Western Reserve University) is associate professor in the Department of Social Work Education at California State University, Fresno.

Lacey Sloan (MSSW, PhD, University of Texas at Austin) is a policy research consultant and political activist in Limerick, Maine.

Maggie Tang (MSW, University of Alabama) is a doctoral student at the University of Alabama School of Social Work.

Stephen P. Wernet (MSW, University of Connecticut; PhD, University of Texas at Austin) is professor in the School of Social Work at Saint Louis University.

Diane S. Young (MSW, PhD, University of Washington) is associate professor in the School of Social Work at Syracuse University.

■ Index